Sex in an Old Regime City

Sex in an Old Regime City

Young Workers and Intimacy in France, 1660–1789

JULIE HARDWICK

OXFORD
UNIVERSITY PRESS

Oxford University Press is a department of the University of Oxford. It furthers the University's objective of excellence in research, scholarship, and education by publishing worldwide. Oxford is a registered trade mark of Oxford University Press in the UK and certain other countries.

Published in the United States of America by Oxford University Press
198 Madison Avenue, New York, NY 10016, United States of America.

© Oxford University Press 2020

All rights reserved. No part of this publication may be reproduced, stored in a retrieval system, or transmitted, in any form or by any means, without the prior permission in writing of Oxford University Press, or as expressly permitted by law, by license, or under terms agreed with the appropriate reproduction rights organization. Inquiries concerning reproduction outside the scope of the above should be sent to the Rights Department, Oxford University Press, at the address above.

You must not circulate this work in any other form
and you must impose this same condition on any acquirer.

Library of Congress Cataloging-in-Publication Data
Names: Hardwick, Julie, 1962- author.
Title: Sex in an old regime city : young workers and intimacy in
France, 1660–1789 / Julie Hardwick.
Identifiers: LCCN 2020008319 (print) | LCCN 2020008320 (ebook) |
ISBN 9780190945183 (hardback) | ISBN 9780190945206 (epub) |
ISBN 9780190945213
Subjects: LCSH: Sex—France—History. | Courtship—France—History. |
Man-woman relationships—France—History. |
Youth—Sexual behavior—France—History. |
Working class—Sexual behavior—France—History.
Classification: LCC HQ18.F8 H37 2020 (print) |
LCC HQ18.F8 (ebook) | DDC 306.70944—dc23
LC record available at https://lccn.loc.gov/2020008319
LC ebook record available at https://lccn.loc.gov/2020008320

Contents

Acknowledgments   vii

Introduction: A Foundling's Garter and the World of Young People's Intimacy   1

1. Sourcing Intimate Histories: The Social World of Young Workers   18
2. Peril Stories: Licit Intimacy, Space, and Community Safeguarding   43
3. Holding Men Responsible: Fertility, Community, and Court   78
4. "Remedies" and Remedies: Managing Out-of-Wedlock Pregnancy   110
5. Intimate Labor: Paid Work and an Intimate Economy of Reproduction   140
6. Foundlings and Makeshift Coffins: Community Complicity and Dead Babies   169

Conclusion: The End of the Old Regime?   201

Notes   211
Bibliography   259
Index   273

Acknowledgments

I was working on two books for several years and, if they are both the better for the synergy, that strategy also delayed the progress of each manuscript so this project has been a part of my life for a long time. I thank Susan Ferber at Oxford University Press for her enthusiastic support of my work and indeed for her broader commitment to work in my field as well as for the many ways her guidance improved it. The press readers generously shared their enthusiasm and expertise, and I am very appreciative of their input.

I could not have completed this book without the financial support of many institutions. My academic home at the University of Texas at Austin funded many research trips and a semester of leave. The Gender and Work group at Uppsala University generously underwrote my stay there. Many institutions paid my way to give talks. A University of Texas at Austin Subvention Grant awarded by the Office of the President supported the book's publication.

I had the incredible good fortune to work on this project during an extended dialogue with the Gender and Work in early modern Sweden group. My initial talk at their meeting in Stockholm in 2012 led to a generous invitation to spend a marvelous three months in Uppsala in early 2014, and I returned to give a workshop on a book chapter in the summer of 2016. The intellectual creativity and analytical sharpness of that group profoundly impacted the shape of this book and indeed my whole early modern worldview. I thank Karin Janssen, Dåg Lindstom, Sofia Ling, and in particular my host, Maria Ågren.

Lyon's amazing archives made this book possible. The staff at the Archives Municipales de Lyon and at the Archive Départmentales du Rhône do wonderful work in making their incredible records accessible and in providing very friendly and efficient service to researchers.

Lyon also brought me the wonderful company of Cathy McClive and Anne Verjus for our intersecting adventures in motherhood, feminist scholarship, and gender and family history. Cathy began to work on Lyon as I was moving into full gear with this project. It is been a privilege to share the Lyon archives with someone whose excitement about the records there matches my own. In particular I am grateful for her generosity in sharing her photographs of investigations into possible infanticide cases and for an incisive reading of the second half of the book that helped me shape the final form. Anne read the first half of a late draft of the manuscript with her usual vigor, and I very much appreciated the many helpful suggestions and the enthusiastic endorsement.

I have benefited enormously from the comments, questions, and suggestions that arose at the many talks I have given about this project. I thank Amy Erickson and Laura Gowing for an invitation to the women's history seminar at the Institute of Historical Research in London where Judith Bennett, Cynthia Herrup, and Catherine Hinchliff also provided invaluable feedback. Rafe Blaufarb hosted and Nina Kushner coordinated a fabulous meeting about Sex and Gender in French history at Florida State University that gave me the chance to try out some big frames in my plenary. I learned a lot from participants' engagement with my work as well as from discussion of other papers. Wonderful discussions with all the participants at Katie Barclay's University of Glasgow symposium about the history of marriage and emtoions , "Institution to Intimacy: Courtship, Marriage, and Marriage Breakdown in Historical Perspective," pushed me to consider more fully the emotions of young couples in this project. Laurie Nussdorfer invited me to a workshop at the University of Connecticut on early modern masculinity that reshaped my thinking. Michael Kwass invited me to return to the Johns Hopkins History Department Seminar 30 years after I gave my first year graduate student paper there, and I appreciated all over again the vigorous and expert discussion that characterizes that meeting. Toward the end of my work on the book, I benefited from opportunities to present parts of it at a very invigorating conference funded by the AHRC titled "Women Negotiating the Boundaries of Justice" held at the University of Swansea, at a "Domestic Space" workshop hosted in Thun by Joachim Eibach and his team on the SHF-Sinergia "Doing House" project, and at the "Family and Justice in the Archives" symposium organized by Eric Reiter and Peter Gossage at the University of Concordia in Montreal.

I have lost track of all the helpful conversations I had with so many people about this project over many years and I appreciate all the input. Conversations with Nina Dayton encouraged me to think about and be bolder about some key issues in this project. Megan Armstrong and Jotham Parsons gave me a lively, fascinating tutorial on the role of friars and internal missions in France over glasses of wine at a conference. Nina Kushner provided an early incisive reading of a draft of the first chapter that was enormously helpful. A conversation with Sally Holloway was critical in helping me puzzle out the foundling baby's token. Julia Gossard, Alex Taft, and Laurie Wood, current and former PhD students, provided essential intellectual labor of all kinds along the way. Alecia Seidel broadened my thinking about the ways in which young people's relationships were embedded in coverture as a legal and culture structure. Conversations by email and in person with Mary Fissell and Matthew Gerber were enormously helpful. Benjamin Breen generously made the map for me. To everyone who talked to me about this project, I extend my sincere thanks.

Karin Wulf read and discussed many versions of many papers and chapter drafts as well as the whole manuscript in its last but one round. Her imprint on this project is profound, matched only by the way in which we have shared so much personal and professional solidarity over three decades now through rough times and good times.

My own life has moved through family cycles as I worked on this book. In Austin, Martha Newman's friendship encompasses our work and our households. Far away from our families, I have appreciated the life my family made in Austin with the Newman-Weinbergs and the Hedrick-Hunts as all our babies became adults. Over thirty years of two-careering and almost twenty-five years of co-parenting with Bob Olwell has made my work possible and worthwhile. In particular in this round, he wrangled our daughters endlessly in Lyon and at home while I was in the archives or otherwise on the road. Rose Hardwick Olwell and Grace Hardwick Olwell grew up with this project. During many summer stays in Lyon and dinner conversations at home, we talked about the "girls" who were my historical subjects. The learning, labor, and love of my particular experience of motherhood as my little girls became young women never ceases to amaze me, and I dedicate this book to them.

Sex in an Old Regime City

Introduction

A Foundling's Garter and the World of Young People's Intimacy

Perhaps the most evocative of the surviving artifacts left with children who entered the foundling hospital (the Hôtel-Dieu) in Lyon in the long eighteenth century is a pink silk ribbon decorated in beadwork with rural motifs and the message: "I am going away but not leaving you."[1] It was a very particular kind of ribbon—a garter that could be tied above or below the knee to hold up a young woman's stockings. How did such a garter come to be left with a foundling? Did the mother buy it for herself as small personal adornment or was it a gift to her from her intimate partner? Was it chosen as a token to leave with a foundling because it was distinctive enough to identify the baby in the future, because it linked the father and mother to the baby, or because it was something personal to accompany a newborn baby being dispatched to an unknown future? Garters came in pairs so the mother perhaps poignantly held on to the other one as a reminder of the child she had to give up and of her broken relationship with the partner who failed to marry her. This memento is a tantalizing connection to the elusive world of young people's intimacy in Old Regime France.

The garter is a material and emotional link to a particular time and place. Its beaded decoration was typical of skilled workers in the Lyonnais, and silk was the primary textile produced in Lyon. Many young women as well as men worked in silk production and the associated trades that produced decorative items of all kinds. Garters were made alongside myriad other quickly created fashion items of the kind that became very popular in the eighteenth century. Cheap ribbons were common expressions of affection and or self-adornment that a young person could purchase at a market stall or from a street seller.[2] They offered fun and suggestive ways to demonstrate affection and connection between intimate partners.

The baby was admitted with a copy of his baptism record and a "ticket" that recorded an agreement to admit him to the Hôtel-Dieu as well as the

A foundling's garter. AML HCL HD G85 27 April 1768.

garter. The ticket was dated four months earlier and did not name the parents. The date indicates that the father or another party had negotiated ahead of time with the Hôtel-Dieu administrators to accept the baby, probably with some payment or commitment to pay. One or the other of his parents saved the ticket carefully for four months, valuing its guarantee of a spot for the baby and perhaps finding it a constant reminder of their intimacy and an intention to marry that did not work out. For the father, this arrangement might have met the minimal acceptable standard for taking responsibility for his commitments to his partner when he did not marry her. The infant boy was surrendered to the Hôtel-Dieu one day after baptism, so likely at no more than two days old. The baptism record noted that the local surgeon who brought the baby to the church claimed not to know the names of either the mother or the father. Yet the surgeon and his wife served as godparents and the child was named Jean.[3] The surgeon was probably preserving the privacy of the parents and whoever negotiated the unborn child's eventual transfer likewise gave them anonymity by describing them on the ticket only as a "poor young woman and poor young man." Like most Hôtel-Dieu foundlings who were sent to wet-nurses, he likely died long before he could wonder about the baptism record and garter that survive as the reminders of his parents' youthful intimacy.

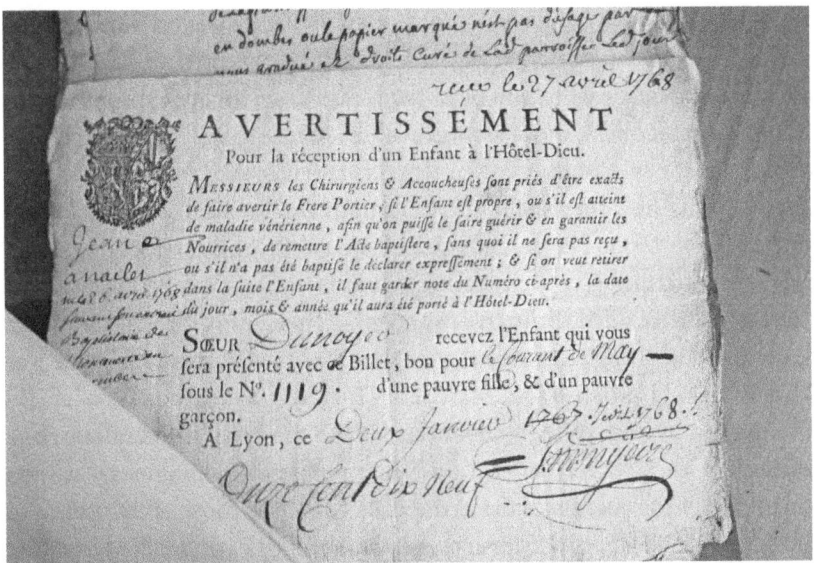

A ticket (*billet*) for the foundling hospital, the Hôtel-Dieu. AML HCL HD G85 27 April 1768.

Whether the garter was a fashion item and/or a suggestive gift and whether it was repurposed as an expression of regret or a continuing bond or a functional means of identification, its changing circumstances—from production to purchase to wearing to accompanying a baby being given up to institutional record and eventually to an archive—point to the shifting experiences of young people's intimacy in its many forms. The kinds of youthful intimate relationships that produced the foundling and his garter are explored though many extraordinary stories of the ordinary lives of young people's work and intimacy in Old Regime France. These stories reveal the histories of young people's work and intimacy in many forms. They are extraordinary only in the sense that such very ordinary events usually went unrecorded. They show that young people's relationships were embedded in work and in community; they involved intense and often roiling emotions, their sexual histories, and women's reproductive health.

In the early 1680s, Marguerite Vignon worked in a large building "long known for manufacture of silk stockings." Those stockings would of course need garters to stay up. It was a typical building on a typical street in Lyon, much like those found in most early modern cities: multiple stories high, divided into many apartments and workplaces with shared stairways, balconies, courtyards, and wells. Many other young female co-workers lived in the building's apartments, as did young male workers and the master silk stocking maker who employed them all. About eighteen months after Marguerite met one of those young men, the journeyman Pierre Barbier, he started—as she said and as their co-workers and neighbors noticed—to keep company with her. They spent many evenings and Sundays walking around town, often to Lyon's new public squares and along the quaysides of the two rivers that ran through the city center, or to the hamlets around the city's perimeter that were filled with gardens and inns. Their co-workers, friends, and sometimes kin accepted a wide range of intimacy as appropriate. Pierre was "always making promises" to Marguerite that he wanted to marry her. He even said so in front of their co-workers. With the expectation of marriage established, they started to have sex. Their relationship no doubt was similar to that of the parents of the garter baby as well as those of thousands of young people working in Lyon and elsewhere. Yet by early 1683, Marguerite was telling her story of everyday heterosociability in a local court when she found herself pregnant and Pierre proved reluctant to keep his promise. She asked friends and co-workers to corroborate her claims. Barbier found himself imprisoned while the legal investigations into his erstwhile girlfriend's allegations proceeded.

Meanwhile at the same time on the same street, Rue Tupin, in a similar building in a neighborhood in the parish of St. Nizier that where many Lyon textile workers lived, Louis Deroche and Marianne Mignot started keeping company. Friends, neighbors, and Mignot's widowed mother saw them having "great familiarity" with each other for a couple of years, and all expected they would wed. Mignot's mother asked Deroche outright about his intentions and he told her that he wanted to marry Marianne. With marriage on the horizon, the young couple started to have sex and she became pregnant. Deroche said he could not marry her immediately, but made some inquiries in their neighborhood about alternative arrangements. He leased a room for a short term from a fifty-year-old woman who lived nearby. The next day he told her he had rented it for a young lady and and arrived the next day with the pregnant Marianne. Within a few days, a baby girl was delivered by a midwife. Deroche visited daily, and a servant brought Marianne soup and other necessities. The baby was baptized, with a friend of Deroche's acting as godfather and the eleven-year-old daughter of the landlady as godmother. The baby was quickly dispatched to a wet-nurse while Marianne moved back to her mother's apartment. She and Deroche picked up their lives and resumed their relationship for a while without marrying. Their daughter was still at the wet-nurse's five years later.[4]

By 1759, when Catherine Eure's baby went "missing," many elements of young women's experiences remained very familiar. Catherine worked as a servant for a schoolmaster and his wife, helping care for the students and staff who lodged with them. She began a relationship with one of her co-workers, a tutor named Sr. Bruiaire who in time promised to marry her. She became pregnant, and "it was the talk of the neighborhood that they must marry."[5] They did not marry and the whole household turned instead to other ways of managing their situation. The schoolmaster and his wife both wanted Eure to leave because they needed the tutor to teach while the schoolmaster was ill. All opposed Eure publicly naming Bruiaire as the father. These concerns were perhaps rooted in the worry that their business might be negatively affected if potential clients heard about the out-of-wedlock birth. The schoolmaster's wife visited a nearby baker's wife several times to inquire about a place where Eure could deliver her baby. A seamstress who lived next to the baker recommended a silk worker who lived on the outskirts of the city. Catherine told the baker's wife that although Bruiaire had promised to marry her, when she told him she was pregnant he threatened to break her arms and legs if she named him as the father. She told the seamstress that he wanted her to name a student as the father. The silk worker and Eure agreed on a price for the lease of a room where she could deliver her baby. Eure claimed that she had tried to visit one of the administrators of the Hôtel-Dieu to explain her situation, but he was not home so she would try again.

Catherine moved the short distance to the silk worker's neighborhood where her temporary landlady delivered the baby. Before the delivery, the schoolmaster's son-in-law visited her and advised her to make a declaration to the Hôtel-Dieu administrators. A neighbor who worked for the son-in-law advised her likewise. Catherine was reluctant to name Bruiaire as the father to the Hôtel-Dieu officials because she was afraid that, if she did so, her employers would pay her wages to the Hôtel-Dieu to cover the costs of her delivery. The neighbor told Catherine to ask her employer's son-in-law for her wages.

A few days after the delivery, Catherine left her host's home without the baby. She asked the daughter and son-in-law of her former employers if she could stay and work for them. She told them she had delivered the baby and paid someone (without naming the person) six francs to abandon the baby at the Hôtel-Dieu. They agreed to help her in the short term. The three women who had helped Catherine prepare for delivery did not admit to inquiring about the baby's fate, although they had heard neighborhood gossip that the baby had been abandoned. Someone informed the legal authorities about the missing baby, a complaint that generated the surviving record of the events. Officials questioned Catherine, the family she worked for, and the three women who had helped her. Catherine said she did not know she was supposed to declare her pregnancy when she had told many people, had acted in good faith, and had nothing to reproach herself about as she had made sure "to keep her baby safe." She claimed that she had asked the schoolmaster's family or the tutor through a third party to pay her delivery costs but they had responded with threats. She insisted that she had used her own wages to pay for her room and the delivery. No explanations were recorded for the absence of the baby's father. The court officials declared that she should be charged with "the disappearance of a baby" (*suppression d'enfant*), a capital crime. However, seemingly no prosecution took place as no other evidence survives.

Intimacy and Young Workers in the Old Regime

These small stories of young people's intimacy woven into the garter, into the mystery of the missing baby, and into broken promises to marry and their reproductive consequences were embedded in larger Old Regime patterns of urban life, production, and reproduction as well as in the political, legal, and religious matrixes of the early modern authorities and communities. They provide backstories about the usual course of relationships and circumstances of young workers who were intimate partners and also demonstrate that many local people and local institutions were involved in regulating young couples' relationships and helping them manage out-of-wedlock pregnancies. Between foundlings, broken promises to marry that were eventually litigated in court, extralegal solutions like the private arrangements for short-term rented rooms, and criminal investigations were some of the by-products of the social worlds of young workers in an old regime city. Young couples' relationships and their fertility were matters of tension, threats, intense emotions of all kinds, and neighborhood as well as official attention. Some of the essential management of young people's intimacy and its reproductive consequences involved paid work as well as the investment of unpaid time, energy, and emotional involvement from a wide range of people.

The extraordinary stories of young workers' ordinary intimacy reframe multiple aspects of the Old Regime. Their experiences challenge the centrality of the disciplining of female sexuality as a critical early modern project of state formation and religious reformation, the history of a sexual double standard in local and long contexts, the history of marriage as a transition from pragmatic to romantic, and the trajectory of the role of law in politics writ large and small of communities and institutions. Their lives also illuminate many more specific debates—for instance, about the history of emotions, infanticide, attitudes to illegitimacy, pre-modern workplaces, and the body. They center on sexuality and intimacy as important ways to understand all of these issues.

This book explores the intimate world of young workers primarily through what I term an "archive of reproduction." These varied materials associated with pregnancies made public records of events that were usually undocumented and they cross standard cataloging lines or research paths. The records of the "archive of reproduction" are unusual only in the sense that they make visible what was well known to people at the time, even if written records were rarely made—or at least not records of the kind that are extant in modern archives. This archive includes many different kinds of records generated by reproduction. Young single women's legal claims for paternity against their consensual intimate partners form the backbone of this material. Court officials documented the finding of babies' cadavers and often included surgeons' reports about the possible circumstances of the infants' deaths. Initial investigations into possible infanticides sometimes survive even when no prosecution followed. Pregnancies could also lead to encounters with the staff of Hôtel-Dieu where pregnant women could deliver their babies or where consensual partners could arrange to leave their babies in the care of the Hôtel-Dieu or engage the administrators as mediators with their partners. Artifacts of pre-modern youthful intimacy that have almost never survived for working people were sometimes deposited as evidence in paternity suits and occasionally are still filed with the archived records. They include letters, promises to marry, billets-doux, tickets for babies to be surrendered to the Hôtel-Dieu, copies of parish register records for baptisms, and extra-judicial private settlements signed at notaries' offices. All of these documents also constituted the material culture of intimacy produced, saved.

Paternity suits and other related documents offer timelines that reveal rich evidence for the ordinary course of intimate relationships between young workers and the many possible solutions to out-of-wedlock pregnancy. A range of documents about courtships gone awry fill thousands of pages of the Lyonnais archives and indeed can be found in virtually every historical time and place and certainly across early modern Europe. Yet even when relationships did not end in marriage, most also did not end up in court. Many such resolutions were handled informally and without generating any legal record or any written record beyond a baptism certificate. Only a minority of them involved a legal action or other event that led to the creation of official records that are sometimes extant. In the Deroche-Mignon case, for example, the couple made a private accommodation as was common. It was five or six years later, when Marianne's mother finally had enough after discovering that Mignon had not only delayed marrying her daughter but was about to marry someone else; this knowledge induced her to petition the court for compensation. Yet these solutions were not secret: family, employers, friends, neighbors, landladies, midwives, wet-nurses, servants, legal officials, clergy, and the staff of social welfare institutions all participated in them.

This archive of reproduction is voluminous and provides compelling evidence about persistent patterns in young people's intimate relationships and their communities' management of them. The extant material coincides with the late seventeenth- and eighteenth-century decades termed in French history as the Old Regime, from around 1660 to the late eighteenth century. It illuminates observable patterns and includes hints at some changes over time as well as a powerful sense of enduring dynamics. I have selected a few typical illustrative examples of broad, persistent patterns across the time period to include in the text. Signals of emerging changes are highlighted when they are evident. The patterns also highlight, however, the persistence and significance of gendered patterns and gendered power between intimate partners as well as between young couples and their communities.[6]

Unraveling the pre-modern history of quotidian sexuality is a challenge because our primary access points have been though the archive of the legal regulation of sexuality in terms of criminality or illegitimacy, a viewpoint that highlights the problematic rather than the ordinary. Historians have access to extensive documentation about the work young people did but much less in the way of their own accounts about their personal lives. The recovery of their personal lives through the prism of illegitimacy has led, as Carolyn Steedman argues, to an eighteenth-century historiography of "sex, love and desire that proclaims . . . female virtue in distress, coercive masculinity and a yielding (mind-less and certainly body-less) femininity."[7] Although historians have made clever use of court records, a gap persists between the much-studied regulation of sexuality and the more elusive practices of everyday sexuality for working people.

In contrast, the history of early modern sexuality as a matter of early modern prescription and politics, whether legal, religious, or cultural, has provided a wealth of insights into early modern and Old Regime French history (and in many other regions) as have the dynamics of specific groups. Pioneering work has explored male same-sex sex, prostitutes, and elites as well as issues like fertility and reproduction.[8] This range of work has also explored how sexuality as a historical category of analysis illuminates many other large themes. State regulation of sexuality and the criminalization of particular forms of sexuality, for example, demonstrate the political and legal concerns and dynamics around reproduction and extra-marital sexuality.[9]

The varied materials in the archive of reproduction, however, reveal the everyday backstories of intimate partnerships through the narrations of actions of young women, sometimes their partners, and often the neighbors, friends, and co-workers who had watched their relationships grow. Their experiences point to the need to re-conceptualize early modern quotidian sexuality in some of the ways historians of sexuality have intimated. Nayan Shah suggests that we should unsettle our conceptual stabilizations and problematize rather than assume gendering of sexuality. "Multiple sexual cultures," as Nina Kushner argues, co-existed and sometimes of course overlapped.[10] The particular sexual culture of young urban workers was important because of the size and visibility of this group for contemporaries, even if silences often seem to shroud their lives beyond their work.

Paternity suits revealed the usual trajectories of relationships in the timelines of months or years as well as details of strategies for informal and extra-judicial negotiations.[11] Young women (and occasionally their male partners) narrated their relationship histories, indeed their sexual histories. They and their community witnesses recollected intimate conversations and actions that are suggestive windows into the emotional worlds of emerging young adults as they experimented with intimate relationships on the path toward marriage. These records demonstrate that the routine courses of intimate relationships between young workers could be rough as well as smooth. They reveal common causes for negotiation and contention.

If much is known about the work lives of seventeenth- and eighteenth-century young men and women in the silk trade and other occupations, strikingly little is known about their intimate lives. Silences exist in the absence of written records that were either never made of routine matters in people's personal lives (other than baptism, wedding, and funeral records) or were regarded as ephemera of daily life and discarded. Some record-keeping silences may have been due to attempts at discretion. Professional archival practices created other silences when archivists valorized some records and disregarded others or made cataloging decisions that makes the documents' content opaque.

Silences are also powerful and historically specific practices, however. What communities discuss with whom and what they record or leave unwritten change over time, place, and rank. While gossip is a well-known early modern mode of information exchange and informal discipline, the failure to gossip or highly selective exchange of informal information were also critical modes of community exchange and regulation.[12] Silence did not inevitably mean secrets because people also chose not to talk about matters that were quite widely known. This book takes up the challenge of writing histories that have not usually been written, in part because they did not involve legal solutions and in part because secrets and especially silences have always been integral to family and community life. Silences have been especially potent around issues of interrupted reproduction in its many forms.

This book focuses on emerging adults in the decade or so before they got married and about their relationships before marriage—and when they did not get married after pregnancy occurred. Its subjects are ordinary people, young workers, and their ordinary physical and emotional intimacy in consensual relationships between young people. Young workers routinely formed a series of intimate consensual relationships in the decade or so between leaving their parents' homes and getting married. Their lives reveal the fundamental integration of quotidian intimacy in terms of the social, public space; work; religious practices; and life course. Rank, labor, and leisure intersected to configure young working people's lives. The worlds of production and reproduction of workers, families, and ranks were tightly interwoven in the lives of young people. That is, this book explores the specific contours of the long history of gender and sexuality in terms of early modern contingencies and structures.

Young couples' relationships were embedded in their communities. From the start, a range of people were involved in their relationships as observers, monitors, regulators, and interveners who I term "community safeguarders." These safeguarders ranged from neighbors, employers, friends, and kin to clergy, notaries, and administrators of the Lyon Hôtel-Dieu. They sought to ensure the stability of the couples' lives and of their communities. They were quick to provide support and facilitate solutions and slow to discipline. Communities realized that young couples' intimacy was inevitable and appropriate and they accepted the inevitable outcome that young people's experiments with intimacy would sometimes lead to pregnancy before marriage or would not be followed by marriage despite broadly based efforts to secure that outcome. Community members practiced communal complicity, that is, they chose to let some things pass or to refrain from telling anyone in authority if they deemed the risk of disruption was greater than the costs of accommodating the predictable reality that young couples would sometimes not marry and some babies would be born out-of-wedlock.

The first two chapters explore how specific forms of intimacy as daily practices were an integral part of young people's lives. They formed couples and engaged in a range of behavior identified as appropriate and respectable. This behavior was actively monitored and regulated by young people themselves; by their families, neighbors, and communities; and occasionally by authorities. The first chapter establishes the parameters of this huge community of young workers in one of Europe's largest and most important economic centers, the city of Lyon. The second analyzes the particular forms of consensual intimacy and the ways in which young couples and communities sought to structure and enforce the extent and limits of pre-marital sexuality.

The last four chapters explore some of the complexities that could unfold when young couples who began an intimate relationship that seemed headed to marriage found themselves as expectant parents. Communities had an elaborate set of practices and resources to manage the risk that licit intimacy in its Old Regime forms entailed, that is, it would likely lead quickly to pregnancy and perhaps before the couple married. In most such cases, couples did marry, even if not immediately. In others, however, couples, together or independently, interrupted social and biological reproduction through practices that everyone knew about at the time but that are very elusive today. On other occasions, they did not marry. While some of out-of-wedlock births were the result of casual encounters, many were the products of stable, consensual relationships when the intimate partners could not or did not want to go forward with marriage: 5-10% of babies in Old Regime Lyon were born outside of marriage, and such births were likely under-recorded elsewhere.[13] A dense web existed of community expectations, informal regulation, avenues of support, and acceptable behaviors in a variety of situations from courtship to efforts to disrupt untimely pregnancies. Clergy, municipal officials, and legal system personnel were all part of this network.

Couples who had access to local networks could mobilize energy, knowledge, and resources about how to manage when a young woman's pregnancy became clear. Intimate partners and especially young women experienced reproduction in a variety of ways from a quick affirmation of marriage through uncertainty and delays to efforts to terminate their pregnancies or come to some other agreement (in court or outside of it) about what would happen next or indeed to abandonment or infanticide. These possibilities were not linear, and couples could and did try more than one option in a variety of orders. The third chapter focuses on the ways in which many forms of community safeguarding sought to reinforce male responsibility for the consequences of sexual activity and the transition to parenthood as the couple shifted incrementally from courting partners to spouses. The neighborhood expectation of marriage as the outcome of licit intimacy usually came with multi-pronged efforts to scaffold matrimony as the desirable outcome when a young woman became pregnant with her longtime intimate partner or even before pregnancy once the couple began to have sex. Kin, neighbors, and employers sought to encourage or press young men to marry their partners and local courts allied with them to ensure that young men would take responsibility for their sexual activity through marriage or financial support.

When couples for many reasons did not marry, young women and men had a swirling set of choices about how to handle out-of-wedlock pregnancy, and they might often have utilized more than one option in endlessly differing sequences. The disciplining of young women for inappropriate sexuality was very rare in practice, and indeed both lay and religious officials seems more concerned with pastoral care than punishment of wrongdoing. Even in the very rare cases of criminal investigations, most ended before prosecution. Community practices supported young women who would be unwed mothers, continued to hold young men responsible for their role in parenthood, and sought to protect the babies born to such unions in a variety of ways.

Local knowledge about how to handle such situations was highly developed. A variety of options existed that helped maintain social order and mitigate the risk to young people's lives and the life of the unborn baby. Young partners could pragmatically pursue, together or individually, a variety of possibilities that were structured, regulated by the community, and well

INTRODUCTION 13

known to everyone. Young couples and communities grasped the reality that out-of-wedlock pregnancies would happen and used these well-established options to handle what they saw as inevitable consequences of young couples' licit intimacy pragmatically rather than as crises.

Chapter 4 explores the "remedies" available to manage out-of-wedlock pregnancy. Young couples might try to interrupt untimely reproduction. They might turn to a variety of "remedies" to restore women's periods through actions that in fact terminated the pregnancies. Even if they did not understand interruptions of pregnancy before quickening (when a woman could feel the baby move which they thought was about eighteen to twenty weeks) as abortions, the efforts to interrupt reproduction early in pregnancy were in fact terminations. Both male and female partners believed they could end untimely pregnancies and participated in efforts to make that happen. All kinds of people—family, employers, friends, local legal and religious officials—sought to reach other kinds of remedies by brokering agreements that would provide a different kind of remedy by safeguarding the futures of the couple and the safety of the baby.

Chapter 5 explores the labor of providing paid services for out-of-wedlock pregnancies, a work niche that provided livelihoods for the purveyors of care through pregnancy and delivery, and afterward for the newborn. Landladies who specialized in providing short-term rented rooms for unmarried mothers offered shelter, advice, pre- and post-natal care, and help in arranging for midwives, baptisms, and wet-nurses. Out-of-wedlock newborns were usually rapidly dispatched to rural wet-nurses as also were legitimate babies and infants abandoned to the Hôtel-Dieu. Some midwives worked for the court as medico-legal experts who made official reports to confirm or deny the allegations of pregnancy made by women who brought paternity suits. Their reporting made them gatekeepers to the legal system. Purveyors of such services made possible a routinized, respectable handing of out-of-wedlock pregnancies and they worked hand in hand with other community safeguarders.

Chapter 6 examines the ways in which neighbors gossiped, provided support, and yet looked the other way or did not ask questions were all key elements of the ways in which communities, for the sake of reputation, pastoral care, or income, deployed pragmatic, structured practices to handle out-of-wedlock pregnancies and births. The depositing of babies at the Hôtel-Dieu could be negotiated with a variety of brokers. Pathways even existed for handling the incidental/situational/intentional deaths of newborns born to unmarried women. Certainly, many babies were anonymously abandoned, despite all the efforts of the staff to admit foundlings through regular routines. Some babies were informally and anonymously buried, having perished from lack of care, perhaps intentionally withheld sometimes, or premature birth. Occasionally, women engaged in active infanticide and concealed the bodies in drains or rivers. In all such outcomes, the young partners and their communities mobilized local knowledge, but the pragmatic practices that tried to ensure the well-being of all parties also depended on the select silence of many people about what they knew and who they told.

Even couples who did not marry were usually involved in negotiations and conflicts about how to proceed, and many women who gave birth out-of-wedlock were far from isolated and alone, as shown by Catherine Eure's case. Young men rarely simply abandoned the scene when they did not marry, and their reputations—and those of their partners—depended in part on how they reacted to the responsibility of parenthood by their choices, often brokered by many other parties. Indeed, the ongoing presence of a partner, even with no marriage, made a critical difference to young women's situations before and after delivery. Yet these were surely fraught months for both partners, often filled with frustration, anger, anxiety, and uncertainty, especially for young women.

Whether the interruptions to biological (pregnancy) and social (marriage) reproduction were pauses, hiccups, or permanent situations, these ordinary events are recorded today only from exceptional occasions when someone reported a concern to a legal official, and a record of some kind was generated that is now part of the archive of reproduction. As with all early modern court matters, usually nobody alerted authorities unless some provocation occurred that was tied to the status of the parties, suspicion or conflict arose between the parties and their communities, or the parties were outsiders who lacked access to the protections and resources of local networks.[14] The futures of their babies once born were extremely uncertain. Surviving records reveal an exceptional glimpse of ways of handling out-of-wedlock pregnancies that were routine for contemporaries.

If communal complicity in its many forms often allowed young couples to resolve their out-of-wedlock pregnancies with their reputations and prospects largely intact and young women were able to resume their lives, the dynamics of youthful sexuality were gendered and the penalties for the young man and the young woman were not the same. Young women who had been in consensual relationships headed toward marriage and their many allies, paid and unpaid, sought to mitigate the long-term impact on them and hold young men firmly responsible for the sexual activity they had justified by the prospect of marriage. This meant that young women had room to explore licit intimacy and their chastity did not require celibacy. Respectable solutions endorsed by working communities meant that young women were not ruined if they gave birth without being married; they went back to their working lives, and they probably eventually married—sometimes to the same partner, sometimes to other men. Nevertheless, in a whole variety of ways, the impact for women was different and more serious. The culture of licit intimacy and support for managing unplanned reproductive consequences was far from the traditional sexual double standard in which women paid the price and men got off scot free, but nevertheless, young women and men were still in a set of asymmetrical gendered power relationships, albeit more complex and nuanced.

Intimacy is at the heart of this book. It involved physical proximity, emotional connection, bodily experience, and sometimes sexual closeness. It requires us to engage the historical specificity of universal human experiences. Young people have always been involved in intimate relationships in which sexuality and fertility were keynotes for them and their communities. Relationships always involve bodies, fertility, and acceptable relationships, but the particular forms are configured and reconfigured over time. Sex between two people was given specific meanings not only between the couple but in the community, both local, clerical, and official. Early modern emerging adults were usually defined as adults when they married, a status that provided men with the legal privileges of adulthood as heads of household when they became economically independent. However, these transitions were incremental as many newly married couples only slowly, if ever, achieved economic independence.[15] Sex also seemed to lead to adult responsibilities as when young men were charged with responsibility for babies they had fathered and young women were able to express desire licitly and engage in sexual activity before marriage without ruining their reputations as long as they followed the conventions of their communities about what constituted licit intimacy.

Power was layered into all forms of intimacy in ways that were historically configured. Gendered power shaped relations between intimate partners as well as between men and women more broadly. Asymmetrical power relations inflected rank, religion, kinship, and workplaces. Between young couples and their local communities, asymmetrical power relations made for important potential resources and providers of support as well as protectors and theoretical discipliners. Conversations about young people's intimacy took place in many sites of asymmetrical power relations—in the confession box, at notaries' offices, of course in court or in prison, and with a wide range of people like employers, parents, neighbors, or Hôtel-Dieu administrators. Power relations also shaped silences, whether in terms of community power to tell or not, or in disciplinary and archival power to reject or marginalize intimacy as important and knowable. Emotions involved practices of power and power factored into the ways communities coalesced or fragmented.[16]

Where were emotions in these young couples' relationships? Historians of marriage as an institution have largely characterized the history of marriage as a shift from pragmatic partnerships based on property to modern companionate marriages based on romantic love. The emotional stakes have been elusive in pre-modern relationships in part because of the lack of ego documents whereas the financial arrangements like dowries recorded in contracts are very visible in extant documents. This book instead explores emotions as observable practices that can be identified in court records or occasional material culture objects.[17]

The archive of reproduction offers an extraordinary window into the ways in which youthful consensual intimacy highlights clerical, state, and community experiences, attitudes and practices around sexuality that alter our understandings of the dynamics of early modern society. Courts, clergy, and communities primarily played pastoral rather than disciplinary roles. Projects of extra-marital pregnancy control were essentially local and highly variable rather than uniform and national. The limited reprimand efforts were focused more on the people who enabled solutions to extra-marital pregnancy rather than the young women themselves. Enforcement was at best occasional and limited to a particular minority subset of out-of-wedlock pregnancies. Young men as well as young women were held responsible for the consequences of their sexual activity. Young women who chose to go to court to make paternity claims leveraged the apparatus of the legal system and the state to secure assistance and to defend their reputations.

This book centers mundane practices of intimacy in many forms to re-examine many key pre-modern topics. It explores the pleasure as well as the many uncertainties intimacy involved, and it revises the historiography of the pre-modern body in terms of the circulation of knowledge among young women and men. It examines workplaces as sites of reproduction, of social practices and procreation as well as production. Practices like infanticide and abandonment are examined as community mediated strategies rather than as occasions for the criminalization of single women or as isolated emergency steps.[18] In all of these regards and more, the ordinary lives of young urban workers involved rank-specific patterns and practices, but working people constituted by far the largest sexual culture in terms of sheer numbers. Lyon's young workers are important because they were utterly ordinary, and their very ordinariness invites us to interrogate the usual as a category of analysis. In its focus on consensual and licit desire, it demonstrates the expansive intimacy young people enjoyed and the many ways in which communities sought to mitigate the risks inherent in permitting that intimacy through community safeguarding and communal complicity. A wide range of people—peers, kin, neighbors, employers, clergy, landladies, midwives, wet-nurses, a variety of legal industry officials and the welfare institution of the Hôtel-Dieu—participated in supporting licit intimacy and risk management. Thinking about the practices of normative heterosexuality reveals not only the experiences of emerging adults but recasts or complicates many of our major historical narratives about law, economy, community, religion, state, and family. The foundling's garter provides a window into the ordinary, if usually elided, world of emerging adulthood that intersected with every aspect of the Old Regime world.[19]

In all of these ways, the issues around young people's Old Regime intimacy had particular valencies, but they also point to the profound persistence of challenges that emerging adults and their communities still grapple with. Emerging adults' intimacy is still often fraught as well as wonderful, still often results in untimely pregnancies, and still involves critical issues about women's reproductive health. Communities, courts, and clergy as well as governments are still invested in trying to manage young people's sexual activity in particular and patterns of intimacy more broadly. Sometimes out-of-wedlock babies are given up for adoption, or on occasion, infant deaths in opaque or explicit circumstances still occur. In Texas, a Safe Haven law passed in 1999 allowed newborns younger than sixty days old to be dropped off at fire stations or police stations or medical centers with no questions asked and no prosecution, and this law became the model for nationwide initiatives to reduce the likelihood of infanticides. In July 2019, a newborn baby's body wrapped in a plastic bag was pulled from the same Lyon river dead babies were pulled out of in the Old Regime. Even as we pay attention to the historical specificity of the young adults in Old Regime Lyon, we can recognize the continuities that shape experiences of sexuality and reproduction.

1
Sourcing Intimate Histories
The Social World of Young Workers

Francoise Bert moved from her native village to Lyon in the late 1670s and found work with a master silk worker. Like many other young women making a living, she "pulled the cords" on looms for male weavers, a role that required skill and experience to keep the weaving process running smoothly. These "draw girls" and many other women were just as essential to Lyon textile production as their male counterparts.[1] They routinely worked with young men employed by the same master, and they often lived in apartments clustered in the same big building. By 1682, one of the journeymen Bert's employer hired, Pierre Aymond, began to court her and eventually they started to talk about getting married. Eighty years later, Anne Rubard, likewise a migrant from a rural area, worked as a draw girl with another journeyman, Jean Claude Fiancon. Their employer and mistress watched their relationship develop as they walked out, went to mass together on Sundays, and sometimes worked very late, long past the midnight hour when their employers and the other workers retired to sleep. They talked about getting married and he wrote her an effusive promise to marry that she kept as a token of his affection and a surety of his commitment. As Rubard recalled later, with the decision to marry seeming firm, they on occasion took the opportunity of late-night work shifts to have breaks for sex.[2]

For couples like these who were partners in production and reproduction, work was inextricably linked with their social lives in space, time, and place. Eight decades apart, their experiences were very similar and typical of those of thousands of young people who worked in Lyon from the mid-seventeenth century to the 1760s when the silk industry and associated trades dominated the city economy. Although court records described both young women as servants, they described themselves as making a living in the commercial production of their employers rather than the domestic labor usually associated with the term "servant."[3] Their journeys to the big city for work were part of a well-established pattern that made Lyon, like most other major

Sex in an Old Regime City. Julie Hardwick, Oxford University Press (2020). © Oxford University Press.
DOI: 10.1093/oso/9780190945183.001.0001

European cities, a hub for migrants. Their domestic, remunerative, and social worlds were tightly braided, as work places also provided sites of intimacy and residential spaces were used for work.

This chapter explores the parameters of urban life and paid work that framed the intimate world of young people in an Old Regime city, and explores the sources that can reveal that intimacy. In a range of documents that many aspects of reproduction sometimes generated, they and their communities narrated many aspects of the practices by which emerging adults formed partnerships and managed the inherent challenges of intimacy. Emerging adults were essential members of the labor force and community as they began to explore personal relationships that might eventually lead to marriage and the establishment of their own households. The emotions that animated their relationships and that their relationships animated in their communities were always important aspects of intimacy and, although usually elusive in the archives, offer a glimpse into an important stage in their lives.

Finding the History of Intimacy in Official Records of the Regulation of Sexuality

The archive of reproduction curates documents that are primarily legal or institutional records although such records and the items occasionally deposited with them could also constitute the material culture of intimacy and they were layered with emotional meanings. Extant records were created by court officials; by the officials of the Hôtel-Dieu; by surgeons, midwives, and low-level court officials making bureaucratic reports as part of the legal process; or by notaries in their role as official writers of legally binding agreements made outside the judicial system. Some materials deposited as evidence, such as records of births and marriages from parish registers or Hôtel-Dieu tickets, were also institutionally generated. Others such as examples of or references to emotional objects that are rarely extant for working people like courtship gifts, letters, promises to marry, and foundling tokens. Even legal and institutional records also represent the material culture of intimacy as well as more obvious examples like garters or letters or promises to marry. Such records in fact were sites of intense emotion for the participants in the decision making and negotiations about intimacy that preceded the making of such documents and in the experience of giving evidence, hearing verdicts, reflecting on the outcomes, and so on.

The records and associated evidence from paternity suits are at the core of this archive and represent an invaluable but complicated history of intimacy, inevitably shaped by the circumstances of a lawsuit and the creation of a legal record. The dossiers of paternity cases could include documents from many different stages of the judicial process. The women narrated their relationships in initial petitions to the court and then called witnesses who could speak to the history of their partnerships.[4] Witnesses' depositions (many from young men and women as well as other employers, neighbors, and co-workers) revealed many aspects of the social practices through which emerging adults formed intimate partnerships. The interrogatories during which judges questioned the plaintiffs (all young women) and the defendants (usually young men although a few were older employers, often already married) sometimes survive. Court orders to hold young men in prison while the investigation continued or until they had arranged for payment of financial orders are sometimes included. (The alleged fathers were frequently held in prison during all or part of the legal process, as was common in early modern court investigations.) If disputes between parties over the release of young men took place, they are noted. The court's final decisions virtually always recognized the young women's claims as valid with the award of financial costs to compensate for the costs of delivery and the charging of long-term custody of the babies to the fathers. Very often, the dossiers are partial, sometimes no doubt due to loss of documents but usually likely because the plaintiff dropped the case and the partners settled out of court.

Paternity suit records illuminate the timelines of very conventional relationships that lay behind the unusual endings in court. Single pregnant women who chose to go to court to make a paternity complaint selected a highly unusual strategy for women in their situations, an important characteristic to consider.[5] They decided to make paternity claims only if they had a feasible chance of success and they might do so as a negotiating tactic or because other forms of mediation had produced no resolution.[6] In fact, many of the female plaintiffs had likely tried one or more of the other options or would do so after going to court so they had also tried much more common solutions.[7]

The relationship histories illuminate the many possible solutions that existed for out-of-wedlock pregnancy between marriage and infanticide, and they locate all phases of young people's relationships as part of a communal project. These extra-judicial strategies are very elusive for historians because many such breakdowns were handled informally and without generating any written record beyond a baptism certificate. Paternity claims often reveal histories in which such strategies had been tried and sometimes succeeded—that is, the matter ended up in court only because of subsequent disputes, often about other matters. For instance, they came into court only via disputes over payments. These backstories demonstrate how working people, whether couples, neighbors, families, co-workers or employers, clergy, or legal officials, engaged informally and in court to define and monitor appropriate intimacy for young couples. That included licit desire as a widely accepted developmental stage for emerging adults, young women as well as young men, and young men's accountability through the legal system and outside it for the reproductive consequences of their intimacy with the clear expectation that male partners were expected to take some responsibility even if they did not get married.

These backstories embedded in relationship narratives also highlight the role of emotions and the place of licit desire in ordinary youthful, consensual intimate relationships. Those narrations reframe the role of emotion in our understanding of marriage formation in early modern Europe and unpack the category of pragmatic partnerships driven by property concerns to explore the ways in which emotional practices integrally braided actions and feelings. Emotions as learned practices played a critical role in early modern courtships, although the expressions of those emotions were often expressed in time specific ways in terms of actions as well as verbal articulations.[8] Affection and desire were intertwined elements of pre-modern emerging partnerships, and a wide range of emotional practices were routine elements of early modern courtships. Accounting for this emotional fabric transforms our understandings of the transition from single to married in early modern Europe at a time when marriage was regarded as of pivotal importance in political, legal, and cultural as well as social and economic terms.

Historicizing the emotions of intimate partners is challenging. Historians (including myself) of early modern marriage have in the main lacked the kind of source material conventionally associated with the history of emotions. Certainly, non-elite early modern young people have left almost no surviving ego documents where individuals wrote about how they felt. Even the few letters that do survive for these young couples raise all kinds of questions about the strategic and conventional tropes that provide filters between the historian and the emotions of the writer and reader. Young women's initial petitions occasionally included some discussion of the emotions of both parties. Witnesses described what people did, often in great detail, but rarely commented on feelings they expressed.

Emotions as practices, however, can be identified in attentive readings of many legal and other kinds of sources that recorded observable actions.[9] The legal setting as always shaped what was said as well as what and how it was recorded. Young women who hoped to be successful in paternity claims needed to emphasize affection, promises, stable relationships, and parental approval in narratives of courtship in order to protect their own reputations as well as present evidence persuasive to the court. Moreover, women who chose to pursue a legal remedy for their broken relationships self-selected because they knew their case fit the legal model and they had witnesses who could speak to these attributes. Witnesses answered specific questions although they also often made many incidental observations. Yet the actions as well as articulations in the records point to conventional expressions of intimate emotions and (apparent) ruptures of those conventions.

The legal logic of the paternity suits shaped who went to court as well as what was said and how it was recorded. Young women needed to be able to demonstrate that they were in stable partnerships with young men of about the same age and rank who were plausible spousal prospects. To do so, they needed to have neighbors, co-workers, and friends who would provide reliable testimony to the effect that their monogamous relationships were approved by the community and seemed to be moving toward matrimony. Pregnancy before marriage was entirely routine and in fact regarded as such. Although historians have seen "pregnancy declarations" as emblematic of patterns of illegitimacy, in fact, over 90% of women who made paternity claims in royal courts were in stable consensual relationships because they had no case via this legal route if they were not. Largely invisible in the historical record is the number of couples who cohabited in stable, monogamous relationships without the legal benefit of marriage after the birth of one or more children and likely sometimes indefinitely.[10]

Consequently, the collection of documents in the archive of reproduction highlights a powerful sense of a sexual culture of heteronormativity. There is no hint in these records of same-sex desire and rarely of casual heterosexuality or overtly transactional sex. Young women who had kissed many boys or had casual encounters had engaged in intimacy of the kind that was not respectable for young single people. They could not hope to make successful cases, and so their relationships were rarely documented in this series of records. Even though young women's narratives of their sexual histories in these consensual relationships consistently presented the pivotal shift from the extensive intimacy associated with walking out to intercourse associated with "marital" sex as a moment of coercion, few other instances of violent or abusive sex were registered because this legal pathway did not engage with those problems.[11] So women who were seduced and abandoned or who became pregnant as a consequence of casual relationships are in fact also largely absent from these records, and such situations were perhaps quite unusual. Of course, these other sexual cultures co-existed with stable heteronormativity and may even have overlapped.

The powerful imprint of marriage as the norm in the archive of reproduction also reflected a society where matrimony had a high political, economic, and cultural value and in which young men in particular, but also young women, gained the legal and other privileges of adulthood only as spouses. Certainly, a few women do seem to have chosen to form households with other women as economic units and perhaps for other reasons.[12] Yet the pull of marriage for the financial benefits of pooling labor and resources as well as its legal and cultural status meant that a powerful sexual culture among working people focused on monogamous heterosexuality, even if this was not the only sexual culture in their circles.

The existence of local networks and rank were two other important variables that shaped how likely women were to choose to file a paternity lawsuit even if they were in stable relationships. Migrants may have been over-represented even though many young women who were born in Lyon also went to court. However, young women from the surrounding rural areas who moved to Lyon as teenagers to work perhaps had fewer connections in the city whom they might call on to help them reach a settlement by one of the many extralegal forms of resolutions young couples used. Families of middling or higher rank rarely used the institutional judicial system as a tool to resolve out-of-wedlock pregnancy. Women of higher status may have been supervised more closely by their families and so were less likely to have experiments with intimacy before marriage and/or preferred private solutions that would avoid gossip about their families that might damage their elite reputations. The occasional paternity suit from a middling or elite family indicates that they resorted to managing the situation by keeping it out of public view in spatial as well as judicial terms, confirming that strategies around young couples' intimate lives were connected to social rank in many regards.[13]

Young women's accounts of their relationships as given to and recorded by court officials are complex texts: they acknowledged what happened and the meanings they attached to it, but they also deployed legal tropes and multivalent filters that served several purposes in a lawsuit. Like all legal records, paternity suits were mediated by the circumstances of a lawsuit and the creation of a legal record. Women's retelling of their sexual histories in a legal proceeding featured the partners coming together as a chaste (but not celibate) couple. Women had to demonstrate chastity as a key to legal success as well as present witnesses who would attest to the existence of stable relationships where marriage was feasible. They used their court narratives in part to defend their honor and to distinguish their involvement in intimacy from prostitution, a distinction that mattered in legal terms as well as community ones. So women's narratives for the purposes of their paternity suits were strategic. Lawyers who advised women (women's cases were allowed to proceed after their initial petitions; court clerks recorded the names of lawyers) and the clerks who recorded the petitions, testimony, questioning, and other evidence also shaped the record of what happened. Yet women's voices, experiences, and especially actions are still legible in these complex texts.[14]

The records of paternity suits in the Lyon archives are extensive and rich but very uneven.[15] The surviving records for the royal *sénéchausée* court begin in the late 1650s and continue until the Revolution in 1789 with thousands of pages of documents and hundreds of records.[16] However, they are not consistent across the decades. The years 1700–1719 are missing completely, for instance. Wide variations exist in the number that survive from year to year and in the patterns. Women associated with the Hôtel-Dieu in some way, for example, made the majority of the claims in the early 1720s. Many complaints include only the initial petition; some include very rich and detailed documentation from plaintiff, defendant, and witnesses. This unevenness does not lend itself to meaningful quantitative analysis but the overall volume produces rich accounts with granular texture that suggest clear patterns.

The Puzzle of Paternity Suits

The archive of reproduction, through the evidence of paternity suits and the other associated material, historicizes Old Regime young women's emotional and physical intimacy as conventional and quotidian and as a matter of negotiation with their male partners in tandem with different groups in their communities. These paternity suits are a very well-known source to historians, but they pose a legal, archival, and historiographical puzzle. Although women who made paternity claims in court used the state's legal system as a means to control their reproductive and sexual lives and discipline their male partners, their legal actions have instead traditionally been coded as evidence of the state's efforts to discipline female sexuality. Unpacking this puzzle is critical to understanding the ways in which paternity suits and the evidence with them point instead to a very different dynamic around women's and indeed young people's intimacy at every level from couples to communities to church and state.

Routinely cataloged and referred to now as "pregnancy declarations" (*déclarations de grossesse*), these paternity suits have become a staple of early modern historiography as evidence for the early history of sexuality and the historicization of illegitimacy and as pivotal elements in an argument that placed the regulation of gender and family as a key element in state formation. The paternity suits that are at the center of the archive of reproduction represent a well-known source in French history. Historians initially used "declarations" primarily to look at illegitimacy. They have focused on the legal outcome—a child born out-of-wedlock—to gauge attitudes toward, patterns of, and causes for the births of natural children in early modern France. The earliest such work truly pioneered an expanded purview for the history of sexuality both as an archival subject and as a more expansive field than fertility and reproduction.[17] Typical single mothers were identified as female servants.[18] More recently, "declarations" have also been used to examine jurisprudence and understandings of the female body.

Many historians, including myself, have claimed that the 1556 Edict on Clandestine Pregnancy made it mandatory for young single women to declare their pregnancies to a variety of public authorities, often with an associated assertion that midwives were required to get their delivering patients to name the fathers of out-of-wedlock babies. This view become received wisdom through a long process that included a legal debate about what the law required, professional archival practices, and a powerful if inadvertent professional confirmation bias. This persistent myth has elided much of what the paternity suits in fact reveal.

The basic premise is wrong: the 1556 Edict was poorly written as many observers have noted, but it did not require single women to declare their pregnancies at all nor did it require midwives to be official witnesses who established who fathers were and made declarations. What it did say was that single women who *had concealed* their pregnancies and childbirths *without having declared* either one *or having had witness* to either one, even as to whether the child was born dead or alive, *and who had deprived the baby of holy baptism* would be assumed to have committed murder and infanticide and punished by death.[19] (Emphases mine.) That is, it confirmed the death penalty for single women who killed their babies and made concealment of pregnancy a key proof of intention. The edict was reissued word for word in 1708 with the added requirement that priests publicize it from the pulpit every three months. The edict referred only to the consequences of lack of a declaration in specific circumstances around a baby's death and offered no specifics of any kind about what "having declared" might mean or what appropriate witnessing might involve. It gave no role to midwives. Historians often acknowledged that the edict was not enforced.[20] However, there was nothing to enforce.

Declarations were in fact generic legal instruments that had nothing to do with the 1556 Edict. They were used for a varied set of purposes: as declaration of facts, as acts that modified previous acts, or as complements to judicial cases. They were common far earlier than 1556 and used in many situations.[21] In practice, the lawsuits archived as "pregnancy declarations" were essentially paternity claims brought in local courts by young women who were pregnant, usually against their consensual partners when promised marriages failed to materialize. They asserted their legal right to repair their honor, secure financial compensation, and arrange for their intimate partners to have physical custody of the babies as well as pay for their upbringing. Moreover, paternity claims were not novelties in 1556 as women had made legal claims for alleged paternity well before the mid-sixteenth century.[22]

Certainly confusion existed in the eighteenth century about whether the edict required a declaration. Educated men sometimes articulated erroneous terms to the edict, and the circulation of their errors contributed to the crystallization of misunderstandings. The error circulated in popular texts, for example, such as Louis-Sébastian Mercier's *Tableau de Paris* published in the 1780s. Mercier discussed the 1556 Edict in his article on midwives—where he noted, "When a girl becomes a mother, she doesn't tell anyone despite the edict of Henri II. . . . The edict of Henri II has fallen into disuse" and hardly one young woman out of a hundred who delivered clandestinely "knew of the old law which condemned her to death for not having declared her pregnancy."²³ Mercier's observations likely contained a web of fiction and fact—young women perhaps did not indeed know of the old law as it did not in fact require them to declare. Eighteenth-century jurists were aware of such misconceptions about the 1556 Edict and experts tried to correct them. Pierre Brillon's discussion of *"grossesse"* in 1727 concluded that the criminal penalties of the edict were in effect only if the baby was not baptized. It was directed at infanticide and not at single women who were pregnant. Jean-François Fournel, a Parisian *avocat*, noted in 1781 in what became the standard treatise on seduction as a legal category, that prosecutors had sometimes sought convictions against women with living babies on the grounds that they had not made declarations. He emphasized, however, that all such cases were rejected because the edict did not allow it. Fournel noted that "declarations" were essentially paternity claims and added that the belief that the 1556 Edict required a declaration was "an error" and making a declaration was "superfluous."²⁴

In the eighteenth century, some municipalities and local institutions did establish regulations that aimed to ensure that young pregnant women did make declarations or that people who knew them did. Nantes (1725), for example, passed a municipal regulation intended to make young single mothers declare their pregnancies whereas Brest (1735) and St. Malo (precise date unclear) created regulations that would require midwives and/or landlords to notify authorities if single women gave birth. In the early eighteenth century, the Grenoble Hôtel-Dieu started to require declarations from the young women it admitted with the hope of making fathers support their offspring. It is unlikely, however, that these kinds of local regulations were ever widely observed. Midwives and landlords and even doctors as a rule had no interest in forcing young women to make declarations, and there was widespread disregard of the municipal prompts.²⁵ That is, most people did not think the 1556 Edict or local legislation required a declaration or should apply to a young woman when people knew she was pregnant and a landlord or midwife who knew usually did not feel the need to report it.

The royal court in Lyon that heard paternity suits attempted to introduce a local regulation for the management of pregnant single women in the early eighteenth century, but its short life undermines the idea that disciplining female pregnancy was a top-down project, even if it may have stoked local confusion in subsequent decades. In 1704, the court passed a ruling that required anyone who received a woman at home to have a baby to notify one of its judge or risk corporal punishment and or a fine of 250 *livres*. As with other local regulations, it focused on the facilitators of out-of-wedlock births rather than on the young women themselves. However, when a Lyon paternity suit ruling was appealed to the Parlement of Paris, the Parlement (France's highest legal court) annulled the Lyon regulation in a 1712 ruling on the grounds that its requirements went beyond the 1556 Edict. The order also forbade the Lyon court from making such regulations. These kinds of top-down restrictions on local initiatives affected other municipalities too.[26]

If the Parlement's ruling did create clarity in some quarters, some confusion clearly persisted in Lyon about the possible existence of some requirement among elites and working people. A 1787 Lyon episcopal guide for parish priests, for example, included the terms of the 1556 Edict and subsequent reissues but made no mention of any additional local regulation, suggesting a clear understanding of the limited parameters of the edict.[27] Yet occasionally midwives mentioned a requirement to inform the authorities, although most midwives certainly did not do so. Likewise, infrequently plaintiffs' petitions or intimate partners in conversations recalled in paternity suits made references to some kind of requirement. When Nicole Armonie told Claude Dambois that she was pregnant, for example, he responded that he would "follow the orders of the king and give her ten *ecus* and take the baby but would not keep his word" (that is, his often-made promises to marry her). When Estimiette Montmain came to court in 1741 when her intimate partner had disappeared to go to his home village to get "his papers," that is, his parents' permission for them to marry, she explained that she came to court "to make a declaration to avoid the severity of the ordinance."[28] It is entirely unclear what young men and women were referring to when they made such statements, but they do attest to a popular as well as an elite cloud of confusion.

Local legal elites did not necessarily give up the desire to expand regulation tied to erroneous understandings of the edict judging by the elliptical indications of a manuscript "book of declarations" for the years 1741–1747 that includes 187 very formulaic, brief statements from pregnant single women. The cover page said nothing beyond "book of declarations" and the contents provide no indicators as to the purpose of the declarations or for what jurisdiction. Women also still used the court system to make regular paternity claims and continued to make the informal settlements that were the most common strategy of all. Yet the two primary signatories of the statements were two judges who also supervised many of the paternity claims in the *sénéchausée* court in the same years and who frequently witnessed the questionings of the young female plaintiffs. The book seems to have been a personal project of theirs for which we have little explanation. One at least was new to the court at the time, having inherited the position from his father a couple of years earlier. The court had begun to show a bit of interest in the possibility of women making false accusations (judging by the rise of that issue in their questioning), as we will see, and people who appeared occasionally made elliptical references to some version of "his majesty's ordinance." Their interest might have been part of a broader elite concern about morality in the mid-eighteenth century, but the impact of their measures did not seem to extend beyond some new language. In other parts of France, it did seem that a new official could imprint the language of the lawsuits.[29]

The Old Regime confusion seems to have caused subsequent generations of archivists and historians to perpetuate the myth about the status of "declarations" and the 1556 Edict. In particular, the Lille ordinance of 1590, an outlier more than a century before other local efforts, seemed to have become mixed up with royal legislation. Lille officials made their regulation during a serious local economic crisis, and they included the mandate that midwives should ask women about paternity while they were in labor and then report to city officials to prevent children being abandoned to the city's care. This local regulation, tied to the city's desire to avoid the costs of caring for abandoned children, seems to have been conflated in the historiography with the efforts of the 1556 Edict to prevent infanticide.[30]

The organization of the French archives has magnified the idea of the significance and visibility of the 1556 Edict for historians.[31] Guides to series B (legal records) in French departmental archives routinely include a separate section entitled *déclarations de grossesse,* a beguiling category that promises to deliver the aftermath of the 1556 Edict neatly packaged into numbered files. This taxonomy emerged from the organization of the archives in the nineteenth and early twentieth centuries, perhaps reflecting the pro-natalism of that era. The catalog category represents the sorting that archival staff did when the document organization was systematized, and in fact, the archivists themselves often added the term *déclaration de grossesse* in pencil on the lawsuit covers above the original description of *plainte,* presumably during that process.

As archivists over decades reorganized and renumbered the city's vast judicial records, the updates to the Lyon series B catalog show an incremental increase in the *declarations de grossesse* category. In 1975, Marie-Claude Phan listed 1720 as the first date for Lyon holdings of "pregnancy declarations" (based on the Lyon catalog at that time) as part of a survey of existing records in many regions. Subsequently, when the entire B series was renumbered, a new guide added three boxes for the decades before 1700 that include almost 2,000 pages of documents.[32] Presumably the archival staff found more *plaintes* for paternity suits of this kind during the review of documents for the new catalog and filed them as *déclarations de grossesse*, according to the categories established in earlier catalogues.

This archival practice generated a fictional distinctive category of "pregnancy declarations" that did not exist in the original documents. In the cases themselves, the simple term "complaint" [*plainte*] was used, and their purpose was to seek redress from the alleged fathers rather than to make a public record of an out-of-wedlock pregnancy. The phrase *déclaration de grossesse* was not used in paternity lawsuits in Lyon until the mid-eighteenth century. For instance, the term *plainte* was used for the cover of the Bert-Aymond complaint in 1682 (with a notation *grossesse* written in pencil in a modern hand underneath that must have been added during a sorting of the papers) while the cover of the Rubard-Fiancon suit in 1762 used the term *plainte et declaration en grossesse*.[33] The only reference to any kind of declaring in these legal actions came in the interrogatory stage when judges routinely asked young women if they had "declared" their pregnancies to their intimate partners, by which the judges were simply inquiring whether the women had told them. Even if the young women said no, the judges were not concerned about a legal violation. The simple descriptive term *plainte* also dominated contemporary usage elsewhere until the mid-eighteenth century. Moreover, even then declaration, as we have seen, meant general legal claim and had nothing to do with the 1556 legislation.[34]

Finally, the power of professional paradigms also seems to lie behind the acceptance and reiteration of the interpretative link between the edict and a mandatory declaration that tied the disciplining of sexuality to state formation. The 1556 Edict gained historiographical prominence in the last thirty years as a key legislative innovation that underpinned a broad early modern link between lawmaking, regulation of family life and female sexuality in particular, and state formation.[35] Historians have repeatedly claimed that it required single pregnant women to "declare" their pregnancies to local authorities and midwives to assist local officials in determining who the fathers were. Failure to do so constituted concealing their pregnancies, a form of behavior that would be taken as de facto proof of infanticide, a capital offense. This claim about the edict was a pivotal element in what has become a powerful historiographical trope about the disciplining of female sexuality as a central project for early modern states as well as for reformed religions. The link between regulation of women's sexuality and state formation first posited by French historians inspired a generation of work for regions across early modern Europe and "pregnancy declarations" became the epitome of the emergence of an early modern disciplinary state in which the regulation of gender, family, and especially female sexuality was a core element of the centralization of state power. Moroever, the strict regulation of female sexuality was positioned not only as a critical project for centralizing states but at the center of understanding of religious change with the disciplining of female sexuality as a central dynamic of both Protestant and Catholic reformations. In this paradigm, women were seen as the source of disruptions with regard to sexuality and were thus the focus of intense regulatory energy as well as prosecution.[36]

Even if a few historians pointed out that the edict did not involve any requirement for any kind of declaration, a powerful professional confirmation bias interested in disciplining as a historical process and in centering gender and family as a way to rethink traditional meta-narratives contributed to the acceptance of the misinterpretation of the 1556 Edict.[37] Historians were interested in disciplinary formations in the 1980s, whether explicitly influenced by Foucault or not. Early modern states were certainly making a wide variety of disciplinary claims through a host of new regulations, as were many reforming religious denominations. In this sense, the emphasis on a state's attempts to regulate family and sexuality and in particular to discipline female sexuality was very much an interpretation for the moment. Moreover, feminist historians (including myself) were ready for an argument that put gender and family at the center of traditional early modern meta-narratives like state formation and religious reformation.[38]

The 1556 Edict was only one element of a large number of new early modern royal regulations that sought to expand state regulation of family and sexuality, but in the main, these regulations were aspirational rather than impactful. New laws introduced in the two hundred years after 1556 also spoke to other aspects of the control of marriage and extra-marital reproduction.[39] Claims were important in terms of the aspirational aims of states, but they did not translate neatly into states' ability to manage what was going on locally (even in the collaboration with elites or families, which early modern French historians have emphasized as key to the rising power of the state). Some expansive state claims, like the ability to impose and extract taxes, impacted families and households very directly. Others like the regulations of sexuality (a moral issue albeit with political and economic implication as elite rhetoric emphasized) had much less impact, not least because local communities, clergy, and even judges often did not agree with the seriousness of the risk or the means of addressing it. The prescriptive impulse of the state's regulations was not necessarily shared in local communities or even local courts, much less translated into quotidian practice.[40]

Nevertheless, the broader concept of the importance of the family as a political, religious and economic subject and agent integral to our understandings of large processes has galvanized scholarship that has remade our understandings of early modern society; and the archive of reproduction, in fact, reveals a different but critical aspect of this reframing. Paternity suits did not provide the occasion for the state to discipline women but for women to seek the protection and assistance of the state to discipline men. This perspective challenges much of the disciplinary paradigm that has linked tight regulation of female sexuality to projects of state formation and reformation and opens up other debates. The records of young people's intimacy do show how central gender, marriage, and reproduction were to political, religious, and economic matters in Old Regime cities, but these matters operated across a far more complex matrix than just an elite alliance to discipline female sexuality. When women brought paternity suits, they not only reached out to the state for assistance, but they also revealed a world of young people's licit intimacy.

A City and Its Young Workers

Young people in Old Regime Lyon lived in a fast-growing city that was experiencing shifting political, religious, economic, and global imperatives. In many different ways, the lives of Lyonnais residents were linked to much wider projects and processes. France fought repeated wars against its neighbors in Europe and across the globe. The French state wrestled with the challenges of building, peopling, and managing an empire that stretched from South Asia and the Indian Ocean to the Caribbean islands and North America. Kings from Louis XIV to Louis XVI headed governments that tried serial projects of economic reform and were embroiled in recurring political contests about the parameters of monarchical governance. The Catholic reformed monastic orders launched "internal missions" in a new phase of the

Catholic Reformation, and their friars became popular preachers who also heard the confessions of many workers.

During these years, Lyon was France's second city in political terms but also an economic and cultural hub in its own right as an international center for European publishing and trade as well as luxury silk production.[41] Even though it was far from the Atlantic ports closely associated with global trade, Asian manufactured goods like Indian cotton and Chinese porcelain (or their French imitators) as well as Asian inspired goods like parasols and umbrellas became familiar sights on Lyon streets. New commodities like coffee from Yemen and Martinique became popular too as did sugar from Caribbean plantation economies. Lyon's own luxury silk cloth production grew exponentially as workers created gorgeous and expensive patterned fabrics for dresses and decoration. In Lyon as well as the surrounding towns, skilled workers also produced many other high-quality textile items like embroidered decorative trim and fashion textile items like the foundling's garter mentioned in the Introduction. As the city's textile economy grew, Lyon became a center of the production and consumption that helped fuel the consumer revolution.[42]

Lyon was a young city whose population grew rapidly from the mid-seventeenth century, primarily through migration. In 1650, it had about 67,000 residents, a number that jumped to 97,000 in 1700, 120,000 by the mid-eighteenth century, and 146,000 by the 1780s. Young people's migration from the surrounding rural hinterland fueled this growth. Young women and young men, often in their mid-teens, moved to Lyon to find work. They lived in rented rooms in multi-story tenements in very densely populated neighborhoods of a city where two rivers and steep hillsides limited sprawl even as the population grew.[43]

The city's residents were affected by many fluctuations in the textile economy and other difficulties over the course of the Old Regime. Across France, the 1690s were a decade of extreme uncertainty in commercial life. Lyon experienced a serious period of food insecurity in 1709. Textile workers often had unsteady work, as it was subject to rapid increases or quick drop-offs. The fortunes of silk had begun to fall by the 1760s, due in part to the competition from "Indian cotton" and domestic imitations of that fabric. The 1780s saw widespread difficulties in Lyon as throughout France.[44]

Amidst all these uncertainties, Lyon workers and their partners struggled to make a living, to maintain their households, and to raise their families. Occasional signs of those larger patterns are evident in references young women made, for example, to intimate partners in Lyon who were soldiers or who had left town to join the army. The difficulties created by the 1760s downturn were evocatively made visible in notes on scraps of paper left with babies or children surrendered to the Hôtel-Dieu. A repurposed piece of card was left, for instance, with Benoit Fleuret "age one month this [leaving him] because of lack of work I baptized him 19th may 1767." A parasol seller and his wife who left their Lyon life, including their debts and their five children, wrote about his difficulties in a letter to his landlord.[45] Their circumstances were similar to those of many other spouses who left. Even though some parents hoped to reunite with their children and did, most of these familial ruptures were likely permanent. Working people in Lyon were always living month to month, with precarity just around any corner if work lulled or illness suddenly derailed income-producing work. That daily struggle is the backdrop to the stories of young workers' intimate lives, even when it was rarely articulated specifically. These realities were persistent throughout the Old Regime, just like many other aspects of young people's relationships. While young people's intimate relationships are the subject of this book, the stark realities of persistent poverty and precarity that were also central to their world cannot be romanticized.

Was Lyon unusual in terms of demographic or work variables that might have shaped a potentially distinctive sexual culture? It was a very large city by pre-modern European standards, dwarfed by London or Paris but much bigger than most cities. The dominance of one industry—silk—and its guild (the *fabrique*) was unusual. The high level of women employed in productive work rather than domestic service may also seem unusual. Certainly, a high proportion of Lyon women worked in silk production. At least 30% of Lyon's workers were in silk production, and many more were in associated trades. Especially for single women, silk work and the associated trades dominated, and only about 10% of Lyonnais women worked as "servants," a contrast to our usual historiographical tendency to identify female servants as typical early modern women workers.

However, Lyon also had much in common with other Old Regime cities and other large European cities in terms of its economy and the nature of gendered work. Many pre-modern cities housed huge numbers of young migrants who had moved there for work, similar to Lyon. It had a long history as an important economic hub for trade, banking, and printing as well as textiles. In many other urban centers, large and small, women did much work beyond the domestic although the full extent of this is still not clear.

Women were critical workers in other sites of silk production like London and Bologna and in the production of many other items.[46] Single women who were pregnant in Lille in the eighteenth century, for instance, also included a high percentage of textile workers. Indeed, the term "servant" itself may have misled historians to imagine such women specialized in domestic labor when in fact they mixed many kinds of productive work with their domestic tasks in a world where production, consumption, and domestic labor occurred in the same spaces. While domestic service is usually regarded as the most frequent form of work for young women in early modern Europe, and a single female servant was just as ubiquitous a part of most Lyon households as they were elsewhere, being a "servant" could mean doing whatever work other household members did. Many Lyon depositions show that young women who were "servants" also did textile trade work at least some of the time. Probably more accurately, servants did the work of the household, which included productive and commercial as well as domestic work. Equally, many women in Lyon identified as textile workers likely also did domestic work.[47] That is, Lyon itself shared with other cities much that was ordinary about Old Regime daily life.

Emerging Adults in the City

For early modern young men and women, the transition phase of emerging adulthood was characterized by a decade or more of work and play as singles between their first jobs in their teens and their marriages in their mid/late twenties. The multi-purpose streets and buildings of the city where they lived had much in common with other parts of pre-modern Europe. The streets were public spaces that were at once commercial, social, productive, functional, and emotional as well as sites of religious observation, revelry, and intimacy. The buildings that fronted on the streets masked complex interior space where public and personal, domestic and commercial were interwoven in shared rooms, courtyards, staircases, and balconies. People, activities, and goods circulated between households that were very porous. The households were sites of production and credit/debt production as well as residential spaces. Both co-operation and friction about a wide range of issues profoundly shaped relations between and within households, and power relations along many axes were integral parts of inter- and intra-household life.[48]

Young women and men developed intimate relationships that were widely accepted as long as the pair observed particular conventions and practices that marked intimacy between them as licit. As emerging adults, they explored heterosocial relationships in the full view of their co-workers, friends, and neighbors, and indeed the public aspect of their intimacy was a key safeguard to their reputations and to a perhaps surprisingly wide range of licit intimacy. For communities, this stage provided young people with an opportunity for that they saw as a normal desire for intimacy and a chance to balance compatibility with the interwoven pragmatic elements of early modern marriage. For young women and men, sexuality was organized around age as well as gender and work.[49]

The transition phase of young adulthood lasted for about ten years: between the mid-teens when young people began to work, often for someone other than their parents and living away from home, to their mid- to late twenties when most people married. These young workers were unexceptional in every regard—except that we know about them today. Both partners were usually in their mid-twenties, an age at which couples in the city and across northwestern Europe generally married.[50] Both young men and young women were primarily textile workers, engaged either in some stage of the silk production that dominated the Lyon economy from 1650 or in one of the myriad associated textile trades.

Age was a key variable in young people's relationships in terms of the appropriate progression of intimacy for them and their communities. The demographics of sexuality and marriage provide key contextual clues in this regard. The average age of marriage in early modern northwestern Europe was mid-twenties and registered illegitimacy rates were very low, perhaps 2% or 3%, although pre-marital conception was very common and indeed not regarded as problematic. These traditional figures for illegitimacy may be low. In eighteenth-century Lyon, the average age of first marriage for women was twenty-seven and a half and the illegitimacy rates were between 5% and 10%. As we will see, parish registers also may often have under-registered out-of-wedlock births.[51] The well-established pattern of relatively late marriage suggests that although sex frequently preceded marriage among couples who were in the age range of feasible marriage—that is, in their mid-twenties—younger single people rarely took their intimacy as far as intercourse. Otherwise, illegitimacy rates would have been higher or the marriage age lower since their ability to control their fertility effectively meant regular intercourse was very likely to be followed quickly by pregnancy.

Among Lyonnais intimate partners who appeared in court, very few women were younger than twenty or older than twenty-five, and men had a wider age range, a gender pattern that points to the age-related organization of sexuality. Only a small number of women were teenagers or older than thirty, usually widows. Men's ages were likewise clustered in the early to mid-twenties although middle-aged men were a bit more visible. These older men were almost without exception the already married employers of the young women who usually had a clear narrative of unwanted, coerced relationships. The records also reveal a few incidents of what we would clearly identify today as rape even between young people of the same age. However, the vast majority of young women who told their stories to the court were involved in consensual relationships with men of their own age who were feasible marriage partners because this particular legal avenue addressed problems in those particular relationships.

These demographic indicators suggest a well-understood progression of conventions of age-appropriate intimate behavior in consensual relationships with both parties in their early to mid-twenties before they engaged in intercourse and had to face dealing with possible pregnancy. Younger intimate partners (teenagers) knew that early intercourse was unacceptable and impractical because marriage was not regarded as feasible. Later puberty (probably at around age sixteen) as well as intense pressure to delay marriage seems to have quite effectively curbed experiments with physical intimacy. Marriage was closely associated with intercourse—in fact, "as husband and wife do" was a common euphemism—but young people rarely married before they were twenty except in elite families. These younger couples likely walked out together, had many outings as part of larger groups with their friends and kin, and experimented with many forms of intimacy short of intercourse. Intimate partners approaching feasible marriageable age (early to mid-twenties) were very likely to agree to pre-marital intercourse in the wake of discussions about marriage, and mostly followed through with marriage if or when pregnancy occurred or before pregnancy occurred.[52]

Pregnancy before marriage was entirely routine and regarded as such. The timelines of the relationships of couples who did come to court in paternity disputes sometimes after years together "living as man and wife" and more than one child hint at the number of couples who cohabited in stable, monogamous, ongoing relationships without the legal benefit of marriage.[53] Communities (from neighbors to clergy and legal officials) were on the whole very supportive of these young women whose redress via institutional recourse in court we can see but whose histories also reveal the many extrajudicial ways in which their struggles were remediated. Very little evidence points to any kind of disciplining of women, and indeed the primary disciplining through the legal process or outside of it was of young men who sought to walk away from the consequences of their intimacy.

Shifting Spaces of Intimacy: Young People, Work and Heterosociability

Workplaces provided key sites where young people could forge intimate relationships with partners as well as friendships with co-workers. Young couples most often said they had met through work even if occasionally they were introduced by friends or at social events. They were co-workers, customer and client, or workers for different employers in different stages of the production process and thus met, for example, delivering supplies or goods. Workplaces generally facilitated consensual relationships between young men and women who were peers—similar not only in age and rank but in shared experiences of work in silk and allied trades. Their relationships developed in full view of their co-workers, employers, neighbors, and bystanders. As Marie Pitra recalled in 1743, she and Pierre Joseph Matton met when they both worked for the same master silk thread maker (*tireur d'or*) in his workshop. (Her father was also a *tireur d'or* so she presumably acquired her skill in his workshop.) Pitra noted that their mutual workplace meant they often "ate and drank together" and "this kind of connectedness" [*espece de connexite*] gave Matton "free access" to her. She remembered that he "ceaselessly" chatted her up while he recalled "that he felt a powerful inclination for her," that is, he was very attracted to her.[54]

If Pitra likely began to learn her trade watching and working in her father's workshop, many young people learned their skills when they migrated to Lyon. Lyon's young female workers occasionally explained how they came to the city and their lives as newcomers as part of the backstories to their intimate relationships. Their trajectories were very similar. Anne Martin explained in 1724, for example, that she came to Lyon from her village in the province of Dauphine a decade earlier when she was fourteen and took a position with a master silk thread maker where she "stayed and worked as an apprentice and *tourneuse*" (a worker who turned the reels of several women as they coiled the silver thread) for four years. She subsequently worked for several other silk thread makers over a period of six years and for each had demonstrated "the regularity of her conduct" and established her reputation as a "good worker."[55]

The high rate of migration likely sometimes impacted relationships between young men and women. If one or other of the emerging adults in a couple had been migrants, they could leave the city to avoid an unwanted marriage (as women often suggested men had done or intended to do when they came to court) or go home to have an out-of-wedlock baby with the support of their families away from their city lives (as women may sometimes have done), perhaps returning to their Lyonnais work without the baby afterward. These latter strategies are very difficult to trace in surviving records. On the other hand, if migrants lacked the dense local networks of contacts and knowledge that allowed young women to to find community solutions to their untimely pregnancies, they may been more likely to go to court or have found themselves isolated and facing very difficult circumstances.[56]

Did the co-ed working environments and practices involved in much of Lyon's textile labor structure particular patterns of intimacy between men and women compared to, say, women's traditional work in domestic service? For men in Lyon, silk work was probably very similar to work in many other trades (that is, the specific skills were different but the structures of work were alike), but women silk workers performed highly skilled, essential labor. Women worked on a piece-work basis and their pay was much lower than that of journeymen, but, despite the striking if not surprising differentials in pay, the importance of reliable, skilled female silk workers was acknowledged in many ways. Masters in silk trades were required to give their female silk workers year-long contracts and to provide them with accommodation and board. Journeymen who married the daughters of silk masters could cut short the years they had to wait to become masters in their own right because the silk guild's regulations noted that "these marriages channel the talents of these girls, raised in the trade since they were young, with the knowledge journeymen have acquired."[57]

Demand for skilled female workers was high, and employers enabled job mobility despite complaining about it. The dependence on female labor and these workers' ability to change jobs could frustrate employers. In 1707, for example, the Lyon community of *maîtres tireurs d'or* complained that their *tourneuses* (young female workers) often left their jobs when work was at its peak and the women had been paid ahead for their labor, a practice that "caused great disorder." They recalled a 1698 local court ordinance that regulated the mobility of female workers by allowing them to leave jobs only with the permission of their employers and forbade other employers to hire them without proof of this permission. They claimed that fines of 50 *livres* had temporarily been sufficient to deter young women and their employers from job mobility but gradually the practice had recommenced. In 1733, the employers complained about their journeymen, some of whom often stopped work or produced defective work that could not be sold. The masters noted that when journeymen stopped work, their female workers stopped too and the employers "were deprived of the labor" of both sexes. Notably they referred to the male and female workers (*ourvirers et ourvrières dudit art de tireurs*) when acknowledging their labor force. Yet despite such frustrations, in practice employers were very willing to pick up skilled women, as the very complaint about their mobility showed. When a young silk worker asked his employer, for example, if he could use another skilled female silk worker, the employer said right away that he would love to and the woman came over the next day to see about working for him.[58]

Yet significant overlap existed between working as a servant and female labor of other sorts. Servants were certainly ubiquitous even in working households, and female servants, despite the essential labor they also provided, were easily replaceable in ways that female silk workers were not. Servants were also very mobile, moving between employers every eighteen months or so on average. The *tireurs d'or* called their female workers "servants" in the complaints of their company interchangeably with specific occupational names like "*tourneuses.*" Servants did the key work of carrying goods for sale or purchase between households and much other labor that blurred the line between domestic servant and commercial producer.[59] In some ways, the fact of working was more important than the type of work.

Female workers narrated different kinds of histories of their intimate relationships, depending in part on the structure of their work and workplaces. Workplace encounters facilitated consensual relationships between young men and women who were peers—similar not only in age and rank but in shared experiences of work, very often both textile workers or working in manufacturing trades.[60] Their workplaces offered opportunities for young couples to be together, which sometimes allowed them to enjoy each other's company and other times to risk their reputations. They took breaks to talk to each other, and enjoyed other couple moments. A silk worker and several of her female co-workers recalled how her intimate partner would call her over to go with him into the cabinet where silk was stored on the pretext that he needed to give her more silk while he had it unlocked. However, the length of time they stayed in the cabinet together—in violation of all the conventions that marked young couples' intimacy as appropriate when conducted in public spaces—was regarded with great suspicion.[61] So the workplace in itself was not a safeguard of what was regarded as acceptable behavior, but working together all day provided ample opportunity for relationships to develop in a public environment in ways that were acceptable to communities.

Women's narratives of intimate relationships with their employers varied in some significant ways from the narratives of their relationships with peers. They talked about the development of a consensual relationship with peers framed around public walking out together, but they rarely cast their accounts of interactions with their employers, married or not, in these terms. Women emphasized repeated pressure and sometimes coercion from their employers as the frame for their intimacy. The issue of commitment to marriage, a key feature of consensual relationships between peers and shifting intimacy, was usually absent in servants' accounts, no doubt because the men were usually already married. City authorities were hostile to relationships between employers and servants, as we will see, because they perceived them as sources of disorder—both because of the inequalities of rank and the likelihood that the situation would not be resolved by marriage. Certainly some servants/textile workers did subsequently marry their employers and may have seen the prospect of such opportunity, as Laura Gowing has argued.[62] Yet the structures of their workplace also exposed them to sexual exploitation and reduced the likelihood of a satisfactory outcome to out-of-wedlock pregnancy whether in terms of matrimony or one of the myriad informal, extra-judicial arrangements made between intimate couples who were peers in consensual relationships.[63]

The ordinary histories of young workers' intimate relationships had many stages from initial courtship to experiments with emotional and physical intimacy to discussions about marriage that were usually accompanied by shifts to new forms of intimacy. Work rather than family or friends provided the introductions, and young people in working ranks were free to choose among peers of similar rank who their intimate partners and eventually marriage partners would be. And since one of the qualities most highly valued in early modern spouses was their assiduousness and skill as workers, these experiences with each other as workers provided a decent basis for making those kinds of judgments about potential spouses. Their experiences were embedded in community expectations about appropriate forms of licit intimacy for young people and in community scaffolding to foster outcomes that sought to safeguard the futures of young men and women. These patterns were gendered in all kinds of ways with differential expectations and experiences for young women and men that were often undergirded with implicit or explicit power. Yet just as textile production masters could not consistently command women's skilled labor, young workers' intimate relationships involved many and ups downs, with pressure on young men as well as young women to meet expectations or remedy mistakes. Young people could choose their own partners as long as they chose within their own ranks and at appropriate ages (still subject to parental consent to marriage) but from the start of their interactions, the maintenance of licit rather than illicit intimacy was a communal project as well as an experiment between the couple.

2
Peril Stories
Licit Intimacy, Space, and Community Safeguarding

Textile workers Jean Pillot and Marguerite Perricaud began to visit each other often in 1723. Marguerite recalled that Pillot "pursued her" for a year and promised marriage. She told him he had to ask her father. Marguerite told a co-worker that he loved her and she loved him. Neighbors often saw them together. One evening, Pillot came into Margeurite's room with a candle, locked the door with a key, and put the candle in a candlestick. As she recalled later, he made many protestations of affection and promised he that he would never have another woman. Then he seized her by the arms, threw her on the bed and, despite all her resistance, "knew her twice carnally" while assuring her again that he would never be with any woman besides her and that she had nothing to fear. They continued to see each other and have sex in the continued expectation, as she said, of marriage. Neighbors noted they were often in a room alone together for extended periods of time. Her father sometimes sent a co-worker in to see what they were doing and her aunt, Pillot's landlady, also kept track of their behavior.[1]

Perricaud and Pillot's relationship thus unfolded in an entirely conventional way: in full view of kin, co-workers and neighbors in the preliminary phase and then in a striking shift to privatized space as their relationship transitioned toward marriage. For an extended period, they had taken long walks together during which they developed a physical and emotional intimacy that indicated they were preparing for marriage. Like most other couples, they associated intercourse with marriage, and so Perricaud's account of their first intercourse was braided tightly into a narrative about promises to marry. Indeed, pre-marital conception was very common and not regarded as a social problem so long as the parents married before the baby was born or not long after.

Like Perricaud and Pillot, single workers routinely experimented with multi-faceted intimacy that included physical proximity, emotional connection, bodily experience, and sexual desire. They registered a vernacular language of affection as an intrinsic part of the progress of their relationships, engaged in a repertoire of activities that served as a non-verbal body language of connection, and demonstrated that a spectrum of emotions defined pre-marital intimacy. As partners and their communities traced the histories of couples' relationships, the narratives of intimacy recorded by court clerks complement the letters, *billets-doux,* or written promises to marry that were sometimes also deposited as evidence. These personal texts provide extraordinary examples of the material culture of youthful intimacy, a key means through which couples expressed their feelings and consolidated or fractured their relationships.

Young couples' relationships routinely involved a wide range of emotions, no doubt layered in complex and shifting ways, including but not limited to uncertainty, conflict, disappointment, responsibility, guilt, and no doubt heartbreak, as well as joy, affection, and passion. The material culture of intimacy clearly indicated a complicated and sometimes contradictory sentimental component along with physical intimacy as routine elements in young people's relationships.

Their consensual relationship histories include elements of licit intimacy that are familiar today alongside forms that are strikingly different. They engaged in an extensive range of intimacy as a part of courtship. They had explicit discussions about sex. Space was a key marker of licit or illicit intimacy as moving from public to private intimacy was integral to the transition to marriage. Male force was a central feature of first-time intercourse. Perricaud's jarring account of her first experience of intercourse was absolutely common. Women routinely narrated acts of sexual violence as pivotal moments of transition between courtship and commitment. Time after time, they described how men's force moved intimate relationships forward, but they continued to stay together, presumably because they expected marriage to come next.

Women's relationship narratives unfolded as peril stories as they identified the expectations, practices, and risks they faced in exploring the partnership and potential feasibility for marriage. Their accounts reveal the constant calibration of opportunity and danger, promise and peril. The configurations of acceptable intimacy, including intercourse as an ordinary part of couples' progression toward marriage, were always tinged with the danger that young men would not keep their promises.

Communities and couples viewed licit intimacy as an avenue through which marriage as a key opportunity was supported and yet risk was mitigated. Community conventions about forms of intimacy that were regarded as licit embodied a socially constructed set of values that were specific to time and place. Many members of working communities served as safeguarders who shared a consensus about licit intimacy that acknowledged intercourse as a calibrated step into marriage, but a step that included risks as well as the promise of matrimony. They validated expressions of emerging adult sexuality as a part of young people's selection of partners, but they also knew the boundaries beyond which youthful courtship could pose risks to young workers' futures and to neighborhood stability.

Intimate partners, their families, and their communities configured a wide spectrum of intimacy as acceptable and clearly delimited behavior deemed illicit. Licit intimacy between young workers in the Old Regime had particular qualities. It took the form of publicly observed, stable relationships between young people of similar rank who were feasible marriage partners and with the knowledge of kin and friends. It centered on walking out together in the evenings and on Sundays or feast days over many months. As relationships progressed, couples and their communities carefully calibrated their behavior, aiming to ensure that their intimacy was appropriate to their not-yet-committed to marriage status or eventually to their definitely committed to married status. Licit intimacy was choreographed, and young people no doubt learned from their elders and their peers and from watching what others deemed acceptable and what seemed to cross the boundaries. When young people were monogamous within these parameters, they did not damage their honor, reputations, or futures.

The city's public spaces, exterior and interior, were opportunities for and safeguards against particular patterns of youth heterosociability and heterosexuality both for couples and for communities. Such spaces provided for licit intimacy as well as economic transactions and commerce in many forms, political life, and law as practice.[2] Among working people, the Old Regime city allowed for and shaped a particular set of practices that gave young people considerable leeway in consensual relationships as long as they involved serial monogamy and public performance of intimacy that ended short of intercourse unless marriage seemed certain.[3]

Interior space played a pivotal, although complex and in some ways contradictory, role in young women's legal narratives of their sexual histories. Even though they detailed the public intimacy leading up to first intercourse, they highlighted the switch to marital intimacy that intercourse represented as an activity laced with risk. If locked doors repurposed the interior space for sleep and sex, the male partner's use of force magnified the potential danger. Despite the previous months of public intimacy and explicit expectation of marriage, the shift to privatized space signaled both a key step in the transition to marriage and a fraught experience with potentially uncertain consequences for women.

While young women in working communities were in many regards given striking room to explore intimacy as they chose their lifetime partners, they were not, of course, equal partners in these relations. The power differences between young men and young women became visible only at particular moments, at least in the conventions of licit consensual relationships. Men were supposed to ask women if they wanted to take a walk; they could apparently kiss many girls, and they were expected to press for physical intimacy to move from touching to intercourse. Women were not supposed to be "familiar" with more than one man as neighbors marked when witnesses carefully noted that they had not seen a particular woman socializing with other men.

Early modern communities were concerned about inappropriate female sexuality, but they were *also* worried about young men's sexuality, and expectations about sexuality were as critical to constructions of masculinity as they were to gendering female behavior. Couples and communities understood licit intimacy as appropriate for men as well as women and recognized the marked boundaries that neither intimate partner could transgress without damage to their reputations. Single women and men were given calibrated leeway for intimacy in many forms built around specific conventions and practices. Nevertheless, in full awareness of potential perils, community members sought to mitigate the potential risks to their young people's futures.

Spaces of Consensual and Licit Intimacy

Space shaped young people's experiences of intimacy in important ways. The choice of space calibrated the stage and appropriateness of intimacy. Workplaces, city streets, public squares, doorways, and many other places were key public sites of licit intimacy that allowed communities to observe young couples and monitor the appropriateness of their behavior. Couples self-identified as stable and monogamous when they started to walk out together. Women remembered that step as pivotal, and communities regarded that performance as a declaration. These walks between emerging adults of similar rank who were feasible marriage partners were key pastimes. A broad, if rank-specific, consensus existed about these features of licit intimacy across gender and generation.

As young people frequently met at or through work, their initial conversations often occurred at workplaces. Estienne Dumaretz, for example, worked as a journeyman for Marguerite Minquet's father, a master silk worker. One of his co-workers observed that Dumaretz "often stopped his work" to go to socialize with Minquet. Sometimes young people met as work partners, typically with women pulling the cords on looms for male weavers. Couples also often met through other kinds of workplace interactions, such as delivering goods or buying workplace supplies. Thus co-workers, male and female, peers or employers, were spectators to emerging coupledom and well placed to regulate intimate relationships.

Walks were a particular kind of public performance of intimate connection that cemented couples' relationships and were the key identifiers of stable, monogamous couples. Women's relationship narratives routinely highlighted the moments when their male admirers had asked them to walk together, a transition from flirting to being prospective intimate partners that was rich with meaning for emerging adults and their communities. Marie Ruedy recalled that when Matthieu Michel asked her to go for a walk with him, she told him to ask her father first. Claudine Rang remembered that a young man named Millot never missed a chance to chat with her for over a year before he asked if she would go for a walk with him.[4] Young couples spent evenings, Sundays, and saints' days walking together.

Co-workers and neighbors often commented on the frequency of a couple's walking out as a signifier of the seriousness and stability of a relationship. A female neighbor who lived in the same building as Helen Ferraud recollected in 1680 that she had seen Laurence Terme there "all the time, every day." The neighbor sometimes walked with them, and another neighbor also recalled he had seen the pair walking. A long-time neighbor of Louise Chauvet said she had seen Pierre De Juif visit "over 100 times." A former roommate of Claudine Joanon remembered in 1688 that she walked with Antoine Marcou every Sunday and every feast day, sometimes with the witness or with their employer's son and his wife.[5]

The performance of walking remained central to the experience of being a couple and to conventions about appropriate expressions of licit intimacy over the course of many decades. In 1724, a fifty-year-old shoemaker recalled that he had seen his neighbor, Claire Valouey, walk out "daily" with Jacques Richard and had watched them talking and kissing. He added he once saw them between 10 and 11 at night and was "scandalized" because of the lateness of the hour. In 1740, three young neighbors of Francoise Clerc recalled that they had often seen her out walking with Phillipe Flacheron frequently, even "every evening," and they saw that practice as an indication that the young couple intended to marry.[6] Comments of this kind showed the close observation of young couples' public behavior as well as the fine calibration of its appropriateness.

Couples' walks in public view, whether of friends, kin, or neighbors in their community, allowed them to explore many facets of intimacy as they linked arms, talked, kissed, and caressed in plain sight without damage to their reputations. When Janne Olier and Jean Guillemin reviewed their two-year relationship before the court in 1683, for example, both emphasized that the outdoors was the respectable site for young people's relationships. Like other young people, their leisure involved strolling together most evenings on city streets, in public gardens, and along the banks of the city's rivers.[7] In the heterosociability of the streets, young people could engage in public displays of "familiarity" (as they were often called) without fear of reprimand or damage to their honor. Licit intimacy that took place in the context of this public space safeguarded reputations and women's bodies.

Evening and Sunday walks followed itineraries that favored particular spaces for public intimacy. Couples walked along the city's quaysides and around the new civic squares that were created from the mid-seventeenth century on. The Place des Terreaux, the square that was the site of the grand new city hall, and the Place Bellecour were about a mile apart at opposite ends of the densely populated neighborhood of St. Nizier where many young workers lived. In Lyon, as in Paris where visitors in the late seventeenth century were amazed to see how busy the public spaces were and how men and women walked around together there, the new public spaces may have fostered the emergence of walking out as a new form of heterosociability.[8] Especially on Sundays, couples also walked through the vegetable gardens and orchards of the *faubourgs* that surrounded the city or strolled up the Fourvière hill that overlooked the city. On Sundays, the walks to the outskirts of the city often included buying food at the various places that offered snacks or enjoying picnics. Jeanne Moulin, for example, remembered that she and Jean Fontrobert had eaten biscuits and grapes in the garden of a seminary.[9]

The seasonally changing light meant the circumstances of evening walks varied through the year. Although long summer evenings allowed daylight walks, for much of the year evening walks much have taken place in public spaces that were dark. From about 1660 on, Paris began to expand street lighting with lanterns, and other cities in France as well as across Europe soon followed. Lyon took part in this urban experiment from about the same time although it is unclear how many streets or public squares were lit or how effectively before installation of the more efficient oil lanterns that were used after the mid-eighteenth century.[10] Nevertheless, couples' evening walks after work must often have benefited from the frequent dark spots on their routes.

The streets and squares were places of shared urban experiences where particular behaviors and values could be endorsed or contested.[11] They were full of people, so couples were always in the company of others, whether friends, acquaintances, or strangers, who could monitor their behavior. Marking licit intimacy as public allowed the community to collectively manage social reproduction by supporting behavior that facilitated the appropriate development of couples but monitoring against slippage into casual intercourse that potentially undermined stability if pregnancy resulted. Communities actively policed the spaces for licit and illicit intimacy. The appropriateness of a couple's behavior depended significantly on the space where it took place. For example, Anne Recorneau went to mass with her neighbor one Sunday morning in 1663 and her partner, Jean Baptiste Favary, knelt besides them at the communion railing. Her neighbor was outraged when the couple whispered about meeting each other after the service.[12] Sunday outings for couples were perfectly routine, but not if the arrangements were made at the altar while waiting for communion.

Observers tolerated quite a wide range of practices of intimacy as licit, age-appropriate desire even if the couples went beyond linked arms, hugs, and kisses so long as they were in view of spectators. The friends of Barthelemy Caron and Elizabeth Demen watched them kiss, and saw him caress her breasts and put his hands down her skirt. None seemed to think anything was amiss, saying only she made no effort to stop him which they seemed to accept as a sign of her consent rather than inappropriate behavior on either of their parts. Marguerite Minquet and Estienne Dumaretz held hands and engaged in "all kinds of caresses, and he kissed her on the face" in front of their peers. None of these expressions of intimate desire was regarded as problematic. Indeed, after explaining that Francoise Namy and Guillaume

Bergeron's relationship included going out most evenings between eight and ten, being "very friendly" with each other, and "kissing and caressing," one acquaintance added explicitly that they had not engaged in any "inappropriate behavior."[13]

Meanwhile both men and young women defended their behavior by insisting they had never been alone in each others' rooms—that is, they had observed the convention that linked licit intimacy with public space. Almost all urban workers were tenants who lived in buildings that resembled latter day tenements where whole families usually lived, usually in one or two rooms, and young workers shared living space with their peers or employers. People ate, slept, had sex, worked, and died in these unspecialized cramped spaces. So especially for young people, socializing outside must have been both practical and liberating, giving them room for personal expression that interior spaces restricted. Jean Guillemin said that he had stood at Janne Olier's door but had never been inside and moreover "had never been in any room with her," a statement that emphasized their propriety and her chastity. Olier contradicted him when she claimed that Guillemin had been in her room once, but she stressed that she had never been in his room and that it would have been very "inappropriate" for her to do so. Ermond Duplot, a journeyman, said that Jeanne Cossard had been in his room several times—but only when the artisan for whom he worked had also been present, often along with his wife and eight to ten apprentices and journeymen from their shop.[14]

The specific use of space was one of the key means by which couples and their communities policed appropriate boundaries, and any seeking of privacy that might suggest intimacy was coded as illicit. In 1684, for example, a neighbor of Barthelemy Florin and her family observed that she had often seen Pierre Cognard talk to Barthelemy in the street in front of their building and noticed they took frequent walks together, sometimes even with the neighbor's own daughter. This neighbor had asked Florin's father so as to confirm what "all the neighbors" thought—that they would be married. She also remembered that three or four months earlier, she had seen Cognard take Florin by the hand behind their building where they remained for about ninety minutes and then left separately. When Barthelemy was known to be pregnant, the neighbor's recollection connected the disappearing out of view and the subsequent pregnancy.[15] Prolonged disappearance—ducking out of public view behind buildings, in alleys, or into the rooms where either one slept—quickly led to skepticism and criticism about what a couple was up to. Privatized space, internal or external, was a no-go zone for pre-marital intimacy.

Licit intimacy also entailed avoiding intimate relations between social unequals for whom marriage would be an unlikely outcome. Vital Delphin was an apprentice stocking maker and Jeanne Quentin, the daughter of his master, also worked in her father's trade. When she became pregnant, Quentin's father made no reference in court to the long intimate history between his daughter and his apprentice (who had been together as a public couple for four years according to their account), but highlighted his recent discovery that his daughter was six months pregnant. For her father, it was the "fault" of Delphin. Quentin *père* wanted "repair" for the harm because this situation was "a big crime on the part of a domestic worker against the daughter of his master."[16] Apparently the father perceived unequal rank as a valid obstacle to marriage. Clearly he had thought the apprentice should have been aware that the status gap between them meant their relationship should not cross the line of intercourse with its implication of marriage.

Young people were well aware that unequal rank marked relationships as illicit and often sought to emphasize their relationships as between peers. Marie Maugard, a seamstress, recalled how she and Jean Ravier, a cook, had explicitly discussed their equal status as well as his intentions (all honorable) as two important issues that meant no obstacles existed to their relationship. She consulted her kin. They and her neighbors knew they were a couple who walked together on many evenings, kissed, and even engaged in more intimate behavior, as when Ravier touched her breasts. Their behavior was regarded as licit because it was public knowledge and indicative that they were of similar rank and feasible marriage partners. Sometimes neighbors explicitly commented on the rank issue. A widow recalled that Louis Estodat often came to meet Elizabeth Tronchet, who used to lodge with her before they went out for walks. Estodat told Tronchet's landlady that they were keeping company with an intent to marry and she claimed that she had "believed him because they were of the same rank."[17]

In the context of stable, ongoing, monogamous relationships conducted in public spaces filled with casual or close observers, couples of equal rank enjoyed the ability to go out together and to engage in a wide range of intimate behavior. Young single female workers were not chaperoned nor were they kept home to preserve their reputations and chastity, in part because these public spaces provided what everyone agreed was an acceptable safeguard against potential couple trouble. The licit intimacy of public walks found cross-generational acceptance among Lyon's working people, both men and women. Communities saw young couples' experiments with desire, female as well as male, as a licit, typical developmental stage as long as they were in public sites and in public view.

Mitigating Risk: A Community Project

Communities supported the emerging intimacy of young people as long as it met their expectations for appropriate behavior, and community members were quick to question, warn, and scold when they saw young couples engage in kinds of intimacy they judged illicit. Friends, co-workers, neighbors, and family members were watchful and judgmental about developing relationships. They were usually protective of women, conscious no doubt of the likely unequal costs of intercourse without marriage, and quick to call out men as they registered community recognition that male sexuality was a potent potential source of family disorder. They watched closely for shifts in intimacy that might lead to untimely parenthood associated with sex before clear commitment to marriage or no path to marriage because of rank differences. Community safeguarding of young people's relationships required broad participation when experiments with intimacy were regarded as predictable and quotidian. If awareness of the risks of youthful intimacy was embedded in stereotypical early modern popular print in the form of the threat women's sexuality posed to men, the lived experience of Old Regime working communities established that the potential costs were greater for young women.

Intimate partners themselves calibrated their intimacy as they marked the boundary between licit or illicit. Even in the "she said, he said" crossfire magnified in the process of litigation and the record of it, Vital Delphin and Jeanne Quentin agreed that in the four years since they had shared a household as apprentice and daughter of a master stocking maker they had constantly kept company with each other. When he recounted their relationship in court, he acknowledged that he "had crossed the limits of decency" with her. Separately she explained for the judges' benefit that "the love in her heart" made her weak so she agreed to his "liberties." She also noted that he had never missed an opportunity to tell her he loved her and did not want anything more than to be united in marriage with her. She claimed she had no sexual experience before him. He admitted they had kissed on the mouth, but claimed that he had no experience so she "had taught him things of which he was until then ignorant and which decency does not permit him to describe." Vital confessed to his priest who told him to leave his job to avoid any "shameful commerce" with her. While he followed this advice, she was already pregnant. Two of his friends recollected that when they told Vital that it was a "nice business" he had had with Jeanne, he "smiled," said he was ready to marry her if her father wanted, and acknowledged that he "had done wrong by her" in having intercourse.[18]

Jeanne and Vital recognized the boundaries of licit intimacy even though they disagreed in their testimony about who had breeched them. She used two common euphemisms to calibrate the stages of intimacy: "liberties" (caresses that were short of intercourse) and "last favors" (intercourse). Delphin likely feigned innocence in his recounting to the court when he said she had persuaded him into "impure touches" and "indecent practices" in the months before they had intercourse, given that in the earlier bar chat with male friends, he framed intercourse as a mistake and his wrongdoing, albeit an error he was willing to fix through marriage. Nevertheless, he, like Jeanne, distinguished what was acceptable from what was inappropriate.

Young partners' efforts to self-regulate their intimacy were ubiquitous even if predictably not 100% successful. Young women and their communities often used the word *sage*, meaning sensible or prudent, to assess what they saw as good female management of intimacy. During Anne Roussin's relationship with Jean Chabanassy in 1680, several of their female co-workers warned her not to go into a cupboard with him under the pretense of getting supplies because that was "suspicious." When she came out "all disheveled," her co-workers were quick to suggest to her that they thought she was more *sage*. Joseph Ramel, a baker, claimed Marie Chana "had not been *sage*" with one of his journeymen, although he had reminded her to be *sage* and warned her that if she "did something mad" with young men, he would send her away. Jeanne Maugard described herself in 1725 as "too *sage* and prudent" to begin an intimate relationship with Jean Ravier without first being assured that he was sincere in his intention to marry her and not just "playing with her." However, a *sage* young woman could openly engage in licit intimacy with a view to marriage with a young man who was, as Maugard went on to say, equal in rank and with no other obstacles to their eventual matrimony.[19] *Sage* indicated that a young woman was wise in the sense of careful, cautious, and self-aware in managing her interactions with young men but this definition allowed women considerable room to explore intimacy with appropriate partners.

Certainly *sage* young women could also anticipate trouble and take steps to avoid a misstep from broad physical intimacy to intercourse if marriage was not in the future. They recalled telling young men not to come around anymore if they were not sure of their intentions to marry and sometimes even moved jobs or addresses to put some space between themselves and relationships that seemed to have shifted from promising to perilous. A neighbor of Claudine Grissonet remembered that she had hidden in a closet one day to avoid Benoit Peyssonaux when she felt it had become clear that his persistent interest in her was not with an eye to marriage.[20]

Young men and their interlocuters meanwhile were clear that engaging in intercourse in an ongoing consensual relationship committed them to matrimony. As Claude Michaud noted to several neighbors and coworkers in 1741, he "was obliged" to marry Laurence Ripert because he got her pregnant.[21] In stable consensual relationships, responsibility for pregnancy was usually attributed to the men who themselves accepted it as their fault, saying it was their "work" [*oeuvres*] or "he put her at fault" [*la mis en faute*].

Observers across gender and generation felt free to speak up when they saw signs that youthful intimacy might be slipping toward intercourse. Men as well as women regulated couples' behavior as they marked and re-marked the boundaries of appropriate intimacy. Phillipe Guy, the fifty-year-old neighbor of lacemaker Philberte DeLuis, for example, noticed that Rene Gaultier "continually" spent time with her and often went into her room, "which obliged" Guy to speak to Gaultier at the door to ask him what he was doing. Gaultier insisted he had no "bad intentions," but Guy nevertheless said he did not want Gaultier to visit DeLuis anymore without making a promise of marriage.[22] In these and innumerable other similar situations, both men and women actively intervened to monitor young couples' relationships and safeguard their futures.

Women's girlfriends, whether co-workers or co-residents, were often important mediators of relationships. Sometimes young women introduced men to their friends, often on the endless walking around that was a part of youthful sociability as well as a key activity for couples. Girlfriends watched as relationships developed and gave the same kind of endorsement or warning that other community members did. Fleurie Gillet and Drie Robert, for example, were first friends and then four-year roommates who split the rent although they worked independently. Robert recalled that she had often seen Gillet and Jacques Feraud walking out, kissing, and cuddling. Robert accepted their behavior as appropriate as she had "no reason to doubt" they were on the way to marriage. In contrast, Julienne Millon, a twenty-one-year-old silk winder, watched on several occasions as Felicité Durand and her partner took walks together with all the usual "familiarities," but when she saw them sitting close together in a street kissing while Riviere held her neck, she was concerned enough to "warn" Felicité's parents. Perhaps she spoke to Felicité too, even if she did not specify that when giving her account later as a witness. A friend of Antoinette Chabry did recall telling Antoinette bluntly that she was seeing her boyfriend "too much."[23]

Young men's friends were also facilitators, observers, supporters, and regulators of relationships. Co-workers often made introductions, although these ties were often elusive later. Antoine and Phillipe Flacheron, brothers who were both *tireurs d'or*, provided a rare articulation of these networks of work and sociability when they both recalled in different paternity suits in the summer of 1749 how couples met through co-worker mutual friends. Jeane Priere recalled decades earlier that she had asked Antoine Rambaud's friends to speak to him when he continued to resist keeping his promises to marry her even after the birth of their two children. After those conversations with his male friends and with the permission of his father, Rambaud finally agreed to marry her.[24]

Young people themselves were well aware that their conduct was a matter of community scrutiny. Anne Tillart, who sold wine in her uncle's bar, often visited Pierre Gaylart, a journeyman weaver, at his workplace where they cuddled and kissed in front of the other workers, as did other people who lived in the same building. Their physical intimacy was completely acceptable in terms of its public setting and particular forms. Yet when a female customer entered the bar and could not see Tillart until the couple got out of a bed at the back, Gaylart kissed Tillart (perhaps in a cheeky effort to assure her he had her back) and asked the visitor not to tell anyone.[25] Gaylart's actions nodded to the pleasure of intimacy and acknowledged that they were not supposed to be in bed together.

Observers were constantly making judgments about whether the boundary between licit and illicit intimacy was being observed or being crossed, and the line was critical for the reputations of both young men and young women as well as a potential risk marker for their futures. A male co-worker of Pierrette Duchene remembered he had seen Claude Poully "kiss her on the face and mouth" and had seen them go into a room together with the door closed "for a long time." He noted that he had never seen her visit with any other young men and had queried Poully, who told him they were going to be married. A stonemason on the same street likewise observed their intimacy and remarked that "everyone in the neighborhood" knew they were going to be married. Their commitment to marry allowed them to extend their intimacy to being alone in a room.[26] Benoite Chaville pulled the loom cords for Antoine Planet, and one of their co-workers recalled that she had often see them be "very familiar" with each other and sometimes arrive at work together "which made her suspect [something]." Nevertheless, she had not heard anything to make her think Planet had bad intentions (that is, he did not intend to marry Benoite) so she did not say anything to their employer or his wife. In this case, the co-worker judged their behavior to be acceptable because Planet intended to marry Benoite. A neighbor of Antoinette Chabry observed that he "would have disapproved if they were not getting married" because she was often alone in a room with her intimate partner.[27]

When emerging couples' intimacy seemed to be heading toward illicit, a whole range of people felt empowered to step in, including superiors like parents or employers as well as peers like friends or co-workers. Employers took an active role in regulating the intimate behavior of young people. When Marie Berger went to live with a woman to learn to make stockings, she met Bastien Chappuis who also worked there. Another young woman recalled that she often saw Chappuis "be very familiar" with Berger and put his hands on her breasts or under her skirt and often heard him say he intended to marry her. Her employer, Catherine Leroy, recalled that she had often seen the couple caressing each other. She recalled that one day she "surprised them" in bed. Even though the spouses knew that Berger had been buying household goods to prepare for marriage and Chappuis tried to assure them that he would marry her as she was a "respectable" (*honnete*) girl who had not been with any other men, the employers decided to fire her.[28] The interactions between employers and workers about the practices and intentions of youthful intimacy illuminate the active supervision that both allowed young couples to enjoy intimacy as they moved toward marriage but also empowered observers on occasion to mark a hard boundary. The young woman lost her job despite the evidence of her partner's words and her actions that they were intent on marriage, a telling reminder of the potential for uneven gendered consequences even when young men were expected to be responsible for the reproductive consequences of their sexual activity.

Landlords or often landladies, like employers, were supportive of moving toward marriage but were quick to check behavior that was problematic if marriage was not in view. Marie Allegret's landlord often saw her with Jerome Caillat and noticed "their familiarities" with each other. He asked them both what was going on and he recalled that they both emphasized that they were going to get married. He added that the extent of their public intimacy had made for plenty of neighborhood gossip, and in doing so articulated explicitly the many layers of communal observation in which young couples' relationships were embedded. Likewise, Elizabeth Tronchet's widowed landlady often saw her boyfriend come to take her out for walks and he indicated to the landlady that indeed he was seeing Tronchet with the intention that they would be married.[29]

Such community safeguarders of young people's future often wanted to speak to both the young women and the young men. Claudine Grissonet and Benoit Peyssonaux, for example, had been neighbors for years and their intimate relationship was well known in their vicinity. A *marchand fabricant*, who was only thirty-three himself, often visited her family and saw the couple cuddling and caressing. He first questioned Claudine about who her beau was. She replied he was a man she was seeing with an eye to marriage. A few days later he ran into Peysonnaux with his family on the street and asked him when they would be married. In all these kinds of interactions, observers expected young men as well as young women to respect clearly established expectations about their intimate behavior, even if they were alert to a greater potential consequence for young women.

If they did not do so and began to have intercourse prematurely in the eyes of their communities, safeguarders could take swift action. When a butcher's wife went up to look for something in the attic, she found Jeanne Pichon and Claude Lucenay "doing something that isn't respectable" (and of course in violation of the expectation that respectable intimacy took place in public view) and she slapped Pichon. In another instance, a crowd of evening walkers noticed Jacques Issac and his partner engage in what they took to be intercourse on a river quayside. Their efforts to break them up caused a fight between Issac and some of the interveners.[30]

Intercourse was in fact one highly policed pole of a wide spectrum of expressions of desire that were quotidian, some tied to promises of marriage and some not. Even intercourse was not considered illicit when followed by marriage. No mention was ever made of anyone—parents, court officials or community members—finding pre-marital sex inappropriate in the context of a clearly established existing agreement to marry. A similar pattern of high rates of pre-marital sex when tied to promises of marriage existed across early modern Europe. Lyonnais women steadfastly claimed in court that they had engaged in intercourse only with promises of marriage secured. Their clarity spoke to the broad understanding, if not always perfect observance in practice of course, of this key connection. Young people's intimacy, and even intercourse, became illicit only when pregnancy was de-coupled from marriage.

The Material Culture of Intimacy

The letters, *billets-doux* (love notes), gifts, and written promises to marry that couples exchanged expressed and reinforced couples' connections but also could become symbols of their tensions. Young women occasionally deposited such items as supporting evidence in paternity suits. They provide extraordinary and rarely surviving examples of the material culture of young workers' relationships. Young partners expressed their intimacy through their actions as well as words and their exchanges of material culture artifacts emphasized their emotional as well as physical connections in pursuit of what we might call compatibility and connection, if not the modern construct of romantic love. The material culture of intimacy was braided with emotions of all kinds in the roller coaster of excitement, uncertainty, anxiety, enjoyment, hope, and fear that characterized young people's relationships as much then as it usually does now—even in the smoothest of circumstances—although configured in ways that were specific to their rank and era.

Young women's articulation of their emotions survive primarily in the relationship narratives in paternity suits in which they often specified the warm feelings that developed between couples as well as their actions as indicators of stable intimate relationships. They used a variety of terms to articulate these sentiments, all variants on the "love and affection" phrase. They even sometimes used a phrase *faire l'amour* that translates literally as "make love" although at the time meant to court. They also used different constructions with *amour* or frequently used the noun *amitié* which was a common euphemism for love and affection.[31] The use of the word "love" with a verb helps illustrate that their relationships were built on emotional practices that included the exchanges of texts and letters and evocative language as well as the endless walks.

Women often referenced having received written promises to marry as well as the ubiquitous verbal promises and these provide an illuminating window into the world of young adut intimacy.[32] In a 1680 written commitment, a silk worker, Antoine Flacheron, acknowledged his relationship history with Ysabeau Martin, whose work as a servant was probably mult-facted like other servants. He promised to marry her: "in a true and loyal marriage as soon as she or her kin asked him to in order to keep the verbal promises he had given earlier. Moreover subsequent to those I recognize that she allowed me to visit her often and to have sex with her following which she became pregnant by me." The note ended with the assurance that "In faith of which [promises] I have signed this present [note] although it is written in another hand."[33]

The promise was small, about 4 by 6 inches, and the tax stamp at the top indicates that Flacheron recounted the details of his sexual history with Ysabeau to a notary he hired to write it. Notaries were party to many intimate conversations about young couples' relationships and often made written records for clients about many matters, even though such documents did not

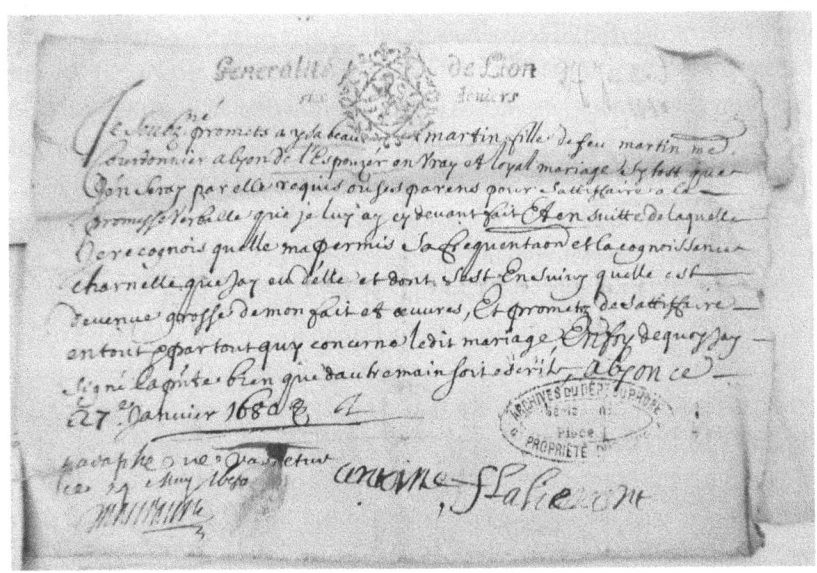

A 1680 promise to marry. ADR BP3541 14 May 1680 Dossier of Berchet and Flacheron.

have official legal standing.[34] Such a promise did carry a kind of legal association, however, as it probably gave added weight about the couple's seriousness and it involved a financial cost that might also have been seen as an indicator of commitment.

The emotions associated with a written promise to marry could evolve as in the case of Flacheron and Ysabeau who had had an entirely conventional relationship. They were co-workers who shared the same employer and lived in close proximity. They had known each other for two years and she recalled that he had "fallen in love with her" (*rendu amoureux*) and promised to marry her. She noted that his persuasiveness and "violence" led to "carnal knowledge" and she became pregnant. Flacheron's promise was written in the wake of that unsurprising development. Then he gave it to her and she had kept it carefully as proof of his commitment. When she deposited it in her paternity suit, its status changed to legal evidence. No doubt its emotional meaning also shifted as it signified broken promises rather than a token of commitment. Ysabeau never got it back from the court. It survives as a painful reminder of the risks of intimacy that always underlay the initial stages of the transition to marriage.

The promise leaves many questions unanswered. What discussions preceded the decision to have it written? Did Ysabeau Martin want something more concrete than Flacheron's verbal promises or did he offer it as proof of his commitment? While written promises to marry were common, it is unclear how often a couple would have used a notary to record it. Why did Flacheron pay a notary to write his promise rather than have a literate friend or co-worker write it for him? His signature is a bit awkward suggesting that he was not a fluid writer. A notarial version cost money, however, so he or she must have thought it had some greater credibility even though it had no more official legal standing than any other written promise.

Eighty years after Flacheron promised to marry Martin, Jean Claude Fiancon included a similarly sized promise to marry in a letter missive to his fellow silk worker Anne Rubard. On the back of the second page, Fiancon wrote a straightforward five lines that included: "Promise I made to Mlle Rubard... that I promise to keep... and nothing will get in the way of carrying it out," and signed it.[35] Did Fiancon write his note himself because of rising literacy rates among working people and/or to stress his sincerity with a self-authored commitment? Had Flacheron used a notary because of the perceived additional value of notarial writing? The reasons for their different choices are elusive.

Fiancon's tone in the three-page letter part of his text was quite different. He promised Rubard if she "agreed to what I have asked [intercourse presumably]" he would marry her and "never abandon her." He chose some dramatic rhetoric to convey the intensity and seriousness of his commitment: "The kingdom of God would never be his if he left her" and "he would a thousand million times rather the devil take him away than he not keep his commitment to her." He continued, "It's with the best of my heart my lovely sweetheart that I make this oath to persuade you that I will never leave you." Nevertheless, he apparently thought such sentiments were not sufficient so he composed the more formal brief promise to marry too.

Such written promises were common material expressions of intimacy that gave concrete form to a couple's commitment and had an emotional connotation that could shift as a relationship waxed and sometimes waned. Paper promises to marry represented a physical embodiment of the connection between the couple that shaped as well as reflected it. Written promises to marry were a form of proof of a couple's emotional connection and an articulation of their future together. They represented in a material form the verbal promises to marry that were pivotal in a couple's shift from physical intimacy short of intercourse to having sex. For young women, the physical evidence may have cemented the sense of security about the future course of the relationships. They kept these tokens carefully, sometimes showed them to friends, and told people that written promises of marriage had been exchanged. For young men, the written marital commitments magnified on a different level the promises they had made in conversation and confirmed them in a less heated moment. For young women, they were part of their strategies for managing the pathways of their intimacy, physical, emotional, and reproductive, with their consensual partners.

The artifacts of material intimacy reveal the undulating intimate topography of emotions in young people's consensual relationships. Only one-half of correspondence between young couples usually survives: the letters or notes men wrote because women deposited the letters as evidence. For women, handing legal officials the letters, notes, and promises in which their beaus expressed their feelings must have been fraught with emotions of disappointment and perhaps anger. Young men certainly articulated intense feelings of affection and passion. A. Chaboud, for example, wrote three brief love notes on small pieces of paper in a very informal style to Pierrette Sibert as they conducted a relationship while working for the same employer. He addressed her as "my dear love" or "Tender Heart," and he claimed that "his heart deprived of her absence for a few days was in a state of continual suffering." He promised that his love would be long lasting and referenced his affection, respect, and attachment. In a letter, he said that he could not wait to hold her in his arms and that he dreamed about her.[36] Variations on the same terms of endearment filled other letters.[37] Such language does not preclude a pragmatic bent to their marriage choices, but it acknowledged that they were interested in a sense of connection with each other as well as other forms of compatibility. Women's decision to deposit the letters as legal evidence in their favor indicates that this language of love was regarded as broadly appropriate.

Other letters illustrate the complexities and uncertainties of young couples' relationships. In the middle of a long, complicated, messy breakup, Louis Mollard wrote an angry letter to Benigne Dubois in which he used terms such as "a slut like you" and said he would never marry her. Francois Cadet addressed Marie Dutremblois as "My dear heart," proposed a meeting to talk a few days later, and proclaimed that he loved her and would love her for his whole life. However, between those lines he attached to the letter the ticket that would be needed for their unborn baby to be accepted at the Hôtel-Dieu as a foundling.[38]

The exchange of gifts between young people as a practice of intimacy has a long history, but did such exchanges have ambiguous meanings for Lyonnais workers? Historians have argued that the exchange of tokens was a ritual step in the conformation of developing relationships that implied material responsibilities as well as emotional commitment.[39] Yet in Lyon, judges always asked women if their partners had given them anything and they routinely answered no. That is, judges seem to have associated the giving and acceptance of gifts with promiscuity, perhaps bordering on quite casual prostitution. Young women's consistent denials in court proceedings likewise acknowledged the undertones of such a transactional interaction. The number of such gift exchanges mentioned in these records is very low.

Nevertheless, witnesses' incidental observations demonstrate that young intimate partners in consensual, stable relationships in Lyon did sometimes exchange jewelry and ribbons that, like garters, were clearly associated with flirtation, confirmation of affection, and transitions between stages in relationship. Matthieu Bernier gifted Marie Cottelier a pair of silver earrings, for example, which his sister explicitly said were given "as witness of his affection." Bernier also gave her a silver ring and ribbons, which were a universal early modern symbol of love. Daniel Devaux gave Isabeau Decert "a ring with a green stone and two diamonds." Jean De Juif gave Louise Chauvet a pair of silver earrings, a gift a witness recalled as one of many demonstrations of affection, including many walks with her as well as kissing, caressing, and attending a dance with Louise hosted by the men in his trade. The "two Grenoble handkerchiefs" Jean Chabanassy gave Anne Roussin were also well-known tokens of affection that carried and consolidated warm emotions.[40]

Even gifts of money could have multiple meanings, sometimes being defined as "presents" (rather than payments) and sometime as a legitimate step on the road to marriage. Despite its connotation of prostitution, a gift of money, rather than a promise to marry, was occasionally specified by young women as the pivotal condition of their shift to intercourse. Clearly some exchanges of money were part of a conventional series of steps toward marriage, and these gifts were freighted with expectation about commitment. Antoinette Rozet recalled that Charles Michaud went with her to her home village outside of Lyon to see her father where Michaud gave her five *livres* "as a mark of the certainty of marriage" in the presence of her father. Likewise, Claude Ponsu gave Louise Billon "six *livres* as a mark of the commitment to marriage as is the custom in this region." These amounts of money constituted roughly a working man's wages for a week (although early modern wages are notoriously difficult to establish), so they amounted to a significant act of commitment by young men. They also hinted at the mutuality of quotidian family economies where women and men both contributed their resources and managed household finances.[41]

Whether these gifts had an emotional or transactional valency may not have been stable then, much less clear now. Sometimes the meanings of the exchanges were opaque, perhaps even to the couple. Helyen Lyonnet claimed that over four months Jean Moulet had pressed her to have sex, promised she "wouldn't lack for anything," admitted he had developed affection for her, and offered to marry her. She admitted he "sometimes" also gave her money when they had sex.[42] When young men were being pursued for paternity claims, they retrospectively framed money transfers as transactional exchanges that implied sexual commerce although they may have meant something different in the moment. Their claims show the slippery nature of gifting: an exchange that began with affection could be repurposed to have another meaning later. Louis Mollard alleged that other young men had given Benigne Dubois a range of gifts; he associated the presents with her being easy when he asserted "It's easy to make babies when you are doing that," and called her a slut. Pierre Peyssillon and Lucie Peyrieu were both silk workers for the same employer in the late 1650s and conducted their relationship at work as well as elsewhere. Peyssillon admitted that he had slept with Peyrieu, but claimed he was very surprised to learn that she thought they would be married because he "had given her money and she is a *fille de joie*."[43] What he meant by calling her a *fille de joie* is unclear, especially in the context of defending himself against a paternity claim, but he did admit he had given her money.

The term *fille de joie* had a broader and more ambiguous set of meanings about sexual availability over the course of the Old Regime than simple prostitution. Louis-Sébastian Mercier used it 130 years later to describe young shop workers who had sex with their boyfriends in return for small gifts. Certainly, young female workers in the seventeenth and eighteenth centuries (and later) likely supplemented their meager wages with gifts from their boyfriends, but this did not constitute prostitution. Possibly Pierre meant that Lucie had had several previous suitors or perhaps he simply used the term to undermine a legal claim that rested on her ability to show that they were a monogamous couple headed to marriage. Notably the court awarded her the usual compensation, clearly unmoved by the exchange of money despite their routine questions about gifts.

All these tokens, whether they were love notes, promises to marry, or gifts like ribbons, garters, and rings, had emotional meanings for the young partners that were fixed by context.[44] When a pregnant Pierrette Sibert moved from the rented room where she lived, her employer found Chaboud's three short love notes as well as a longer letter that she had left behind.[45] Did she leave them behind by accident during the move or did she deliberately abandon them as they had become unhappy reminders of the breakup rather than emblems of affection and intended marriage? Regardless of the reasons, all these surviving texts were likely imbued with anxiety, anger, and frustration by the time they were deposited as part of a legal proceeding.

The changing status of written commitments and gifts shows the ways in which youthful experiences of intimacy and emotion were about heartache as well as hope, rupture as well as connection. When young women handed over to the court the promises to marry their intimate partners had given them or letters sent to them, they had likely experienced emotional roller coasters. Young women kept them, treasured them no doubt, reframed them, or occasionally weaponized them in court and no doubt more often out of court. The material culture of intimacy was one expression of a kaleidoscopic emotional web that "love" only hints at.

Sex Talks

As young couples' relationships progressed, they began to have frank talks about sex as well as their other forms of physical intimacy. The vernacular language of sexuality demonstrated how young partners both calibrated the extent of their intimacy and framed their expressions of licit desire in gendered ways. They shared a common basic knowledge about sex and reproduction and explicitly discussed having intercourse and at least sometimes about managing fertility. Their sex talks coded power relations between them as gendered and revealed their explicit awareness of the significance of the transition to intercourse in terms of promise and peril. They understood that starting to have intercourse involved a commitment to marry and a danger of pregnancy. For both partners, but especially young women, these conversations involved risk management as well as relationship management.[46]

Knowledge about sex in working communities certainly included some uncertainties. The mother of one young man, for example, asked a surgeon if a young man could get a girl pregnant without ejaculating, because her son told her he had not ejaculated so he could not be the father of his girlfriend's unborn child. The surgeon assured her that her son was correct.[47] Women frequently claimed in court, perhaps implausibly, that they did not know whether the purpose of remedies they had taken was to regularize their menstrual periods (a common health concern) or to interrupt reproduction (a common goal of remedies that "regularized" periods).

Young women's awareness of the promises (marriage) and perils (pregnancy not accompanied by marriage) associated with a shift to intercourse was abundantly clear. Young women consistently used the passive voice to emphasize their lack of agency in initiating the shift and emphasized their active if futile resistance to sex, at least until or even when the promise of marriage seemed firm. They explicitly referenced gendered power, repeating terms such as a male partner "took advantage of the weakness of her sex" or his pressure, verbal and physical, "had obliged" her to have sex. Women framed intercourse as "he had carnal knowledge of her." In doing so they drew of course on the available language to talk about respectable women's behavior in paternity suits whose success depended on their good reputations, but they also echo the cultural convention that pre- and postdated the Old Regime—men's role in the progression of physical intimacy was to push while women's role was to brake.

Their language included specific euphemisms that calibrated different stages of their experimentation with physical intimacy in ways that also captured how gendered power shaped their relationships. Young men did the asking for the walking together that marked the start of a meaningful performance of coupledom and these walks included "linking arms." As relationships progressed to stable courtships that were plausible preludes to marriage, young men took "liberties" that included hugging and kissing, and even touching parts of the body through or under clothes. Observers would often characterize these behaviors as "she permitted him" to take these kinds of liberties. Young women granted "the last favors"—that is, intercourse—as a consequence of elaborate negotiations about marriage as well as reiterated requests.

The explicit nature of these negotiations demonstrates that young women and young men understood that the stakes of intercourse were quite different from the stakes of even expansive caressing short of that. Women often recounted the discussions of marriage and intercourse as intertwined. That is, a man asked his partner (often repeatedly) to grant the last favors and promised to marry her if she did, or she agreed to the last favors only after he had promised to marry her. Louise Official explained that she had had "carnal knowledge" with Antoine Pinardy after his many requests and promises to marry her and insisted "she would not have agreed without the promises to marry." Claudine Rangeard described how Philibert Mercier had "attested to his love for her and asked her to agree to the last favors, promising her he would marry her if she succumbed to his desires."[48] While telling these details to a court official certainly shaped women's versions of events, in practice they also knew that they needed to clarify as far as possible men's intentions about marriage (through verbal promises, preferably in front of others, or written promises that offered concrete proof) before they had intercourse or risked uncertain times ahead.

Young women's accounts emphasized that they themselves indeed sought to regulate the levels of physical intimacy very carefully to secure the consequence they wanted (marriage) and to avoid the consequence they sought to avoid (unwed pregnancy). In these ways, women were at pains to demonstrate to their partners, their communities, and, if need be, eventually to the courts that they had not been carried away in the heat of the moment when they started to have sex. Certainly, the insistence on careful calculation in part reflects who made legal paternity claims. On the whole, they were women whose relationships were feasibly preparatory to marriage and whose communities supported their experiments with physical intimacy as appropriate and respectable in that light. They also wanted to emphasize their virtue in the legal context by rejecting any implication of casual sex rather than intercourse as a key step into marriage. Nevertheless, the high value on women's management of sex as an explicit element of the commitment to marry was not simply a legal ploy.

Young women and men rarely acknowledged, in surviving records at least, what was evident in their actions and in observers' comments—that their relationships included a pleasurable bodily connection as well as the enjoyment of their partner's company on walks and conversations. A young man's letter in which he admitted how he longed to hold his partner in his arms offers an exceptional extant written expression of the physical pleasures associated with these relationships.[49] Within the conventions of carefully monitored and calibrated stages of licit physical intimacy, young women as well as young men enjoyed and were allowed to enjoy the experience of desire without damage to their reputations.

Yet women's narratives marked intercourse as a pivotal moment of matrimonial commitment, one that often preceded explicit parental permission or a marriage contract, much less the readings of banns in parish churches to announce upcoming weddings. If young couples' intimacy in many forms was an acceptable expression of youthful desire within the framework of feasible marriage and intercourse was tightly correlated with commitment to marry, first intercourse marked a potent shift in relationships whose significance was marked by space and place, both conceptual and literal.

First Intercourse in Consensual Relationships

When Agathe Laumosnier remembered the first time she had sex with George Piot, she detailed how on a Sunday the previous April, he found her alone in a room, closed the door and put the key in his pocket, "violently seized her," threw her on the bed and had sex with her. She framed their first intercourse as a turning point in what had been a long established consensual relationship that she, like other women, routinely continued afterward. Like Laumosnier, young women narrated their sexual histories in court records as peril stories that positioned the transition to intercourse as pivotal. The peril lay in the routine use of force as well as the possibility of uncertain consequences and the danger of pregnancy not followed by matrimony. The promise lay in the clear step toward marriage. Pre-marital intercourse also held some consequence for young men, who were expected to take responsibility for any resulting pregnancies, but the rewards of marriage were also a prospect.

The shift to intercourse for young couples was entwined with the decision to marry and a new location for licit intimacy. When young women used the phrase "carnal knowledge" to demarcate intercourse and equated that explicitly with "what happens between a husband and a wife," they clearly marked intercourse as distinct from a spectrum of acceptable activities for courting couples that ranged from talking through expansive physical intimacy.[50] The use of a temporarily repurposed interior space as the site for first intercourse reinforced that association as marital sex took place in the beds used for sleeping albeit in rooms that were usually used for multiple other purposes during the day.

Young women narrated the arc of their sexual histories with a particular trajectory: consensual relationships that involved experiments with licit intimacy, discussions about marriage, the use of force in initial intercourse, and subsequent intercourse as part of a continuing expectation of marriage. Typically, they recounted a lengthy history of sociability and intimacy in the form of "caresses" and "liberties," "keeping company" (usually in the form of frequent walks), and requests for "the last favors" that were repeatedly repudiated. A stark single episode followed in which a young man typically found his partner in a room alone, used force (often some version of him taking her by the arms and throwing her on the bed), promised marriage, and had intercourse despite her resistance. Young women acknowledged that intercourse continued subsequently as they expected to get married, so marriage still seemed a desirable option after their experiences. Perhaps, despite the use of force, the possibility of pregnancy and closer prospect of marriage made their commitment firmer.

These distinctive sexual histories must be understood in the context of the legal requirements that occasioned the telling, the ubiquity of violence in relationships, and the impact of the subsequent failure of their relationships. The narratives reflected a particular historical moment in terms of intimate relationships, when experiences of them and meanings attached to them were specific to a certain time, place, and rank.

Young women's descriptions of the use of force as key to first intercourse occurred in cases heard before a wide range of jurisdictions across many early modern regions, and their accounts point to the routine use of force as part of women's lived experience in intimate relationships that seemed to be leading to marriage. Even with young women who found themselves in court to make legal claims in paternity suits and needed to tell their stories in a certain way to be successful and to maintain their reputations, their narratives about their sexual histories have to be understood in the context of the well-established practice of using violence as an integral element of intimate relationships. Men routinely "disciplined" wives, servants, children, and apprentices, for example, as a part of the obligations and privileges of adult masculinity.[51] The use of force as a mundane staple of first intercourse was part of the same spectrum of legitimate uses of force, and not simply women strategically mobilizing a legal trope.[52] Tellingly, when court officials questioned young male partners, they never asked them to address the allegations of force. That silence suggests that legal officials took coercion in consensual relationships as a norm. In doing so, court officials endorsed forced sex as licit intimacy that met community conventions in the context of a consensual relationship leading to marriage.

This particular use of force was apparently regarded as quotidian and likely predictable. None of the young women apparently cried out for help to summon their neighbors in the way battered wives did. They did not allege that they had been raped, nor that the intercourse itself dishonored them. The very different narratives that framed criminal trials for rape show very different conventions as did the rare instances in which charges of *rapt* and or seduction (which indicated intercourse with the intent to abandon and dishonor) were made.[53]

The complexity of the use of force in accounts of first intercourse in relationships headed for marriage expressed a deeply embedded notion of legitimate force as well as a rhetorical stance or legal strategy. Old Regime licit intimacy for young workers who were partners included forced sex in a way that is jarring to us but was predictable for contemporaries. In fact, male force was likely a routine part of Old Regime sex as one more site where male power and privilege was acknowledged. Sharon Block has argued for early America that coercion was always a part of sex as a key element of male dominance, and Garthine Walker noted that prosecution for rape in early modern England required "beyond normal" sexual aggression.[54] In the early modern world, the wide association of intercourse with the use of force was one of the reasons that prosecution for rape was rare and difficult to win.

The routine use of legitimate force as a normal expression of adult masculinity was part of a cultural sexual script in working communities and of a broader legal script around coverture that shaped conventions and expectations surrounding the shifting ground of intimacy and the decision to marry. Young men's sexual scripts for first intercourse included expectations that use of force would be required and that young women likely shared these expectations. Women probably anticipated that men would take their virginity, and young men expected they would have to coerce the granting of "the last favors," even though women in consensual relationships had already expressed their desire with public intimacy for months, and had anticipated intercourse when they engaged in explicit discussions in which they agreed to "the last favors" as part of the commitment to matrimony.

Indeed, the explicit link to marriage guaranteed men sexual access to women's bodies as they became part of the property of coverture. Coverture was the key form of family property law that empowered men to discipline and manage their wives' bodies as well as other aspects of household life. Men could not rape their wives because the law gave them access. In this way, the incremental transition to marriage that began with promises and the shift to intercourse then proceeded through contracts and the reading of banns prior to the religious ceremony meant that the establishment of the varied property rights of coverture took place incrementally. Men, whether judges or textile workers, were assured that the privileges of coverture encompassed marital sexual violence and differentiated that use of force from types of behavior that could lead to legal and community constraints on men's privileges.[55] Women's endurance of such behavior was a part of their larger experiences of violence as a common feature of many marriages. While early modern communities and courts calibrated and regulated what they defined as the "excessive" use of force in intimate relationships and other aspects of community life, sexual violence was broadly accepted as a predictable initiation rite in intimate relationships between young couples.

As with Margeurite Perricaud and Agathe Laumosnier, young women's accounts of their sexual histories associated the new site for intimacy with the new use of force, linking them as integral elements in the shift to intercourse with its expectation of matrimony. Just as space was essential in marking the courtship intimacy as licit or disreputable, it was a critical marker of the meanings and experiences of the shift to intercourse. The women's narratives—he found her alone, locked the door, and used force while whispering sweet nothings and promising again to marry her—highlight the uncertainties and dangers of the new location. Women located their experiences of first intercourse inside rather than in the public spaces, whether interior or exterior, that framed licit intimacy for courting couples. Sex in a bed in a space also used for sleeping was clearly "what a husband and wife do." This spatial distinction was important in associating sex with marriage rather than just a roll in the hay in the fields that might be consensual but not associated with matrimony. However, specialization of interior space was rare outside of elites so the space that working people slept in was used for other purposes too, whether eating, having visitors, or working. Moreover, individuals did not usually have their own rooms; usually someone else slept there too, whether a family member, co-worker, servant, or the person who paid the other half of the rent. These rooms were spaces in which young people lived all aspects of their lives—slept, ate, socialized, and likely also worked. They were not specific or private domestic spaces in the modern meaning of bedroom.

In this context, locking the door had multivalent meanings that might have changed over time or even perhaps in the same episode: was he locking her in or locking other people out? Privacy in early modern society was fraught in terms of meanings. Secrecy was often associated with deceit or wrongdoing, but it is also clear that community conventions accepted quite a broad range of intimacy in public and also regarded intercourse as an appropriate private matter. Yet it was very difficult to make a shared multi-function interior room into a personal or private space.

When a young man locked the door, his action had multiple possible meanings and those meanings were not necessarily stable over time. Households as material and constructed spaces shaped couples' intimacy. As young men and women knew that they should not go into each other's rooms when they were single if they wanted to preserve their reputations, being in a room with a closed door marked an important new phase, pre-marital sex, in the transition from single to married. On one hand, men established temporarily private personal spaces appropriate for acts of marriage. At the time, they likely associated that with desire, excitement, and anticipation; and their intimate partners probably experienced some of those feelings as well as anxiety and fear. For women, the legitimized use of force and the risks of intercourse that was not followed by marriage made the situation potentially perilous. For young partners, these sleeping spaces were sites of desire and danger to be managed by at least interrupting with a locked door the routine coming and going of other residents, neighbors, or co-workers.

However, when women later recollected the door closings in the wake of the subsequent failure of the projected outcome (marriage), they processed the locked door and use of force as a peril story that highlighted men's unpredictability. The danger was at the forefront of women's minds when they looked back because of subsequent failure to marry; and in this rearview mirror, interior space with the barrier of a locked door was a trap where virtue was threatened rather than an intimate space with connotations of matrimony.

Early modern women surely had more than one reaction to any situation, especially such a fraught experience as young couples' first intercourse. Nevertheless, Old Regime communities articulated and internalized conventions that choreographed the experience whether in the anticipation, excitement, discussion, and negotiation that preceded intercourse or in the locking of the door and routine use of force to coerce sex. The subsequent failure of the relationship as well as the legal context of a lawsuit shaped recollections of what had happened. In highlighting the locked door and the use of force, young women elided their own desire. Licit intimacy required young women to wish for marriage and agree to sex only because of their desire for marriage, not from any desire for expanded physical intimacy per se.

If sexual violence punctuated consensual relationships as a key transition step into marriage, the opening and closing of the room was a register of danger as well as desire. If the promise associated with first intercourse was marriage (with all its broader signifiers), women were also aware of the potential perils. They routinely noted that after the first coerced intercourse, they "continued to have sex in expectation of marriage." Intercourse was supposed to seal the marriage bargain but it might also lead to pregnancy, an event that opened another moment for negotiation and uncertainty between young couples. Judges routinely asked young women if they had told their intimate partners that they were pregnant and how the men had responded. The women almost always claimed that they had told their partners. They recalled varied responses, most commonly some version of "That's fine" and "We'll get married." Even in relationships that ended in paternity lawsuits, men frequently said that, although they also sometimes stalled or made excuses as to why marriage was not possible. Strikingly, women often recalled that men acknowledged female anxieties in such situations by saying, "Don't worry" or "You have nothing to fear." These references to newly pregnant women's worry and fear, even in relationships with clear commitments to marry, highlighted both men's and women's awareness of the perils of intercourse in terms of fertility. For women, of course, the stakes were higher in terms of the danger pregnancy posed to their health or their lives as well as the threat of single parenthood, even if Old Regime men would also be held responsible for out-of-wedlock pregnancy.

Old Regime Changes and Continuities in Narratives of Consensual Relationships

When Claudine Grissonet recollected her experience with Benoit Peyssoneaux in 1740, she said he had "lit a passion in her heart" although their first intercourse occurred when he found her alone in a room, locked the door with a key, and used violence to throw her on the bed and have sex.[56] Grissonet's relationship narrative showed potent continuities that would persist throughout the Old Regime and pointed to emerging new constructions of partner intimacy that became apparent by the early 1740s. For partners who promised matrimony, intercourse continued to precede marriage, and equal rank continued to be seen as the key basis for feasible marriage. Exterior and public space continued to be viewed as respectable for expansive intimacy short of intercourse, and privatized, interior space as appropriate for marital sex. The risks of pre-marital sex remained, as some men would continue to ignore their earlier fervent promises of matrimony. However, from the early 1730s on, single women occasionally began to use a language of emotional connection linked to the persuasiveness of caresses as reasons for their consent to intercourse instead of emphasizing physical coercion. New sites for youthful heterosociability also began to emerge, especially in commercial dance halls overseen by dancing masters. The shifts were incremental, with many accounts of relationship histories mixing new and older elements. However, these shifts suggest new elements developed in young couples' licit intimate partnerships.

While couples continued to take walks together, the popularity of dances overseen by dancing masters hinted at the emergence of new forms of more commercial opportunities for young people's intimacy. Men or women began to sometimes say they had met at the dancing master's or that they went to the dancing master's together. Pierre Vincent remembered that he met Barbe de Moulin a year earlier in a dance hall (*salle de danse*) where she went every Sunday and feast day. Catherine Trenet recalled that she met Jean Baptiste Francois "at a dancing master's" where he approached her with compliments and he subsequently began to visit her. In 1740, [no first name given] Milot recalled how he and Claudine Rang had taken walks and had picnics as young couples had long done, but he also "took her to dance halls." In earlier decades, couples occasionally mentioned dancing, usually on feast days or at artisans' "balls," but these were less commercialized and less choreographed.[57]

Advertisements in Lyon's classified newspaper show that "dance halls" were in fact temporarily repurposed rooms in one of the city's multi-story tenements, often not even on the first floor, where dancing masters hosted and taught lessons for a few hours. In this way, dance halls were one more example of the constant repurposing of interior space that characterized life in Old Regime cities. Dance masters taught dances like minuets that required couples to dance together and offered a new activity for youthful intimacy that mandated physical contact and brought fun and pleasure. A traveler to Paris in the 1780s described the scene at a new dance hall. Young people enjoyed "dances and quadrilles . . . guided by the dancing masters" while others sat at benches at the sides to watch. The popularity of dancing of this type was also clear in advertisements for schools or training programs that explicitly included dance lessons. Three sisters ran a *pension* for girls, for instance, where they trained them for key textile jobs, teaching them "to make all kinds of linens, different embroidery and even embroidery of gold or silver" while also promising to give their charges lessons in dancing and writing.[58] The shift to specific interior spaces where entertainment cost money marked a step away from the free pleasures young couples had enjoyed and hinted at future re-alignments of courtship dynamics whereby young men covered the expenses and expected their female partners would reciprocate with intimacy.[59]

From the early 1730s, women occasionally began to use a new language of affection and more frequently started to emphasize the impact of caressing as well as verbal persuasion. In doing so, they emphasized an explicit physical connection and implicit pleasure that they elided when their accounts of first intercourse highlighted force as the critical element. Gabrielle Bornelier provided on early example in 1730 when she emphasized how Nicolas Burel had expressed his "feelings of love for her" and gave her a written note of their engagement when he promised to marry her. When they found themselves alone, she recalled, "he redoubled his caresses" along with continued promises of marriage—and they had sex and went on having sex.[60] Women's reference to caresses as part of the reason they had sex became more frequent after the 1740s. This new version of young women's sexual histories reframed relationship stories to emphasize a language of love and actions that were defined as persuasive caresses even in the context of careful continued attention to commitment to marry as key.

By the 1740s, young women increasingly defined themselves as willing partners in the shift to intercourse, even if they still used passive voice, and occasionally began to use a specific language of consent. Marie Anne Cagny described how she and Phillipe Gonnet had started to have intercourse by saying "she let herself go with him due to [her] warm feelings [*amitiés*] and [his] promises of marriage." So she slept with him because she liked him a lot and he had expressed sufficient commitment to marriage without any indication that force was involved. Claudine Brun had been spending a lot of time with Michel Bodet for nine months and they had talked about marriage when one day he found her alone "and due to his caresses she agreed to his request to" have sex. Anne Thillier recalled in a very straightforward way that after months of Pierre Gaylart frequently expressing "warm feelings and love for her" and their discussions of marriage, one day when they were alone he asked her to have sex and promised to marry her if she did, so she "consented."[61] In these new narratives, women exchanged sex for the precious gift of a husband.

The mid-eighteenth century was a transitional period as some women's relationship narratives continued to pivot on the use of force, some mixed the emphasis on force with newer elements, and others omitted any mention of force. Suzanne Anger's narrative in 1740 could equally well have been from a century before. She explained that her co-worker, Benoit Blain, pressed her constantly for sex, talked about marriage, and one night when they were alone pushed her on the floor and forced her to have sex. Claudine Privat mixed old and new elements of intimacy. She emphasized Jean Lefebvre's repeated caresses and reiterated promises to marry, but also insisted he used force to throw her on the bed where she "would not have given herself to him ... without his violence." Then she added that "she wouldn't have succumbed to" him "without the promise of an establishment." Her hopes for matrimony with him mixed the promise of a good match for pragmatic reasons, the persuasiveness of their physical intimacy, and his use of force. Claudine Blanc and her partner worked together as embroiderers, and their year-long relationship had included many walks together, discussions of marriage, and his entreaties for sex. She recalled that he pressed her "to agree to the last favors," but she "never consented although he made all the promises a man can make." She explained the turn to intercourse as a result of a time "when she could not resist due both to the violence he used and the warm feelings [*amitié*] she had developed for him in view of all the promises he had made." [62] A couple of decades later, Michelle Favard claimed that she and Francoise Belleville "loved each other reciprocally," and he pressed her for fifteen months to have sex which she resisted until "the pressure of his requests and promises meant she consented." These mixed narratives indicate both the incremental nature of change in practices or rhetoric and the persistence of long-standing conventions rooted in gendered power as well as community preferences.

Factoring the economic advantages of marriage also persisted even among the emerging new rhetoric. In 1769, the purse-maker Jacqueline Thervenin recalled how her intimate partner, Sr. Martin, the son of a master stocking maker, had framed their marital futures together. He claimed that he had already consulted his parents and pointed out that "the talent she had and the commercial experience he had together with some property he had access to would enable them to secure a comfortable life with resources that would significantly augment their financial situation." When in the wake of this commitment she became pregnant, she told him they "would have to accelerate their plans to marry."[63]

The slow shift away from force as a predictable element of first intercourse in young women's retellings did not mean that coercion necessarily disappeared as the meaning of their "consent" was fraught and perhaps layered. Their acknowledgment of their own willingness and newly articulated passionate emotional attachment may have led them to want to shift to intercourse or may have made them feel like they ought to agree. Women often emphasized that their intimate partners badgered them for intercourse. It is possible that the language might have changed although the experience remained the same. They may have wanted to avoid references to force or to add other factors as a new set of expectations for relationships began to emerge. They may have consented due to sexual desire or because they wanted to be married. Women's emphasis on how hard men pressed them may have been a performance of chastity as they wanted to show they were not "easy," or it may indicate how difficult it was for women to say no even without physical coercion.

When Francoise Clerc came to court to make a paternity claim in 1740, she was clear that she had not been dishonored nor damaged her own reputation by having sex with Phillipe Flacheron as a single woman. Their relationship had all the hallmarks of licit intimacy that observed the appropriate conventions in an ongoing consensual relationship that included intercourse when a commitment to marriage was clear. She had been dishonored only when he failed to follow through on his promises to marry her.[64] Her distinction highlights the Old Regime calibration that allowed young women and men to experiment with intimacy in all its forms as part of the experimenting with potential marriage partners. Her recounting this story in court reveals the ways in which licit intimacy's potential for marriage also inherently involved a fundamental risk of peril young women and their communities. The sense of youthful intimacy as a community project in which many people felt charged with a responsibility to safeguard a young couple's behavior and future remained very potent.

The shift to marriage took the form of an extended transition with various elements rather than a sharp distinction before and after a wedding day, and intercourse was strongly associated with spouses. As couples progressed toward matrimony and began to have sex, fertility issues took center stage. Indeed, young women's peril stories highlight another critical issue: the agreement to intercourse based on commitment to marriage was a kind of hinge between a transition to matrimony or a precarious phase of extramarital pregnancy. Community safeguarders continued to play important roles in encouraging marriage or facilitating alternative solutions to marriage that would preserve the futures and reputations of young men and young women - if they continued to observe communal protocols about how they should behave when pregnancies occurred that for many reasons were not followed by legal matrimony.

3

Holding Men Responsible

Fertility, Community, and Court

When young women in stable consensual relationships on the road to marriage realized that they were pregnant, they routinely informed their intimate partners of their new status as expectant parents. In the vast majority of relationships, the men must have customarily answered as Elie Reposte did when he told Jeanne Rougemond—that he was fine (*aise*) with her news and that she would be his wife. (Otherwise illegitimacy rates would have been higher.) Sometimes the responses were more ambivalent. Anne Transchard's news led her partner to respond that she should "conserve her fruit" (a euphemism for avoiding trying to end her pregnancy) and he would take care of her. Occasionally, these initial conversations were causes for great upset if the men immediately reneged on their promises of marriage, as Jean Francois Chosellard did when he responded to Antoinette Silvestre's news by calling her a whore and claiming he was not in a position to marry her, or when men subsequently left town.[1]

Women recalled these initial exchanges when court officials routinely asked if they had "declared" their pregnancies to their partners. In fact, the only time court officials inquired whether a woman had "declared" her pregnancy to anyone was in specific reference to her partner. Women's attentiveness to this question as well as the judges' consistent interest over the entire course of the Old Regime hints at the gendered power relationships embedded in consensual intimate relations and at the layers of expectations about the conventional course of events in young people's relationships. Fertility was a predictable outcome of intercourse for young couples in an era without effective contraception, and it had important inevitable and potential consequences for both men and women. In an era of high maternal mortality, women faced the physical stress of reproduction as well as the dangers of pregnancy and childbirth. Women in late term pregnancies sometimes pointed out in court that they were no longer able to do the intense physical labor that employment as textile workers or servants involved.

Pregnant women were quite likely to lose their jobs if employers perceived that marriage was not in their future. Single working women could not earn enough money to support a child. And if men abandoned them completely— that is, left them without any help to manage the pregnancy even if they did not marry—their reputations as well as their financial circumstances were at stake.

Yet men too felt pressure, as working communities and local courts had explicit expectations that men who engaged in intercourse associated with promises to marry should carry through with their promises, even if they had to be imprisoned while the legal system investigated their intimate partners' paternity claims. For women to invoke even the possibility of resorting to "justice" posed a potent threat for men because of the possibility of detention in prison. Men's ability to preserve their reputations depended on their willingness to accept the consequences of their sexual activity, preferably through marriage or if not, by providing for their intimate partners and offspring outside of marriage.[2]

Not yet married couples were not usually isolated as they sought to manage the new stage that fertility entailed. Courts and community safeguarders worked together to encourage male responsibility, to mitigate the risk of pre-marital conception to women and their communities, and to amplify the normative expectation that men's promises of marriage should lead to marriage or some other form of acceptable support. Neighbors, co-workers, employers, and friends encouraged, incentivized, and pressured couples to marry. Mostly they acted informally within the community, but if necessary, they appeared as witnesses in paternity suits to confirm women's appropriate behavior and their credible expectations of marriage. Throughout the Old Regime, community safeguarders advocated marriage as the preferred course of action when young couples' intimacy resulted in pregnancy. Their efforts show that the outcomes were perceived to have high stakes for more people than just the couples and their families. Indeed, statistics on low illegitimacy (even if the 5% to 10% rate in Lyon was a bit higher than usually reported elsewhere) but high rates of pre-marital conception indicate that on most occasions men did marry their pregnant partners, whether willingly or with informal or legal encouragement. If marriage did not occur, community members worked to ensure that men at least took financial and usually custodial responsibility for the children.

Local courts worked in ways that aligned with community priorities to reinforce the expectation that men were responsible for paternity either through marriage or through paying their partners' costs and taking custody of the offspring. While most couples did not end up in court, the possibility of legal action always existed for women in stable consensual relationships where marriage had seemed likely. Judges imposed penalties that disciplined recalcitrant male intimate partners and allowed single women to re-start their lives. By holding men responsible, however, the court also reduced a wide range of bad male sexual behavior to a single form of wrong addressed by a simple penalty—a financial provision for the woman and custody of the baby to the father, a practice that maintained gendered power differentials within a system that was generally very supportive of single women.

Women's fertility prompted negotiations with intimate partners and communities as well as occasional engagements of the legal system to assist in the project of emphasizing male responsibility that reframe our understanding of the intersections of sexuality and state in the seventeenth and eighteenth centuries. The regulatory and disciplinary pressures on some expressions of women's sexuality were only one part of a larger mosaic of efforts to delineate some forms of male and female sexuality as inevitable and usual while seeing other kinds of sexuality, especially extra-marital reproductivity, as a threat for which men as well as women were held responsible. The disciplinary potential of expanding the regulation of sexuality in early modern Europe has received much attention.[3] However, a common project also existed to mitigate the risks of intimacy in ways that complicate the idea of a gender double standard centered on female sexuality.

The politics of fertility, parental permission, and property among European elites were transparent when timely and legitimate reproduction was closely associated with political stability and diplomatic alliances. Similarly, the power issues embedded in daily negotiations about fertility had implications for ordinary people who were intimate partners and for their families and communities. Young men and women had their reckoning, parents and property were potential obstacles as well as potential supports, and a range of community safeguarders sought to encourage the transition to marriage. Gateways had to be navigated before young couples could marry. In working communities, marriage depended on appropriate financial situations as well as other property issues, and parents had to consent. These negotiations involved an emotional roller coaster for intimate partners even when they went relatively smoothly, and these issues could derail plans even when the couple wanted to marry. Paternity suits offered a legal avenue to procure marriage or acceptance of responsibility. In all these ways, women's fertility provided a marker, a milestone, and a malleable process integral to the ambiguous and complex transition in emerging adults' consensual relationships between walking out and matrimony.

Fertility as a Key Site of Negotiation and Transition

The reality of a new pregnancy opened a pivotal phase for young couples in consensual relationships. As their earlier discussions anticipated, it often pushed them to move forward officially with a planned marriage. However, female fertility also marked a phase of negotiation and sometimes contention between the intimate partners, their families, and their communities. Paternity suits by their nature highlight situations where the path to marriage became bumpy but the backstories they reveal highlight the routine ways in which pregnancies occasioned uncertainty, negotiation, and different impacts for men and women.

Throughout the Old Regime, judges consistently asked women if they had "declared" their pregnancy to their intimate partners, and the consistency of that question over a century indicates how pivotal the telling was in terms of the relationship and its future. Women reliably responded that they had indeed told their partners and they recounted the responses. Partners could confirm a smooth progression toward matrimony (probably the usual response with the low illegitimacy rate but frequent rate of pre-marital conception), or equivocate, or sometimes immediately demur about marriage despite all the promises. Evidence drawn from paternity suits probably overrepresents difficulties in the transition to marriage, and certainly women seeking legal relief via paternity suits were perhaps especially likely to emphasize clearly that they had communicated the pregnancy news.

Telling pregnancy news to intimate partners was fraught with uncertainty and potential peril for not yet married women. They used the occasion to reiterate the expectation of marriage. Jeanne Mulatier, for instance, recalled in 1682 that she had told Andre Priou "as soon as she realized she was pregnant so that he could keep his promises [to marry her]." In the same decade, Elizabeth Demen said that she had told her partner before she told her father so they could talk about it first. Francoise Bonnard four decades later recalled that she told her partner and "invited him to keep his promises." The same year, Andree Girard remembered she had told her partner that "he had to do the right thing."[4]

Anxiety and even fear must have been common elements of newly pregnant single women's emotions about sharing that news, even in relationships where commitment to marriage had preceded the shift to intercourse, because women understood the difficulties they faced if men abandoned them instead of marrying them. If some women recounted how their partners had acknowledged that uncertainty by responding with endless versions of "Don't worry, we will get married," other conversations amplified anxiety. Anne Roussin, for example, wailed to her friends that "she was dead" after a private conversation with her intimate partner, and they attributed this despair to his refusing to marry her when she told him about the pregnancy. Some women articulated their fears when they noted that they could no longer work when they were pregnant or worried that their employers might terminate them if their pregnancy did not seem to be followed by marriage. Anne Martin explained in 1723, for example, that she had not been able to work as a draw girl due to her pregnancy.[5]

Moreover, women knew that single mothers whose intimate partners did not support them and who had no other help quickly faced a subsistence crisis. Marie Groble's lawyer provided a rare detailed accounting in 1741 in her claim that the 33 *livres* her partner had paid did not cover the cost of her delivery and that she needed 17 *sous* per day to pay the wet-nurse, who was threatening to send the baby back due to non-payment. Groble also lamented that the butcher would not give her any meat and the baker did not want to give her bread, presumably meaning those food suppliers had cut off her credit.[6] The costs of delivery and childcare by wet-nurses alone were crushing for single women without partner support, let alone feeding and housing the children later.

Men who were upset on learning the news also sometimes compounded women's fears by threatening violence if they were identified as fathers or asking them to name other men instead. Joseph Perron offered Antoinette Lachausee 150 *livres* if she did not identify him as the father. When Jean Royer, a weaver, asked Jeanne Burraud not to name him or to identify another man as the father, despite their year-long relationship and his repeated promises to marry her, she recalled that she "realized he had deceived her and started to take the legal actions necessary to repair her honor." Francoise Lerat explained that when she told Antoine Champetre that she was pregnant, he suggested that "she accuse another [man]," but she had not wanted to "have a false declaration," and he abandoned her without any support. Catherine Malgendre's partner asked her not to name him but promised to take care of her. Many neighbors of Anne Martin and Antoine Louis recalled that their conventional courtship had created the community expectation that they would marry and he had repeatedly promised to marry her. Yet she claimed he threatened to kill her if she named him as her baby's father in a paternity suit and told her "he would settle with her and in a word she would die by his hand." He wanted to pay her ten *ecus* and be done with the matter.[7]

These conversations illuminate how quickly the potential perils of intercourse linked to marriage could manifest. Louis's violent threat highlighted the potential damage to women's bodies and men's reputations. Women knew that their conversations about pregnancy might be a moment when their relationship could start to fracture, no matter how long and firm their prior discussions about marriage had been. Men's reactions, whether threats or efforts to hide their involvement, highlight the risk to their reputations an out-of-wedlock pregnancy could pose if they did not marry their intimate partners. The possibility of men's unpredictable reactions illuminated a fault line around pregnancy that made women vulnerable even in well-established, seemingly stable, and on the road to marriage consensual relationships.

Women must also have known that some men who at first responded favorably might still balk before marriages were completed, so first conversations that went smoothly were no guarantee that men would not resist later. Even in relationships that led to paternity suits, men had usually initially confirmed their intention to marry their partners. By the time Francois Falconnet told Francoise Legout that he would not marry her and would rather be in prison, they had signed a marriage contract and had the banns called twice at their parish church. She duly granted his wish by starting legal action and successfully requesting that he be imprisoned during the investigation.[8] In many other situations, men changed their minds or admitted they had changed their minds after the initial acknowledgment of pregnancy when they were faced with the realities of matrimony and parenthood.

Some pregnancies led to stable cohabitation instead of legal marriage. This arrangement was almost certainly more extensive than extant documents indicate because women tended to come to court only when something about their long-standing monogamous relationship became unsatisfactory. By 1670, for example, Madelaine Vacheron and Jean Paul Hugonin had been together for over a decade during which time they had had four children and she was pregnant with the fifth. Their neighbors took it for granted that they were husband and wife. Their stable, respectable, long-term co-habitation was effectively an extra-legal marriage that was likely not uncommon when various obstacles could prevent couples from marrying or when they simply did not bother with an official ceremony.[9]

Pregnancy then marked the start of a period of transition and negotiation even if most men who were in stable, consensual relationships with feasible marriage partners replied affirmatively to what must have been predictable news. Elizabeth Rozet, for instance, who sewed for a living, recalled her relationship with Jean Bouin, a dyer. They had known each other for several years when he started stopping by to see her and soon said he wanted to marry her. She told him she "wasn't her own mistress and he would have to speak to her father." Bouin assured her his intentions were honorable so she had nothing to worry about as he only wanted her to be his wife. She agreed to start taking walks with him, and he began to proposition her to "let him enjoy her," which she resisted for a while. Then he overcame her resistance and they started having intercourse. When she told him she was pregnant, he said he was not at all bothered by that and he would marry her soon.[10] Nevertheless, Rozet's acknowledgment of her father's role showed one way that initial conversations between intimate partners about fertility were only the start of a longer set of discussions and negotiations that, even when marriage resulted, always contained the potential for fraught feelings and uncertainty as well as excitement and happiness.

Gateways to Marriage: The Emotional Work of Parental Permission and Property

When Benoist Mallet learned from Magdelaine Fournais in 1720 that she was pregnant, he replied (as she recalled) that he was "delighted" (*bien aise*) because that news would make his kin consent to their marriage.[11] Mallet's response spoke to the larger set of considerations for young partners hoping to wed whatever their promises and best intentions about marriage: parental permission and property. Couples as well as their kin clearly acknowledged the importance of the so-called pragmatic concerns that historians have regarded as central to early modern marriage partnerships, but these considerations were also emotionally weighty for young partners. Likewise, their emotional attachments involved pragmatic commitments. Both men and women articulated the significance of practical financial concerns and the need for parental permission as well as more general approval from their families and communities. Friends, neighbors, and employers as well as kin all confirmed the importance of those issues. The distance between couples committing to marry and the associated shift to intercourse and marriage could be very significant in terms of time, effort, and emotion. Even in a straightforward transition toward matrimony, their observable actions indicate that emotional practices (whether hope, uncertainty, anxiety, relief, happiness, and pride as well as deference and responsibility) were symbiotically associated with pragmatic issues in configurations could shift in the same relationship or vary between relationships.[12]

Both parents and offspring were invested in parental permission as a legal, cultural, and emotional practice that was a key step in which responsibility, affection, and deference framed negotiations about the transition from courtship to marriage. The issue of parental (usually paternal) consent was a constant theme in decisions about marriage for Lyon's young working people, even when the parents lived out of town. The early modern French state mandated parental permission as a requirement for marriage in a series of legislative acts that raised the age of legal majority well into the twenties, and notaries carefully recorded that consent in marriage contracts.[13] In addition, working communities expected such approval, and young people felt emotionally obligated to receive it.

Men as well as women talked about the need to get permission for marriage from their fathers or families, and they identified lack of permission as a common obstacle to the fulfillment of their wishes. Louis Poullin, for example, wrote to his father, Marcellin (who lived in a village outside Lyon) to seek permission. Louis and Lucrece Morel's courtship followed the usual path—their promises to marry each other, and thus to start having sex, led to her pregnancy. Although Poullin was twenty-eight and earned his living selling wine and Morel was already a young widow, Poullin explained to his father, "I have a favor to ask you which is to give me your consent to marry Lucrece." Poullin justified their marriage to his father in terms that pointed to community expectations that men should meet their responsibilities to marry pregnant partners: "I have no doubt she will accept[,] I want to tell you she is four months pregnant [and] all my friends advise me to marry her." Poullin combined urgency and deference in his request: "I beg you to give me your reply soon [and] I will be infinitely obliged to you for the permission.... [W]hile waiting to hear from you I am with respect and submission your very obedient son."[14]

Young women likewise framed the need to secure their family's permission to marry as integral to emotional practices between generations. Madeline

Bruyart remembered how after Evremond Picart asked her to marry him, they both went to visit her father in the nearby town of Vienne where they made a marriage contract and arranged to have the banns called there as well as at their own parish church in Lyon. Antoinette Berthaud explained that she had not become engaged to Louis Poulet because it "would make her father and mother angry" if they had not given permission. Antoinette Rozet and Charles Michaud went together to ask her father's permission—but he said no.[15] In these and many similar instances, women's recollections point to the complex feelings that the acknowledged need for parental permission could entail. Deference and responsibility were inseparable from parental consent, and parental ability to withhold approval was also a powerful emotional dynamic.

Even when young couples and their communities attested to their emotional attachment, the couple nevertheless acknowledged that their financial circumstances could be and probably should be a potential brake. Financial issues were pivotal to determining marriage partners and timing. Single women needed dowries to marry, even if they had to earn them themselves because their parents were unable to afford such costs, and men had to wait until they were able to make their livings in some way independently. Silk workers Pierrette Sibert and A. Chaboud, for example, whose two-year-long relationship was well known to their neighbors, co-workers, and employer, had affirmed their emotional attachment to each other in love notes. But when their employer quizzed Pierette about their intention to marry, she explained "the time wasn't right because there was not enough work to cover the costs." Their employer testified that he subsequently allowed their visits to each other to continue because he was persuaded they did mean to get married—that is, he recognized that financial resources as well as established companionship were integral pre-conditions for matrimony. The set of emotional practices about these material pre-conditions for marriage could take a variety of forms. Jean de Juif, for instance, told friends that he wanted to marry Louise Chauvet, but he could not yet because his mother would disinherit him and he needed her to buy him a shop so he could become a master in his trade.[16] Obedience and deference as well as affection and compatibility underpinned pragmatic decisions in a dynamic that could be difficult for young couples to navigate.

The thousands of surviving marriage contracts that dryly record property and permission hide the inevitable and sometimes difficult negotiations that went on beforehand. These legal instruments provide historians' easiest window into early modern marriage formation, but they also provide a classic example of how our sources highlight some aspects of a process and elide others. Many couples made marriage contracts before notaries in which the specifics of dowries—as well as other property matters, like provision for widows—were agreed. But, of course, no dowry meant no contract—and typically no marriage. No marriage of course usually meant no record. Estimette Colombet told the court flatly in 1673 that the father of her baby had promised her "a considerable sum so that she could get married" and asked that he be ordered to pay for 500 *livres* in restitution to provide her with a dowry. Colombet's explanation highlights an unusual situation in which the baby's father would pay a dowry for the mother to use in a subsequent marriage, but it confirms that women themselves were aware that dowries fundamentally shaped their marriage prospects and that property was an essential feature of marriage in the manner that marriage contracts highlight.[17]

However, marriage contracts were also inevitably the subject of intense emotions; court records reveal this whereas the concluded contracts do not. Young people were sometimes apprehensive about whether their parents would agree to the marriage, felt their parents' anger and disapproval, or were frustrated by their refusal. Other times, no doubt, they relished their parents' approval or even acquiescence. Negotiations could cause resentment or anxiety between the partners as well as across generations. Occasionally men who had signed marriage contracts subsequently refused to marry their partners, so the contracts came to represent failure and anxiety. The securing of parental permission and agreement about the terms of marriage also provided occasions for relief and jubilation. Emotional work of many kinds was integral to pragmatic considerations and decisions and vice versa. Pragmatic concerns were inherently imbued with emotional meanings in shifting configurations that could produce competing demands for the couple hoping to be married.

Community Safeguarders and Scaffolding Progression toward Marriage

As young couples' intimate partnerships unfolded with intercourse following marriage promises, communities mobilized to encourage their progression toward matrimony, even before and certainly after pregnancies provided a red flag alert that possible derailments of plans should be averted. Community safeguarders of the futures of young couples and their offspring made multi-layered efforts to channel couples into marriage just as their birth families did. These safeguarders could include co-workers, employers, neighbors, male and female friends, parents, and others. The same communal networks that monitored couples' relationships while they were walking out ensured that, where possible, marriage would follow the commitments made.

Multiple people stepped in, for example, to encourage Pierre Vincent to marry—and, if not, support—Barbe Moulin. Everyone acknowledged that their marriage was expected and feasible, given the behavior of two young people of similar rank. Barbe recalled that Vincent had "much love" for her, visited her at her parents' home, walked out with her, promised to marry her, and pressed her for intercourse. When she told him she was pregnant, he said she had nothing to fear and he would marry her. He delayed and delayed so they were still unmarried when their baby was born. The midwife who delivered Moulin's baby, Bartheleme Perrouset, asked Barbe's mother who the father was. Moulin's mother said Vincent and invited the midwife to go with her to visit him. The two women went together and Vincent agreed to pay the midwife later that day, no doubt after both women reinforced his responsibilities. A young friend of Barbe's who had spent a lot time with them saw Vincent in a local square and asked him if he was going to marry her. He said he no longer planned to but he would pay for everything if Moulin agreed. A female neighbor who had helped Moulin get to the midwife's saw Vincent and he told her he would pay for everything. When the neighbor saw him the next day, she asked him if he was going to marry her. Vincent said he could not "because the times were too difficult" (that is, he did not have enough work) but he did want to marry her. The next day the neighbor and her mother went to visit his employer.[18] At a minimum, judging simply by who was mentioned in court, her mother, the midwife, a neighbor, one of her girlfriends, and Vincent's employer were all involved in pushing him toward marriage.

Similar interventions also took place well before the birth of babies and did not depend on parents' presence, an important issue since so many workers in Lyon were migrants from surrounding areas. When Benoit Blain delayed keeping his promises to marry Suzanne Anger, who had moved to Lyon without her parents, her neighbors, employers, and co-workers supported her. Anger had worked for the same silk master for three years and he also employed Blain. The silk master and his wife, both involved in overseeing the workers, were quick to clarify their expectations with Blain. Each of them said they had "reproached" him. Blain told his mistress (the silk master's wife) that he wanted to marry Anger, and he asked his master if he could marry her without his parents' permission as he was of legal age. The employer explained that he could not, so Blain said he would go home to get their consent. Two journeymen who were their co-workers also talked with the couple. Anger told one that she was pregnant and subsequently Blain admitted he was the father, said he "loved her very much," and he was ready to marry her if his kin agreed. The second "reproached" Blain when he learned Anger was pregnant but Blain assured him he would never abandon her, would help her learn a trade, and would marry her.[19] In all these conversations, Blain received the clear message from his elders and peers that the months of courtship, promises to marry, and intercourse constituted a firm commitment to marry Anger in the eyes of their community. The accumulated messaging about male responsibility in the form of questions, reproaches, and discussions of arrangements no doubt added up to real pressure on men that warned them of the cost to their reputations if they failed to follow through.

Young people were not usually living with employers but often resided in the same multi-story building, creating a physical proximity and supervisory potential that positioned employers as key monitors and safeguarders of youthful relationships. Fleurie Berger and Joseph Duplaignant, for example, both worked for the silk merchant Jean Vert. Their relationship was well known to their co-workers and employer. A co-worker recalled that he had seen them being "very familiar" with each other and kissing on the mouth. Vert's son, who also worked with them, remembered that his father had told Berger several times that "this is not how a good girl should behave," to which Berger replied sassily that her employer was "unbearable." Vert subsequently fired them both on the grounds that they had "spoiled" some of his fabric, perhaps using that alleged production problem as an excuse to get rid of them when he did not like their behavior. Yet when Berger's pregnancy became local knowledge four months after their employment was terminated, Vert, his son, and a male neighbor (also a silk merchant) as well as Berger's brother-in-law all participated in trying to persuade them to marry or at least to arrange an extra-marital solution. After the neighbor discussed the situation with Vert and Duplaignant, Duplaignant promised to give Vert 50 *ecus*, presumably for Berger, but the next day Duplaignant had changed his mind. Berger's brother-in-law summoned Vert junior to a bar where they agreed to call Duplaignant and Berger so the four of them could talk together. Vert senior (the employer) joined them. Berger's brother-in-law proposed that Vert junior provide 200 *livres* in return for which Berger would sign an agreement (a *desistement*) to "end this business." However, Vert junior offered only 100 *livres*, so he and his father left with the situation unresolved. Two days later, Berger and her brother-in-law visited the Verts again and were offered 150 *livres*.[20] Even the former employer here felt some responsibility for the events that had happened on his watch. Duplaignant later alleged he only consented to offer money because Berger's brother-in-law and others had threatened him.

The involvement of multiple people in managing Berger and Duplaignant's relationship illustrates the frictions that communal investment in individual relationships could create as well as the way ties of residential proximity and employment led to efforts to find satisfactory solutions. Young people resisted and frustrated their safeguarders as well as benefiting from their advice and efforts. Persuasion could take the form of conversation, money, or threats. These informal efforts were presumably often successful with men held responsible to make some arrangements to take care of their intimate partners and newborns, and the relationships dissolved without any extant written record.

As other young women did sometimes when informal negotiation failed, Berger sought the assistance of the state a few days later when she filed a complaint for a paternity suit against Duplaignant. She explained in her initial petition that she was six months pregnant and he had made no effort to keep his many promises to marry her so she had to seek recourse in court. Eventually she was awarded 120 *livres* as a "provision" as the court termed the financial awards that were designed to cover women's costs, a sum less than her brother-in-law had declined from the Verts. Berger's experience highlighted a key pattern: single women who went to court were routinely successful in securing provisions, but the size of the awards were low, perhaps lower than extra-legal mediation might have produced. However, Berger might have appreciated Duplaignant's being arrested and held in prison during the investigation, a public shaming that perhaps offered her a different kind of satisfaction. Community safeguarders were also critical in providing support in court cases as women could not hope to take successful legal action without people who were willing to testify that their stable relationship, was expected to lead to marriage.

Women in Court: Policing Paternity, Repairing Honor, and Securing Futures

Florie Brouillard worked for a surgeon in Lyon and in 1697 came to the court to ask that Claude Duvert, her co-worker and intimate partner, be held to account. She recounted a classic relationship narrative: he had started to "frequent" her, he asked her to take walks with him, they discussed marriage, and she had sex with him when she was certain his promises about matrimony were solid. Yet when she told him she was pregnant, he refused to marry her. As women routinely did, she asked the court to require him to pay the costs of her delivery and to charge him with the care and upbringing of their baby. Neighbors served as witnesses to confirm their steady courtship and the feasibility of their marriage. They detailed community efforts to persuade him to marry her and his claims that his parents were opposed. The court agreed with Brouillard that Duvert should be held responsible; he was detained in prison until he paid her and took responsibility for the baby. The outcome affirmed a sense of men's reproductive responsibility that was widely shared in actions and articulated explicitly, as when Phillberte Maison said Jean Lauren had not kept his promises to marry her "like a respectable man [*honnete homme*]."[21]

When young women like Brouillard and Maison went to court to enforce that male responsibility, they asserted their legal right to repair their honor, secure financial compensation, and arrange for their intimate partners to be charged with financial and custodial responsibilities for the babies. They were not simply trying to avoid the presumption of guilt embedded in the 1556 Edict because the vast majority of them were not thinking of depriving infants of baptisms or of keeping their pregnancies secret or indeed of giving birth alone, all essential pre-conditions for the judgment of infanticide the edict sought to address. Young pregnant women went to court for reasons that bore no relationship to the edict in fact. For men, their intimate partners' legal actions entailed public shaming and often prison as well as financial penalties and the costs and care of bringing up the babies. Women's decisions to pursue a public, institutionally brokered solution in court were double-edged. Occasionally they sought to leverage their partners to marry them but they always sought to defend their honor, recover their monetary costs, and restore their ability to work. Collectively, they also used the opportunity to reinforce marriage as the normative outcome of young adult intimacy.

Women's decision to take legal action occurred in the context of complex backstories with many actors and possible routes to solutions. This complexity played out in ways such as the wide variation at the point in their pregnancy at which women came to court. Some women made legal claims as soon as they could reasonably think that they were pregnant at four or five months while others waited until they were near term, until after the babies were born, or occasionally for years. The wide timeframe also hints at the many motives women who went to court might have. Some women hoped to use the pressure to get the men to marry them; others wanted financial support for themselves and discharge from bringing up the babies; a smaller but notable group came to court as part of a dispute about another matter completely, such as the father's failure to pay for landladies, midwives, wet-nurses, or other promised costs. Some women went to court because their partners had left town or they feared they would depart from the city. In these ways, paternity suits had much in common with all forms of litigation as a lawsuit was only one of many strategies that also could include extralegal settlement efforts before, during, or after shifting to legal action. Going to court could be as much a negotiating strategy as a pursuit of a sentence and indeed many paternity lawsuits were settled out of court in a common pattern in all early modern litigation.[22]

Why or when a single pregnant woman might press a court complaint depended on many factors. Women often said they had been "advised" to have recourse to the law. Although women and sometimes their parents or Hôtel-Dieu administrators did refer to the loss of honor and the repair of honor that a court decision in women's favor signaled, the decision to pursue a legal avenue may have depended in part on an economic calculation: did the man in question (or his family) seem to have the financial resources that would make it worthwhile? Instances where partners previously had a baby or two together without litigation clearly illustrate that going to court to make a paternity claim was used only selectively.

Many of Lyon's young workers referred to the need to go home to rural areas to get permission to marry, but these departures nevertheless could be deeply worrisome for young women. Daniel Devaux, for instance, told Isabeau Decert in 1676 that he had to return to his birthplace to get his father's permission before they could marry. Jeanne Rougemond said Elie Reposte told her he needed to go home to get the "papers necessary" for them to get married. Yet the timeframe for the returns from these visits home was usually fluid. Jacques Berthet said he would be back in two weeks, and when he had not returned soon after that, Dimanche Bourjon began to doubt his intentions. The absences could cause other people to speculate too. Rougemond explained, for instance, that she had come to court in the wake of Reposte's departure "to have greater certainty [about his responsibility toward her] and to prevent anyone insulting her." In some instances, the need for permission provided a cover for a man to escape a courtship and its consequences, or perhaps his family persuaded him that marriage at that time or to that particular girl was not a good idea. On other occasions, men left to go home and clearly intended to abandon their pregnant partners.[23]

Men's potential or actual departures from town were one spur for women to go to court to procure a legal remedy as male partners' absences made women's situations especially precarious. Sometimes women acted out of an abundance of caution as the men's return dates were uncertain or their absences seemed suspiciously long. Both Antoinette Laurat and Estimiette Montmain came to court a week apart in 1741 to address such absences. Antoinette and her partner had signed a marriage contract with a notary and had the banns read three times in their parish church when he left Lyon to go back to his village to get his parents' consent. He had been away for two weeks without sending her news. Wondering if he had decided to leave permanently, she came to court to seek to ensure that their marriage contract was executed. Estimiette had begun a relationship with a soldier who also lodged with her landlady. After a few months, they had made plans to marry and for him to work as a carpenter in a village outside of Lyon. He had gone home "to get his papers" and she had not heard from him since. She came to court "to make a declaration to avoid the severity of the ordinance," a phrase that highlights again local confusion about legal requirements for single women.[24] Women who feared their partners might leave town also used court action to halt such plans. In 1677, for instance, Claudine Goujardy explained to the court that her partner, Jean Jacques Bonjour, persistently refused to keep his promise to marry her and, as he was "from another province," she feared he might leave Lyon and so she asked the court to bring him in. The next year Eleanor De Renauol told the court that Pierre Lacoste was "on the point of leaving town" so she came to court. In 1723, Marguerite Perricaud said she had repeatedly pressed Jean Pillot to keep his promise to marry her but he persisted in refusing and was about to leave town.[25] Over the many decades of the Old Regime, women sought to use state power through the court to force men to take responsibility.

Sometimes the decision was a family one or the woman or her family might consult with other people about whether to pursue a legal case, though such deliberations are rarely visible in surviving records. Claudine Privat's lawyer claimed that her mother had consulted "the most skillful jurisconsults, notaries and close kin" who advised her to pursue a court case in order to make her partner marry her since the families were equally in honor, that is, no obstacle existed to their marriage.[26] In this case, the lawyer articulated the premeditation, a rare explicit hint at the calculations involved about whether to bring a lawsuit.

For a couple of decades from the 1720s, the Hôtel-Dieu administrators appeared as a key factor in women's pursuit of paternity suits in Lyon as in other French cities.[27] If women were in contact with the Hôtel-Dieu, the staff wanted to hold someone responsible if possible for the cost of delivery and for the baby becoming a public charge. Hôtel-Dieu administrators were very active mediators between expectant mothers, their intimate partners, and their kin, and they resolved many situations no doubt outside of formal court complaints. However, if no informal resolution was reached, the administrators wanted women and may have required women to take legal action against intimate partners in order to receive some financial compensation. Although only a tiny fraction of women who delivered at the Hôtel-Dieu brought paternity suits in court, the resulting provisions were often directed to be paid directly to the Hôtel-Dieu administrators. Clusters of cases originated by women who had given or would give birth at the Hôtel-Dieu dominate surviving paternity suits in the mid-1720s. This pattern demonstrates that this association was an important trigger for a particular subset of paternity suits. By the 1740s, the Hôtel-Dieu was much less often a party to paternity suits.[28] It is unclear whether this shift reflected a change in legal strategy, represented a change in recording format, or was a misleading artifact from the uneven survival of records.

Women's goals for legal action likewise varied. Many times pregnant women waited, negotiated, and pressed their intimate partners to marry them, often with the assistance of their communities, and they only registered their legal complaints late in their pregnancies when it appeared that these other strategies had not worked. Louise Chauvet was pregnant for the second time when she filed a paternity suit against Jean De Juif because of "his perfidy" as she had come to see that his repeated promises to marry her were lies.[29]

However, women sometimes went to court quite quickly and may have seen the instigation of legal action as a negotiating tactic rather than a preferred solution that might lead to marriage or an out-of-court settlement. A majority of paternity suits did not reach the sentencing stage, another pattern common to all early modern litigation. Some of these women litigants may just have dropped their actions, but many of the cases were probably settled out of court. Out-of-court settlements were occasionally noted on the cover sheets of paternity suits but far more often, as in other kinds of litigation, the sudden end of records midway through a lawsuit points to an out-of-court agreement, and no documentation survives about what happened next. Certainly some couples did subsequently marry, although it would be very difficult to document that without searching all extant city parish registers. Others reached extra-judicial agreement outside of court to arrange a settlement of finances and child custody either informally or with the assistance of a notary.[30]

Some women who initiated paternity suits had not necessarily given up on marrying their intimate partners but rather saw a legal process as another form of pressure to marry. Sometimes this strategy worked even if we might wonder about the desirability of marriage to someone who has to be held in prison to agree. In 1674, M. Barrot told the court official who walked him from prison to respond to the judge's queries about his partner's paternity claim that he had "made a mistake" to have promised to marry her but, since he had promised, he would do so. Phillippe Ballet had a conventional relationship with Madelaine Degoin through promises of marriage to intercourse and pregnancy. When she told him that she was pregnant, he at first said he wanted to marry her but his guardian would not agree. Neighbors recalled that they seemed to be living together to all intents and purposes as man and wife and that he had told at least one neighbor that he had changed his mind (regardless of his disapproving guardian—or perhaps the guardian was always an excuse). Nevertheless, he delayed. A month after Dugoin initiated a paternity suit in 1741, Ballet was arrested and held in prison. When the judges questioned him he said he was not the father and, although he had promised to marry her, he did not want to because she was a girl of loose morals" [*mauvaise vie*]. Yet after a month in prison he signed a marriage contract with her and the judge agreed to release him.[31] Probably much more often, in ways unrecorded but evidenced by suits that did not proceed beyond the initial complaint, the act of filing a paternity suit was a sufficient tactic to get reluctant grooms on board. Even before that, no doubt men knew women had the option of going to court, and at least sometimes women used the legal possibility as explicit negotiating leverage. Marie Aymin recalled, for instance, that she had told Claude Francois that "if he didn't keep his promises [to marry her], she would go to justice."[32]

Women expected that the public endorsement of a paternity suit, with its recognition about the appropriateness of their behavior in a stable consensual relationship, would restore their reputations and rehabilitate their honor as well as provide financial support for costs incurred and charge fathers with custody of the offspring. A few women asserted, like Fleurie Gillet in 1730, that their "honor could only be repaired by marriage," but much more often women like Marie Mann came to court "to seek reparations proportional to the outrage he has committed to her honor" . . . "and [to] repair her honor." Women were clear that the status of single motherhood could dishonor them if their situations appeared to be the result of casual sex associated with loose morals. It was that possibility, rather than being pregnant before marriage, that they expected their communities to be concerned about. Sometimes women anticipated such a loss of honor and came to court pre-emptively, especially if their partners had absented themselves from the city.[33] Women repeatedly described themselves to the court as "dishonored" by their intimate partners' failure to carry out their promises of marriage and asked the court for "reparations" that would remedy the challenges posed to their honor (and finances).

Single women saw paternity suits as a way to restore their reputations even if their partners did not marry them. They acknowledged that their reputations would be damaged if men abandoned them without taking responsibility, and demonstrated that they had behaved respectably in good faith expectation of marriage. They and their witnesses established their own good behavior and preserved their reputations by establishing that they had waited to have intercourse until marriage seemed certain—in other words, their partners were to blame for the situation. The court's acceptance of their appropriate behavior would repair their reputations even if matrimony did not occur. They valued their honor and they could fight to repair a threatened loss of honor by defending their own behavior in court.[34]

Women also sought financial compensation usually to cover the costs of their delivery and any legal costs. They typically requested relatively modest amounts of a couple of hundred *livres* but were usually only awarded around 100 *livres*. Requesting a larger sum did not persuade the court to make a larger award. Francoise Faury, for example, requested a provision of 500 *livres* in 1721. She and her partner, Barthelemy Matteron, were silk workers and both sets of parents (also all silk workers) consented to their marriage, but Matteron continued to delay on the basis that he was "too young." Her request for such a relatively high amount perhaps suggested extreme frustration that even four parents could not get Matteron to keep the promises he made during a two-year courtship. Nevertheless, the court awarded her just 150 *livres*, only slightly above its usual range.[35]

The court's persistence in awarding modest provisions suggests the judges had an informal scale that they were reluctant to vary from, regardless of the size of a financial request or the degree of men's reprehensibility. Whether this stable award reflected what young working men or their families could realistically pay or a commitment to keeping the provisions tied to reimbursement for costs, the sums awarded were consistently within 20 *livres* of the 100 *livres* range for many decades, only edging slightly higher.

Finally, women sought to commit their intimate partners to take physical and financial custody of the baby. They asked the courts to extend men's responsibility to the upbringing of the child, and the courts routinely agreed. These requests meant that men would pay for the newborns to go to live with wet-nurses, usually in rural parishes outside the city, and then—if they survived the sky-high mortality rates that beset such nurslings—returned to their fathers for child-rearing. Very occasionally, the court record mandated that the men were supposed to report the whereabouts of their offspring every three months, a safeguard against infanticide or abandonment. It is unclear whether this was a routine expectation or if it was ever enforced. However, women who brought their cases long after their pregnancies usually said they had never seen the babies and often did not know where they were. Madeline Vacheron, for example, asked the court to require her partner to tell her where the baby was and the name of the wet-nurse. She also remembered that someone had told her that a previous baby she and her partner had together had died. However, she noted that she knew her partner sometimes visited the children at the wet-nurse, often with a friend of his.[36] The practice of paternal custody as a permanent arrangement was as routine as the legal assignment of paternal responsibility. Consequently, for single women, the successful court settlements usually meant permanent separation from their newborns.

These threefold goals of paternity suits allowed single women to recover their lives, defend their reputations, and go back to work as they were compensated for their financial costs and relieved of the labor of motherhood.

Many babies probably died at their wet-nurses' rural homes with their deaths unrecorded in parish registers.[37] Lyonnais married working couples also routinely used rural wet-nurses and many of their babies died there too. If the practice was not at all unusual, the experience was different when single fathers had custody because the unmarried mothers apparently did not visit or send letters in the way at least some married parents did, nor did babies who survived usually return to their birth mothers. The emotional valency of these practices for unmarried women remains elusive. They were able to resume their lives by returning to work, and they often got married and went on to have more children. Did they long remember the separation as a silent wound or were they relieved to move forward with their reputations and modest prospects intact? Certainly it is important not to essentialize maternal feeling and automatically project modern sensibilities onto a premodern context.

Going to court, then, was a highly unusual outcome for young women whose consensual relationships ran aground after they became pregnant. Their prospects rested on the willingness of community safeguarders to speak on their behalf and on the attitudes of the judges who heard their cases. They found a legal system that in many ways was highly predisposed to be supportive of their plight and ready to provide a remedy, albeit within limits that privileged men while holding them accountable for the reproductive consequences of their sexual activity.

Courts Police Paternity: Prison, Penalties, and Privilege

In 1670, Madeline Vacheron asked her local court in Lyon to imprison her long-term partner, Jean Paul Hugouin—unless he paid her 1,500 *livres* or married her within three days. They had been together for more than a decade and she was pregnant with their fifth child. Hugouin sought to use a classic sexual double standard defense. He alleged that Vacheron had been someone else's mistress for three years before their relationship started, implying that her credibility and virtue were so corrupted that he should not be held responsible for subsequent events. However, the royal prosecutor on behalf of the court summed up the case by focusing not on her earlier history, her failure to make an official statement to any authority figure about her previous four pregnancies, or even her long out-of-wedlock intimacy with Hugouin, but instead on his behavior and legal strategy. It was, he said, "ill-judged" for Hugonin to use the excuse of her history before they met when they had been together for years with several children and had "a life so conforming to that of a husband and wife." That pattern had "deceived" her to expect marriage and indeed had deceived their neighbors into thinking they were married. For Hugouin's accusation to carry any weight against her claim, the royal prosecutor continued, "it would be necessary that he had not abused her impudently for so long." The judges ordered that Hugonin "be condemned to marry the said Madeline Vacheron or pay her 1,500 *livres* and take responsibility for the children"—and had to choose the option he preferred in three days or she would get to choose.[38]

Vacheron's request that Hugouin be imprisoned along with the court's articulation of male responsibility are key themes of the dynamics of the legal process in paternity suits. When women in consensual intimate relationships resorted to the legal system, the courts were highly supportive of them and consistently judged in their favor in assigning financial support to cover their costs and charging their intimate partners with the costs and custody of the offspring. Women routinely asked that their intimate partners be held in prison at some point during the investigations and the court routinely agreed. For men, their intimate partners' decision to go to court meant a temporary loss of their freedom in many instances during investigations as well as legal affirmation of their responsibilities as fathers and damage to their reputations for having failed to meet their obligation without the pressure of a court case. Yet there were also limits to the court's reparations as judges almost always flattened out a range of men's illicit sexual behavior to simple issues of paternal responsibility. Even in a legal process that systematically supported women who could show they had been in stable consensual relationships when they became pregnant, male privilege limited the calibration of penalties to a flat remedy with little regard for the level of violation.

The young men jailed in Old Regime prisons were held during part or all of the investigations to prevent their flight from responsibility. Sometimes women requested their partners be held immediately as part of the initial complaints or midpoint in proceedings after medical experts' reports confirmed their pregnancies and witnesses confirmed their stories. Others were threatened with imprisonment if they failed to appear to answer the court's questions or until the money awarded to their partners was paid. Marguerite Joubert complained to the court in 1663, for example, that she had known Jean Bonjour about six months and slept with him after he promised to marry her on numerous occasions, but when she found out she was pregnant he did not want to keep his promises. She asked the court to bring him in to respond to her complaint and "further to keep him in prison until he had kept the promises he often made her," that is, until he married her.[39] Very occasionally men were held until they married their partners but even the request that they do so became less common over the decades of the Old Regime.

Although relatively few men who were unmarried expectant fathers or had out-of-wedlock babies went to prison, even the possibility served as a harsh reminder to men to meet their obligations. Men who were ordered to be imprisoned because of unmet paternal responsibilities were publicly shamed when bailiffs arrested them in view of all their neighbors and co-workers. The state of Old Regime prisons was deplorable, and all kinds of prisoners were held together. While alleged fathers might be released the same day if the judge came to hear their responses to a set of routine questions, sometimes they endured a stay of many weeks or even months. Even the average stay of a week or ten days was definitely something anyone would want to avoid. In a typical sequence, Antoinette Duon came to court on December 20 to make her complaint, and she and her lawyer asked on December 21 that Jean Eyroux be held in custody while the paternity suit was in process. The court ordered him to prison on December 24, he was questioned on December 30, and released under the guaranty of a supporter the same day when he (or the guarantor) paid Duon the 140 *livres* that the court assigned to her.[40]

Men's irritation at the legal pressure they could experience because of pregnant women's paternity suits indicates that they saw these court actions as threats to their reputations and perhaps their futures as well as to their liberty during the course of the investigations. Francois Benoist denied the allegations of paternity and bluntly told the court in 1688 that if "he had made an error" with Henriette Gabet, he would "repair it." Joseph Ramel claimed that he wanted his honor restored publicly after being held in prison while the court investigated Maria Chana's case against him. Other men were very cognizant of wanting to avoid the potentially damaging public knowledge associated with such claims. Pierre Julien came to court voluntarily, for instance, to complain that "people" had told him a girl he claimed not to know had made a complaint to the court about his alleged paternity of a child. He said he would answer any and all questions, but asked the court to forbid its officers to use force to bring him in. Jacques de la Frasser turned himself into prison at 5 A.M., hoping to avoid Marguerite Carler's allegations becoming public knowledge.[41] Their desire for discretion demonstrated the public cost men could pay if neighbors saw court officers deliver notices to them to appear in court for paternity suits.

Men liked to claim that women were able to get the courts to act on very little evidence. In May 1659, Claude Puzin complained that the court had him imprisoned on the allegation of Marie Bourdain "without any information or other procedures." He asked that her *procureur* be required to deposit a copy of papers at the court records office (the *greffe*) in three days or release him. Others alleged that women used this legal avenue unscrupulously. Pierre Peyssillon and Lucie Peyrieu were co-workers, and he responded to her allegation by admitting they had indeed slept together. However, he denied he had promised her marriage or anything else, saying "Every day we see girls like her who accuse this person or that person to extract money off getting them pregnant.... And then they move on to the next guy." Jacques Marest combined such allegations of unscrupulous use and no information when he asked to be released from prison because the complaints of Marguerite Tatier and her mother Etiennet Blanchi against him were the result of "pure animosity." Exceptionally, the judge released Marest a few days later after the women failed to provide any evidence.[42]

Elite judges have often been associated with morality campaigns in the seventeenth and eighteenth centuries in which the use of the courts to discipline female immorality was a common theme. This sentiment did exist among the elite judiciary in the Lyonnais region. For example, in the 1658 suit between Francoise Beaujollon, and her employer, the silk merchant Louis Bichon, the royal prosecutor wrote a tirade about men's vulnerability to women's deviousness, especially sexual. If her "simple statement" that Bichon was the father was taken as "sufficient" without proof of other kinds, the prosecutor said, it would "create a maxim with perilous consequences" that would encourage similar women to prostitute themselves more easily in the hope that their children would be supported. Moreover, a woman who accused her master in this way was capable of "abandoning herself to others" against whom she would make similar accusations.[43] Almost a century later, the prominent lawyer Joseph Michel Antoine Servan railed against the judicial presumption that women told the truth when they made paternity complaints. In a 1760s pamphlet published in Lyon, Servan claimed that the habitual acceptance of single women's claims was "an astonishing exception to the ordinary rules of probability and to our judgment." Servan asserted that in "our big cities" conniving women used their fertility "as a new kind of commerce" where false accusations of paternity against the most reputable men produced financial reward.

Nevertheless, this kind of view seemed to have no impact on legal practice in the Lyonnais region, where judges over the course of more than a century routinely accepted that women in ongoing consensual relationships made legitimate claims against the men who had fathered their children. The moralizing prescriptive view is visible today, probably because it survives in printed material, but usual judicial practice at the time continued to support women. Although elite jurisprudence in bastardy cases, at least until the early eighteenth century, sought to protect women and their families by penalizing extra-marital fathers in a number of ways, including compulsory marriages, judges in local courts preferred to support working women who made paternity claims throughout the Old Regime with financial provisions and charge fathers with custody.[44] The Lyon court rarely made marriage compulsory even in the seventeenth century when at most it sometimes offered men the choice of marriage or paying a provision and taking custody of the child, and the issue of marriage was rarely raised in the eighteenth century.[45]

These local practices were likely also seen as protecting the offspring of such untimely pregnancies. The action triggered by a woman's "declaration" to one of Lyon's church courts highlights with unusual clarity the gap between intense official rhetoric and pragmatic local action. Local officials subsequently "heard" that the woman, Marie Joseph Butavna, was a widow pregnant by her late husband's natural son. Court officials went to visit her and the officials asked if, "fornication being the most atrocious crime, she was guilty of having given herself to" him. She admitted it, saying her weakness was because she intended to marry him. The court prosecutor noted that her pregnancy had caused "an enormous scandal," the local vicar had refused to marry them, and their actions amounted to incest. However, the officials accepted her explanation that they were ignorant of their relationship, not having realized that he was the son of her first husband because his mother had died a long time ago. Their record noted that instead of imposing the "full rigour" of the law, the officials limited themselves to ensuring the safety of the baby, requiring her to show the baptism certificate and provide proof every three months. (Of course, the baby was sent to a wet-nurse and soon died there according to Marie Joseph.) In fact, the push that led someone to inform the court of the unusual situation in the first place seemed to be less outrage over the relationship than a dispute over 300 *livres* in her husband's will that he left to the same son.[46]

Lyon judges routinely accepted women's paternity claims as reliable and consistently awarded them financial support, just like the judges Servan complained about in Grenoble. From the 1720s, judges occasionally asked women if anyone had asked them to make a false accusation, a new line of intermittent questions that suggests an increasing interest of the court in the possibility of false accusations, but women testified that men asked them to name other people, too. Nevertheless, judicial decisions continued to endorse women's stories and award them financial compensation. Moreover, in contrast to Servan's rhetoric that deceptive women were the source of false allegations, some men originated fraudulent declarations when they sought to deflect the threat of an unwanted pregnancy by suggesting their partners accuse someone else, as we have seen.

Over the many decades of the Old Regime, the court had little patience with men's excuses as to why they had not married their intimate partners and the excuses remained similar. Men who challenged paternal responsibility in court used three main justifications: alleging female debauchery, denying intercourse had taken place, refuting promises of marriage, or some combination of the three. Jean Renaud, for example, claimed that Aymee Joannin had slept with other men and "her reputation is not as good as she wants to persuade you." Jacques Richard said he had learned Claire Valouey had slept with other men. Vital Delphin claimed Jeanne Quentin had become enamored with him and was more experienced sexually so she had led him. Benoit Riviere admitted he knew Jeanne Chazey as they lived in the same building and he had asked her father for permission to marry her, but he denied that they had had intercourse. Antoine Louis acknowledged knowing Anne Martin as they both worked for his father, but he denied he had asked her to marry him.[47] However implausible or plausible such denials of responsibility were, men's arguments had no effect on the judges' decisions to award women financial provision and to assign custody of the babies to the fathers.

In fact, judges were so broadly supportive of women who were pregnant and single that even when young women whose relationships were not as clearly headed toward marriage brought suits, judges sided with them and assigned the usual remedies. Claudine Rang, for example, claimed she and a man the court named only as Milot had been seeing each other for a year when during a walk to the outskirts of town, they took a break to pick nuts to eat and drink wine before he forced her to have intercourse. No witnesses were called and Rang said her parents had abandoned her (although she did not explain why). Rang alleged an ongoing consensual relationship and the continuation of sex after their first coerced intercourse. If she recounted many elements of the usual trajectory of couples' relationships, she did not mention any promises to marry or associate the site of their coerced first intercourse as a bedroom with its clear association with marital intimacy. Nevertheless, the court still awarded her the usual provision.[48] Claims that missed key elements of commitment were uncommon, but they could be successful.

Royal courts clearly expected single fathers to take responsibility for their newborns' physical care and expenses, a perspective shaped by law as well as community expectation. A Lyon royal prosecutor clearly articulated this practice in a 1658 case, noting explicitly that women who were successful in their complaints were "discharged" of the feeding and care of their babies. Legally, men were expected to meet their obligation to support their natural children.[49] The legal obligation aligned perfectly with community expectations, and informal arrangements made out of court observed the same paternal custody arrangements as we will see. In paternity suit after paternity suit, men were assigned custody of the newborns, which usually meant that they sent the babies to wet-nurses outside of the city.

If the strong proclivity of the court to believe women and hold men responsible persisted from the 1660s through to the later eighteenth century, there were important limits to the kinds of penalties the court was willing to impose regardless of the spectrum of men's behavior. They assessed a wide range of male sexuality and violence as adding up to the same penalty—that is, a modest provision that covered women's costs and charged men with responsibility for the offspring. This same response varied little regardless of how much women had asked for as provisions or of how egregious men's behavior had been. The court contained the seriousness of women's allegations in almost every regard, including listing women's legal actions as straightforward complaints (*plaintes*) on the cover summaries of cases, even if a woman or occasionally her father or lawyer had framed her pregnancy as the result of the specific crimes of *rapt* or *séduction*. Royal legislation in the early seventeenth century categorized *rapt* as such a serious matter that it merited capital punishment whether in the form of *rapt de violence* (abduction for an immoral purpose) or *rapt de seduction* (straightforward immorality and/or immorality committed by an adult on the person of a legal minor).[50] Yet, in practice the Lyon court bundled such allegations with routine paternity suits as examples of male irresponsibility for which the court's discipline was the award of a simple provision. Local royal courts responded to infractions of sexual morality with little or no attention to royal edicts that sought to criminalize such behavior.

What kind of behavior the court might accept as *rapt* was very slippery as the court primarily defined what was not unacceptable in rejecting claims. Both lawyers for and fathers of female plaintiffs occasionally expressed frustration with the court's umbrella policy of presuming all claims that included out-of-wedlock paternity could be resolved by a modest financial provision for costs and charge of the baby to the father. Royal prosecutors for the court, for example, argued in two 1670s paternity suits that the male partner owed his female companion financial maintenance when the baby was the result of libertinage but ruled that the incident did not constitute *rapt* because such claims could not be made between people of unequal rank. In 1688, a no doubt exasperated father brought a claim for his daughter after she had a second baby without her intimate partner keeping his promises of marriage. That second "seduction" of his daughter, Etienne Gabet claimed, merited punishment as a crime of *rapt*. The court did not agree that a second failure to marry met the standard and ruled instead for a simple provision.[51]

When young women alleged their intimate partners' behavior amounted to *rapt* (usually in the form of seduction), they usually associated the immorality involved with age. They were younger than twenty-five (the age of legal majority) and their partners were older. Not surprisingly these kinds of claims did not persuade the court since in fact both partners were of feasible marriage age and women who were working and living independently were de facto adults. Sometimes women in their early twenties (or the small number in their late teens) did not articulate their experience to the court as *rapt*, but did claim that their partners had "abused the weakness of their young age." This strategy likewise had no effect.

Fathers who brought paternity suits with or for their daughters often alleged *rapt*, and they were usually obviously very irritated and pointed out that the daughter's condition merited a serious penalty because of damage to the father's honor as well as their daughter's, financial costs, and untold emotional tolls. One father, for instance, wanted reimbursement for supporting his daughter as well as for the deliveries and burials of her twins in a claim that sharply points to the usually elided emotional costs as well as the transactional ones when men failed to meet their responsibility for the outcomes of their sexual activity. In 1687, Jean Aurilloz alleged that Vincent Berty had committed *rapt* against his daughter, Eleanor, "a young woman under the authority of her father whose probity is so well known and conduct so free of reproach that *he* [the father] cannot suffer this injury without requesting reparations." Francois Ferlat likewise complained that his good family lived without reproach so Jacques Prevallier's behavior with his daughter, Izabeau, was "a *rapt*" that required him to go to court. On one occasion, a young women's lawyer complained that the "jurisprudence" of *rapt* was not being enforced and young girls continually fell for the promises of marriage.[52] The court thought otherwise in all these instances and assigned provisions.

In fact, the court's judges remained consistently unmoved and committed to holding young men financially responsible and charged with custody of the baby, often after being held in prison during the investigations, even when their behavior was particularly egregious. Marienne Didier went out with her shoemaker partner for two years and their relationship followed a track that seemed destined for marriage, as he repeatedly assured her. When she became pregnant, not only did he not marry her but he left her for another woman. It was, she said, a "crime of *rapt* which deserves most severe punishment" and she also asked for an unusually high provision of 300 *livres*. The court's penalty however was limited to the lower end of its usual modest provision, 80 *livres*, and charge of the baby. Ten years later, even the rectors of the Hôtel-Dieu could not pressure the court for a more severe punishment when they petitioned in 1741 for Jeanne Revilly, a former ward of theirs, whom they had apprenticed to a silk worker whose son they claimed had taken advantage of her age and his status. They argued that "the honor of a girl is her most precious property" and hers could only be repaired by marriage—any other action would be an "imperfect repair"—and noted that *rapt* was a capital crime. They demanded that he pay "considerable damages to repair her honor" if he continued to refuse to marry her and asked for 3,000 *livres* or marriage. The court awarded her its usual remedy of provision in the usual range at just 130 *livres*.[53]

Similarly, in the small minority of cases brought by women against their employers, the court leveled the behavior out to award simple provisions, even if the women (with the assistance of their lawyers presumably) resorted to even more dramatic and explicit language about the undermining of acceptable norms found in master-employee relationships. Marie Chana's complaint against her married employer, Joseph Ramel, involved an unusually extended legal exchange between them and many witnesses. Ramel denied involvement on several grounds, including accusing one of his apprentices and claiming he [Ramel] could not have been guilty because he never got his wife pregnant. No doubt frustrated, Chanu dismissed his denials as "the usual artifice of the guilty" and articulated the core issues. If what he alleged had been true, it would have been his duty as master to prevent such wrongdoing. His married status and age did not excuse his actions but made his crime worse. It was "the corruption of the century" that there was so much tolerance for masters who abused servants when they should have been supervising their morals and conduct and keeping them away from opportunities for sin. She compared the abuse of authority to a guardian's over his ward or a prison guard over an inmate. Likewise, Anne Martin, who worked as a *tourneuse* for Antoine Louis, a journeyman *tireur d'or*, asserted that what she called his "criminal undertaking . . . deserved the outrage" of the court because it went against human and divine laws."[54] Judges were not, however, outraged, or at least not enough to impose a harsher penalty.

The court also routinely released young expectant fathers from prison before they had paid the awards or even before the awards were assigned if they had a guarantor, a policy that, like the testimony of witnesses, integrated the practices of community safeguarding of young consensual partners' futures with the legal system. Kin or employers usually provided the guarantees. Jean Viegerard was released under the guarantee of his widowed mother and Francois Benoist under that of a master *patissier*. Balthazar Berger, an apprentice candle-maker, was released in 1697 "under the guarantee of his uncle, a silk worker, who signed and promised to return him to prison if so ordered and to pay what was ordered." Like other aspects of the handling of out-of-wedlock pregnancy, the pattern of releases continued through the Old Regime.[55]

Sometimes young women were not satisfied with the court's routine handling of young men who had backed away from their responsibilities. Yet when their lawyers objected, they found no traction with the judges, no matter what reason the lawyers gave. Janne Olier's lawyer opposed Jacques Guillemin's release, for example, and insisted that if the court agreed to it, someone with the means to pay had to be named because the proposed guarantor "did not have a penny." Aymee Orset's lawyer opposed Antoine Reydellet's release because he was Orset's employer, presumably implying that their employer-employee status made the situation more serious or perhaps that it was unlikely an employer could be relied on to pay for a female employee.[56] Generally, the court's handling of paternity suits aligned with the community acceptance of the reality that some young people would not in fact get married and some out-of-wedlock births would occur, so judges and communities aimed to stabilize the situations and get both young people on track for the future.

A father noted in 1740 that "if the court lets go of appropriate rigor" about men's behavior, it is "disastrous to repose of families," but his daughter's intimate partner claimed he was the one who deserved the protection of the judges because her claim lacked evidence.[57] Their differing views about the legal dynamic illustrated how, despite the court's limited disciplining of young men, single women's ability to use the courts could be the source of plenty of gender conflict between intimate partners. Pregnant single women and their communities were willing and able to use a tightly calibrated set of official means to sanction young men for what they defined as illicit sexuality if they thought circumstances warranted pursuit of a public, legal remedy. They were ready to see the young men imprisoned as part of that solution. What courts did was not to introduce a top down state-driven disciplinary impetus, but—even by physical confinement in royal prisons—to work with communities on shared expectations about desirable outcomes, or more likely the least undesirable outcomes.

Holding young men responsible for the reproductive consequences of their sexual behavior in monogamous consensual intimate relationships was a foundational element of community and court practices throughout the Old Regime. Pre-marital intercourse was conventional practice in young couples' relationship as a part of the step into marriage, but the risk of allowing licit intimacy that included intercourse made women's predictable fertility a key spur for negotiation and decision making between young couples, their families, their communities, and the court system. Young single women who could persuasively claim commitment to matrimony used litigation with no fear of being disciplined. In paternity suits, young women themselves framed marriage as the normative outcome. Young men knew that reproductive accountability was key to their reputations even if its limits exemplified gendered power. Community safeguarders and local courts steadily supported young women when they were pregnant but not deemed at fault. Intimate partners negotiated with each other, but they did so in the context of practices that served to mitigate risk by amplifying marriage or if need be orchestrating backup solutions that still held men responsible. Intense emotions for various community safeguarders as well as the intimate partners were integral to discussions about parental permission, property issues, and legal actions.

The resort to prison for reluctant male intimate partners, likely common throughout France, tellingly highlights the range of ways in which managing sexuality by enforcing paternal responsibility was a pivotal element of masculinity for young working men in early modern communities as was the insistence on men's custody of offspring.[58] Literal imprisonment was at one end of a spectrum of ways in which young men's sexuality was calibrated, monitored, and, if necessary, penalized as well as young women's. The prisms of elite print culture and criminal prosecutions of women as primary sources led historians to emphasize women as the target of policed sexuality. However, male sexuality was also policed because of the entwined economic and political as well as social stakes involved. Young working men's reputations rested on their willingness to take responsibility for the consequences of their sexual behavior, at least with women whom they seemed to have intended to marry.

Regimes of extra-marital pregnancy control were essentially local. Local courts and communities had little interest in disciplining young women for extra-marital sexuality.[59] They did have a big investment in stabilizing the lives of young couples (and in turn the communities that would be affected if they were not stabilized). In Lyon as elsewhere in France, local judges in royal and ecclesiastical courts were strongly supportive of unwed mothers.[60] Lower court personnel were attuned to their local communities, and the state had very little capacity to enforce its new legislation about morality. In practice, individuals and communities usually chose when to—and when not to—use the court system.[61] Throughout the Old Regime, the management of young people's sexuality and its consequences remained primarily a matter for individual, family, and local community.

Yet sometimes—for a variety of reasons—couples did not marry even when pregnancy occurred, and nor did they rely on a court to formalize their extra-marital arrangements; instead a host of community safeguarding practices that still emphasized men's responsibility sought to help find an acceptable solution. While abandoned single mothers are very visible in court records, the many ways in which young men were expected to remedy extra-marital pregnancy—through marriage or by other means—and in fact very often did so were rarely documented but were very well known in their communities. The negotiations between most couples took place entirely outside of the institutional legal system because it was a choice to use the courts and they most often chose not to do so. The decision not to marry led to a series of other decisions. Intense emotions were integral to these sets of negotiations, too.

4
"Remedies" and Remedies
Managing Out-of-Wedlock Pregnancy

When young expectant parents deferred marriage or did not marry, they faced an array of possible options and they often used more than one of them. In February 1688, for example, a priest recorded the birth of a baby boy to Francois Benoist, a shoemaker, and Henriette Gabet in the St. Nizier parish register. Benoist, godfather Jacques Blanc, and godmother Antoinette Bremond went to see Gabet after the baptism and they all ate supper together. It seemed an everyday affair in all regards. However, the priest's routine brief parish register entry elided the fact that Gabet and Benoist were not married.[1] They had had a perfectly conventional relationship. They met at a dance and started to walk out together; he promised to marry her and said he would never have another woman. When she became pregnant, he said they could not marry yet because his father would not allow it. In the expectation they would marry eventually, she had the baby at her parents' house and continued their relationship. As he avoided marriage, she still said she would follow him anywhere, but he turned to a wide variety of people as he explored alternative solutions. He had recruited the godparents from among his peer cohort. He had placed the baby with a wet-nurse, bought a cradle for that baby, and tried to persuade Henriette to go live with his mother in a village outside Lyon where the new baby would, he promised, want for nothing. He consulted a legal official (a *commis au greffe*) about how to make an out-of-court settlement. Even at the church during the baby's baptism, Francois discussed with the godmother whether he should put his name as father on the baby's birth certificate. She assured him that, since he was the father, it made no difference. His decision to list his name and the priest's decision to register the baby as legitimate created a written public acknowledgment of his paternity and the settled status of the couple; Henriette eventually presented a copy of this register in court to support her claim.

Over sixty years later, young couples faced the same dilemmas. Anne Julliard and Francois Page were not ready to get married in 1753 when she became pregnant after a conventional courtship. To interrupt reproduction, he gave her several "remedies," and she endured several rounds of bloodletting. Those efforts made her so ill that she recalled she thought she would die and she almost fainted twenty times. Weeks later she felt the baby move and told Francois that she was still pregnant. He gave her a dose of a "white liquid" as the previous efforts had not worked and told her it should induce a miscarriage.[2] Their efforts to end her pregnancy through an early abortion (which was understood as "restoring" women's health by restoring their menstrual cycles) or after quickening (which was legally and spiritually defined as an abortion) provide a rare explicit glimpse of couples' efforts to manage fertility. While Julliard lived to tell the tale, women undoubtedly found their health and sometimes even their lives threated by such efforts to induce abortions in untimely pregnancies. Whether such efforts were successful in inducing terminations or harmful to women's health or indeed killed them, the outcomes usually did not generate any documents, so they are shrouded in silence.

The events before and after babies were born out-of-wedlock reveal some of the many actors, men as well as women, whom intimate partners could turn to for help in finding solutions when, for whatever reason, they would not in fact marry. Many conversations, negotiations, conflicts, and resource-finding efforts were involved, but rarely do records of these survive. Those that do point to some of the multiple strategies and many actors involved in the management of intimate partners' out-of-wedlock fertility. Networks of men (intimate partners, lawyers, clergy, employers, and friends) as well as women provided "remedies" that restored menstrual cycles and facilitated remedies of other kinds by circulating information and providing a wide range of assistance for intimate partners facing the challenges of out-of-wedlock births.

These issues intersect with many different topics including youth culture, gender and sexuality, and the extent of a disciplinary impetus in state law and reformed Catholicism. Historians have often emphasized the role of midwives and other women in early modern management of fertility, and women were very involved in the management of out-of-wedlock births as landladies, midwives, and wet-nurses—and no doubt there were friends who offered advice or assistance during early stages of pregnancies. However, networks of men—peers, employers, legal workers of various kinds, and clerics—were also integrally involved in the management of untimely pregnancies.[3] Historians have emphasized the commitment of the legal system and the Catholic church in disciplining early modern sexuality, especially of women.[4] Yet when intimate partners' pregnancies were not followed by marriage for whatever reason, legal officials and local clergy sometimes chose to become partners whose work aligned with neighborhood practices to employ well-established, flexible, and pragmatic solutions to mitigate the damage to couples and their communities. These efforts were often seemingly sympathetic or non-judgmental rather than disciplinary.

This chapter explores the relationships between intimate partners and their communities around the management of reproduction outside of marriage amid what were often times of high tension and conflicting emotions. It examines how couples sought to manage their fertility outside of marriage through a range of "remedies" to interrupt reproduction. Early modern people used the term "remedies" to mean specific medical interventions to improve general health, and it was also a euphemism for abortifacients when used to restore menstrual cycles if untimely pregnancies were suspected. These "remedies" indicate a gray zone around fertility that was likely familiar ground to many intimate partners, a familiarity that belies the seemingly straightforward link between intercourse and marriage that demographic statistics suggest. Alternative kinds of remedies were also possible to access. Notaries and other legal officials could help intimate partners find solutions to out-of-wedlock pregnancy. Clergy—both parish priests and friars—acted as mediators who helped manage the consequences of fertility; and peer relationships helped support couples. All of these supports involved discussions about intimate relationships not only between couples, but also among young people and a range of interlocuters.

In these ways, the community safeguarding that supported young couples' relationships as they developed continued to coalesce about "remedies" and remedies. When not yet married women became pregnant, the risks of youthful intimacy became apparent for everyone as did the potential gendered impacts. Couples' intimacy was the subject of conversations, whether these were negotiations or conflicts, occurring among a wide range of people beyond the couples themselves. Young partners individually or together were often able to draw on established community practices and local knowledge networks to resolve the challenge of out-of-wedlock pregnancy although these efforts usually went undocumented. They relied on their networks for help in managing information. Many people were complicit in assisting couples manage out-of-wedlock pregnancy, and they did so in part by selective discussion of these personal situations because silence was often a helpful way to smooth their paths. Above all, communities were attuned to the reality that pre-marital intimacy would sometimes not result in the endpoint of marriage, and this should not necessarily be ruinous.

"Remedies": Efforts to Regulate Fertility during Pregnancy

In 1722, twenty-five-year-old Leonarde Bergeron, a servant, began to see Antoine Soutel, a gardener who worked just outside the Lyon city walls. Their courtship took all the usual forms and, as the months passed, he began promising to marry her. With this firm expectation, they started to have sex. Soon she found herself pregnant. When she told him, he said he would have to talk to his uncle about getting the necessary legal permission to marry. By the time she was six months pregnant, she began to press him to keep his promise. One evening he brought "a bottle of Spanish wine" for them to share and claimed it was from the cellar of his employer. When she drank it, she noticed it had "an unnatural taste" and seemed to have some sand or salt in it. He gave her some bread to eat with it, perhaps as a snack or to counter the taste. She suspected he had some "evil plan" and threw the bread away. Soutel left without saying anything. Leonarde examined the bottle closely and noticed it contained "a liquid similar to wine" with "some substance that looked like sand, salt or powder." She gave a drink of the liquid to a cat and the cat died a few hours later. She herself was very ill even though she had drunk little of the liquid.

Leonarde left much unsaid in her account to court officials of their relationship and of the "remedy." She hinted at the danger abortifacients posed to women's health. She avoided discussing the negotiation and conflict that presumably accompanied Soutel's stalling, leaving their marital status unresolved as her pregnancy progressed. She did not mention other conversations that preceded his storming off without a word, as she claimed, after she declined to imbibe more of the grainy wine.[5] She did not suggest or perhaps did not know where he had procured the potion that he hoped would resolve the problem her pregnancy seemed to have raised for him.

Nevertheless, Bergeron highlighted the ways in which fertility sometimes led young intimate partners to explore ways of handling the reproductive consequences of their relationships outside of marriage and pointed to the prominence of male intimate partners in efforts to find solutions to untimely pregnancies. These searches for "remedies" were documented in paternity suits when female partners and witnesses of both sexes provided narratives about how pre-marital conception was handled. The legal logic of the cases meant that women often described themselves as reluctant parties to these efforts. Yet they often also had vested interests in delaying parenthood if they were not going to marry or were not yet ready to marry.

Women's retelling of the efforts to interrupt reproduction were shaped by pressures that usually remain invisible, such as generational conflict and conflict between partners, as well the legal context of the record. Antoinette Berthaud, for instance, had not been in touch with her father, Guillaume, for three years before he discovered in 1685 that she was cohabiting with Louis Poulet just a few blocks away from her family residence. Her angry father forced the matter into judicial view when he brought the lawsuit against Poulet, perhaps with significant reluctance on Antoinette's part. Intense generational conflict likely marked her (and likely her intimate partner's) experience of managing reproduction. However, her account to the court of their multiple efforts to manage fertility elided that conflict with its connotations of an unruly and disobedient daughter. Instead she framed their courtship as a typical and respectable one, feasibly leading to marriage. She cast Poulet as a model suitor who chatted with her at church every morning for a long time, made every appearance of *amitié*, and often proposed marriage. She claimed that she had been reluctant to commit to him without her parents' permission because it would make them angry—an accurate prediction—but this narrative also represented her role as blemish-free.[6]

Convention as well as situations specific to individual cases and the reality that the use of "remedies" was legally peripheral to the paternity suits powerfully shaped courtroom discussions of the use of "remedies." To persuade the court to find in their favor, unmarried pregnant women needed to demonstrate that they were respectable because they had feasible expectations of marriage when they engaged in intercourse. The court officials sought to determine that by asking the woman a routine set of questions about the history of the relationship, about whether she had told her intimate partner that she was pregnant, and about whether she had previously had sex and babies with other men. Court officials did not initiate questions about the use of "remedies" as that subject was not pertinent to the issue at hand, so it was the women who occasionally introduced the issue. Presumably, they did so as part of their strategy to defend their reputations while explaining their situations and emphasizing the many ways in which their intimate partners had acted wrongfully toward them. Women's narratives to the court always emphasized that they were shocked and dismayed by their intimate partners' suggestions to use "remedies." They claimed to be surprised to realize that what their partners proffered was a "remedy," or they suggested that the men had tried to dupe them. If a single woman had admitted willingness to consider "remedies" to end the pregnancy, she might have appeared to be guilty of the kind of easy sexual behavior associated with girls who had many partners, and her case might have been dismissed. Similarly, men who had declined to marry their pregnant partners also needed to emphasize their own upright behavior and thus distance themselves from the provision of "remedies." They routinely and consistently denied to the court any intent to do anything other than restore health, or they disclaimed any role in providing "remedies."

Yet these sources provide compelling evidence that couples who could not or did not want to marry used such "remedies" whether consensually or reluctantly, despite the challenges of using complex, layered legal texts to recover intimate practices to interrupt reproduction. These solutions sometimes worked, probably simply by making the woman so ill that she spontaneously miscarried. Intimate partners clearly saw the use of "remedies" as a feasible and legitimate option early in pregnancy, and court officials usually ignored such references or at most were ambivalent about them. These outcomes usually did not generate any written record. The decision to go to court was highly unusual for women even when they were pregnant, and the shift to a legal action no doubt sharpened and spotlighted the contestation between couples. The extant record reflects a particularly contentious subset of a much wider practice.

Women's narratives of their experiences with these "remedies" meant to interrupt pregnancy illustrate the practices and meanings attached to the management of female fertility outside of marriage. Even if early modern men and women had very few effective tools to control their fertility, they clearly sometimes wanted to and the imperative was likely especially pressing for couples who were not yet married. Intimate partners often discussed and practiced possible strategies to control their fertility. They purchased "remedies" or purchased the services of medical providers to perform the bloodletting that was thought euphemistically to restore menstrual cycles. Men engaged with contraception as a concept—they thought they could interrupt pregnancies—and practice—they took active parts in attempts to interrupt pregnancies.

Women's narratives highlighted two kinds of "remedies": the use of bloodletting or taking liquids or powders. Both strategies fit with early modern medical practices of purging the body as the cure for many health issues. They occupied a nebulous zone between restoring menstrual cycles and ending pregnancies. Correcting menstrual blockages was regarded as key to female wellness for which various forms of purging were routinely employed. Meanwhile, abortion was legally and religiously defined as intervention only after the baby could be felt moving at about four or five months' gestation.[7] So the use of "remedies" early in pregnancy allowed intimate partners some flexibility in dealing with untimely pregnancies.

Ambiguity about reproduction provided a critical context for the uses of "remedies," including the complex construction of menstruation and the typical uncertainty over a diagnosis of pregnancy.[8] Women's accounts identified the "remedies" simply as "remedies" or as "drinks," "powder," "drugs," "purging remedies," or "bleeding" (usually in the foot if specified). They were usually cryptic about using them with the intent to interrupt reproduction. Anne Julliard, for example, said her partner had given her "remedies to prevent hydropsy." Antoinette Berthaud claimed in 1685 that Louis Poulet often gave her "remedies" and had also had a surgeon come to bleed her eight or nine times. She remembered having "two losses of blood," but said she did not know if the bleedings and "remedies" had "drained" her of pregnancies or if she had ever been pregnant.[9] In part because interventions were made to restore women's periods as routine health measures as well as deal with untimely pregnancies, the relationship between "remedy" and reproductive status seemed amorphous or was left unarticulated—perhaps sometimes between partners as well as in the legal record.

Women's claims to ignorance about the intentions of their actions can be parsed in several ways. Perhaps some saw a "remedy" as a way to restore their health, a project not incompatible with ending a pregnancy, as restoring menstrual cycles was thought to be important for women's well-being. Some were perhaps gullible and taken in by their partners. Given the uncertain knowledge around pregnancies, it is also plausible that they were not sure they were pregnant. Perhaps some edited their recollection to suit the contexts of a court action. According to the account Antoinette Berthaud gave the court, for example, perhaps shaped by her desire to present herself as virtuous and committed to a relationship that she expected to end in marriage or perhaps simply naive, she claimed that she realized the "remedies" were tied to possible pregnancies only when she and her partner ceased having intercourse for five months.[10]

However, some women openly acknowledged that their partners provided "remedies" with the intent to terminate their pregnancies, even if the women claimed reluctance to use them. Marie Antoine Faure, for example, said her intimate partner gave her "powder" after she told him she was feeling ill, which presumably they both took to be a symptom of pregnancy. When she got pregnant a second time, she declined to take what he offered her as she had been so ill the first time. Louise Blanchet alleged that Gilbert Behal made "black propositions," telling her to buy drugs to end her pregnancy with money he gave her and that he wanted to "abort her fruit" (the usual term for a foetus). Louise Chauvet claimed Jean De Juif had advised her several times to "take remedies that would damage (*faire fonder*) the baby in her." Anne Julliard said she was "horrified" when her intimate partner gave her a white liquid that would "injure" her. Antoinette Berthaud said the realization that the "remedies" were designed to damage her fruit "caused her great grief." These accounts drew a fine line between restoration of health early in pregnancy and late pregnancy termination as well as taking advantage of the trope of female naivete and gullibility.[11]

Young couples were sometimes persistent in their efforts to resolve the problem of a suspected pregnancy by undoing it. In the case of Antoinette Berthaud, she and her partner frequently resorted to "remedies" over the course of their nearly three-year-long relationship. Francois Page and Anne Juilliard made repeated efforts over at least several weeks to interrupt reproduction. Explicit accounts of such repeated efforts are rarely extant, perhaps because such persistence may often have been successful and certainly because the women usually had no reason to provide a full accounting to the court.[12] Yet these attempts were very likely common, and not only in working communities.

"Remedies" to interrupt reproduction involved risks to women's health and well-being, and young women sometimes recalled how sick the "remedies" made them, an important pointer to one of the differential gendered impacts for intimate partners. Anne Julliard's recollection that she thought she would die aligned with other indications of serious physical impairment. Antoinette Berthaud claimed the "remedies" she took sometimes made her retch until she vomited blood. A widow-neighbor's elliptical reference to Izabeau Marquet's two-week stay in her room after taking "remedies" indicated the high level of discomfort such interventions could cause for women.[13] This physical debilitation was one of many ways in which negotiations and actions involving fertility before and after birth had different implications for women and men.

The number of women who died during attempts to induce abortions is impossible to calculate, but the severity of symptoms indicate that no doubt some did die as women always did in the era before safe and legal abortions. Parish registers did not record causes of death, but young women's deaths would not be suspicious in an era of high mortality when they sometimes died unexpectedly as did people in every demographic group. For women who survived, the effects of such "remedies" could damage their physical health in the short or long term. Even in the archive of reproduction, silences largely shroud these possible consequences.[14]

The providers of women's reproductive health "remedies" were male in these accounts, whether intimate partners or surgeons or apothecaries. The midwives who historians often highlight as providers of resources for fertility management were noticeably absent from the records either as sources of "remedies" or as witnesses. Male partners were seemingly able to procure "remedies" either from surgeons or apothecaries under the cover of purchasing purgatives to restore health. They could also hire surgeons to come to do the bloodletting. Perhaps vernacular knowledge about the powers and liquids that would work circulated among men too.

The roles of surgeons or apothecaries, like many other people who provided support for young couples, were often elliptical and seemingly involved a willingness not to ask too many questions. They were very rarely called to testify in women's court actions. A surgeon, Louis Oriel, testified in 1685 that when he had visited Catherine Faure, a servant, because she was "very uncomfortable," he learned that she had previously been visited by a doctor who had bled her in the foot and given her a potion, and he did likewise. He was called again to see her, but found her "drunk," and so he told her to rest because she was "not in condition to take a remedy." On a third visit he bled her from an arm and gave her a drink "as he did not believe she was pregnant and nobody said that to him." Certainly, the surgeon seemed to want to deny in court that he had been involved in knowingly ending a pregnancy, suggesting some unease with being publicly associated such actions. A subsequent 1700 prohibition forbade surgeons to bleed unmarried women without proof that they were not pregnant. The existence of the regulation spoke to the widespread belief that bloodletting could interrupt a pregnancy. It seems reasonable, however, that he must have suspected that a boyfriend who called a medical provider four times for his girlfriend might have been trying to "restore" her menstrual cycle.[15] Just as priests chose to accept babies as legitimate if their fathers were present at baptism, surgeons could choose to see their treatments as restorative.

Couples, their communities, and legal professionals saw the resort to "remedies" as familiar and frequent, and they were largely resigned at worst or accepting at best about their use. A widespread community ambivalence existed about the use of "remedies" early in pregnancies and a complex attitude about later interventions. Legal officials had at least a tacit sense that "remedies" to restore women's health even in these circumstances were commonplace. The kin and neighbors of Anne Julliard had often seen Francois Page visit her; they knew she had been "ill," and they saw him bring "remedies" and instruct her grandmother to make sure she took them twice. Her uncle told a female neighbor she was pregnant and Page was the father, which led the neighbor to inquire whether Page's "remedies" were not meant to "injure" Julliard, that is, induce a miscarriage. She recounted that the uncle replied they were not because the couple had kept company with the intention of marriage—and he would not have put up with the "remedies" if he thought that they were for that purpose. Another female neighbor observed similar events and even saw Page try to bleed her in the foot. She did not know why, but when she learned that Julliard was pregnant, she asked if that was why she had taken the "remedies," and Julliard replied she did not know why Page had given them to her.[16] Such discussions show a widespread awareness of the circulation of "remedies" as antidotes to untimely pregnancies as well as some ambiguity in sentiment. However, many family members and neighbors watched Julliard and Page negotiate their fertility, and most seem to have chosen to take the treatments at face value as restorative (in the early modern purgative sense) rather than intervene to object. Such efforts were likely sometimes successful for other couples or not spoken of in court.

Legal officials in these kinds of cases seemed strikingly unconcerned about references to "remedies" or even to intentions to damage "fruit." Even if they occasionally voiced skepticism about the veracity of testimony that denied all knowledge and responsibility, no evidence of legal follow-up exists. Court officials were skeptical, for instance, that Gilbert Behal had given Francoise Blanchet money to buy drugs to abort her pregnancy, "as one can't assume" that if he had seduced her, as she said, he would next have given her money to use "so badly as she has told us." A midwife recalled that she had chastised him for giving Blanchet money "to abort her fruit" and he had not responded.[17] In court, Behal denied giving her money with "such pernicious advice" and said "she had told him she was pregnant and asked for the money to buy remedies she promised were for a malady." Although the court officials remarked that giving money to terminate a pregnancy was "a very serious and very punishable action," their judicial commentary seems to have been meant only to acknowledge the he said/she said quality of the dispute. They released Behal from prison as he requested and ordered him to pay her costs and take charge of the baby as she requested—a mundane outcome to such legal disputes. The wide latitude of such outcomes was likely rooted in broad cultural attitudes to early stages of pregnancy and perhaps in the consensus evident in other ways that the marriages of young couples were not always feasible or even desirable.[18]

Elite awareness existed of the religious and legal divide between restoring menstrual health and termination of pregnancy, although how widespread it was is less clear. Certainly examples of elite concern about "remedies" were occasionally articulated. Jean-François Fournel, a jurist who wrote the definitive late eighteenth-century text on "seduction," rehearsed the historic distinction in law and theology between termination of "the hope of a man" and of "a man." However, he acknowledged that in the eighteenth century only the latter carried criminal punishment and conceded that abortion "by drinks, drugs or deadly efforts to prevent the accomplishment of motherhood" was a well-known practice. A century earlier, the mayor of Dijon (about 125 miles north of Lyon) acknowledged that "remedies and potions" were "often" used to end pregnancies. Like Fournel, he was discomfited by what he saw as a serious crime. He asked for a special kind of judicial order (a *monitoire*) to be issued to compel witnesses to come forward to provide information.[19] Both men focused on the mother as the liable criminal party, and the Dijon mayor indeed associated the use of "remedies" with women of "libertine ways," indicating perhaps another reason that young women sought to distance themselves in court from active involvement in using "remedies."

Yet court officials who heard references about the use of "remedies" apparently just shrugged and moved on to deal with the issue of financial compensation and the baby's upbringing. Only three possible cases of abortion were prosecuted in Lyon between 1720 and 1790, while prosecutions in other cities were also highly unusual.[20] The judiciary shared with the community a practice of pragmatism toward young people's efforts to deal with the predictableness of untimely fertility. Again judges appeared to be partners with working neighborhoods in a broad communal complicity that helped young couples manage out-of-wedlock pregnancies.

Young couples also explored other kinds of solutions during the terms of pregnancies when their out-of-wedlock conceptions were not going to be followed by marriage, and male intimate partners and other men were likewise actively involved in remedies of this kind. Various legal actors, especially notaries, were frequently consulted, as were clergy. Young men's friends and kin also provided a range of assistance. These legal, clerical, and peer actors were invaluable partners in shaping strategies that accepted that some pregnancies outside of marriage would result as long as the community defined licit intimacy to include pre-marital intercourse as one of the steps into marriage,

Remedies: Legal Officials and Out-of-Court Settlements

When Francois Benoist consulted a lawyer about making a private settlement with Henriette Gabet, he explored a solution to out-of-wedlock pregnancy that many couples used but discovered he could not afford one. His reference to the consultation and cost highlighted an important reality: legal assistance was available, but at a price. These forms of "help" by legal officials were work for them, and usually they expected to be paid for it. Nevertheless, many young unmarried men and women together and individually used legal professionals—mostly notaries—to make binding agreements about how to handle their prospective parenthood without going to court. Intimate partners' motives in seeing such agreements could be varied and were often multiple. Such agreements could provide out-of-court settlements to end judicial processes. They were a way to avoid going to court altogether but still produced legally enforceable settlements. They offered a more private solution than a court case. The terms could be negotiated so they could differ from the very standard elements of a paternity suit decision. The use of a notary (or occasionally another minor legal official) was cheaper than the costs of a lawsuit when lawyers and court fees had to be paid.[21] In all of these ways, intimacy became a legal matter, just as it did in a court case.

Legal officials provided many services outside of the formal legal system, including mediating between intimate partners without the generation of a formal written record. For example, Marie Roze, a stocking maker, went with Marie Arthaud, to see an *avocat* to "take advice about what she could do in her situation." The lawyer sent Arthaud to find Marie's reluctant partner, Eustache Croste, who duly accompanied her back to the lawyer's office. As Marie recalled, the lawyer told Croste he had to repair the damages he had done to Arthaud and pay her.[22] Although the practice of such lawyer mediated efforts to settle arrangements between young couples was documented only when women, like Arthaud, subsequently went to court, no doubt many intimate partners reached agreements in such circumstances without any confirming record.

A variety of petty legal professionals besides notaries might also have facilitated the out-of-court settlement of cases or made records of declarations. A man who worked as a court recorder (*greffier*), for example, visited Anne Chevallier to record her "declaration" as part of a settlement with her intimate partner. Pierre Scarron used a *greffier* as the middleman to give Izabeau Bremont the money he had promised. In an interesting illustration of other uses women might make of their "declarations," Marie Fleuri Beuajollit made her declaration "at the greffe" in 1773. She later went to a church court to request an order to have a *greffier* make a copy for her so she could give it to her parish priest and get her baby baptized.[23] *Greffiers* also had a formal role in legal cases when they would collect the money young men were sentenced to pay for the costs of delivery and then pass it on to the young women. When they helped wrangle extra-judicial settlements, they extended unofficial assistance that likely had an aura of legality by association.

Young women could also be taken advantage of by unscrupulous legal officials who were, in theory, helping them. Antoinette Buy, for example, moved to Lyon in 1761, hoping to get more work than she had found elsewhere. She lived with and worked for a *passementiere*, and one of their clients, Sr. Duvernay, a merchant, often stopped by. Buy claimed that her employer encouraged or arranged their relationship. When Buy became pregnant, the employer said she had to leave, so she went to live and work with a widowed needlewoman. About six weeks later, Buy asked a *huissier* named St. Morice to broker a settlement with Sr. Duvernay regarding their unborn baby. Presumably she had learned via local knowledge that St. Morice had a sideline in making such arrangements. The couple met at St. Morice's residence where Duvernay agreed to pay Buy 168 *livres* "to avoid gossip and get an out-of-court settlement" while she in return promised not to make any legal claims against him. A notary drew up the agreement and Duvernay gave St. Morice the money in the notary's office. However, the *huissier* gave Buy only 90 *livres*. He paid the notary six *livres* for his work and kept the other

72 *livres* for himself as payment for his services, taking a commission of over 40% without prior agreement and twelve times what the notary charged.[24] As a newcomer to town with little in the way of a support network, Buy was probably more vulnerable than some of her peers to such exploitation by men whose sideline income included mediation of private agreements, but the informal nature of this work facilitated the possibility of extortion.

More commonly, young men and women exploring solutions to out-of-wedlock pregnancy sought out notaries who were familiar neighborhood resources for private legal services. Early modern families routinely used these professionals to draw up legal instruments for many domestic and commercial issues, such as marriage contracts, wills, residential leases, inheritance settlements, loans, commercial agreements, apprenticeship contracts or reconciliation of guardianship spending. Although most acts notaries wrote were formulaic and the templates were included in widely circulated "how to" guides, notaries also tailored written records for the particular needs of their clients for a wide range of purposes. [25]

Sometimes a young woman might pay a notary to make a "declaration" of her pregnant status and a young woman who made this choice presumably saw some strategic negotiating value in having written evidence of her acknowledgment of her pregnancy. A young woman's "declaration" did not involve any association with the 1556 ordinance even if she was pregnant. Claire Dolan has noted that a "declaration" was a legal instrument that could be used in a variety of different ways: as a declaration of fact, as an act that modified previous acts, or as a complement to judicial cases.[26] Young women in fact used notaries to make "declarations" as instruments that functioned in all these ways, and for varied purposes. Jeanne Bezan, for instance, had had two babies with Jean Croizat and was pregnant with a third when she went to a notary to "declare and affirm" under oath that the baby she carried was Croizat's. Her pregnancy was already a public matter. She recorded a declaration with a notary not to avoid charges of concealment but because the officials of the Hôtel-Dieu—where she expected to give birth—had made a request to Croizat to pay her costs and those of their care of the baby, and he had had "the bad faith to deny" his involvement.[27]

Women could also use notarized declarations as negotiating chips to pressure their recalcitrant intimate partners into marriage or commitments for support. Marguerite Riboullet, for instance, recorded a "declaration" with a notary in January 1689. She had worked for a year doing washing and other jobs for Jean Quinet, a tanner, during which time he solicited her and made many promises to marry her. The reason that Marguerite, who was eight months pregnant, recorded her situation with a notary was not to prove that she was not concealing her pregnancy. Rather, she did so to lay out her demands—Quinet had to marry her as he promised or else take and raise the baby at his expense; he had to pay her costs as well as acknowledge that he was the baby's father, and she had already spoken to a lawyer who would act for her in a paternity suit. Riboullet intended to use her declaration to pressure Quinet to keep his promise to marry her or at least support her and the baby by showing she was ready to initiate a public lawsuit. For Marguerite, the declaration was an opportunity to document her integrity, her intention to make her intimate partner accept responsibility, and to list her demands.[28]

Sometimes young women used a notary as leverage to make their intimate partners come to an agreement. In February 1685, for example, Francoise Phillipon, went to a notary with a male companion, a glassworker, to make a legal record that she had appointed a *procureur* "to work for her in the case she intends to bring in the Lyon royal court." The notary's act recorded that Francoise was "acting as a major and as mistress of her rights" and laid out her claim: the "carnal knowledge and cohabitation" she and her partner had had after his promises of marriage had left her seven months pregnant and yet he had not in fact married her. She wanted him to marry her or provide support. Neither she nor the person who accompanied her to the notary's office were able to sign their names, but presumably she brought him along for support. She filed her complaint with the court the same day.[29] A surgeon who quickly visited her to confirm her pregnancy filed his report confirming her condition. The next day the court gave her permission to proceed with her suit by gathering depositions. No subsequent documents survive. Likely Francoise's rush of legal actions convinced her partner that he would have to step up, whether to marry her or at least to agree on a financial settlement.[30]

For young couples who would not marry despite the pregnancy of the female partner, notaries provided a variety of services in mutually binding out-of-court agreements variously called *accords*, *accomodements*, or *desistements*. Either or both parties in an out-of-wedlock pregnancy might seek a notarially customized record of their agreement about how to proceed. By the second quarter of the eighteenth century, such agreements between young intimate partners had become such a routine part of the notarial workload that templates for them began to appear in professional handbooks. A 1720s reissue of an older guide that promised "new models in the formats of the most skillful notaries and in the most used terms" included for the first time a form for a "mutual agreement to settle out of court by a young man and young woman of a promise of marriage when the young woman has had a baby whose father is the young man" [*Desistement respecitif par Un Garcon et une Fille, d'une promesse de marriage lorsqu'il est issu un enfant de la fille provenant du fait de garcon*]. The 1752 edition of a guide for notaries first published in the late seventeenth century added a template for an "agreement between a young man and a young woman due to an ephemeral romance followed by pregnancy" [*accord entre un garcon et un fille pour raison de galanterie suivie de grossesse*] although no such forms had been included in earlier versions.[31] This template for a relationship that had not involved promises to marry followed the standard terms of paternity suits, although some were spelled out more explicitly than in the usual court decision (father to pay costs of mother, father charged with custody of child and to prepare child for a trade, father to bring child up as a good Catholic). It also added a clause that went beyond paternity suits in requiring the father was to bring the child to the mother (and her father) whenever they wanted.

The example given in the state-of-the-field 1728 notarial handbook, which claimed to have the most up-to-date and most used forms, suggests clients might have had greater flexibility in a private arrangement than in a court decision. Although judges routinely ordered young men to take full financial responsibility for the costs of the delivery and the upbringing of the baby, including custody, the 1728 guide provided a template by which both intimate partners renounced their promises to marry, the father paid half of the costs of upbringing and apprenticeship, and the baby apparently stayed with the mother.[32] If this template was indeed typical of the ones that notaries wrote for young couples, an out-of-court settlement could spell out the future responsibilities of the partners in ways quite different from those of a court action.

Intimate partners could negotiate private extra-judicial settlements at many different moments: instead of or before going to court, in which case women promised not to take legal action, or during legal proceedings when they agreed to settled out of court rather than continue with the judicial process. The wife of Jacqueline Faure's employer, for example, noticed Faure was pregnant, and Jacqueline told her who the father was. Her employer and a friend of the about-to-be father conferred to have a notarized "act" drawn up that committed Faure's partner to pay both her rent for a short-term stay with a midwife and the costs of delivery.[33] Such written records of agreements had the advantage of being legally binding, and thus offering more security than the early modern equivalent of a handshake, but they remained private unlike judicial proceedings.

An agreement made after a lawsuit was under way, known as a *desistement* (literally a commitment to desist from legal action), was a legally binding renunciation of whatever claim had previously been made in court or in a contract as well as an agreement to the terms of a compromise.[34] The majority of court actions started by single women against their intimate partners were not resolved by judicial decision, and the absence of further records after the initial legal documents signals that some other solution was found. Very occasionally, a note on the cover of the lawsuit made that explicit. A note on Jacqueline Ballard's dossier, for example, recorded that a notary had made an agreement so there was no need for further judicial action because it had been "settled" (*accomode*).[35]

Young intimate partners sometimes reached these settlements while young men were held in prison during paternity suit proceedings. Matthieu Marcel was imprisoned during the investigation into his intimate partner's complaint, like many other young men. He and Marie Ruedy settled when both signed a *desistement* by which she agreed that her accusations were unfounded (a boilerplate phrase referencing accusations of bad faith, not to the fact that he was the father of her child) and he promised to pay 100 *livres* to the Hôtel-Dieu to cover the cost of the delivery and upbringing of their child. The court agreed to release him on evidence of the agreement and the receipt for his payment. Likewise, Anne Martin filed a complaint against Antoine Louis in late October 1683. She claimed that he threatened to kill her if she accused him of paternity and that he had failed to keep the promises that had led her to have sex with him. Within four days of her petition and testimony from witnesses, the court awarded her 150 *livres* and ordered him to prison if he did not pay. Five weeks later, with Louis in prison, she signed a *desistement*. He was released the next day when a copy of it was deposited with the court.[36]

Although it was exceptional for the female intimate partners to be imprisoned, the same incentive for settlement no doubt existed no matter who was in prison. Matthieu Deleon responded to Rozette Blanquemette's petition by alleging she had stolen property from him, an allegation that led to her being imprisoned during the investigation. They nevertheless settled with a "*traite de l'accord*" where each promised to drop the charges, she agreed he was a gentleman, he attested that she was virtuous, and he paid the 100 *livres* the court had awarded her.[37]

The interplay between judicial and out-of-court notarized settlements that had legal weight was often no doubt ongoing, though it is only occasionally highlighted in extant documents. Magdelaine Fontanel filed a petition against surgeon Charles Rey which came to court "when he did not want to keep his promises" to marry her. Three days later in a notary's office she agreed to "desist" in all claims made and not to make any claims in court or for expenses in future. Her change of heart, she said, was "to discharge her conscience" because what she said was not true and because Rey would be "worried and troubled" by her lawsuits. The agreement did not include any payment to her. However, the presence of another surgeon as a witness—presumably as a proxy for Rey, who did not attend or sign—suggests that this boilerplate accord was probably to hide a more complex agreement. Certainly, Fontanel did not see the renunciation of legal action as the end to the matter. Two months later, after the baby was born, she, her midwife, and some other women brought the baby to Rey's shop and left him there. Their de facto extra-legal resolution by literally charging him with the baby indicates that Fontanel and her female friends felt neither legal action nor notarized renunciation nor any private agreement had been sufficient to compel Rey to correct his error in fathering her baby without marrying her. When Rey complained in court and asked the judges to investigate her "crime" of abandonment of the baby, the court agreed to open an inquiry but required him to take all necessary care of the baby. No further court records survive, presumably because abandonment in a safe place like a shop was not in fact a crime. Perhaps they finally agreed to resolve the matter without going back to court.[38]

Notaries did more than record such agreements. Witnesses occasionally explicitly recalled that notaries actively mediated to encourage the intimate partners to come to agreements as well as hosting, articulating, and recording what the parties wanted. A notary's wife described how her husband "had taken many steps" to get Pierrette Tripier and David Bourgeois to come to agreement after the notary heard of the pregnancy. These included conversations between the intimate partners at his office. A surgeon explained that he had been at the notary's when Tripier's mother and aunt came in to meet Bourgeois, and he had promised in front of the notary and surgeon to make particular payments to Tripier to get a *desistement*.[39]

Notaries on occasion refused to be drawn into disputes when they were wary of the circumstances even though they routinely were hired as facilitators to make private legal arrangements between unmarried couples. If notaries regarded involvement in making legal arrangements for out-of-wedlock pregnancies as ordinary work, they could be sensitive to what they perceived as possible illegalities. Indeed, recording a false legal instrument (a *faux*) was considered a serious professional violation for notaries. Marie Salloman recalled, for instance, that Louis Ragon wanted her to make a written declaration that the father of her child was another man and offered her 300 *livres* to do so. She initially demurred because it was not true. Ragon threatened her and said he would pay her rent, so she went with him to see a notary, M. Perrichon, who duly drew up the act. She still did not want to sign, so claimed she did not know how as an excuse. Many working women were illiterate and did not sign for themselves, so her refusal apparently made the notary suspicious as he subsequently refused to add his official signature. Ragon then visited "five or six notaries who refused to sign" before he found one who was willing to draw up the instrument on the terms he wanted.[40] His persistence and eventual success suggest that notaries were not uniformly vigilant in handling such matters.

The coded and formulaic language of the agreements elides what must often have been intense and unpredictable negotiations across generations as well as between intimate partners. Anne Julliard, a pin maker, and Francois Page, a journeyman surgeon, had a conventional courtship: they spent time together, he expressed fond feelings for her, he promised to marry her, they had sex, and she got pregnant. He said he had talked to his family, they had made some arrangement with his mother, and they agreed to meet at a notary's to make a marriage contract. Anne's uncle and aunt, with whom she lived, went with her to the notary, expecting to meet Francois and his father. Instead, they found only the father. The aunt and uncle asked him where the son was. The notary "proposed that instead of a marriage contract, they make an agreement or a promise to desist from legal action." The aunt and uncle felt this suggestion was "no doubt prompted by the father" and was "contrary to the promises" Francois had made so the threesome walked away.[41] This was surely a very tense meeting filled with conflicting emotions and differing goals, even if surviving records are very flat. For Anne and her kin, the occasion must have involved surprise, disappointment, and apprehension while Francois's father likely felt anger and frustration. The rare record of the backstory illuminates the many different parties and intentions involved in negotiations.

Many varieties of family and/or intimate partner tension played out as settlements outside of marriage were sought and, even if documentation is rarely extant, such meetings must have been common as couples used notaries as facilitators and their offices as meeting places as well as recorders if agreements were reached. One such example was a long, tumultuous relationship in the 1750s between Louis Mollard, an *emballeur*, and Benigne Dubois, *a lingere*, that included the births of two babies while he stalled about marrying her. Her exasperated father made repeated efforts to put an end to their relations despite her willingness to repeatedly take Mollard back after breakups. The threat that she (or even her father) might go to court and the possibility of an out-of-court settlement were key sources of friction. Mollard was concerned that she would file a paternity claim against him in court and at one point he stopped her father on the street to ask him to agree to a *desistement* that would allow them to come to terms. Her neighbors had watched every stage of their relationship and knew that when Mollard came to ask Benigne to go with him to sign a *desistement*, she refused, and he was so angry that he hit her. He took the key to her room, forcing her mother and a neighbor to run after him. Mollard wanted to take Benige by force to a notary to make her sign the agreement.[42]

The variations were endless. In 1685, for example, Claudine LaCroisette "renounced" (*se desiste*) all claims made against Francois Massias in a suit filed three months earlier that alleged he was the father of her baby. Her *desistement* said he had nothing to do with the baby and that the father was someone absent from the city. She asserted that she had identified him in the lawsuit due to her obedience to her father and his paternal influence. Now she claimed she wanted to "discharge her conscience of the false accusation she made," as Massias should not have to "suffer such an accusation and a thing so contrary to the truth." She signed the agreement at the residence of a widowed midwife, and a copy was filed with the court the next day.[43] The settlement reflects generational tension between father and daughter, but it also suggests a tumultuous process from the decision to file a court complaint to the determination that the couple would settle out of court.

Extant documents only hint at the scale and customization of notarized private resolutions between intimate partners, and notaries as keepers of family secrets contributed to the invisibility of such agreements for intimate matters in particular.[44] Legally, notaries were required to register all the acts they made. A 1693 *Contrôle des Actes* law obliged them to "control," that is, to register, acts made within two weeks, or face fines as the French state sought to regularize and enforce a long-standing requirement to register. However, clearly notaries continued to not register all of their acts, although again extant evidence is usually indirect. The intimate partner of a Grenoble apothecary, for example, recalled his advice to her: "One makes a declaration before a friendly notary and he keeps the secret until the baby is born and then tears up the papers and a woman's honor is preserved." A notary in the Loire Valley in 1720 explained that he had not registered acts involving young people's out-of-wedlock intimacy because "he almost never [did so] with acts of this kind." The widespread lapses in notarial compliance with the registration requirement were evident in the occasional prosecutions of notaries who had failed to register their acts—acts that contemporary jurists had recorded—and in the repeated re-issuance of the 1693 requirement to register that appeared in other judicial pronouncements. Copies of these acts are rare in the notarial registers because numerous notaries who wrote such agreements did not see the need to report them.[45]

The provision of templates in manuals for notaries about arrangements for out-of-wedlock pregnancies confirms both how widespread out-of-wedlock pregnancies were and how they were treated routinely as situations to be managed, not as crises or causes for young women to be shamed. Notaries, like communities and courts, insisted that young men take responsibility for the consequences of their sexual activity. They explicitly expected fathers to take responsibility for out-of-wedlock as well as legitimate children. Copies of the notarial agreements subsequently included as evidence with court records offer a glimpse into settlements for young couples negotiated outside the judicial system but facilitated by legal professionals. Notaries, like their neighbors, knew that predictable fertility could make for unpredictable consequences even when employers, neighbors, and friends watched and regulated young couples' relationships. When notaries did not keep track of the settlements in their public registers, they silenced the events for posterity. Notaries were parties to information that was held among quite a number of people who thought there was nothing to be gained by speaking further of it when births had passed and arrangements settled. In many ways, notaries and Catholic clergy had similar roles as both prioritized safeguarding the future of young couples with minimal disruption. They were parts of networks that sought to maintain reputations, order, and the well-being of expectant parents and their infants.

Remedies: Priests and Friars as Mediators of Out-of-Wedlock Pregnancies

Clergy were also an important resource for young partners to mobilize, individually or as a couple, and they might help in a variety of ways. As we saw when baby Benoist-Gabet's baptism was registered as if he were the legitimate son of married parents, priests could help smooth the situation even at the baptism font. Parish priests and friars were often collaborators with young couples who helped manage the situation in ways they deemed least likely to disrupt individual lives and communities. A striking tension existed between Catholic Reformation official policy and discourse, which was heavily invested in disciplining extra-marital sexuality, and actual clergy practice, which was often rooted in obligations for mediation, pastoral care work, and sometimes close personal relationships.[46] Friars in particular saw mediation and reconciliation as important parts of their mission as Christian reformers. The friars and priests who worked with young couples actively participated as partners in helping young men and women to navigate the challenges of out-of-wedlock pregnancies.

Parish priests played important roles in young couples' ability to manage out-of-wedlock pregnancies, above all at the moment of baptism, and their own situations as well as judgments about the young couples' behavior shaped their decisions. The baby born to Benoist and Gabet was far from the only one priests baptized as legitimate although born out of wedlock. A priest baptized Louis Mollard and Benigne Dubois's baby as legitimate in the same parish. Many other babies were baptized in their fathers' names with no reference to their own status and therefore appear in the registers as legitimate. Parish priests who entered the details of the baptism into their registers were key on-the-ground arbitrators of a child's legitimacy.[47] Priests may often have judged it appropriate not to mention a baby's status if the parents were a stable couple who seemed like they would marry or had all other attributes of marriage in terms of living as man and wife. As long as the father was present at the baptism, priests may have accepted that the couple was transitioning into marriage. In a rare explicit acknowledgment of this practice, a priest who had baptized a baby as legitimate acknowledged later that he did so even though the parents were not yet married because he had called the banns announcing their intention to marry. Priests may also have had their own motives. Subject to regular evaluative episcopal visitations from the seventeenth century as part of the Catholic Church's commitment to reform, priests were incentivized to minimize the rate of illegitimacy in their parishes, as a high rate could be taken as a reflection of the clergy's own shortcomings in leading their flocks. This priestly discretion continued throughout the old regime. In 1788, for example, Catherine Brillat produced a copy of her baby's baptism registration in which the priest described her as the wife of her partner, Francois Sallier.[48]

In Lyon and many other French cities, moreover, Catholic reform initiatives included the arrival of large numbers of friars, such as the Dominicans and Capuchins, who were committed to "internal missions." They directed their missionary work to the metropolitan French laity as a complement to global external Christianizing missions. These friars were popular preachers and became popular confessants too. Their training emphasized reconciliation and mediation in and out of the confession box. They brought a spiritual and moral authority to their involvement in the lives of their penitents and could be effective brokers both because of their emphasis on mediation and because they were hard to say no to.[49]

From the late sixteenth century, many people in Lyon and elsewhere chose to make their confessions to friars whom they could pick based on their preferences and personal chemistry rather than to the priests assigned to their parishes. By 1700, over 1,000 Capuchins lived in the diocesan province of Lyon. They brought new forms of prayer, lived on alms, and rejected the wealth and tithing of the established Catholic Church in stark contrast to the traditional clergy. Their appeal in working communities seems to have rested in part on these "novelties" as a mid-seventeenth-century Capuchin noted in his history of the order in the Lyon province. The friars often developed very close relationships with their penitents, young women as well as others, and came to be common, even dominant, providers of confessions. In some cities, the number of friars associated with the reformed orders far exceeded the number of parish priests.[50]

For young people in Lyon, discussions during confession could help navigate out-of-wedlock pregnancy challenges. A new wave of confessional manuals that were designed to provide advice for both confessors and penitents gave special attention to young unmarried men and women. Jean Eudes's *Le Bon Confesseur*, directed specifically at friars engaged in missions, was published repeatedly in Lyon between 1669 and 1689 as were other of Eudes's works. He was a very influential figure in seventeenth-century reformed Catholic circles, with work published in many editions all over France.[51] Eudes advised confessors to encourage their penitents to tell them everything, even if it was uncomfortable, because it was necessary for their well-being.

Eudes provided specific directions for questioning young unmarried men and women that revolved around the behaviors young people routinely engaged in the course of their relationships and echoed the concerns of other community members about managing the boundaries of licit behavior. His queries for young men were predictable—had they had unclean thoughts and wanted to act on them; had they acted on them and, if so, with whom; if it was a long time ago or recently; if they looked at images or printed material and had inappropriate thoughts, and if they masturbated. Eudes also suggested questions that were specific to young people's intimate relationships—had they taken young women to dances or balls and had their parents given permission, had they given them "unwise" kisses, or had they advised anyone or procured anything that would "prevent reproduction or make the fruit perish" (that is used a "remedy"). He recommended that young women be asked all the same questions, and others such as if they had ever worn clothing that exposed their throats and breasts, if they spent too long dressing, if they had spoken too freely to men or spoken one on one with them in a remote spot, or if they let men touch their breasts.[52]

Confessors were committed to secrecy and were obliged to take care of the spiritual well-being of their penitents, but Eudes's questions pointed to even broader responsibilities. The confidentiality of confession created a relationship with penitents that could cut across institutional dogma and highlight the complexity of their own situation as members of the local community as well as the institutional Catholic Church. They might have developed personal relationships, sometimes over years, with their parishioners, and they were invested in their pastoral obligations to provide care. They sought to protect, mediate, and offer practical assistance as well as weigh salvation and sin. They may have grown up in the neighborhoods they served or have kin there, and certainly friars as well as priests were intimately familiar with the practices and challenges of their communities

In these ways, the confession box was a key site for discussion of intimate issues related to out-of-wedlock pregnancy as well as other challenges of youthful heterosociability. Evidence of what was discussed in confession boxes is, of course, elusive, but occasional references demonstrate the existence of rooted relationships that included intimate conversations. When Catherine Bariou, for instance, discovered she was pregnant and she and her intimate partner agreed they could not marry, she consulted her confessor, Gaspard Charier, an Antoinin friar who had heard her confession for eighteen months. He in turn discussed Bariou's situation with at least one other of his penitents, Elizabeth de Beaulieu, whose confession he had heard for four years. Both women made a point of emphasizing the length of their penitential relationships with him in their recounting of subsequent events in court.[53]

Young women may have had ongoing discussions with their confessors about intimate details of their relationships over long periods of time and sought advice and guidance which their confessors duly dispensed as part of their pastoral care. Friars and priests provided a variety of advice and assistance related to the challenges of youthful intimacy. Sometimes confessors simply advised their penitents to remove themselves or their intimate partners from the situation, especially when they were employer-employee. Richard Du Colombe told his confessor in 1685 that he and Florie Solore were having sex and the priest told him to have her leave his household—which he did. Catherine Faure confessed in the same year that she was having sex with her employer, Joseph Foretz, and she recounted that her confessor told her to leave because of the damage to her "conscience and honor" and "remedy the disorder and put her conscience at rest." Marie Chana likewise said her confessor had "ordered her to leave" when she told him her employer, Joseph Ramel often "caressed her." [54] These three situations that involved married employers violated the conventions of licit intimacy between equals for whom marriage was feasible, and priests recognized the best outcome was to separate the two.

Priests could deal in matters of conscience and practicality at the same time. Genevieve Chevallier had made a court claim for paternity and claimed the usual recompense against a M. Sirol. She subsequently told her confessor that her employer was in fact the father of her baby and she had named Sirol at his suggestion in exchange for a promise of money. The priest said she had to withdraw her legal action before he would give her absolution to discharge her conscience, and she duly made a "declaration" to that effect.[55] This sequence of events suggests that the network of clergy as well as legal officials provided strategies and resources that were rarely documented but well known in communities.

Generally, clergy seemed inclined to mediate on behalf of penitents for whom marriage was feasible, and occasional references point to young women seeking advice and help from their parish priests when they were pregnant. Francois Berthellier wrote to Jeanne Revilly to express his surprise that the vicar of their parish, St. Nizier, had come to speak to him and tell him she was pregnant. The vicar apparently also reported that she was planning to go to the court. Berthellier asked her to meet him the following day at the church where "we can settle on a price" (that is, make a settlement). Whether he expected the priest to be present when the young couple talked is not clear, but the choice of the church as the meeting place for negotiation certainly opened that possibility. Francoise Patra had also talked to her priest in a different Lyon parish and he likewise went to visit her partner, Pierre La Fay. The priest told La Fay she was on the verge of despair and about to miscarry so he needed to "restore her tranquility" by marrying her. La Fay must have resisted this priestly suasion as Patra went to court and eventually signed a *desistement*, signaling they had agreed to settle out of court, after he had been held in prison for six weeks.[56]

The priority on pastoral care and often long relationships positioned friars to provide assistance as messengers and mediators. Marguerite Loubat said that "the first person she had revealed her disgrace to was a holy father and no doubt he had told her grandfather," who must have subsequently told her father. Loubat did not mention the context for the conversation so perhaps it was not covered by the confidentiality of the confession box, and it is unclear whether she intended the friar to intervene in this way. On other occasions, clergy might be drawn on explicitly as mediators. In 1689, Florie Brouillard and Claude Duvert did not marry because, he claimed, "they had nothing [no property] between them." After he left town, Brouillard became concerned he intended to abandon her, and she went to a scribe's where she asked the scribe's wife to get him to write a letter on her behalf to Duvert. Brouillard engaged a friar ("Father Maxime, [an] Augustin") to take her letter to Duvert. Duvert admitted to the friar that he indeed was the one who "had put her in difficulty" and was ready to marry her, and the friar carried back Duvert's message that he would be back soon to "put an end to the worries" she had.[57] It seems safe to assume that the arrival of the friar, as much as his intimate partner's letter, persuaded Duvert to promise at least to meet his responsibilities.

Sometimes clerical assistance involved delivery of material items and finding resources as well as mediation. Marguerite Ruffard, a silk worker's daughter, and Pierre Gay, the son of a grocer, had been courting in the conventional way when she came pregnant in 1684 following Gay's promises to marry. Gay assured Marguerite and her widowed mother that he intended to keep his promises. Subsequently he spoke to a "Reverend head father of the Capuchins" about their situation. Gay gave the friar a gold *écu* coin to give Ruffard "to buy whatever she needed and promised that she would want for nothing and he would marry her." Friars might even be in contact with care workers to smooth arrangements for the baby's arrival.[58]

These fleeting glimpses illuminate how clergy, whether as friars or parish priests, provided critical forms of assistance to couples managing out-of-wedlock pregnancies in ways that suggest at least some clergy provided a sympathetic, pastorally inspired approach rather than a disciplinary one. They did so in confession boxes, in nearby residences, with lawyers, and no doubt elsewhere, and their willingness was surely well known to their communities. Their efforts to manage and support unwed expectant parents were aligned with and often embedded in those of kin and friends as well as lawyers and surgeons.

Remedies: Kin and Peer Mediators

Friends and family were also important resources for young men and women dealing with out-of-wedlock pregnancy, sometimes with medical and legal professionals or clergy and sometimes without. Male networks provided young men with many forms of assistance in this phase of couples' relationships as well as the help they might give to young women. The role of female friends remains more elusive in extant records, although no doubt it existed. Yet the assistance of family and friends, although essential at the time, is all but invisible now because it usually generated no legal or written record of any kind.

Nevertheless, male kin and friends provided many forms of assistance for unmarried expectant fathers. Monsieur Saunier had his "friend" and "confidant," Monsieur Berger, "do a favor for him . . . as his friend" and bring Saunier's partner to a room rented for her to deliver their baby. Francoise Bert claimed the brothers of her intimate partner "had threatened to kill her" and one had abused her physically in the street because she wanted to take legal action against her partner. Male kin and friends served as guarantors for young men imprisoned during a suit so that they could be released. Guichard Gras recruited his brother and sister to be the godparents of the baby he had out-of-wedlock with Catherine Bouvier.[59]

The range and texture of fraternal co-operation to produce workable remedies could be infinite. Having siblings willing and able to help was a big advantage for young couples facing the challenging situation of out-of-wedlock pregnancy, even if not every brother could be mobilized. Brothers featured as godparents, as companions providing moral support, as sources of practical help, as would be-enforcers, and no doubt as assistants in other ways. Andre Priou, for example, tried to find a new job for his girlfriend, Jeanne Mulatier, when she became pregnant, likely anticipating that her employer would ask her to leave or she would want leave. He and his brother visited another master silk worker to say that since Priou and Mulatier's own workshop had little business, a skilled female silk winder was available to work for him. The silk master replied that he absolutely could use another skilled female worker and they arranged for her to start work the next day.[60] The presence of Priou's brother for this visit suggests how fraternal support to sort out the situation could come in many forms.

No doubt young women also received many kinds of advice and assistance, but this is even more hidden in surviving records. One of Jeanne Mulatier's brothers had in fact introduced her to Priou. The couple went out together for a couple of years, presumably with her brothers' knowledge, and they discussed marriage. When Mulatier became pregnant and Priou resisted following through on his promise, she must have told her brothers. They looked for Andre Priou to tell him that he had to "settle the matter," pay the costs of the delivery, and take charge of the baby. (That is, they requested the arrangement that the court would also usually require.) They also spoke to his employer who told them that he had discussed the situation with Priou who had promised to pay for the delivery and take the baby if she did not go to court. Even though their attempts to sort out the matter for their sister came to naught, these kinds of endeavors no doubt did lead to private—but unrecorded—settlements in many other instances.[61]

The remedies and "remedies" that young intimate partners could draw on to manage out-of-wedlock pregnancies were varied and multi-sited, and they involved many people. Fertility remained an ongoing issue for negotiation and contention when it transpired that young partners would not marry even though the young woman was pregnant. Young women and young men believed they could interrupt reproduction and they sometimes tried to make that happen. Their efforts are an important part of the long history of abortion that demonstrate the inevitability of the desire to control reproduction and the dangers to women's reproductive health involved before safe legal abortions were possible. Widespread pragmatic attitudes existed even in the clergy and judiciary as well as among family, friends, and neighbors that focused on the safety and well-being of the young people—and the infants to be born—rather than on scapegoating, outcasting, or disciplining young women. Young men were still expected to take responsibility even if that took the form of extra-judicial settlements outside of marriage. The safeguarders who monitored young people's relationships at all stages continued to be involved to mitigate the negative impact of youthful intimacy in the out-of-wedlock pregnant stage. The success—or failure—of such strategies involved high stakes for both young partners, but higher for young women whose health and futures could be impacted.

Young intimate partners viewed the abortifacients they called "remedies" to interrupt reproduction as a commonplace practice in consensual intimate relationships. Collaboration, negotiation, and conflict about the use of "remedies" were part of young couples' struggles with untimely pregnancies. Men shared in (not always valid or reliable) contraceptive knowledge and practices. Historians have examined the availability of such remedies and their place in the medical lexicon of early modern vernacular and learned science and positioned midwives as key popular actors in a female world. Yet young single people's efforts to manage their fertility reveal that pragmatic grassroots practices were critical too. Knowledge about the use of "remedies" was widespread in working communities and was at least tacitly accepted among the broad ambiguities about the status of pregnancies and the wide acceptance of purging as the cure for many amorphous ills.

In all these many forms, young couples in stable relationships were supported in managing out-of-wedlock pregnancy. Pragmatic but well-known options existed to manage untimely reproduction that were broadly regarded as acceptable if not desirable. At least some local clergy and local legal actors were more inclined to emphasize pastoral care and pragmatic common-sense responses to single expectant parents than to engage in a moralizing discipline of extra-marital intimacy. Although the disciplinary commitment of the institutional leaders of reformed Catholicism might have been clear, local clergy and friars in particular viewed young people's relationship complications as predictable and manageable rather than as opportunities for prescriptive scapegoating that would mark them as illicit or sinful. They provided young men and women with another kind of intimate relationship built around the confidential discussions in confessions that involved a commitment to meditation as well as pastoral care. Local legal officials were likewise more concerned with mediation and support than discipline.[62] Friends, employers, kin, or clergy surely brokered many informal settlements as well as the ones recorded with notaries or in court.[63]

Communities developed practices and structures to limit the collateral damage in face of the commonplace event that young intimate relationships for whatever reason led to pregnancy but not marriage. Notaries and clergy were keepers of personal and family secrets, and their clients might have sought private arrangements both as matters of discretion and flexibility. These affairs were not secret in the sense that nobody knew, and indeed many people were involved in discussions about the intimacies of young people's reproduction, but they were secret in the sense that people who knew were sometimes willing not to say anything. This same dynamic of communal complicity continued to support young intimate partners around the delivery and care of newborns.

5

Intimate Labor

Paid Work and an Intimate Economy of Reproduction

In 1688, Claire Bariou initiated the chain of events in which many people in her neighborhood would mobilize to help her and her intimate partner, Jean Dumas, manage an untimely pregnancy. She first explained her predicament to a friar, Gaspard Charier, who had been her confessor for about eighteen months. She was the daughter of Antoine Bariou, a *juge des gabelles* (a minor state official), and Dumas was a silk worker. The two years of their courtship had the typical trajectory of young people's relationships. He visited her frequently and a neighbor often saw them "caress passionately." A servant saw them lying in front of the fire together one evening while her parents were asleep and often noticed them "courting." Claire recalled that Dumas promised to marry her, so they started to have intercourse and she became pregnant.[1] Although her parents must have known about their relationship, the couple anticipated that her father would oppose their marriage because of the difference in their ranks, a familiar obstacle to marriage, and chose a different path.

Claire's confessor first suggested she should tell her father but, when she demurred on the grounds that her father would be angry, he moved on to helping the couple make alternate arrangements. He consulted another female penitent to ask her if she knew a place Claire could go to have her baby. (He may of course have asked several women but the legal record identifies only the one whose advice he accepted.) Elizabeth de Beaulieu had given her confession to Charier for four years. A surgeon's widow who taught in one of Lyon's charity schools for the poor, she was so devout that people referred to her as "sister." Over the course of three weeks, Beaulieu provided key information and assistance. She introduced Charier to a local midwife, Catherine Bruyere, who agreed to rent a room to the couple. Subsequently, Beaulieu walked with Bariou about half a mile from where she lived with her parents to where Bruyere lived with her glover-maker husband. Bariou stayed for almost three months before and after the delivery of her daughter without telling her parents. In October, the friar ordered Beaulieu to escort Claire to a convent at the other end of the neighborhood, a mile or so from her parents' residence. Beaulieu and Bruyere also went to the wet-nurse's to pick up the baby who was later abandoned at the Hôtel-Dieu. Bruyere first claimed that she had taken the baby to a rural wet-nurse and later that Dumas had directed her to take the infant to the Hôtel-Dieu although he disputed this account.

Bariou's situation and location were well known to neighbors living in the same building, to other people on the street, and to people who knew her parents. Dumas visited regularly as she recuperated. The baby was baptized at the neighborhood parish church with Bruyere as godmother and a silk worker (presumably a friend of Dumas) as godfather. Bruyere took the baby to a nearby wet-nurse who sometimes brought the baby to visit her mother. Neighbors thought Dumas was variously the baby's father, as Claire told some, or a relative, as the midwife told others. Claire and the midwife told at least two people who knew her parents, a surgeon's wife, and a former servant of theirs about her pregnancy and delivery.

Bariou and Dumas, like other young couples, made use of an intimate economy of reproduction to manage their out-of-wedlock birth via paid services that were widely known, if largely elided from the historical record. Paid providers of intimate labor were integrated into safeguarding networks that included other hired helpers, like legal officials, and unpaid facilitators, like clergy and family, employers, and friends. Indeed, Charier provided pastoral care when he located pregnancy services for Bariou as his penitent by tapping into the local knowledge of his other female penitents. Only a dispute about payment for Bruyere's work pulled the events into the legal system and thus documented one instance in an economy that largely functioned unrecorded.[2] Undoubtedly, many other such out-of-wedlock births were handled without the creation of any written record except perhaps the baptism registration of the baby.

The record of the Bariou-Dumas relationship also combined routine actions in terms of men paying for their partners' costs and taking custody of the babies with unusually explicit discussion of the emotions of the couple and other participants in their out-of-wedlock circumstances. Bariou and Dumas continued to see each other frequently at the landlady's, so the decision not to marry had not ruptured their relationship. The confessor suggested that Claire was afraid to tell her father because he would be "angry" and indicated that her "unhappiness and despair" led the confessor to help her by tapping into local knowledge about available rented rooms. People who knew her parents suspected that they were "very upset" by her unexplained departure and so they did not convey news of her to the parents. Bariou *père* duly said he was "enraged" when he found out what had happened. The wet-nurse recalled Claire "asked her to take good care" of her daughter, a request with an implicit emotional register.

The issue of intimate labor around out-of-wedlock pregnancies intersects with topics that are often considered separately: gender and work, illegitimacy, emotions, community morality as well as sexuality, law, and state building. Out-of-wedlock births have variously been seen as sites of local conflict in which women were threats to each other or allies, and as matters of state and shame. Indeed, the stigmatization of illegitimacy, above all for mothers, has become a given. Meanwhile, women functioned within, between, and alongside many sectors of the economy including food provision and textile work in Lyon as in other cities. Care work has emerged as an important form of female labor. As Clyde Plumazille notes, much of the work women did was in "intermediary economic spaces where formal and informal economies and licit and illicit practices were imbricated."[3]

When Elizabeth de Beaulieu directed her confessor to Bruyere, she connected him with one of the many women who made their living, at least in part, through their work in a specialized niche of the economy devoted to the business of reproductive bodies. Women's narratives of their out-of-wedlock births were full of landladies who rented rooms short term where these women awaited the delivery of their babies, recovered, and went back to work. The landladies provided pre- and post-natal care. Midwives delivered babies. Almost without exception, babies born out of wedlock were immediately placed in the care of wet-nurses who did childcare as well as providing nutrition through breast milk. Landladies, midwives, and wet-nurses provided essential services for early modern working communities by assisting couples who faced out-of-wedlock pregnancy. For contemporaries, it was a well-known system that met many needs.

Female workers supported what were seen as appropriate strategies for young couples whose babies would be out-of-wedlock births. Reproduction was indeed a site of conflict and tension for intimate partners, their kin, and their communities, but those same people coordinated with care workers in the business of reproduction to manage unwed pregnancies as predictable events. The legal, economic, and cultural work of extra-marital reproduction was local and pragmatic. It allowed men and women to address the consequences of their intimacy outside of marriage while protecting the lives of infants. Rather than shaming young women, it safeguarded the reputations and futures of unmarried parents by offering a respectable option through which young men could meet their responsibilities and gave young women the chance to restart their lives. Couples who took this route could avoid the association with destitution involved in giving birth at the Hôtel-Dieu.

The use of specialized female intimate care workers for out-of-wedlock deliveries impacted expectant mothers differently than fathers. Young women might not necessarily have endured the shaming so often associated with single motherhood, but they moved residences and gave up their jobs while their male partners did not. Childbirth put women at risk of dying or experiencing severe physical consequences. If the use of rented rooms was regarded as licit in terms of community expectations and preserved the reputations of both partners, women often faced uncertainty about payment of their costs and the status of their relationships. At least until the mid-eighteenth century, women usually gave up custody of their newborns permanently as that practice freed them up to go back to work. Just as with the use of force in first intercourse and the use of "remedies" to interrupt reproduction, women experienced the power asymmetries at the heart of even consensual relationships when they were "put in a room" for the births of their babies instead of being married. For all the pragmatic ways in which reproduction as a business was effective for couples, communities, and care workers, the negotiations, movements, decision making, and uncertainties were filled with mixed and intense emotions.

"He Put Me in a Room": Landladies and Their Unmarried Boarders

Not yet married women's accounts of their out-of-wedlock reproductive experiences frequently featured landladies with whom they stayed briefly while they delivered their babies and recuperated before returning to their regular jobs and domestic situations. For the landladies, payment for their space and services was a key source of revenue. For the out-of-wedlock parents, the secured accommodations were essential for pre- and post-natal care. These services and their purveyors were well known in neighborhoods. Residents of early modern cities typically rented accommodation that they could and often did sublet to lodgers, using tenants to provide all or part of their earned income. However, some women (who might have been subletters themselves) specialized in short-term reproductive care work that allowed the common arrangements that young pregnant women framed as "he put me in a room" to function as a licit alternative to marriage.

Landladies routinely provided advice and assistance on reproductive issues, taking their part in community safeguarding and in the kind of informal mediation that notaries, friars, kin, and others also did. Anne Recorneau boarded with Claudine Berger, who often saw her walk out with Jean-Baptiste Favary. In due course, Berger took it upon herself to tell Favary that "he would have to help" Recorneau since she was pregnant by him, and she and Recorneau's mother met with Favary's employer to try to sort out a solution to the out-of-wedlock pregnancy that was acceptable to all parties. Marguerite Perroud, the widow of an *emballeur*, recalled in 1687 that Louise Chauvet, a Lyon *passementier*'s daughter, had rented a room from her for twenty-two months for 20 *sous* a month. She often saw Jean De Juif visit over a period of many months and saw them do what courting couples did. About two weeks before Chauvet moved out, Perroud noticed she was pregnant and "wanted to say something to her about it." Chauvet at first denied it but later the same day confirmed she was about four and a half months pregnant and De Juif was the father. Two or three days after Chauvet moved out, both came to Perroud's room where "they all agreed he was the father," and he promised he would never leave her and would marry her now if not for his parents' opposition, so they would have to wait. Another neighbor who saw them on the same visit told De Juif "he had only moved her because she was pregnant," and he replied he would take care of her and visit her at least once a day.[4] For Chauvet's landlady and their neighbor, the shifting from her usual accommodation to a temporary base under these circumstances was a routine move that they observed and participated in through directed commentary, perhaps offering suggestions about where such short-term rooms might be available.

Nevertheless, landladies who specialized in short-term reproductive care worked on different terms. While most domestic leases were for at least a year and payable every three or six months, the landladies of pregnant women and/or their intimate partners rented their space for short terms, payable by the week or month. No formal lease agreements seem to have been made, even in the notebook form common in working communities. The rent may have been higher than such accommodation would otherwise fetch. The motives of such landladies are elusive (male landlords did not seem to offer this type of accommodation). Perhaps they could not find long-term tenants, or they had come to specialize in this kind of essential community service work, or they found it more remunerative than their other options—or some combination of the three.

Landladies working in the intimate economy of reproduction were usually widows or at least had absent husbands, and they were rarely identified as such in terms of occupational description. They were occasionally also midwives, but usually different women provided these indispensable services. Rather, they were identified as "hosts" of inns, as washerwomen, or as not having a particular occupation. For instance, Anne Recorneau, a seamstress, rented rooms from two different widows whose occupations were identified as "seamstress" and "silk-seller" in the legal record. Occasionally, the women themselves described what they did as taking in "boarders" even when that term was not applied as an occupational tag. Gabrielle Chou described the lodging and food she provided for Louise Charmeton as "the profession she followed," that is, she identified her work as that of a landlady in the specialized reproductive care niche.[5]

These landladies were actively involved in the reproductive well-being of their short-term tenants and performed a variety of tasks beyond providing shelter and often discretion. They brought in midwives for deliveries. They sometimes provided food. They or their children often agreed to be godparents. They likely provided some newborn care. They hired wet-nurses and sometimes took babies to them. They must have cooperated with the babies' fathers, who almost always were the ones who paid and visited, whether regularly or irregularly. In 1689, for example, a notary, M. Saunier, "put" Jacqueline Faure "with Madame Gayet, a midwife" and agreed to pay her 24 *livres* a month until the baby was born. After the baby's birth, Gayet took her to "a certain woman" (presumably a wet-nurse) before the baby was even baptized, while Faure stayed at Gayet's to recover for at least two weeks.[6]

Discretion was often key in landladies' success with the rented room option for handling out-of-wedlock pregnancies. Francoise Perne recalled that the woman who rented a room to her and her partner, Claude Guerin (a notary's clerk), "thought they were husband and wife" and claimed he had used "false titles" (presumably referring to her as his spouse) to establish this marital frame. It is difficult to imagine, however, that the landlady-washerwoman who took their money did not have some suspicion about the reality of the situation. Likewise, when Louis Deroche rented a room for Claudine Mignot, the landlady agreed on the condition nothing "indecent" should happen.

Deroche gave his assurances, but nonetheless arrived the next day with his pregnant companion, who soon after gave birth. The landlady agreed that her eleven-year-old daughter could serve as the godmother for the baby.[7] The landlady apparently did not consider anything "indecent" in all of that and was paid for her work in handling the out-of-wedlock pregnancy.

For women and their community, men assumed paternal responsibility when they "put" them in rooms as an alternative to marriage. The verb "put" to describe the dynamic of the move is elliptical in terms of negotiation and decision making. It may have been a rhetorical strategy that distanced women from the planning when they explained the situation to court officials. It may perhaps indicate a less than consensual dynamic in cases when the about-to-be father insisted on not marrying and the woman would usually have preferred marriage. This passive phrasing parallels women's use of passive voice in retelling of their initial experiences of intercourse. It may also have served as a widely understood boilerplate shorthand for a particular set of routine arrangements between unmarried couples in such situations. The phrase may have encompassed all of these meanings. Certainly, male partners usually played a key role in facilitating the arrangements by paying and sometimes by finding the room.

Pregnancy not followed by marriage merited strategies to protect young men's as well as women's reputation when they seemed like feasible marriage partners, and temporary housing in rented apartments served several purposes for single mothers and the babies' fathers. Family, friends, neighbors, and co-workers regarded this option as acceptable and—if not as respectable as marriage—far better than men abandoning their partners completely. This path allowed women (and the men involved) to return to their usual work and even domestic situation with their reputations largely intact. Some couples, such as Bariou and Dumas, seem to have collaborated to choose a mutually agreed on strategy. Benoiste Blanc's employer and a neighbor in the same building saw Blanc talking to Pierre Frillat outside their windows one Sunday evening. The next day Blanc asked her employer for permission to leave. She and Frillat headed south and chatted casually with a married couple they met when both couples stopped for refreshments. Frillat told the couple that they had rented a room for a month and even how much they paid for it. For the observers of these events, the Sunday talk, the request the following day to leave a job, and the journey to a rented short-term room all indicated that the couple had made a plan they viewed as routine.[8]

For couples who felt they could not yet marry, for whatever reason, the nearby rooms offered a discreet, even respectable, well-known way to handle the situation. Jean De Juif freely told many acquaintances who noticed that Louise Chauvet was pregnant that he was the father of her baby, intended to support her, and would marry her when he had inherited money to buy a shop of his own. Indeed, far from hiding it, they continued to walk out together publicly. Yet he also told one female acquaintance that he was "unhappy she was still living on *rue de bois* [her original residence] as it was prejudicial to him because of her pregnancy." Thus for the sake of both of their reputations, she moved to a short-term room. Co-workers Aymee Joannin and Jean Renaud had taken all the usual steps toward marriage in the two years of their relationship when she became pregnant. When she told him, he said he could not marry her yet but that she "had nothing to fear because he would marry her." He put her in a room where she had the baby, who went two days later to a wet-nurse. Joannin explained that she "very much wanted to hide knowledge of her delivery from the public, hoping that he wouldn't fail to marry her after all his promises."[9] Even if the couple eventually broke up, this strategy likely helped keep alive the prospect of future marriages.

Employer-employee intimate relationships, always frowned on, gave the expectant fathers clear motive to gloss over resulting pregnancies. Andree Ganot explained that she had her baby, whose father was her employer Sieur Mazard, in a short-term rented room because she was "ashamed to be pregnant in front of the neighbors." Florie Solore returned to work for Richard Du Colombe (and had another baby with him two years later). Married gardener Jean Bourdillion took Marie Crespu, who worked for him, to stay with his cousin who lived about a six-hour horse ride outside of Lyon. Marie's father, another gardener, felt that Bourdillion had taken her so far away "to try to cover his crime." Bourdillion denied any crime because he claimed that Marie consented and he told his cousin he was the father, but he told the court he had sent her away for a month "to avoid dishonor on both their parts."[10] Antoine Reydellet, a silk worker, was not married but arranged for Aymee Orsee, who worked for him, to stay with the wife of another of worker. Although he denied he was the father and claimed he did so to help her, the court was skeptical and asked if his real intention had been to hide her pregnancy from her kin. He admitted he had given her kin a false address for her whereabouts so they would not find her, but claimed that was her idea.[11] Whatever the truth of their relationship (where the indisputable facts were that he employed her, he paid for a room for her to have the baby, and he had given her siblings a false address), they both had some investment in concealing her situation because they could not marry. These kinds of relationships were inherently shameful, unlike those between two young workers, as employers were often married men or the employer and employee were of unequal rank. In these cases, both partners violated the community consensus about licit relations.

Couples did not necessarily agree on not marrying or on resolving the situation by the expediency of renting a room for a delivery that would be conveniently (if locally) out of sight, even if such disagreements are often absent from surviving records. Marguerite Granger and Francois Berne had a long-term relationship that both accepted had all the usual qualities of moving toward marriage, and she had even had him sign a written promise that he would marry her. However, when she told him she was pregnant, he declined to keep that promise. They both agreed that he offered to put her in a room with a midwife who lived about ten miles south of Lyon, promising to pay all the costs and take charge of the baby. He said she had gone there and then changed her mind (persuaded he claimed by other people), but she asserted that she did not like the plan. The tension between them produced a written record only when she came to court to file a complaint. She deposited his written promise to marry as proof of his express commitment and got a court order to have him imprisoned while the legal investigation took place. Many other couples no doubt also argued about how to proceed before the rented room plan was acted on.

The trajectories in these relationships varied. Some couples seemed to have initially agreed on one plan until some other problem caused a rupture. Henriette Gabet, for instance, had her first baby with Francois Benoist, a shoemaker; when she became pregnant after the usual promises of marriage, he claimed that he did want to marry her but his father would not give permission. He put her in a rented room and covered the costs for her care and for the baby to be dispatched to a wet-nurse. They resumed their relationship and had a second baby, which he also "had her deliver" in a rented room, and again the baby was sent to a wet-nurse. Only when he ceased to pay the wet-nurse, leaving Gabet to pay, did she appeal to the court to secure financial support from him.[12]

Young couples usually made decisions about using the temporary rented room solution in consultation with other people. Anne Allary's mother acknowledged that she had suggested to her daughter's partner, Jonot Laval, that he put her in a rented room for the delivery. Allary and Laval both worked for a *maître tireur d'or* and lived on his premises, so they moved her away for the delivery. Allary's mother did not explain in court why she had pushed Laval in this direction. For some reason, all parties seemed to assume that marriage was not an option since she said Laval had "misused" her daughter to get her pregnant; however, he agreed he was the father and would assume all costs.[13]

The lived experiences of young women in Lyon—who gave birth in these rented rooms with their intimate partners as the financial supporters, visitors, and the ones ready to take custody of the children— demonstrate that routine alternatives to shame and secrecy for unmarried mothers did exist. Couples themselves told a variety of people, if not everyone they knew, what they were doing; visitors came and went, and neighbors observed the goings-on. A seventeenth-century royal midwife, Louise Bourgeois, warned her midwife daughter never to have women deliver in their homes, even if they asked, because of the association with prostitution but to be sure to deliver them in respectable homes.[14] So the working cooperation between landladies and midwives served their reputations as well as those of their clients, neighbors, and visitors.

Care Work: Midwives and Wet-Nurses

Along with landladies, midwives and wet-nurses provided vital intimate labor. For the wet-nurses and midwives who made a living through the work of reproduction, discretion was an attribute just as it was for landladies and notaries. They sometimes facilitated informal out-of-court solutions as well as providing essential reproductive services for women, both married and unmarried. Most midwives who delivered out-of-wedlock babies lived in the city while wet-nurses usually lived in the rural parishes around Lyon, but they were all part of the business of reproduction network.

From the middle of the sixteenth century, regulation of midwives increased although, as with many early modern new legal requirements, these rules were seldom honored. Treatises by male doctors and other specialists were filled with criticisms of the ignorance and incompetence of midwives. In part in response to such critiques, Lyon and many other communities followed Paris and began to appoint licensed midwives who had demonstrated some basic knowledge and were often paid a yearly fee by the community for their services.[15]

Women who worked as midwives in Lyon were sometimes registered officially by the municipality and sometimes worked outside that licensing structure. The legal actions single women brought against their intimate partners routinely included claims for the costs of delivery, clearly identifying the activities of midwives as paid work. Their work was described in different ways in legal records. Anne Caneu, for example, who delivered both babies for Gabet and Benoist was the wife of a master *patissier* who "made her profession as a midwife." Jeanne Julien was not identified by the court as a midwife but her actions indicated her work when she offered to deliver the baby after learning that her neighbor's daughter was pregnant. Midwives who did work for the courts were identified in that context as "city midwife" (*matronne de la ville*), and they presumably had been examined to ascertain their competency and might have been paid a yearly fee by the city for their work as was the case elsewhere.[16]

Like landladies, midwives kept their own counsel about their work when they felt the situation required it. Midwives usually did not house the women they delivered, and this probably worked to the advantage of both landladies and midwives. Catherine Brosset gave birth in a room rented short term by her intimate partner and recalled that she did not know the name of her midwife because she had delivered the baby without talking to her. Bruyere explained that she did not know Claire Bariou's last name until she asked Bariou's confessor for payment some time after the baby was born, because Dumas had told her only that she would be well paid for her work because Claire came from a good family.[17]

On some occasions, midwives—like other community safeguarders—dispensed criticism, advice, and other forms of assistance along with their core work, and they focused on men's failure to meet their responsibilities rather than on sexual immorality. Anne Caneu criticized Francois Benoist for delaying too long in calling her to assist his partner with the birth of their second child. She noted that the neighbors were chagrined and he would incur the wrath of God for letting her suffer. Benoist responded defensively, if indirectly, about his role, saying he would send the baby to live with his mother where it would want for nothing. Magdelaine Fontanel and the surgeon Charles Rey had a contentious conclusion to their relationship in 1687 when she found herself pregnant after, she claimed, several months of keeping company with Rey and his promises to marry her. They had extensive negotiations in and out of court. What lay behind all this is impossible to know for certain. Rey claimed her allegations of paternity and false promises of marriage were "prejudicial to him as a married man with children and even a public man." Her withdrawal of the legal claim in favor of a private settlement could have provided a public restoration of his reputation. Rey likely agreed to pay her and take custody of the baby in return for her dropping the lawsuit. However, when he did not meet his responsibility after she gave birth, Fontanel's midwife "named Lamotte" and "some other women" went with her to his boutique in one of Lyon's public squares and left the baby boy there, literally charging the surgeon with responsibility for the baby. Her midwife and other women were seemingly outraged enough that he had misled her twice to think the only solution was literally to leave the baby with him. Their actions might signal a wider customary practice because by 1705 the Grenoble Parlement (not far from Lyon) allowed new mothers to get legal permission to leave their unsupported babies on the babies' fathers' doorsteps.[18]

The wet-nurses who provided the paid infant childcare without which the entire out-of-wedlock economy of intimate reproduction would have foundered usually lived in rural parishes outside the city. The hiring of wet-nurses in no way singled out unmarried parents as married couples routinely employed wet-nurses across early modern Europe, and the practice was very widespread in Lyon. Yet little is known about these workers except in prescriptive and demographic terms. Archival research on early modern England has rebutted the traditional framings of Voltaire and other eighteenth-century critics, refurbished by family historians like Lawrence Stone, that the practice involved alleged parental indifference and neglectful wet-nurses.[19] Nevertheless, although many parents who sent babies to be wet-nursed never again saw their infants due to high infant mortality, wet-nurses who took babies born out-of-wedlock were charged with infants who were permanently in the custody of their fathers and whose mothers usually did not see them again even if the babies survived.

The wet-nurses who accepted babies born out-of-wedlock are an even more elusive group than their peers who nursed legitimate babies or foundlings because their work generated little in the way of records. When parents were married, even those of very modest rank, fathers sometimes recorded family histories, including details of their children's births, baptisms, and financial arrangements with wet-nurses. In mid-seventeenth-century Lyon, for example, Claude Page recorded that he and Catherine Hedelin sent every other one (four in total) of their nine babies to wet-nurses while she nursed the other five at home "with the help of

God." A century later, the Lyon parasol seller, Jacques Bertin, similarly recorded the details of his children with Marie Delaurys.[20] The men noted the agreed on per month payments and Bertin also noted the arrears. However, out-of-wedlock babies were not written into the family histories, and their wet-nursing arrangements generated little in the way of records, making the evidence of the backstories recorded in paternity suits especially significant.

Clearly, wet-nurses who provided outsourced childcare for babies saw their activity as paid work. Guichard Gras, for example, admitted to the court that his daughter with his co-worker Catherine Bouvier had been sent immediately after baptism to a wet-nurse where she stayed for three months, but when he did not pay the wet-nurse, she turned the baby over to the Hôtel-Dieu. Decades later, a baby's admission certificate at the Hôtel-Dieu explained that a wet-nurse, who had agreed to take in the baby of a widow whose young partner still insisted he wanted to marry her, had come to Lyon to seek payment after the father defaulted but could not even find the mother. So she left the baby as a foundling.[21] In fact, private extra-legal arrangements that later foundered when the wet-nurse was not paid were one of the ruptures that could lead to lawsuits, as when Bruyere's desire to be compensated led her to ask Bariou's father to pay. Wet-nurses emphasized the primacy of payment whether their charges were legitimate or out-of-wedlock babies. Surviving letters show that wet-nurses communicated with the parents of their charges as employees, asking for more supplies to do their job (such as clothes for the children or extra money for grain) and payment for their labor.[22]

By the second half of the eighteenth-century, rural wet-nurses solicited for city customers in Lyon's new weekly newspaper. Newspapers full of classified advertisements, like Lyon's, appeared across France. Purveyors of breast milk trumpeted its commodity qualities: the general good health of its source, the young age of the wet-nurse, and the death of her original baby. A would-be wet-nurse offered "milk that was two and a half months old, her baby has just died, she is in the best health," and a twenty-four-year-old woman advertised for a nursling with the pitch that her baby was dead and her milk was only two months old.[23] Embedded in such sales pitches was the reality that the work of wet-nursing was intertwined with the emotional labor of neonatal deaths.

Like midwives and landladies, wet-nurses of out-of-wedlock babies probably asked few questions of prospective customers beyond payment.

Wet-nurses' occasional legal testimony evinced little interest about the personal situations of their employers. The wet-nurse of the Bariou-Dumas baby claimed that she agreed to take her without knowing who the parents were and, even though she several times took the baby to Bruyere's where she saw a woman who claimed to be the baby's mother, she did not know her name. Jeanne Grange, the wife of a peasant who lived in a village outside Lyon, recalled how she was initially hired. A surgeon came to their residence and asked her husband to go with him to talk to the father of a woman. The next day, her husband came back with a baby for her to wet-nurse. A week later the baby's father arrived to say he wanted the child to go to the Hôtel-Dieu, and Grange went with him to deliver the baby there.[24]

Space and Silences: The Geography and Politics of an Intimate Economy of Reproduction

Multiple spaces and many people's silences shaped the participation of partners, landladies, midwives, and wet-nurses in the intimate economy of reproduction. Young people did not hide their pregnancies, so many people knew about them and they were not secrets. Communities clearly saw the provision of financial support, safe spaces for delivery and recovery, and clear plans for the baby as the responsible and expected solution to out-of-wedlock pregnancies when couples did not marry. Female workers' paid intimate labor made these strategies possible. Most moves to rooms were local, barely out of the immediate neighborhood, and many observers and reproductive economy workers were careful about whom they talked to.

The Bariou-Dumas episode, for example, played out through several locations in the same vicinity as Bariou moved around her neighborhood through the course of her out-of-wedlock pregnancy. Lyon's *presqu'ile* was a rapidly growing, densely populated peninsula between the Rhône and Saône rivers, with the established old city neighborhood across one river, growing exurbs across another, and the slopes of the not yet densely developed Croix Rousse neighborhood to the north. Many silk workers and other skilled or unskilled workers in endless variety lived and worked in the neighborhood's multi-story tenement buildings that were typical of many cities. Bariou and her family lived on a corner of Place Bellecour, a large public space that marked the southern edge of a densely populated area but not yet the grand square it became early in the eighteenth century. She visited Charier for confession at his church a few hundred yards away. The schoolteacher, Beaulieu, lived about the same distance on the other side of the church. The landlady/midwife, Bruyere, lived on a street that Beaulieu might well have taken to walk to confession or to her charity school that was near the cathedral in the old city. When Beaulieu took Bariou from her landlady's to the convent, they walked a little farther north past her street to the slopes of the Croix Rousse. There Bariou stayed at one of several convents on the hill. Meanwhile her baby daughter moved the other way, first a few blocks away to be baptized at the local parish church of St. Nizier, then to the home of her wet-nurse, who lived around the corner from the midwife, and finally back to the Place Bellecour square where she was conceived, this time to be charged to the care of the Hôtel-Dieu.

All of these locations were within about a square mile. The peninsula was perhaps half a mile across and the distance between Bariou's family home on Place Bellecour and the convent was little more than a mile. Claire and Dumas had lived, walked, and worked in those streets for their entire lives, and her parents were also well known there. In the five months between the time Claire left home and her father filed the court case against Dumas, she lived among people who knew the couple and her parents. Her baby was born, baptized, wet-nursed, and abandoned in the same very familiar urban space where many people were well aware that she had given birth, even people who testified in court that they knew Claire's parents—and as presumably many others did too.

The geography of rooms rented short term for the purpose of out-of-wedlock deliveries varied: some were in the middle of the city's densely populated parishes, and some were well out of town. Marie Crespu's father said she had gone "to the mountains." It may be that the out-of-town strategy was more common than it appears since it was even less likely to generate any record. Louise Charron, for example, was a servant who took a boat down the river to St. Colombe, about twenty miles south of Lyon, where she asked someone to help her get in touch with a midwife there whom she knew "by reputation." She said she did not want to give birth at the Hôtel-Dieu, where the situation would be more public, and "decided to come to St. Colombe to keep it secret."[25] Such fragmentary evidence suggests that local knowledge networks about female intimate labor providers covered wider regions than the immediate city.

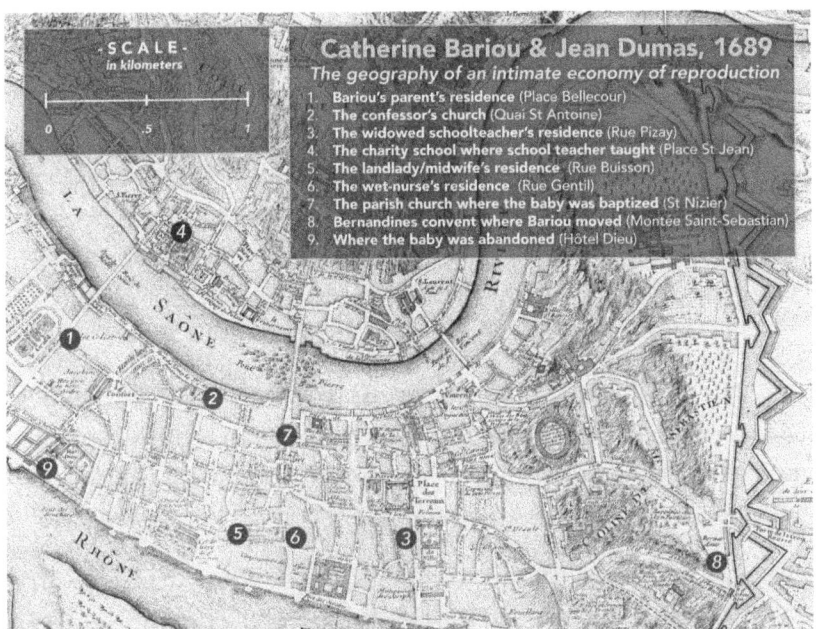

Map of Old Regime Lyon with details of the Bariou itinerary. Map by Benjamin Breen based on Plan de Lion. Ancienne colonie des Romains qui étoit sous leur Empire une des plus celeb. Ville des Gaules; Elle est a present la Seconde Ville du Royaume de France Capitale du Lionnois, Forest, et Beaujolois. Il y a un Archevêché, qui a quatre Evêchez suffragans, Mâcon, Châlon sur Saone, Langres et Autun / Dessiné sur les Lieux par le Sr. Delamonce Architecte; et gravé par C. Inselin. 1750. Wikimedia Commons.

However, rooms rented for this purpose were more typically close to where a couple usually lived as matters of practicality and propriety. A short, easily walkable distance from the regular domiciles of the couples would be a more manageable journey for a pregnant woman and would permit the intimate partner and perhaps other friends to visit easily. Pierre Dolin and Jeanne Volet, for instance, lived together for six months on a street in the center of the city before he moved her to a room a little over a mile away to the northern edge of the old town when she was pregnant.[26] Catherine Bouvier and Guichard Gras had been living at their employer's in the city center, and the room he arranged was on a street on the south side of the old town.

The short distance from the usual lodgings also marked the respectable option for young men who were not going to marry their intimate partners and was a discreet, if far from secret, way for women to wait for the births of their babies and recover. It enabled participants and bystanders to claim a cloak of anonymity. In the Bariou-Dumas episode, for instance, the friar asserted that he did suggest that Claire tell her parents, but as he did not know her parents' names, he could not tell them himself, and he also claimed not to know Dumas. The schoolteacher also said she did not know Claire's name or the name of her parents. The monk, the teacher, and the wet-nurse all said they did not know anything about the baby's abandonment at the Hôtel-Dieu. In the midwife's own building, which had many units, numerous people had observed the events, even just counting those who later testified in the paternity suit. The midwife told a former servant of the Bariou household that she had delivered the baby. A bookseller whose wife was the midwife's sister-in-law knew Claire had had the baby there. Claire told him Dumas was the father, and he saw that Dumas visited her. The same bookseller also knew the baby had been baptized with a silk worker he did not know as godfather and the midwife as godmother. A widow saw Claire move in, knew she had delivered the baby and that the baby had gone to a wetnurse, and saw Dumas visit her almost daily, although Claire told her he was her brother. A silk worker's wife likewise had seen Dumas and Claire there, and the midwife told her Claire was from the country and Dumas was a relative of hers. A surgeon's wife saw Claire at the midwife's on the eve of delivery when the midwife and another women she did not know asked her to keep it a secret to avoid bringing "bad luck and loss" to Claire. She knew Claire's parents and thought of telling them, but decided not to say anything because she knew they were upset about their daughter's disappearance.

This public knowledge of a personal matter was another form of safeguarding the intimacy of emerging adults and was one component of communal complicity about out-of-wedlock reproduction. Just as the urban spaces of Lyon structured licit intimacy for young couples, the same density that provided oversight of courtship also provided oversight of extra-marital pregnancies and births. The work of landladies, midwives, and wet-nurses in the intimate economy required some discretion about the situations. Their reticence may have been rooted in community preferences for handling such practices in these ways, and indeed, midwives swore not to reveal family secrets as part of the oaths they took when they were licensed.[27] However, their ability to maintain such superficial acquaintance was embedded in the consent of their neighbors who could easily have told but did not. The many adults who participated in these networks as active participants or observers guaranteed the safe management of the birth and newborn period for young couples.

Intimate Labor and the Law

The business of reproduction meant multiple roles for midwives beyond delivering babies in and out of wedlock. A few of them served as gatekeepers of access to the legal system. They occasionally worked with the state as medico-legal expert witnesses in criminal cases and routinely prepared expert reports for paternity suits. As medical experts in court, they would certify—or not—women's allegations that they were pregnant, a confirmation that was necessary for any paternity suit before evidence could be gathered from witnesses. Yet uncertainties about the requirements of the 1556 Edict also shaded the work of all purveyors of pregnancy and newborn care services. The persistent myths and confusion about the idea that the edict introduced a requirement to declare pregnancies also developed around the role of midwives, and some local efforts were taken to regulate midwives' roles in delivering babies of single women.

When the court quizzed Claire Bariou's landlady/midwife about events, the official asked "if she didn't know it was forbidden on pain of exemplary punishment" to deliver women without knowing who they were. She claimed she did not.[28] This was no surprise because no such law existed. What the judge's question highlighted was the persistent fiction that midwives were required to play a role in policing single female sexuality by the terms of the 1556 Edict. Like the issue of declarations, this myth confused Old Regime subjects and more recent historians. Louis-Sébastian Mercier's book about Paris in the 1780s discussed midwives and the 1556 Edict where he claimed that Parisian midwives delivered women without asking their name or status. Even though they were not required to, no doubt like their Lyonnais peers they sometimes delivered babies without asking too many questions. Modern historians have also linked midwives to the 1556 Edict and a state policing of female sexuality.[29] However, in fact the edict did not mention midwives and nor did the subsequent reissuings include any legal requirement for midwives.

In some cities, by the eighteenth century, municipal officials began to pass local regulations that sought to locate landlords, midwives, and other tenants as key actors in the management of out-of-wedlock pregnancy. In Brest, in

1735, a municipal official (*lieutenant de police*), for example, required "the owners and tenants in buildings where unmarried girls and women live who they discover to be pregnant as well as the midwives who would deliver them must make declarations about it and are forbidden . . . to make the said declarations to anyone other than us on threat of a fine of 20 *livres*." Similar municipal requirements were established in St. Malo although municipal administrators there repeatedly lamented that they were ignored: they noted that midwives did not declare out-of-wedlock deliveries and sometimes arranged for babies to be abandoned while individuals continued to rent rooms for the explicit purpose of out-of-wedlock deliveries. In Lyon, a requirement was established in 1704 (well after the Bariou pregnancy) that anyone who delivered a single woman had to register the delivery, but the Paris Parlement annulled it in 1712, saying it went well beyond what the 1556 Edict intended.[30]

Enforcement of all such local requirements for declarations was at best patchy, likely occasional, and perhaps non-existent to all intents and purposes in Lyon and elsewhere.[31] A 1758 letter to Didier Landry, the head of the Lyon's corporation of surgeons, complained about a surgeon who harbored and delivered a pregnant single woman in his home. Although Landry said he could not intervene because it was a "police matter," he observed that "every town has rules about the subject of pregnant girls which surgeons must observe or be reprimanded by the judges charged with overseeing such abuses."[32] He noted that the surgeon who sheltered and delivered single pregnant girls had obviously not taken "the required precautions" without saying what they were. Landry added that the professional group had no jurisdiction, but local officials did not seem at all inclined to enforce the regulations either.

In Lyon, even if court officials visited, they seemed fine with the arrangements as long as the babies were safe, and no evidence indicates that anyone was charged or fined. Two mid-seventeenth-century reports (*procès-verbaux*) survive of officials who visited landladies and their female boarders and in both cases the officials seemed intent only on verifying the safety of the baby (that is, that no infanticide had occurred or might be about to recur). On both occasions, officials said they "had heard" a pregnant woman was staying with a landlady (one married and with her husband also present). They reprimanded the landladies for having women stay without their permission, but the landladies said they did not know they were supposed to get permission. The officials asked who the fathers were, told the women and landladies to ensure the safety of the babies, and left with no further action beyond recording reports.[33] The emphasis here, as with notaries and clergy, seemed to be on pastoral care—for the babies in this case—and not on disciplining the expectant single mothers or their landladies.

Licensed midwives worked regularly for the local legal system as official legal medical experts in court-ordered inspections of the reproductive status of unmarried women who chose to make legal claims to determine whether they were in fact pregnant. Early modern courts relied on experts of many kinds, and midwives occasionally worked alongside doctors and surgeons as legal medical experts in criminal cases.[34] Much more often, however, they were employed to make the expert visits that were the basis for official *rapports* to the court that were essential first elements of the legal actions as proof of the legitimacy of a woman's assertion that she was pregnant. They were identified in these reports as a "city midwife" or midwife of the Hôtel-Dieu.[35]

Midwives had prominent diagnostic and bureaucratic roles in the evidentiary visits. Occasionally surgeons alone or midwives alone made these reports, but the reports often noted that both had visited, which the regulations in fact required. When Francoise Roland went to court in 1687, for instance, a midwife named "the widow Roux" visited her at home the next day with a surgeon. They observed that she was twenty-seven, "small size with brown hair, pale face, hard breasts, and a big stomach which assure us that she is four and a half months pregnant." Both the surgeon and Roux signed the report. The next year the midwife Francoise Zacharie accompanied a surgeon to visit Elizabeth Charavay. The report described her size and hair color as well as "hard and big breasts, hard and taut (*tendu*) stomach and we felt the movement of a baby." They estimated she was eight months pregnant. The surgeon signed the report but Zacharie did not.[36] The reports were usually brief, less than a page as the medico-legal experts recorded specific observations that identified the women by physical description and gave medical information considered to be key indicators of reproductive status, such as the state of the breasts and stomach. Women who brought paternity suits had to endure these examinations of their breasts and stomachs in what must have been an embarrassing and perhaps uncomfortable consequence of their decision to go to court.

Pregnancies were in fact notoriously difficult to identify with certainty, a problem that filled many a medical text, and the value of midwives' expertise with women's reproductive bodies was acknowledged in their role alongside surgeons in verifying pregnancies as the essential first step in paternity suits. Occasionally, the visits led to ambivalent reports, saying the pregnancy could not be diagnosed for certain yet and/or might be something else like a false conception (*mole*). Very rarely, the visit led to a report that the woman was not in fact pregnant. A surgeon declined to confirm Marie Pitra's claim that she was about three months pregnant in 1742, for example, on the grounds that her three missed periods were not proof of pregnancy because "the flow or lack of flow of such discharges only determined pregnancy after the fourth month."[37]

The format for the reports was laid out in the 1670 criminal ordinance and reiterated in numerous guides for writing surgical reports published between 1684 and 1764. All of these guides stated that midwives should be present at the examination of women's reproductive bodies, and that a surgeon or physician should oversee them and make a separate report. Clearly these procedures were not always followed. Moreover, the surgical corporation of Lyon did not seem to control who the midwives working as medico-legal experts were. Rather, the midwives seem to have been appointed by the judges on an ad hoc basis, as happened with surgeons who testified in rural areas outside the control of surgical corporations.[38]

From 1723 on, female plaintiffs more often explicitly requested a report by a midwife in their initial petitions, and court clerks more often noted in writing that such permission had been given—in both cases alongside the traditional recording of requests and permissions that the plaintiffs be given permission to depose witnesses. This shift might have been a change in reporting rather than a change in practice, or it might have been related to a 1723 law that clarified the role of surgeons as experts and the supervision of surgeons' corporations as a whole. Either way, the reports for post-1723 made explicit that midwives often—perhaps usually—did the visits and reports on their own. In 1724, for instance, Magdelaine Phillipe asked the court for permission to proceed in a complaint against Louis Pretement and to assign a midwife to make a report about her pregnancy. The court appointed Justine Motton, who duly reported that her visit confirmed the pregnancy. Pretement challenged her report and asked for a surgeon to visit. Such a challenge was very unusual but it indicated that midwives usually visited and made reports without an accompanying or supervising surgeon.[39]

Justine Motton, the midwife whose authority was challenged, was the most commonly appointed medical expert in paternity suits at the time, according to extant records. The name of the medical expert was not recorded consistently even after 1723, and the full documents, including medical reports, from many lawsuits do not survive. Motton, however, served as the named expert in at least 80 suits between 1724 and 1731. She was identified as a midwife for the Hôtel-Dieu and may have specialized in cases where women had or would have some contact with the hospital by virtue of either delivering there or charging their babies to the institution. On three occasions she was referred to as "sister," suggesting she may in fact have been a nun as were many of the care workers at the Hôtel-Dieu.[40] Motton's extant reports were usually brief statements certifying that she "recognized" that the plaintiff was pregnant and estimated how many months the pregnancy had advanced.

Midwives had active bureaucratic as well as medical roles in drafting and delivering the expert reports as well as examining the female plaintiffs. Courts relied on midwives along with surgeons and sometimes midwives alone to write and transport the reports, despite the regulation requiring surgeons to accompany midwives on these visits. After the midwife named as "the widow Roux" left the court-ordered examination of the plaintiff's body, she alone walked to the *greffe* (depositary of legal records for the courts) where the clerk noted he had "accepted the delivery of Roux's report which she has sworn to be true and signed." A petition in 1686 included a specific request that "a midwife who it pleases the court to choose will visit," along with the ubiquitous request for permission to proceed to collect depositions. The court clerk subsequently noted permission to proceed with the depositions and "to have made a report by the surgeon and the [blank—filled in later as "named Gayet"] midwife [and] she will come to confirm the report." [Presumably she would deposit it at the *greffe*]. This petition provides an unusually clear articulation of a practice that was often murky in the reports. In this exchange, the plaintiff (or her lawyer) and the court clerk expected that a midwife could be an investigator <u>and</u> recorder of the legal medical report. Occasionally the receiving official at the *greffe* noted that the midwife had affirmed the truth of the report, a likely indication that the midwife delivered it and sworn to its veracity while the surgeon went on to do something else.[41]

Moreover, as court appointed medico-legal experts who produced reports, midwives were paid when they submitted the reports to the *greffe*. The standard fee was three *livres*.[42] As with other essential services workers provided in the intimate economy of reproduction, this work was a way of making a living. It could supplement income from deliveries of babies and perhaps from providing other kinds of women's health services.

The courts did not find fault with the midwives, landladies, or wet-nurses who worked in the out-of-wedlock pregnancy marketplace. Their services were embedded in the need to make a living and the demand for reproductive services that safeguarded young partners' futures. The court, for example, accepted the focus of Claire's father on Dumas, the boyfriend, when he brought a legal action. The midwife was briefly held in prison, but not because of her involvement with the out-of-wedlock pregnancy. She quickly appealed, claiming Bariou *père* was annoyed that she had requested payment of 200 *livres* she was owed so he made a false charge against her. She was released. The court made no effort to pursue prosecution against any of the other participants. In this instance as in others, the courts accepted intimate labor, even when it involved out-of-wedlock births, as legitimate. The focus of discipline was firmly on expectant single fathers if they seemed to be trying to evade taking responsibility for the consequences of their sexual activity.

Perhaps the clearest indication of the legality of intimate labor in this sector is an absence. Courts demonstrated virtually no interest in the activities of these reproductive care workers and rarely even called them as witnesses. Even when landladies, midwives, or wet-nurses were questioned, the court's occasional questions about if they knew they were required to provide notification seemed to be asked as a matter of information rather than as a precursor to action against them. Indeed, they worked without any evidence of harassment from authorities. Instead, some midwives were licensed and served as legal gatekeepers whose confirmation of pregnancies allowed unmarried women to access the legal system where they could pressure men to take responsibility.

Over the second half of the eighteenth century, the business of verifying the paternity claims of female plaintiffs based in their pregnancy shifted away from midwife participation and toward the exclusive domain of surgeons and doctors. Not only were midwives shut out of earning money for this work but they were also denied the performance of expertise and authority that had accrued to those working as medico-legal experts.[43] Their exclusion was part of the official sidelining of midwives as male doctors claimed a monopoly of professional authority in reproductive matters. No doubt some midwives continued to practice in their communities even as they lost their recognition as legal experts and the accompanying revenue stream.

Crying and Caring: Emotional Labor and the Business of Reproduction

In June 1686, Anne Allary cried as her intimate partner, Janot Laval, and her mother, Claudine Chenu, discussed their future. He said she was a "good girl" (*honnete fille*) and he would never abandon her. Chenu suggested he put her daughter in a room and of course pay for all her expenses, as well as take charge of the baby, to which he immediately agreed. Laval asked Allary why she was crying when he had agreed to all this and said he would not forget her. Two years later, Henriette Gabet and Andre Benoist had not married before their baby was born, although he continued to promise to marry her when they were appropriately situated. When Gabet became so ill that she and Benoist both expected her to die, he cried by her bedside, and she asked him to take care of their baby as she kissed the infant goodbye.[44] These accounts of intimate unmarried partners crying as they worked out their plans for out-of-wedlock births and their aftermaths point to the complex emotions that couples experienced while they were clients of service providers in the intimate economy of reproduction. The documents present unusually clearly recorded observations about the emotions that accompanied the young people's use of these well-established pathways for hiring care workers to assist them.

The legal record does not indicate how Allary responded or if even she did, and to everyone's surprise Gabet survived. Their co-workers and neighbors recollected these emotions as well as the other very conventional aspects of their relationships. Like other couples, these included walking out together, physical intimacy, expressions of warm feelings, promises of marriage, use of force as a feature of their first intercourse, and pre-marital pregnancy. The lack of follow-through to marriage at this stage and the births of babies in rented rooms were quotidian events in the city.

Laval's question to his intimate partner about why was she crying provides a glimpse of the situations from a young man's perspective as his sense was that he had done what he was supposed to do. Laval had either agreed or had offered to do what men were supposed to do—pay to rent a room short term from a woman who specialized in that kind of work; pay the costs of his female partner for delivery; take custody of baby, which initially meant to pay a wet-nurse in the nearby countryside. By providing for her financially, he expressed responsibility and commitment, and he met the community expectations of men who did not marry their pregnant partners. His actions were repeated by other men in numerous similar situations throughout the Old Regime. Laval and his counterparts saw this kind of providing as an expression of respect and even sometimes perhaps affection, albeit outside of the commitment to marriage.[45]

Even having made the appropriate commitments, young men were reminded that these arrangements were the minimum to maintain their reputations, and marriage would almost always have been regarded as a better outcome. Three observers recalled as witnesses later that they told Laval he had "done wrong by" Allary when he would not marry her after all. He apparently found the larger situation and the immediate negotiation stressful and was perhaps surprised by Allary's crying. A neighbor recounted how Laval said he felt suddenly "seized by weakness" and asked for a glass of water. Another neighbor remembered telling Laval that he had to do something so Allary could sleep at night—providing a glimpse into the stress, anxiety, and uncertainty women experienced in these situations. Was Allary crying with relief that Laval would take financial responsibility and custody of the baby so she would be able to resume her life, with sadness that she would be separated from the baby, with fear for her future, or with disappointment that they would not be married? Perhaps she experienced all of those emotions at the same time.

The farewell of Benoist when he thought Gabet was dying, as recalled by neighbors in testimonies, also shows the range of mixed emotions that couples could experience. His care for her and hers for the baby occurred in a context where she, as a single woman, delivered in a rented room that he had paid for after he had failed to keep his promises of marriage. Again, he had met his responsibility for his sexual activity by providing financially for his partner and agreeing to take custody of their newborn. Like other couples, their feelings for each other included warm affection as well as, no doubt, the many emotions associated with the delay of marriage and the labor of childbirth that imperiled her life.

If young men defined their role in part as keeping promises "never to abandon" their intimate partners—at least in the sense of providing financial and perhaps emotional support of some kind through the delivery as well as taking custody of the offspring, young women's emotional experiences of this way of dealing with out-of-wedlock delivery are challenging to recover. Many fathers visited their partners frequently, often daily, in the short-term rented rooms. They carried the babies to parish churches to be baptized. The failure to marry before the babies were born did not necessarily denote a breakup, although it certainly introduced uncertainties that brought anxiety for many young women.

Yet the birth of a baby to Benigne Dubois and Louis Mollard in 1752 offers a glimpse into a largely unrecorded world where such events were generally taken in stride. They became parents after a conventional courtship where neighbors and co-workers saw them walking out, and he often said he would marry her. When Benigne told Mollard she was pregnant, he said they could not marry for two years, but they continued to see each other and he carried the baby to her parish church where she was baptized in his name as legitimate. Two journeymen silk workers who attended the baptism went with Mollard afterward to the place where Dubois was staying. They recalled that her father thanked them, Mollard held the baby, and they all ate supper together there.[46] Even though this couple did not eventually marry, others no doubt did wed later, or they engaged in long-term cohabitation.

The Old Regime context in which young women separated from their newborns was very historically specific, and modern observers' inclination to project a sharp sense of loss at such separation complicates our ability to understand their experience. In fact, the use of wet-nurses was very common among married couples as well as out-of-wedlock parents, and so it had a quotidian normalcy. Certainly, this strategy allowed young men and women to go on with their lives as if nothing had happened—even though the pregnancy and birth were known to many people. The fathers arranged baptisms and (in tandem with landladies) the dispatch of the babies to wet-nurses. As we have seen, women usually did not see their babies again, not only because the fathers were charged with their custody but because they were sent to wet-nurses where, like all wet-nursed babies, many must have died. No evidence suggests that mother and child were later re-united. When disputes came to court long after the babies' births, women said they had never seen their babies again and did not know where they were. Women sometimes mentioned not being able to work because of their pregnancies, and these arrangements—sending the newborn to a wet-nurse and having no further connection with the child—allowed them to return to work after the birth.

In the longer term, some and likely most of the intimate partners had very conventional lives, either with each other or with different spouses. About a quarter of the women who gave birth out of wedlock in two rural parishes outside Lyon, for example, did subsequently get married in the same parish. Just over half of the women married the fathers of their babies; and the others, after an average gap of more than three years, married other men.[47] The proportion of women who married was likely far higher in practice because if they moved—back to where they worked in a nearby town or city or simply to the next village parish—they disappeared from the parish register that recorded the birth of their babies. So even the verifiable marriages suggest that single mothers' reputations were recoverable. These outcomes—resumed work and subsequent marriages—suggest that the safeguarding strategies, beginning with the concerned, involved members of the neighborhood and culminating in the specialized services of short-term rented rooms, were effective at preserving the reputations and futures of women as well as men.

If single women usually never saw the babies again, perhaps neither did most single fathers. Many city babies effectively disappeared in the Lyon countryside as they mostly died in the care of the wet-nurses but rural priests rarely recorded the deaths of babies who were not permanent residents.[48] The intimate emotions associated with that likely outcome remain very elusive, and differed perhaps from married couples' experiences of the same high mortality rates for wet-nursed babies. Young people experienced these kinds of out-of-wedlock pregnancies no doubt as emotionally fraught as well logistically difficult, but they were not inevitably catastrophic in terms of futures nor necessarily experienced as disasters.

"Put her in a room" was a shorthand for a common practice that compressed a sequence of events, negotiations, decisions, advice, complex emotions, and paid work. Throughout, community members worked together to manage out-of-wedlock pregnancy as a quotidian and not crisis situation; clear pathways existed about appropriate and even respectable (if certainly not ideal) ways for young intimate partners to navigate their circumstances. Although many such resolutions of out-of-wedlock pregnancies were handled informally and without generating any record beyond a baptism registration, these solutions were not secret. Many people participated in making them happen, even if they were often the subjects of discreetly chosen conversations or deliberate silences. As community safeguarders watched over women's reputations, they were also instrumental in pressing men's responsibility consistently, from the start of intimacy through courtship to marriage or other outcome.

The purveyors of services needed to manage an out-of-wedlock pregnancy did the care work that allowed intimate partners to manage their situation outside of marriage in ways that were both legal and supported at least implicitly by their communities and even often their families. In most cases, young women who found themselves pregnant and unmarried were not isolated: their intimate partners were still on the scene and were involved in some kind of solution while their co-workers, neighbors, and often some kin knew the details of the situation. Bringing legal action was an unusual choice, not routine, much less mandated. The usual course was to mobilize a range of people and resources to either ensure marriage (as we saw in an earlier chapter) or to find another solution, like renting a room short term and hiring the necessary facilitators for the birth.

The intimate labor at the heart of the business of reproduction was part of an economic sector whose services were well known, at least by word of mouth if not by licensing or regulation. Some of these service providers clearly seem to have specialized in out-of-wedlock services. Bariou and Dumas surely were not the first couple to rent a room from Bruyere to deliver a baby since Bruyere was recommended for that very purpose. The women who provided the intimate labor essential for out-of-wedlock childbirth were part of a much larger group of women who filled critical jobs and whose work is slowly being integrated into our understandings of the early modern/Old Regime economy. Like Lyonnais food trade workers, the activities of these care workers were common knowledge, their legality at worst amorphous, and the attitudes of the local authorities toward them ambiguous.[49] They provided essential, quotidian services that helped avert crises in a range of ways from leasing rooms as landladies to providing expert opinion in legal cases.

These helpers in the intimate economy of reproduction functioned openly and without penalty, situated in a complex legal topography. If elite authorities increasingly stigmatized illegitimacy, many people in working communities where out-of-wedlock pregnancy was not uncommon seem to have been pragmatic about strategies that helped manage out-of-wedlock situations and pro-active about mobilizing them.[50] Would-be enforcers of sexual morality for unmarried women were not agents of the state of any kind via the 1556 legislation but perhaps makers of municipal regulations. Such piecemeal, local efforts were pushed by elites whose concerns were as much economic as moral, but the implementation was at best haphazard and occasional. Meanwhile on the ground, intimate partners and their paid service providers did not see anything illegal in their behavior, no matter how many times they heard the 1556 Edict read at mass, because out-of-wedlock pregnancies were very far from being concealed. Midwives played a variety of roles in facilitating the management of out-of-wedlock pregnancies, but none as enforcers of state-initiated disciplinary projects.

The complex and contradictory emotions—among them affection, optimism, uncertainty, and fear—that were routine elements of early modern courtships were also elements of the intimate economy of reproduction. Young women and men who began as intimate partners who articulated conventions of warm feelings and expectations of marriage no doubt faced the complications of childbirth outside of marriage with shifting emotions that could be anger, frustration, and sadness as well as relief and at least on occasion continued emotional investment in each other. Women who recovered and returned to work permanently separated from their newborns have left little evidence as to how they experienced these separations. Much as we might be inclined to essentialize maternal emotion and project heartbreak, single mothers in the Old Regime shared with married couples a routinized parenting practice that relied heavily on wet-nurses.

Yet gender certainly shaped the routinized process in asymmetrical ways. Pregnancy and labor posed physical dangers and potential long-term health damage for women. When pregnancies ended in rented rooms instead of with marriage, the refusals of marriage occasionally came from parents and sometimes from male partners but apparently very rarely from women. Women as plaintiffs were visited by midwives, with or without surgeons, who scrutinized their bodies closely to determine whether they were pregnant. Their ability to access the legal system to redress their situations depended on their enduring this violation of their persons.

The business of reproduction was at the heart of communal complicity in the management of out-of-wedlock pregnancy. It was not that nobody knew about babies born outside of marriage, but the people who knew spoke selectively and acted supportively or looked the other way. Accepting intercourse before marriage as a part of licit intimacy brought ubiquitous and predictable risks that would inevitably lead to some out-of-wedlock births, despite energetic safeguarding. However, communities did not think that sexual activity should ruin young people's lives if they acted in ways that were accepted as responsible. The same pragmatic communal complicity and safeguarding extended to other ways in which the young men and women chose to resolve the dilemma of out-of-wedlock pregnancy whether through abandonment or situational infanticide.

6
Foundlings and Makeshift Coffins
Community Complicity and Dead Babies

When Marie Dutremblois and Francois Noel met in the early 1740s, she quickly fell for him and "did not hesitate to trust him," even though she said a family issue meant they could not talk publicly of marriage. She claimed that they "lived together under the veil of a marriage of conscience," a euphemism that likely encapsulated a traditional Catholic notion of marriage as a matter between the two partners and rejected the early modern law requiring parental consent as well as an assertion of the reality that "marriage" in working communities was an incremental process. She soon became pregnant and he refused to marry her. At around seven months, she "miscarried," and the dead baby was put into a small box. Noel visited repeatedly during the two weeks she was ill in bed, as attested by friends and neighbors who heard their conversations. During one visit, he noticed the makeshift coffin and asked Marie what she "was going to do with the box." He reportedly continued that he was "happy it had happened this way because it saves us both embarrassment."[1]

Much about this interaction remains opaque. Had Dutremblois used a "remedy" to induce a miscarriage or was it a natural event? The verb used (*se blesser*) commonly meant both induced interruptions of pregnancy and natural miscarriages. Was the pre-term infant born dead or did it die from lack of attention or its premature birth? How did Marie respond to Noel's question about the box? The friends and neighbors who visited must have seen the box too. Did one of them do something with it? When she later filed a paternity suit, nobody recounted what had happened to the box nor did the judges ask any questions about it or the infant cadaver it contained. Dead babies in boxes that were de facto makeshift coffins were likely tragically common, dealt with by local networks and practices that are opaque now but were very familiar to people at the time.

Living babies were sometimes found abandoned, like a one-day-old baby who was left on the bench outside a bakery in 1723. His parents, Helaine

Berthier and Nicolas Estephe, had had a very conventional relationship for four years. He promised to marry her, and she described their first intercourse as involving force, but when she became pregnant, he responded that he could not marry her until his father consented. In the meanwhile, he arranged to put her in a room in the home of a shoemaker, and a nearby midwife delivered the baby. The shoemaker's spouse and their female journeyman who lived with them saw Estephe visit often and heard him promise that he would take care of everything. Helaine claimed he introduced her for the baby's delivery "with the status of his wife." He agreed to take custody of the baby as was the respectable practice for unmarried fathers. However, instead of sending the baby to a wet-nurse, Estephe used the contacts of the shoemaker's wife who was the care worker to broker the delivery of the baby to the Hôtel-Dieu. The midwife she hired alerted the Hôtel-Dieu about the out-of-wedlock birth on the day of the delivery, so the rectors were ready for a possible arrival. The shoemaker explained later that he had "arranged with the rectors of the Hôtel-Dieu to take the baby and paid them."[2] Even then, the baby was left—as many others were—on a bakery bench, a common spot whose attraction was presumably because bakers worked at night and babies would soon be found, and subsequently carried to the Hôtel-Dieu.

The Berthier and Estephe sequence of events, like many others, show that the options for intimate partners who faced an out-of-wedlock delivery were not neatly linear. They faced a swirling series of possibilities, strategies, constraints, decisions, and time to engage more than one or move through several sequentially, as the fragments of evidence demonstrate across the archive of reproduction. Many couples surely went back and forth. They might have tried "remedies" or sought informal settlements mediated by kin, clergy, employers, or legal officials, and in fact some did end up with out-of-court-agreements even after contact with the Hôtel-Dieu and the judicial system. Couples could choose to resort to the services of the Hôtel-Dieu or even to situational infanticide by failure to provide a newborn with essential care. The details of many of these practices were usually recorded only if some later event led to the filing of a paternity suit. Helaine Berthier waited six months, for example, after her baby was born, going to court only after she learned that Estephe had contracted marriage with another woman. Marie Dutremblois did not seek legal recourse until after she had had a subsequent baby with Noel only to find that he still refused to marry her. In most similar situations no record was ever created, although the occurrences were very well known to contemporaries, and only later paternity suits provide evidence of the options intimate partners might consider.

Abandonment and infanticide may seem very different from "remedies," or remedies like short-term rooms, but all of these choices often involved mobilization of local knowledge, negotiation, networks, economies, preservation of reputation, and strategic silences and secrets. Many of the same community safeguarders were involved. The participation or absence of the father was an important variable. The term "abandonment" does not cover the many ways the Hôtel-Dieu functioned in out-of-wedlock pregnancies. Infanticide too, especially the infanticides for which nobody was prosecuted, involved decisions that were shaped in part by access to assistance or the lack thereof. Participants and onlookers might keep silent although many people would know that infanticide was a possible way of managing out-of-wedlock pregnancies that couples might resort to. Although abandonment and infanticide might seem like spur of the moment crisis decisions, they could also be pre-meditated and negotiated processes.

While the high levels of abandonment have been well established, hints of the frequency of unexplained infant deaths are embedded in many records. Church officials, for example, acknowledged the routineness of these deaths when they ordered that babies' cadavers discovered around the city should be buried in the part of churchyards put aside for that purpose. Accidental discoveries, such the remains of eighty babies' bodies found during the renovation of the Rennes drains in 1721 or a baby's body discovered during the renovation of an old barn, suggest that most infanticides were not prosecuted.[3] They speak to the likelihood that an unknowable number of infanticides went unrecorded due to community silences and the involvement of people besides the delivering mothers in disposal of the bodies.

The historiographies of abandonment and infanticide are rich but incomplete. The early modern establishment of foundling hospitals may have revolutionized abandonment by removing the children from public sight. The high rates of early modern abandonment of children and the steep increases in the eighteenth century are clear in Lyon and elsewhere; children charged to foundling hospitals died at very high rates, significant even among the already substantial levels of childhood mortality generally. Matthew Gerber's important study of illegitimacy as a legal and political problem in early modern France argues that the emergence of the Paris foundling hospital reflected an official tolerance of illegitimacy, perhaps as preferable to infanticide. Tokens and notes left with foundlings demonstrate that married parents in crisis, widowed fathers who could not manage without the labor of their wives, and unmarried parents left children with foundling hospitals. Parental sentiments and goals in such situations were complex, making it difficult to judge emotion from such evidence.[4]

Poorhouses/hospitals like the Lyon Hôtel-Dieu and the children they cared for are better understood in terms of institutional perspectives than from the perspective of parents, married or unmarried, and especially women who delivered their babies there. Poorhouses, originally seen as disciplinary sites that enclosed people regarded as troublemakers, have been recast as social service providers. Emerging research is expanding beyond a demographic focus for a better understanding of these institutions: parents used them when they could no longer manage unruly children, but the poorhouses also provided for the care, education, and work placement of abandoned children, as in Lyon.[5]

The early modern increase in prosecution and execution rates for infanticide across Europe is well documented as is the quintessential early modern infanticidal parent: an isolated single woman who was often an outsider to the community with no intimate partner on the scene. Eleven times as many women were prosecuted for infanticide as witchcraft in the region of France around Paris. Most work traces a chronological and conceptual trajectory where sharply increased levels of prosecution and condemnation of mothers as evil characterized the late sixteenth and seventeenth centuries across Europe with declining prosecution and execution rates and more sympathy for mothers beginning in the late seventeenth century.[6]

Yet overall prosecutions for infanticides were rare in France, even in the earlier period associated with high rates, and unprosecuted infanticides were distinguished in part because they usually involved the cooperation of at least one other person besides the mother. In the jurisdiction of the Parlement of Paris, around 1,500 women were executed for infanticide in the 125 years between 1565 and 1690.[7] The average of twelve a year indicates that executions were in fact highly unusual, considering the size of the population (roughly 10 million, that is about half of the total population) and the huge geographic area (almost half of the entire kingdom). For an infanticide to be prosecuted (as for witchcraft and all early modern criminal prosecutions) a community member had to make a complaint to legal officials, and sometimes nobody did so. In situations where the infanticide was prosecuted only long after the act, it is clear that sometimes communities knew and no legal action was taken until something happened to lead someone to alert the authorities.[8] Unprosecuted infanticides continued long after the formal prosecution rates dropped and even today infanticide persists.

This chapter focuses on the uses of the Hôtel-Dieu and the practices of unprosecuted, situational infanticide from the perspective of young women, their male partners, and their communities. It shows that abandonment encompassed a varied set of relationships between the couples dealing with out-of-wedlock pregnancy and the Hôtel-Dieu. The stories of women like Helaine and their partners highlight the multiple roles such institutions played beyond sites for anonymous abandonment of babies. Unmarried women and sometimes their male partners interacted with the staff of the Hôtel-Dieu in ways ranging from punitive to precautionary. The Hôtel-Dieu's multi-faceted role included holding men responsible for the outcomes of sexual activity, providing emergency maternity care for single or married pregnant women with no resources, mediating for couples faced with out-of-wedlock pregnancy, and accepting charge of the resulting infants. The stories of those like Marie that involved infant deaths in opaque circumstances that were sometimes situational infanticides were conflicting and conflicted. These practices were closer to the usual range of strategies than outliers. They were dependent largely on local knowledge, conventions for handling such situations, assistance and communal silences, and sometimes secret keeping. Community attitudes were key to young people's intimacy, and communal complicity—or lack thereof—was a critical element in the resort to abandoning babies and committing infanticides.

The Hôtel-Dieu and Policing Illicit Sexuality

The experiences of not yet married men and women with the Hôtel-Dieu and the practices of its staff show that while the Hôtel-Dieu was concerned with policing illicit sexuality, the administrators perceived only specific kinds of sexuality as contravening acceptable intimate behavior. Paternity suits and the evidence submitted with them provide invaluable backstories about the dynamics at the Hôtel-Dieu.[9] The Lyon administrators had a hierarchy of concerns about out-of-wedlock sex involving both men and women, and their concerns had financial as well as moral aspects. Their discipline was primarily concerned with what they perceived as female debauchery, defined as having multiple sexual partners or engaging in prostitution, and men's illicit sexuality, considered mainly to be employers who sexually exploited their female workers or single men who sought to avoid the consequences of their sexual activity. The administrators were far less concerned about women's consensual intimacy in ongoing courtships that appeared headed to marriage, even if it involved intercourse and pre-marital pregnancy.

Whether people in Lyon who knew about the births of babies to single mothers were required to report the events to the Hôtel-Dieu was the subject of some confusion, like many other aspects of out-of-wedlock pregnancy. As with local regulations elsewhere, an order in the early eighteenth century (1704–1712) briefly required anyone who had a single woman deliver in their residence to report the birth to the Hôtel-Dieu. But even during those years, there is little evidence of enforcement, and (as we have seen) the Paris Parlement annulled the regulation in 1712 on the grounds that it overreached the terms of the 1556 Edict. Nevertheless, occasional suggestions that midwives should make such reports indicate ongoing confusion. Noelle Jourdan, a city-licensed midwife and widow of a surgeon, testified that when she delivered Berthier's baby in 1723, she "advised" the Hôtel-Dieu as she was supposed to do. When Bartheleme Perrouset, a city midwife and the spouse of a candlemaker, delivered Barbe de Moulin's baby in 1740, she asked Barbe's mother who the father was "for her guarantee of payment [surete]." She then went with Barbe's mother to see the father, Pierre Vincent, when Perrouse told him he had to pay her. He told her he would pay her that evening, a delay that made Perrouse think she might not be paid, and so she went to the Hôtel-Dieu to make a statement. Apparently, she would not have notified the Hôtel-Dieu if she had been paid promptly.[10]

Occasionally, the hospital rectors did serve as a kind of civic moral police who disciplined female sexuality by forcing wayward girls into the Hôtel-Dieu. Nicole Devilliard, for instance, was working as a servant in 1689 when she became pregnant. Two female neighbors remembered that they had seen the Hôtel-Dieu rectors come to take her away. One recalled that she "was very surprised because she thought she [Nicole] was a very sensible (sage) girl," but she had heard since that Devilliard had identified several different men as the father of her child.[11] Seemingly an assumption about the mother's promiscuity, not simple unwed pregnancy, had led the rectors to remove the woman from the community in full view of the neighbors at immediate cost to her reputation.

Yet the likelihood of such a removal was very small. Only fifteen babies registered in the 1652–1670 period (less than 10% of the out-of-wedlock births recorded at the Hôtel-Dieu and a much smaller proportion of all out-of-wedlock births in the city) were identified as children of *filles debauchées*, that is single women who were accused of loose morality. "Debauched girls" and other pregnant women, married or single, were kept in separate wards at the Hôtel-Dieu in a division that emphasized the shame of one category versus the circumstantial situations of the others. The segregation of the "debauched girls" stigmatized them, and prevented them from corrupting the respectable married or single women who delivered at the Hôtel-Dieu. By 1760, the term of "debauched girls" had disappeared as a category in the institution's records.[12]

Yet at least some single working women seemed to be aware of the possibility of being forced into the hospital, even if it was more of a fear than a real prospect. When Pierette Thirugien, for instance, filed her paternity suit in 1724, she asked specifically that the Hôtel-Dieu rectors be forbidden to take her in. The court apparently agreed as she was living at a shoemaker's, likely working as a servant as she had been at the time she became pregnant. Michelle Favard, a *lingère*, asked even more bluntly in 1768 that the court order "everyone, especially the agent of the rectors of the Hôtel-Dieu, not to impede her liberty."[13]

The rectors acted only on tips, so distinctions between immorality and mundane failures to marry depended on community judgment, with the Hôtel-Dieu partnering with working people in the management of out-of-wedlock sexuality as did the local courts. Someone who knew the woman and her sexual activity had to bring her behavior to the attention of the Hôtel-Dieu, and these notifications could come from varied sources. Devilliard's employer seemed to have notified the rectors, perhaps because she identified one of her co-workers as the father. Marguerite Ruffard's uncle apparently contacted the Hôtel-Dieu. The rectors visited the midwife where Jacqueline Faure was still recovering from her delivery, although it is unclear who had tipped them off.[14] The relatively few women classified as "debauched girls" suggests that people in the know about the out-of-wedlock pregnancy (whether employer, friends, kin, midwives, or mediators like notaries and clergy) usually did not report what they knew. They and the Hôtel-Dieu rectors distinguished between what they identified as sexual immorality and mundane out-of-wedlock pregnancy among courting couples.

Certainly single women were vulnerable to a complaint if their behavior had crossed the boundary of acceptability—or if the informant had another grievance and saw a complaint to the Hôtel-Dieu as a way to settle scores. The employer of Gabrielle Vignon's partner, for instance, sided with him in blaming her and supported his refusal to marry her. The dispute was intense. She claimed the employer used a big stick to hit her stomach hard multiple times with the goal of ending the pregnancy, and several neighbors had seen them shouting at each other while he was holding a stick. The employer explained to the court that he had been "on the point of taking her to the rectors of the Hôtel-Dieu" because of her behavior when he heard her ask his employee to marry her. This possible outcome—of being reported to the rectors for false reasons—no doubt underlay the concern some women expressed in court about the possibility of Hôtel-Dieu intervention in their situations. Nevertheless, such actions were exceptional in a city where thousands of men and woman participated in intimate partnerships.[15]

Sometimes the judgment of whether a woman's behavior had been respectable or debauched could be debated between the woman, her partner, their neighbors, and the Hôtel-Dieu. The rectors, for instance, picked up Izabeau Marquet from her mother's residence after someone saw her "in the alley by a *patisserie*" with her intimate partner, Charles Bernard. Other neighbors remembered that the two conducted themselves within the bounds of youthful intimacy when they took walks, ate and drank together, and talked about marriage, so perhaps it was her going out of public view that caused this suspicion, as that was an important breach of the conventions about licit intimacy. Or perhaps the person who reported her had some other grievance against her that spurred the report as a way to settle a different score. Marquet's mother recorded a protest before a notary, complaining that her daughter had been taken to the Hôtel-Dieu "under pretext of declaring her pregnancy" when she intended to keep the baby. The mother promised she would ensure that the child was not abandoned and that her daughter would pursue a legal action to win support. Even Bernard also complained that the Hôtel-Dieu rectors had picked Marquet up from her mother's "against all the rules."[16]

The Hôtel-Dieu leaders were quick to criticize and to seek to punish sexuality they defined as inappropriate when it involved male employers who coerced their female employees and left them pregnant. Although the penalties they sought were nowhere near as severe as the mandatory enclosure of "debauched" girls, the rectors may have highlighted these relationships as problems because they were not channeled toward marriage (either because the employer was already married or because the parties were unlikely to marry because they were not of the same rank). The rectors' rhetoric emphasized both the immediate moral problem and the wider threat of disorder if such behavior by masters was allowed. Catherine Pernon, for instance, had been placed as a servant like many other former wards of the Hôtel-Dieu. The rectors petitioned the court for standing in her paternity suit against Blaise Tardieu "because of the many girls they put out to masters ["to work]." Pernod had gone to work for "the Tardieu spouses," and Blaise Tardieu was a journeyman silk worker. The rectors framed his actions in getting Pernon pregnant as a "punishable crime."[17] Many women who made complaints against their employers without any Hôtel-Dieu involvement also accused them of using their authority as masters to coerce their female employees into sex as a particular violation.

Most frequently, the Hôtel-Dieu administrators aligned with community efforts to make men responsible for their sexual activity when they supported young women's paternity suits for costs in situations where genuine grievances about unfulfilled promises seemed to be involved. The rectors seem to have been motivated by a desire to recoup some of the costs the institution incurred for maternity care and child custody, as well as to hold men accountable for the financial consequences of their sexual activity. Women who brought complaints to court while they were at the Hôtel-Dieu, either shortly before or after giving birth, shared a common narrative in their petitions: they had had conventional relationships with promises of marriage and asked the Hôtel-Dieu for help because for whatever reason marriage had not taken place and they had no resources. They presented themselves as virtuous, poor, dishonored girls who, having no other means, had to ask the rectors of the Hôtel-Dieu to accept them to deliver there for the safety of their babies (*conservation de son fruit*).

The question of uncovered costs seems to have caused the Hôtel-Dieu staff to try to push the situation into court. Staff clearly encouraged and perhaps pressed women who were using the services of the Hôtel Dieu to go to court. The boilerplate language of their initial complaints to the court certainly suggests some conversation with the staff but also reflected the realities of their situations. Marguerite Riboullet, for example, recalled that after she had given birth there, she had been "advised" to go to court.[18] On many occasions when a woman who had been involved with the Hôtel-Dieu brought a paternity suit, the court routinely awarded the usual provision but ordered that it be paid directly to the rectors of the Hôtel-Dieu. The direct payments indicate the financial interest of the rectors in securing compensation, but women's lawsuits also emphasized men's responsibility for their behavior.

The rectors proactively pursued fathers and pressured them to pay before any legal proceeding began, again in interactions that happened outside of the judicial system and usually without any written record. Jean Crozet complained in 1712 that the rectors of the Hotel-Dieu were harassing him to pay and threatening him with a lawsuit. They "alerted" him that Anne Plaicet had made a declaration to them that she was pregnant with his baby and "threatened" a lawsuit, so he had been "advised to avoid a lawsuit and settle" with them. It is unclear who gave him the advice to settle, and he was reluctant to do so because he claimed he was not the father. Nevertheless, the Hôtel-Dieu was probably often quite successful in extracting some financial support by this extra-judicial route.[19]

Hôtel-Dieu Staff as Partners of Young Single Parents

The Hôtel-Dieu partnered with young unmarried expectant parents, sometimes with one of them and on other occasions with both of them. Its staff joined the project to hold men responsible at least financially and they provided emergency maternity care for women with no resources. Sometimes women left with their babies and other times they left them as charges of the Hôtel-Dieu. In many regards, the administrators seemed to view out-of-wedlock pregnancy much as did other members of the community and local legal officials—as something that inevitably sometimes happened, and their role was protecting the baby and getting young people's lives back on track if possible while expecting them to act in what was defined as responsible ways. To this end, they often acted as mediators who—like notaries, clergy, employers, family, and friends—sought to broker settlements between the couples.

In fact, most not-yet-married women who delivered at the Hôtel-Dieu, as well as the married women who had babies there, were simply poor and used the facility as a maternity center due to lack of better options and not because they were coerced or legally obligated. The institutional regulations and guides for workers showed that these "respectable" women stayed completely separate from the "debauched girls." Nuns provided care and did the deliveries except in difficult cases when surgeons were called; their expertise was supposed to be certified by doctors before they were appointed. Women who delivered there (for want of another choice) could not enter until they were close to delivery and they left afterward as soon as they were well enough.[20]

Nevertheless, delivering at the Hôtel-Dieu was certainly a last resort for women, single or married, who often described themselves as without resources to pay midwives and unable to work. Women and/or their partners who could afford them—and their networks—preferred the short-term rented room situations for privacy, visitation, flexibility, and the prospect of one parent retaining in principle at least some role in the baby's future. The institution's regulations required the staff to admit any poor woman who was at the point of delivering, but no visitors were allowed and new mothers were not even permitted to name godparents for their babies' baptisms. The Hôtel-Dieu did, however, provide poor women with some basic medical care, as well as food and a dose of regular prayers, for perhaps a couple of weeks.

Women's voluntary admissions came about in numerous ways—sometimes the women themselves made contact as their delivery date neared, and sometimes there were negotiations between the Hôtel-Dieu staff and various third parties. Most arrangements involved no formal agreement, and so court records provide evidence only on the occasions when arrangements fell through and the mother went to court instead. Expectant mothers and fathers, employers, clergy, midwives, and others contacted the Hôtel-Dieu. It was a well-known possible resource even if no records remain—or even were made—for the vast majority of instances where its staff were involved.

Young men sometimes entered negotiations with the Hôtel-Dieu whereby they promised to pay the costs for their intimate partner's maternity care and/or for the costs incurred in custody of the baby as their way to meet their paternal responsibility. Sometimes these agreements were formalized when Hôtel-Dieu staff issued a ticket that acknowledged the agreement and gave the women or babies permission to be admitted. A letter from a Hôtel-Dieu rector to someone trying to make such arrangements in the summer of 1765 highlighted the concerns of the institution—the woman had to be generally poor, she had to have made a legal statement presumably about paternity (*déclaration*), and the funds offered had to be sufficient to cover the costs. The rector rejected the expectant father's initial offer and signaled what the institution regarded as appropriate and responsible when he lamented that a man of such means wanted to use the Hôtel-Dieu instead of taking care of his responsibilities directly.[21] The woman in question, Pierrette Tripier, had worked as a servant for Claude David, who was described as "bourgeois," when she became pregnant. Her employer and her mother tried to get an out-of-court settlement at a notary's whereby the father would pay them an agreed amount of money and get her admitted to the Hôtel-Dieu in return for her signing the settlement. He did get a ticket from the Hôtel-Dieu but he had not paid the mother and daughter so they apparently regarded the agreement as void. Indeed, the staff of the Hôtel-Dieu had urged Tripier to go to court because David had not paid the Hôtel-Dieu either. In this complex sequence of events, both the women and her kin, local mediators like the notary, and the father were attempting to reach a solution by several tracks, only one of which was the Hôtel-Dieu. Records of these kinds of intricate negotiations are very rare because if they had succeeded, no paper trail would have survived, but surely such situations were very common.

Negotiations between the male intimate partner, whether employer or feasible marriage partner, and the Hôtel-Dieu came in many variations as paternity suits occasionally recorded. Sr. Deporte promised Pierette Thirugien that he would talk to the Hôtel-Dieu staff and pay for all her expenses—as long as she agreed to name someone else as father when she made a declaration. She declined and appealed directly to the Hôtel-Dieu when she realized he was not going to keep any of his promises, but Deporte apparently thought that the Hôtel-Dieu would help him keep the matter quiet. Francoise Bonnard, who was pregnant with her employer's baby, argued with him about how to resolve the matter until she discovered he had given someone a letter to take to the Hôtel-Dieu.[22] Single male intimate partners who had been in ongoing consensual relationships also sometimes entered direct negotiations, secured tickets, and presumably paid in which case no public legal records were generated beyond a baby's admission with a ticket.[23]

The hundreds of tickets that survive with the Hôtel-Dieu records of babies' admissions show that arrangements had often been made far in advance, indicating that negotiations and payments to place the baby in the care of the institution were well established elements of pre-meditated strategies. The date of the ticket was frequently many weeks or months before the birth of the baby. As with the "garter baby" mentioned in the Introduction, turning over a baby to the Hôtel-Dieu was often not at all a spur of the moment crisis decision.

Women also saw the Hôtel-Dieu administrators as potential mediators without using them for delivery or child custody. Some women made precautionary contact, registering often early in pregnancy and then having no further contact if they got married or made an extralegal settlement. Little in the way of records was generated unless something occurred to bring the backstory up in court later. Jacqueline Ballard, for example, alerted the Hôtel-Dieu when she was six months pregnant, but subsequently made a settlement with the father of her baby at a notary's. In such cases, a woman may have used the Hôtel-Dieu as a kind of negotiating chip. Marie Cretin said, for instance, in 1724 that she had contacted the Hôtel-Dieu when she was four and a half months pregnant, almost as soon as she would have been certain of the pregnancy, "in case he doesn't keep his promises"; she subsequently settled out of court. Jeanne Clerc said explicitly that she had talked to the rectors of the Hôtel Dieu but did not intend to deliver or leave her baby there.[24]

These kinds of conversations sometimes led to brokered settlements organized by the rectors, meditations that were surely often emotionally fraught. When Claudine Privat, for instance, discovered that Jean Lefebvre did not intend to marry her after all, she recalled she was afraid to tell her mother, so instead she went to see a rector at the Hôtel-Dieu "to avoid rumor [eclat] and save her honor." She made a "declaration" of her situation to him, and the rector summoned Lefebvre to try to broker a private agreement. Privat remembered she was so persistent that in the end Lefebvre asked her what she wanted. She replied that she wanted him to keep his promises. The rector eventually sent Lefebvre home. However, the men must have resumed negotiations because the next day the rector visited Privat to say he had six *louis* from Lefebvre to pay for her delivery expenses and she would need to sign a receipt as well as agree to settle without going to court. Six *louis* amounted to 144 *livres*, slightly above what the court usually awarded as a provision, so the rector seemed to negotiate behind the scenes at about the going rate for a paternity suit payment. When Privat subsequently told her mother, she did not like the way the settlement had been reached, perhaps because she was not consulted, and they decided Privat would file a paternity suit despite the written agreement she had signed at the rector's behest. Privat recalled that the rector noticed that "the conversation was getting heated" between her and Lefebvre, a rare articulation in the legal record of the high emotions that must have been common, and her mother also was very upset about the course of events.[25]

For unmarried intimate partners, the Hôtel-Dieu provided a variety of strategies to manage the out-of-wedlock pregnancy. It offered a vital maternity service to many working couples whether they were married or not. Women came and went; some left carrying their babies (probably to be sent to wet-nurses), and others left them behind to be sent to wet-nurses employed by the Hôtel-Dieu. Since babies born to couples in rented rooms and to married couples also went to wet-nurses, the consequences of delivering at the Hôtel-Dieu may have seemed routine. Men and women relied on mediators as well as direct negotiations with the Hôtel-Dieu staff to make arrangements. On the whole, the Hôtel-Dieu staff synchronized with the values of community members by managing out-of-wedlock pregnancy in a way that would allow men and women to move forward and ensure some safety for the baby in delivery and aftercare as well to prevent infanticide. They expected fathers who did not marry the mothers of their babies to fulfill their responsibility in other ways.[26] In general, the Hôtel-Dieu served much more on the side of helping expectant mothers caught in a perilous situation than disciplining extra-marital female sexual activity.

Infanticide: Concerns, Safe Place Abandonments, and Prosecutions

On an April afternoon in 1781, a fisherman working in Lyon's city center along the banks of the Saône River noticed a baby's cadaver float past. He pulled it in and sent someone to summon the officials of the nearby cathedral's church court. They described "the absolutely naked body of a newborn baby girl with the afterbirth still attached" and believed, based on the body's smell, that she had been in the water for several days. The officials applied a red seal to her forehead to identify the corpse as evidence. They asked onlookers their names and a series of questions: if they had seen or knew the parents, if they knew who had delivered the baby, if the baby was born alive or dead, at term, what day she had been born or thrown into the river, and if they knew anything else. None of the bystanders admitted to knowing anything. The officials wrote a report for the record and called surgeons to assess whether the baby was full term, whether she was born dead or alive, how long she was in the water, and if she was dead before she was thrown in the water. Surgeons carried out the autopsy on the river bank. The court officials ordered that the body be buried "in the part of the churchyard reserved for that purpose." They asserted the court's right to prosecute either the mother or father, legitimate or natural, or whoever had murdered and thrown the baby into the water.[27] Nevertheless, since no indication of a prosecution survives in the city's criminal records, it is likely that no further investigation took place. The quick burial concluded the legal interest. Perhaps the witnesses on the bank and others talked among themselves about the baby's untimely end, but whoever was responsible for her death successfully avoided prosecution. The baby's body retrieved from the Saône raises a host of questions about the attitudes toward and practices of infanticide. Had the body been thrown directly into the river or had it arrived via the drains that run from communal toilets of the city's big apartment buildings? Might the death have been accidental or was it intentional? Who had handled the baby's body before she was thrown into the river? Why did the authorities not make more effort to investigate?

The pervasive anxiety about infanticide among elites was measured in new legislation that made infanticide a capital crime, in subsequent increases in prosecution through much of the seventeenth century in France and indeed across early modern Europe, and also in other ways.[28] Concerns could involve the fathers as well as the mothers of the babies. Unease about possible infanticide underlay at least in part the systemization of the establishment and growth of institutions, like the Lyon Hôtel-Dieu, to manage foundlings. It also fed the willingness to manage out-of-wedlock pregnancies through the networks of community safeguarders, rented rooms, wet-nurses, and a variety of "remedies."

One strategy to mitigate the risk of infanticide was the tolerance of safe place abandonments in an unspoken but clear agreement between young people, communities, and the courts. Most babies were left in locations where they would be quickly discovered, a pattern that speaks both to local knowledge about acceptable modes of abandonment and to parental premeditation. While some babies were left at the Hôtel-Dieu, others were left on benches outside boutiques, in the doorways of houses, or in church porches, places where the baby was likely to be soon discovered and moved to the safety of the Hôtel-Dieu. In 1760, 95% of abandoned children were left in such locations.[29] Almost all were left at night either because anonymity was easier or perhaps because nighttime abandonments allowed community members to look the other way more easily.

Babies were not necessarily abandoned directly by their just-delivered mothers or their fathers as we saw with the midwife and shoemaker-landlord who communicated with the Hôtel-Dieu staff about the reception of the Estephe-Berthier baby. Catherine Eure, who had moved to a rented room to deliver her baby, paid someone to carry the baby to the Hôtel-Dieu and abandon it there. Men also sometimes solicited other people to help abandon the baby, presumably to preserve some distance and anonymity. A middle-aged female neighbor and her son recalled that Antoine Joauanin had asked them to take his newborn baby and abandon it at the door of a nearby shopkeeper and "knock the door before you leave." Another neighbor knew he had asked a different woman to go to the Hôtel-Dieu on his behalf to "get rid of the problem" and that person wanted the witness to go with her, but she had declined. Jean Dumas asked the wet-nurse of his baby to abandon the baby at the Hôtel-Dieu. These kinds of arrangements, involving the father and not just a single mother in out-of-wedlock pregnancies, probably lay behind many abandonments.[30]

The pragmatic tolerance of safe place abandonment synchronized with routinized official responses that sought to safeguard the children with little investment in criminal investigation. Although abandonment was in principle a criminal action if the child was endangered, there was little concerted effort at enforcement.[31] Usually someone called a neighborhood militia officer who made a record of the circumstances of the discovery, interviewed the people who had reported the event or seen the baby to see if they knew who the parents were, and transported the child to the Hôtel-Dieu to be admitted. When church court officials were called, a similar process was followed. When a newborn baby was abandoned outside the cathedral, for example, a church court official was quickly on the scene. Apparently the baby had only been there for a few minutes but none of the bystanders admitted to knowing anything. The official asked a widow to look after the baby for the night while the paperwork was done for a ticket for the Hôtel-Dieu. On other occasions, the church court officials gave older abandoned babies to a widow described as a female member of the vestry to take care of.[32] The routine processing suggests a philosophical attitude, or perhaps a mundane resignation. When an abandoned baby left in the care of a widow died overnight, for instance, the church officials merely added that fact to their report and ordered the baby to be buried in the cathedral cemetery.[33]

Out-of-wedlock newborns were seemingly only a minority of the children abandoned at the Hôtel-Dieu or at other places in town and taken to the Hôtel-Dieu. Less than a quarter of the children registered there for the two plus decades of 1652–1670 were abandoned in the first two weeks of their lives (just over ten a year).[34] The number of children charged to the Hôtel-Dieu increased steadily through the Old Regime to about five hundred a year between 1700 and the mid-eighteenth century, and then a steady rise from mid-century to well over 1000 a year by the 1770s. During these same decades, the city's population also grew enormously. Many children who were older than newborn continued to be turned over to the Hôtel-Dieu by married parents, although gradually children identified as illegitimate became the majority.[35]

Meanwhile prosecutions of infanticide were rare in Lyon, a statistical reality that points both to the difficulty of establishing guilt and the reluctance of community members to bring allegations to court for prosecution. Community knowledge and judgment about babies' deaths in opaque circumstances shaped the prosecution rates. Likely, Lyon followed the patterns of Paris and Dijon where the number of prosecutions declined after the late seventeenth century; but even at the peak of infanticide prosecutions, they would have been very unusual in any one place.[36] In the eighteenth century, the Lyon court prosecuted only eight infanticides, and these were recorded between 1720 and 1790, with three additional lawsuits for abortions. Given the long history of women's efforts to control their fertility, it is impossible to believe there were not more in a big city of Lyon's size. The high visibility of early modern criminal prosecutions in court records disguises the reality that most instances went unpunished and rarely left any written record.

Criminal records in Lyon, as elsewhere, show that women who were prosecuted were typically extremely vulnerable, having few resources of any kind, human or material. For one reason or another, someone reported what they had seen or thought they knew to authorities. The usual trigger for prosecution in a society where neo-natal mortality was so high that it attracted little attention seems to have been not the deaths of babies born to single mothers in murky circumstances, but a clear indication of what was perceived as abuse (like throwing the body down the latrines) or intentional violence. Neighbors or spectators who believed such violence had occurred seem to have been more likely to notify officials than when such was not the case. Seventeen-year-old Pierette Nicoud, for instance, was sentenced to death in 1763 after she gave birth and threw what she described as "the lump of flesh," down the latrines.[37] In these ways the Lyon prosecutions followed the historiographical pattern that has highlighted isolated single women as key perpetrators of infanticides that were prosecuted.

Sometimes, the difficulty of proof seems to have interrupted prosecution even when circumstances were similar. In 1728, for example, Marguerite Ribourdin, aged twenty-nine, had started to have sex with the brother-in-law of her employer. She claimed later that she left and moved to a different job because she was concerned about the consequences of their intimacy. She asserted that she had not had her period for more than a year and did not realize she was pregnant. After severe stomach pains one afternoon, she "felt relief" and threw the lump of flesh she expelled out of the window without realizing it was a baby. Neighbors found the premature infant on the street. Isolation and ignorance (perhaps willful) surely led to her impulsive behavior. She was arrested and charged, but no subsequent evidence survives of further prosecution.[38]

Authorities did express concern about the possibility of infanticide, usually tied to particular circumstances, like giving birth alone and/or in the latrines. In 1724, Hugette Sage, for example, gave birth on her own in the middle of the night in the cellar of the building where she lived and worked as a journeywoman baker. When she went to court to claim financial support for the cost of her delivery and to support the baby, the judge asked her why she had not declared her pregnancy (not even to the alleged father of the baby) and if she had "given birth in the cellar with the plan to lose her fruit," that is, to kill the baby. Sage denied that allegation and claimed that she gave birth in the cellar because she had not expected to deliver so soon and had been seized by labor pains when she was there. As she gave birth at about 2 A.M., her explanation was not entirely plausible. Probably more likely she was not sure what to do when she went into labor—perhaps sooner than she expected—as she had not apparently told anyone or seen the father for quite a while. The next morning, she did go to the Hôtel-Dieu and tell the staff there what had happened.[39]

Between the time Sage gave birth and the time she went to the Hôtel-Dieu, she may have contemplated many options as the judges intimated with their question about her intent: anonymous abandonment, not providing any aid to the baby, appealing to employers or friends for help, actively ending the baby's life and then deciding how to dispose of the body, or taking herself and the baby to the Hôtel-Dieu. She did say in her initial statement to the court that "for the safety of the baby" (*conservation de son fruit*), she had to ask the Hotel-Dieu to take her and the baby in, a rhetorical frame that nevertheless engaged the issue of possible threats to infants' well-being in such circumstances.

Certainly, communal latrines were strongly associated with infanticide, no doubt because women who delivered alone often chose to go there, in part to deal with the body fluids labor involved, regardless of their intentions toward the baby. Estiemette Chretien claimed in 1715 that she had given birth in the communal toilets after thinking she just had an intense stomach upset. In her narrative she went to the bathroom and the baby girl had fallen into the drains, whereas investigators suspected she had thrown the baby into the toilet on the third floor of her residence. The investigators verified the toilet seat was large enough for a baby to fall down. A physician who was called on to analyze whether she had "maliciously and with a plan" thrown the baby into the toilet found bloody linen where she lived and blood marks inside and outside of the latrines. When he went down to the river and searched through "fecal matter over half a foot deep" at the drains' outlet, he discovered the afterbirth.[40] Chretien was apparently on her own, with no indication that an intimate partner was still involved, although she lived with a widow and had female neighbors nearby who, an investigator noted, she could have called on for help if her pains were so intense.

Concerns about infanticidal intentions circulated through the community too, and centered on the intentions of the fathers as well as mothers. Catherine Bouvier's parents complained to the court that her intimate partner, Guichard Gras, and perhaps his co-workers had "suppressed" (hidden or harmed) the baby as Bouvier's parents had looked for the baby everywhere and could not find her. Their daughter told the court that she did not know where the baby was after Gras sent her to a wet-nurse but she responded negatively to the judge's question about whether he had "suffocated" the baby.[41] Jeanne Garnier said she and Jean Renaud had been together for two years. After their baby daughter was born, he sent her to a wet-nurse. Garnier claimed that he and others had removed the baby from the wet-nurse "no doubt with the intention of making her perish," as she did not know her whereabouts. The commitment to holding men responsible for out-of-wedlock babies fed the suspicion that they as well as mothers might prefer that the baby disappeared.

The term "for the preservation of her baby" (*pour le conservation de son fruit*) was in wide circulation, and its implication about women's responsibility to keep their babies safe echoed with unspoken concerns about infanticide. Versions of this term were used in many forms, although it apparently had no specific legal status. Anne Recorneau claimed in 1663 that Jean Baptiste Favary "refused to provide the assistance needed for the preservation of her baby," despite all his promises, so she resorted to legal action. Catherine Ducat explained that she had to appeal to the Hôtel-Dieu for help "for the preservation of her baby," as many women who went there did in their petitions to the court for financial support from their intimate partners. Francoise Faury recalled that both her parents and Barthelemy Matteron's thought they should marry "for the preservation of her baby," although he continued to insist he was too young. Antoine Riche recalled that when Andree Franque told him she was pregnant, "he thought she must be joking but just in case she was serious he told her to preserve her baby." This type of emphasis on "preservation" contrasted with the more explicit language of intentionally "losing the baby" (*perdre son fruit*) by taking "remedies" or worse. Court officials quizzed Catherine Eure, for instance, about whether she had taken part in a plan to "lose her baby" and she responded that she had nothing to reproach herself about because she had "put her baby in a safe place" by paying someone to abandon it at the door of the Hôtel-Dieu. [42]

The availability of some assistance heavily influenced women's likelihood of avoiding prosecution for what might have been prosecutable actions as a variety of people could help in ways that ranged from active facilitation to simply not saying what they knew. Andree Franque and Antoine Riche, for example, were co-workers for a silk maker, and their affection for each other had been widely observed. Riche acknowledged that they had been having sex and she had told him she was pregnant; Franque's sister recalled that Andree had told her he promised to marry her. One day in the autumn of 1724, Franque went past where Riche was working several times on the way to the communal toilets and finally told him she was no longer pregnant, having "injured herself," a common euphemism for interrupted reproduction as well as natural miscarriage. A co-worker saw traces of blood and what she thought was afterbirth in the courtyard and alerted her employer's wife. The silk master chastised Riche for the "commerce" they had had and said she had to leave or he would "go to justice." That same day, Franque moved downstairs to a surgeon's on the ground floor of the same building, a shift of only a few yards, where she stayed for two weeks before Riche found her a job with another silk worker. Some weeks later, Andree left her new employer and returned to her native village in the Alps. Two months passed before someone told the court that "all the neighborhood" suspected Andree had committed infanticide. By the time legal officials were notified, she was more than two hundred miles away. Although court officials took statements from various parties, apparently no further legal action was taken. Franque was able to recover and move on with her life—with the help of her intimate partner, with the care of a surgeon, and with employers, co-workers, and friends keeping the matter among themselves.[43]

Makeshift Coffins and Opaque Neonatal Deaths

In 1631, a small box with a cross on the top was found at the base of a baptismal font in a Lyon parish. It contained the foot-long body of a baby girl. A police commissioner told church court officials in 1764 that "a wooden box about a foot long in which [there is] a bundle of linen that appears to be the coffin of a small dead baby" had been found abandoned on a stone bench beside the main door of the parish church of St. Croix. In 1788, a tiny preterm baby's body, about eight inches long, was found in a box left by a pillar in a third parish church.[44] Over the many decades of the Old Regime, Lyon officials made reports that recorded such discoveries, usually placed seals on the cadavers to mark the bodies as evidence, asked if anyone knew anything, and ordered the babies to be buried in nearby churchyards. As in most other parts of France, church records have survived only in fragments in Lyon, but the twenty surviving reports of finding the dead bodies of newborns suggest a far more pervasive practice of recording and then moving on with no investigative impulse. Very likely, far more often such findings were never reported or the bodies were disposed of without anyone ever discovering them.[45]

Attitudes of family and friends, as well as the circumstances of the women, often led to community silence about the deaths of out-of-wedlock babies in opaque circumstances. As with many other matters associated with intimate partnerships, evidence about infanticides where nobody was prosecuted is fragmentary. While infanticides were surely not frequent or usual, infanticide was likely far more common than the prosecution records indicate, not only because proof of intent was difficult but because even people who knew sometimes did not report the event.[46] Women, sometimes with and sometimes without their partners, and often with the involvement of neighbors or other members of the community dealt with "situational" infanticides—that is, infant death by neglect, inaction, or lack of help but without overt harm being done—or perhaps sometimes with harm being done. When people knew, their attitudes seemed mostly pragmatic, sad, and even sympathetic; they often had a desire to see such infants buried and even recognized as part of their communities by burials in churchyards or other sacred ground. Such communal complicity also meant that neighbors were very careful about what they discussed and who they talked to. Silences covered events that were not secrets.

The discovery of a dead baby in a chest in 1653 in Nantes, a city on France's Atlantic coast, provides an unusual glimpse of how easily such events could escape written records, much less prosecution. Marguerite Metereau, a widow who worked as a water-carrier, experienced what she claimed as a "shocking surprise" (*sensible etonnement*) when she opened her newly deceased cousin's chest and found a dead baby. Her cousin, Marie Metereau, grew up in a village nearby and had come to Nantes to find work as a servant. A month or so later, she left that job and moved in with her cousin. A few days later, she had a "stomachache" so Marguerite and a female neighbor took her to the Hôtel-Dieu, where she died that same morning. Marie told the nuns who looked after her not to give anyone the keys to the chest that held her belongings, still at her cousin's, unless she died. After her death, the nuns returned the keys to Marguerite who decided with a neighbor that they would open the chest. When they found the infant cadaver, they decided to record their discovery with the local court. The officials pulled the chest into the street, opened it, and indeed saw a dead baby. A week later, the officials questioned several people, asking, among other queries, if they had known Marie was pregnant or had delivered. Marguerite, her twelve-year-old daughter, the neighbor, and a nun all denied knowing anything about these matters. The officials ordered the burial of the baby in the hospital cemetery and closed their report.[47]

All the elements of Marie's tragic story indicate local knowledge, silence, and an almost willful desire not to know on the part of the cousin, the neighbor, the former employer, and the nursing nuns. The cousin did not mention any knowledge of the volume of blood and amniotic fluid Marie's labor would have produced, much less the kind of hemorrhagic bleeding that likely accompanied her "stomachache" and illness. None of them acknowledged that she was pregnant or indicated they suspected the cause of her "stomachache," an illness so serious that she needed to be taken to the hospital. The nuns did not observe for the record that they had thought she looked like she had recently delivered. Marie apparently did not mention her pregnancy or delivery to anyone, although the circumstances suggest she came to town to have the baby there. It strains credulity to believe that any of those involved were truly surprised, although it is certainly easy to understand why they preferred not to know. The court officials accepted their performances of ignorance.

The death of Marie's baby may have been situational or intentional. A surgeon who did the autopsy on the day of the cadaver's discovery identified a baby girl and suggested that Marie did not intentionally harm the baby but failed to deliver routine newborn care such as cutting and knotting the umbilical cord. The surgeon concluded that the baby had lost a lot of blood from an uncut umbilical cord and died "by default." Marie may have known that lack of care would be enough to end the child's life, or perhaps she may not have been well enough to do so or to seek help. Either at her wit's end or intending to carry out a plan when she felt better, she put the naked newborn in her chest. Had Marie lived, presumably she would have looked for another job, taken her chest, and disposed of the baby's body—perhaps by throwing it into the river that ran through the city center or into the drains, or perhaps by leaving the body in a small box in a public place where it would be buried. If she and the baby had survived, perhaps she would have abandoned her daughter at night in a safe spot where she would be sure the baby would soon be taken to the Hôtel-Dieu. If Marie had lived and disposed of the body successfully or if the aunt had disposed of the body for her, no record would have been generated. For whatever reason, Marie did not ask for help. Her intimate partner was presumably in the village she came from or had long disappeared. Although much about Marie's situation is uncertain, nothing was unusual about her situation, and many more such episodes no doubt remain unknown.

Court reports about the finding of dead babies' bodies as well as the incidental observations in paternity suits offer a glimpse into the practices and attitudes around unprosecuted situational infanticides. The actions and, implicitly, attitudes of reporting officials, community members, and the new parents are striking. They point to the existence of local conventions around managing out-of-wedlock pregnancy where a baby died at or soon after birth. The babies were almost certainly born to unmarried mothers although the reports said nothing about the parents' marital status. The deaths of married women's babies did not prompt any legal investigation because high infant mortality rates meant such events were routine. Even if married women did induce abortions or harm their newborn infants, such deaths did not attract attention or documentation nor prevent regular burials.[48] Moreover, married women had no reason to conceal their pregnancies since pregnancy was the usual, recurring condition for married women, and concealment was a critical element in criminal infanticide.

The reports demonstrate that standard official responses persisted over the course of the Old Regime. The court officials and surgeons clearly followed procedural templates in such situations. Church court officials made their inquiries and called surgeons to assess the causes of death. Surgeons routinely did autopsies on site as in the case of the dead infant found in the Saône. When a baby boy's body was found at the gates to the cathedral cemetery, for instance, the officials "saw the impossibility of putting their seal on any part of the tiny body" and carried the corpse into the cemetery. Two surgeons could not tell the cause of death from any external indications, so they opened the baby's chest and stomach and concluded that the mother had induced an abortion.[49] The reports typically ended with orders that the babies be buried in various church cemeteries "in the section reserved for such burials."

The officials lacked any apparent broader investigative interest about why the cadavers were abandoned and by whom. They asked bystanders if they knew or had seen anything, and people always replied no. The officials seemed remarkably unconcerned about who was responsible for the events that had led to the babies' deaths, likely infanticides or pre-term births due to abortions. Indeed, their actions suggest at least resignation about such episodes. When they visited a bar, for instance, where a baby's body had been found in a box, they asked the wife of the couple who ran the bar how long it had been there and if she knew who had left it. She said she had seen the box at about 9 A.M. and was curious about its contents—so she opened it and saw the small dead body of a baby but did not know anything about how it came to be there. The officials left the baby's corpse, the cloth it was wrapped in, and the box with the hostess of the bar. Later, an official ordered the box sealed (as evidence) and the baby buried.[50]

The surgeons' reports after they performed on-site autopsies indicated that death resulted from a variety of reasons: the babies died in their mothers' wombs, perished through efforts to induce terminations, or occasionally died by intentional acts. One report suggested the baby had died due to the "state of decline he had been born in," one recorded that the baby had been born alive after "an unnatural delivery" (*accouchement contre nature*) and died due to umbilical cord bleeding, and a third that the baby was born dead, which the surgeons presumed was due to an "abortion." Occasionally surgeons pointed to more intentional deaths. One described the bruises on a baby's nose and the spots of blood in the nose, and concluded that the injuries had been caused by firm "compression" of the nose—that is, someone had squeezed the baby's nose until the infant stopped breathing. Another noted that the baby appeared to have been strangled and suffocated.[51] The lines between a "remedy"-induced termination or pre-term birth and infanticide or death due to lack of medical help or no effort to help were often blurry given the state of knowledge, the circumstances of such deliveries, and the condition of the cadavers. In any event, no matter what the surgeon reported, no legal follow-up to assign criminal responsibility seems to have occurred.

Seven of the cadavers were found in pine boxes, and paternity suits occasionally referenced similar boxes used to dispose of infant cadavers, hinting at a common handling of such situations by the parties responsible. Pine was commonly used for household goods and furniture as well as coffins, but were the boxes repurposed or procured especially for this purpose? Old Regime households did not usually have boxes lying around unused, so inventories might specify a "box of nails" but rarely registered just boxes. A box of a suitable size could certainly be emptied to accommodate an infant's corpse. Of course, putting an infant's cadaver in a box did offer the simple advantage of disguise and concealment. Nobody would take much notice of someone carrying a smallish box in the street in a world where goods large and small, commercial and domestic, were constantly being carried back and forth. However, depositing dead babies where they would soon be found suggests more than convenient disguise was involved.

Infant cadavers in boxes were often left in noticeable places, frequently in or around churches, suggesting a desire to handle the situation with respect for the baby even in these circumstances and informal, but well-known, community conventions for how to dispose of such dead babies with some eye to an appropriate burial. Wrapping a dead baby in linen and placing it in a pine box followed the kind of domestic preparation of a body for burial that any death at home would involve. Leaving the body in the environs of a church or even at the door of a bar clearly reflected the wish that it would be found quickly—and given a proper burial. For the mother or parents, even out-of-wedlock birth and its complex circumstances did not rule out an effort to provide an appropriate resting place. The parent(s) knew that if they left the baby's body somewhere where it would be quickly found, it would also quickly receive burial in a churchyard.

Twelve of the twenty reports involved babies whose bodies were found in or around churches or other religious sites, choices of locations that seem to suggest an even clearer desire for Christian burial than leaving them in a public place. The bodies were left in churches, hidden in the confessional box, or outside under the porch or by the gate. Infant cadavers not left in boxes were often nevertheless placed on or close to sacred ground. One was left in the sacristy of a church, another by the church wall, and another under a vaulted walkway. Some were buried informally in the gardens of monasteries and convents. Whatever the precipitate cause of their deaths, someone wanted them to have a burial alongside the city's community of Christians.

Of course, other circumstances suggest unknown numbers of disposals of infant cadavers that were never found. Two deep, wide, fast-flowing rivers run through the center of Lyon. Cadavers were found in rivers or in the water that pooled around the pump in a field or in a ditch. A bundle of linen pulled from the river in 1743 included a torso with the head separated and an arm separated and the other arm missing. The surgeon concluded that the cause was likely an abortion that had led to a maternal emergency in which the baby had to be quickly pulled out; the body parts had separated easily because of the baby's pre-term status. He speculated that it was a "clandestine delivery" and that the individuals involved had probably thrown the segmented body into the river a few days earlier to protect themselves from legal action.[52] Any infant cadaver thrown in a river would likely be washed far downstream very quickly.

These deaths were surely occasions for intense and mixed emotions for other parties to the disposal and discovery as well as for the parents.[53] These might have included relief as well as anxiety, sadness, and physical discomfort for the delivering mother, complex emotions for the father if he was still on the scene, and varying reactions among the others who knew or participated but did not break their silence, or the people who discovered the bodies. However, if successfully disposing of an infant cadaver was perhaps not so unusual, that did not mean the experience was routine for the parties involved. A teenage boy who said he was "frightened" when he dug up a baby gave an unusual articulation of what the discoveries were like. The bodies were sometimes putrified according to surgeons, or hard to recognize according to unwitting discoverers who noted, for example, that the linen-wrapped object first seemed to be a cat or a "creature." The two male workers who pulled from the river a bundle of linen with dismembered pieces of a baby's body must have had quite a shock. Despite that, or perhaps because of it, they just buried the bundle on a bank under the steps of a bridge and put a small wooden cross on the spot. They acted quickly and decided, either tacitly or after discussion, not to tell any official; but it must have been an intense experience for them too. (Other people apparently watched them also without reporting, although it is unclear whether they looked to see the state of the body. It was a teenage girl who eventually told an official.)[54] Other discoverers, whether clergy who found bodies in their churches or often teenagers whose manual labor and wanderings led them to find the cadavers, came face to face with untimely fertility and its consequences.

The disposal of cadavers also suggests that the mothers had help from others since newly delivered mothers were unlikely to be in a condition to put their dead babies in boxes and carry them where they might be found and given an appropriate burial, or to dig holes to bury them informally, or to dispose of the bodies in the rivers or elsewhere. Such strategies suggest that intimate partners might still have been involved. Couples certainly did, on occasion, have conversations about such things. When Anne Julliard and Francois Page, for example, were debating what to do about her pregnancy, she declined to take a "remedy" as she had done on a previous occasion because it had made her so ill. Page suggested that she instead keep the baby under the bed when it was born and he would take it away. He added that they needed to keep the plan a secret.[55] He did not articulate—or at least she did not articulate for the court later—what he planned to do when he took the baby away. His emphasis on secrecy does not suggest that he intended to send the baby to a wet-nurse. Perhaps he meant to put the baby in a pine box and leave it by a churchyard gate, and pre-meditation gave him time to locate a suitable box. Noel's question to Dutremblois about what she was going to do with the box that had their dead infant in it, however, points to a wider set of assistants.

Louise Gimet's circumstances reveal how a local knowledge network about the handling of dead babies in boxes helped young women with the disposal of their bodies. Louise had moved to a rented room three months before she gave birth, presumably to keep her pregnancy out of sight of her usual community. She gave birth alone in the room. Her partner had not visited her there but he came the day after the baby was born. Her landlady came home to find blood all over the floor and asked Gimet if she had had a baby or "been injured" (again using the common euphemism for abortion or miscarriage). Gimet denied the birth so her landlady went to get a neighbor who likewise quizzed her. They began to search and found a dead baby girl whom Gimet had hidden, wrapped in one of her bodices, in the privatized narrow space between her bed and the wall where nobody would ordinarily look.[56] The women carried the infant to the center of the room and saw that she was dead. Gimet claimed she was born dead. At 11 P.M. at night, the landlady called another friend to come to see the body and asked her "how to get the baby buried." They decided to tell a rector of the Hôtel-Dieu who in turn came in the middle of the night and, they claimed, he told them to bury the baby. The landlady asked the friend to take the baby to the nearby churchyard of St. Nizier and the friend carried the baby, wrapped in linen in "an old pine box," toward the churchyard. On the way, she met a midwife who said she would take care of it and pay the gravedigger to bury the baby.[57]

The landlady, her two friends, and a midwife as well as, they expected, a church gravedigger formed an ad hoc alliance to assist Gimet of a kind that may not have been unusual and was probably most often successful. (The rector of the Hôtel-Dieu who, they claimed, gave them permission to bury the baby with no legal or clergy involvement was also involved although he later denied he had said that.) For Gimet's immediate community, even a hidden dead baby was no reason to notify legal officials. These events suggest how out-of-wedlock pregnancies that ended with dead babies could avoid legal investigation and even provided the dead infants with churchyard burials in small pine boxes or let the small bodies wrapped in cloth be placed where they would be found to be buried. Regardless of whether Gimet's baby's death was situational or intentional, after delivering on her own and leaving the mess of blood and amniotic fluid her landlady found on the floor, she was likely in no condition to do anything more than hide the dead baby by her bed. (Her circumstances were very reminiscent of Marie Meteyer's placing her newly delivered baby in the chest.) The women who lived around Gimet, however, had the connections, the knowledge, and the willingness to put the baby's body in a box and see that she was buried.

On this occasion, seemingly unusually, someone notified the court as an official intercepted the midwife and had the body returned to Gimet's room where an investigation took place, creating a rare record of the sequence of events and of Gimet's own physical and mental state afterward. Gimet's behavior and statements indicate an unsurprising mix of uncertainty, fear, anxiety, shock, and physical weakness. A surgeon who visited later that same night provided an unusually clear description of how she and other young women would have been after such events.[58] The surgeon found her sitting on the bed, "overwhelmed and sick." Gimet recounted a typical young woman's experience with licit intimacy, intercourse, and its consequences. She and her intimate partner had been going out for a year and had had sex on Sundays and feast days. She explained that she had not told anyone about her pregnancy because for a long time she was not sure she was pregnant, and she claimed she had been about to tell her landlady. She denied taking a "remedy" to try to terminate her pregnancy. She thought the baby had been dead inside her for several days and believed the work she did to make a living might have caused that. She explained she had not made a declaration to "preserve her honor." As she did not mention promises to marry her, she may have felt her reputation was vulnerable. Although the legal officials present suggested that her failure to get help was proof of her intention to harm the baby, she claimed she had no such plan and pointed out how she had placed her carefully in a piece of clothing. The surgeon's professional opinion was that the baby might have been born dead. At any rate, he concluded that the death had "no external causes," disagreeing with the legal officials who suspected the death might have been intentional.

If the frequency of such events is impossible to establish because of few surviving records and the infrequency of such episodes being recorded, the existence of similar fragmentary records elsewhere confirms that other communities shared the practices and attitudes of Lyon's working neighborhoods. Fifty reports found in a single archival folder in Marseilles all show the same patterns. The reports were routinized and they were not followed by prosecutions. The bodies, wrapped in cloth, were left in public spaces where they would soon be found. Some of them were in boxes. Twelve of them were left around churches. In only one case did the surgeon's report identify an overt act of violence (strangling) as the likely cause of death. The community members questioned were very reluctant to provide any information.[59]

The handling of makeshift coffins and infant cadavers wrapped in linen suggests the existence of community conventions for dealing with dead babies in such circumstances; respect was shown for the infant even amid the conflicting, contradictory actions and feelings of the mother and perhaps those of other people who knew about the dead baby. People sought to remove the problem pregnancy and its outcome permanently from their lives, but they were aware of the sad human cost and desired to handle that with care. Many people wanted to minimize the risk to women who found themselves pregnant but not married. Reactions were contingent, dependent on the mother's having a partner and/or a community willing to help her or to ignore what was going on rather than report it.[60] The helpers often wanted the dead babies, born outside of marriage in complicated circumstances if not in secret, to be incorporated into their communities at least in death.

Anne Julliard and Francois Page demonstrated some of the multiple ways in which established couples who were not yet married could manage out-of-wedlock pregnancy—take a "remedy" as she had done; secretly remove the baby from under the covers of the birthing bed, as he proposed; or go to court to get some support as she ended up doing.[61] Couples might also arrange to have the baby in a rented room and send it to a wet-nurse or make an extra-judicial settlement either formally with a notary or informally with the mediation of kin, friends, employers, and priests. Several options were often explored sequentially or simultaneously. Intimate partners used the Hôtel-Dieu in a variety of ways—as another mediator, as a maternity care unit, or as a place that would take custody of their child. After leaving their children at the hospital, very few married parents ever recovered them, and this was even more common among out-of-wedlock parents whose babies had entered the care of the Hôtel-Dieu. Babies who were sent to wet-nurses by the Hôtel-Dieu were even less likely to survive than those sent by married parents.[62] Infanticide, intentional or accidental, of course marked a rupture of a different kind. Yet sending a baby, legitimate or illegitimate, to be wet-nursed involved a high risk of mortality. For young couples, neighbors were integral as regulators and occasionally as discipliners, but also as supporters and assistants. In all of these situations, the regulation of reproduction was local.

How and why couples, singly or together, made the decision to hand the baby over to the Hôtel-Dieu or commit intentional or situational infanticide rather than pursue a different option remains opaque. Other solutions often required at least minimal resources, for example, to pay the landlady for the rented room, the midwife for the delivery, and the wet-nurse for the baby care—or to have a family or employer with such resources. Some workers in Lyon, especially those who were migrants to the city, may have found themselves without even the modest financial and personal resources necessary. Use of the Hôtel-Dieu or even infanticide may have been in part the outcome of these kinds of socioeconomic realities along with a lack of access to human resources. Even among working people, who could afford to rent rooms and hire services, a network of connections and intimate partners with the will to cooperate were important variables. The Hôtel-Dieu as a maternity site was clearly the province of very poor married women, but unmarried women who delivered there were more varied; they included women whose partners had agreed with the hospital to pay as part of settlements, others whose partners were being coerced by the hospital staff to pay via court proceedings, and poor women who had no support from partners.

Surely, no woman or her male partner ever cavalierly entertained the prospect of handing their baby to the Hôtel-Dieu or engaging in situational infanticide, and either of those decisions could also take myriad forms. Women who delivered at the hospital and left with their babies after a couple of weeks, their expenses covered as agreed in advance with their male partners, had one experience; it was very different for women who left without their babies or who abandoned their newborns to the care of the Hôtel-Dieu. Even so, women who used the facility as a maternity ward would surely have preferred to be delivering in a short-term rented room or of course to be married.

Yet the Hôtel-Dieu and its leaders were an important resource for couples and communities in the regulation and handling out-of-wedlock pregnancies; they highlight the alliance between local institutions and communities as well as the local character of the management of out-of-wedlock pregnancy in France. Few women were detained as punishment for debauchery, but the Hôtel-Dieu staff were routinely partners in holding young men accountable for their pre-marital sexual activity. Many women delivered there or, still largely invisible to us, used the rectors as brokers to persuade young men to marry them or at least provide financial arrangements for them through childbirth. The occasional glimpses of such negotiations leave in the shadows the perhaps frequent occasions on which a visit from a Hôtel-Dieu rector was sufficient to make a reluctant young man marry his pregnant partner.[63]

Infanticide practices were more diffuse and varied than criminal records reveal. Infanticide prosecutions were rare in part because proof was difficult and women who were accused were extremely vulnerable in every regard. In many more situations, dead babies were the situational or intentional outcome of women's and/or their intimate partners' uncertainty about their options. Their failure to secure assistance for delivery and newborn care was accompanied by the willful ignorance and intentional silence of people who knew of or suspected their behavior.[64] Yet as with foundlings, clear conventions existed about how these situations could be handled: local knowledge was key, assistance made a difference, and most local officials were more concerned with pastoral care than discipline. The rectors of the Hôtel-Dieu and the officials of the church courts were primarily concerned with appropriate burial of the baby corpses rather than with prosecution of mothers. Perhaps preparations for burial seemed to be a mitigating factor for them and, even with autopsies, no clear evidence could be obtained that would meet a judicial standard for proof of a crime. In many regards, like other safeguarders, their interest seemed to be in getting people's lives back on track rather than in shaming or punishing them. The threat of prosecution by the judicial system or detention by the Hôtel-Dieu staff was real, but in practice such outcomes were unusual. As in all other kinds of criminal prosecution, outsiders were far more likely to be reported to courts than people with strong networks. Working communities regarded as their priority the resolution of the out-of-wedlock pregnancy in ways that would allow both parents to move on with their lives.

For babies born to out-of-wedlock workers, the prospects were grim, regardless of the path the intimate partners chose. Communal complicity kept infant deaths under murky circumstances largely unrecorded, safeguarding the futures of men and women. Extremely high mortality rates were associated with foundlings cared for under the auspices of the Lyon Hôtel-Dieu or sent privately to wet-nurses. For babies whose parents were unmarried intimate partners, early death was by far the most likely outcome.[65]

Conclusion

The End of the Old Regime?

In 1790, sewage workers found a dead baby girl in a pipe that connected a building's communal latrine to the river. The building had many apartments and residents, but according to the initial court document, "a public clamor" accused a young servant who worked there, Jeanne Guilin, of infanticide. She denied it. Two sets of medical experts disagreed on whether the baby had ever breathed or whether the young woman in question had or had not given birth recently or ever. Jeanne was at work at the time the all-male medical experts visited her and they conducted an invasive physical exam that included inspecting and touching her breasts and her genitalia to ascertain the status of her potentially reproductive body. Despite the initial allegation of a clamor, the court's subsequent investigation showed that many neighbors were supportive of Guilin as a respectable girl who worked hard. The identity of the baby's parents remained unknown and nobody was prosecuted for the child's death.[1] The difficulty of ascertaining the cause of the baby's death or even the fact of Jeanne's pregnancy as well as her neighbors' support combined to ensure that the circumstances of the baby's death remained opaque.

As this very Old Regime interruption of reproduction suggests, the patterns of youthful intimacy did not change with the collapse of the political order nor did they disappear in the wake of Enlightenment new ideas about family; rather, key aspects persisted. Young people's relationships were embedded in structures of community safeguarding that worked hand in hand with local authorities, clergy, legal officials, and specialized care services to structure relationships, minimize risk, incentivize marriage, and mitigate impact of out-of-wedlock pregnancies. Ordinary people's decisions as individuals, couples, and members of communities or as legal officials, clergy, landladies, midwives, wet-nurses, or employers profoundly shaped the forms and experiences of intimacy in the Old Regime. Their many micro-decisions, aggregated by the thousand or million, were key in shaping the practices of a rank-specific sexual culture and management of reproduction that defined their version of licit intimacy and mitigated its risks.

Young people's intimacy was ubiquitous in the Old Regime. It was the topic of community, religious, social welfare, and legal conversations. It took place at work, in staircases, courtyards, and streets, and in spaces used for domestic life. Licit intimacy as a practice of community and courts allowed young women and young men to develop social relationships that acknowledged physical desire, emotional connection, bodily proximity, and sexual activity as inevitable elements of young people's lives. There were clearly marked boundaries of licit and illicit behavior, enforced through observation, intervention, and even the threat of prison. Youthful intimacy could also encompass violence, coercion, anxiety, and fear. Asymmetrical power relations were embedded in intimacy, not only between young men and young women but between the many parties to the many conversations and actions that young people's relationships gave rise to.

The archive of reproduction partially reveals the now almost invisible iceberg of out-of-wedlock pregnancy. Paternity suits do not show the scale or dynamics of illegitimacy because a small proportion of women brought them. They do, however, effectively point to the reality that the majority of out-of-wedlock births were undocumented. Most women did not formally declare their pregnancies to anyone, and no other party registered their pregnancies. Even parish priests under-reported illegitimacy, in part by assuming, like couples and their communities, that the transition into marriage was in fact incremental and a baby brought to baptism by its father could reasonably be considered legitimate.

The emotional registers of intimacy for young people remained tightly interwoven with other aspects of their lives. Licit intimacy allowed young women as well as young men to enjoy bodily pleasure and emotional highs as part of their frequent physical proximity. Their walks enabled enjoyment, excitement, and anticipation. They recognized the significance of warm emotional connections that were entwined with pragmatic issues in myriad ways. Their intimacy also brought anxiety, uncertainty, and sometimes fear and force even in the least tumultuous of relationships. The tensions and upsets that arose when out-of-wedlock pregnancy had to be negotiated or when young women ended up taking their partners to court were also central to intimacy. Moreover, all of the people involved in observing, monitoring, regulating, and supporting them could become emotionally invested, even those who were mainly involved for remuneration.

Young couples drew on a largely undocumented world of strategies and assistants when they found themselves faced with untimely pregnancies. Young women and young men were not usually isolated in these situations but could access the resources of their communities and networks to find practical solutions when marriage did not seem likely to happen, and the births and newborns needed to be handled carefully. Supporting young people's relationships involved helping transitions to marriage if possible and mitigating the inevitable risks of normalizing forms of pre-marital intimacy that had the predictable consequence of fertility. Providers of assistance crossed gender, economic, and occupational boundaries. Clerics, midwives, wet nurses, local landladies, notaries, parents, and male partners were all involved in established strategies with one aim in mind: safeguard the young unmarried pregnant woman and her partner as well as the child and find a way to help them get out of their situations and get on with making a living. While the centrality of women in regulating communities and out-of-wedlock births has long been recognized, men also played strong roles as community safeguarders. The ways in which men also participated—as kin, employers, co-workers, neighbors, remedy providers, mediators, and so on—were equally important.[2]

This community support was hidden in plain sight and at least tolerated, even if it was not of course the preferred outcome, as shown in the practices of communal complicity that involved tactful silences and agreement about the minimal involvement of authorities. The strategies were routine and commonplace enough not to be noteworthy unless a further breakdown in relationships led to a claim. A sense of shame that has come to be associated with unmarried mothers was muted, even in situations like attempted abortions or situational infanticides.[3] Single working women in consensual ongoing relationships who became pregnant were not persecuted by their communities as a result of their pre-marital sexual activities and its consequences but instead were offered support. Criminal prosecution was extremely rare, even for for infanticide, and it only occurred when someone in a community decided to alert the judiciary about an individual who had transgressed what was accepted as licit boundaries. Elite discourse about unmarried pregnancy may have been harsh, but elites were powerless to act without the buy-in of local communities. The archive of reproduction reveals everyday practices that were nuanced, complex, and less stigmatizing. Women were only judged for their improper sexuality if it was associated with other kinds of disorder such as venereal disease or promiscuity.

Pre-marital sex in a stable courting relationship was not itself a sign of sexual impropriety. The scarcity of prosecutions clearly indicates that communities mostly felt that common-sense solutions could be found that protected everyone's interests.

The acceptance of young French women's respectable involvement in licit intimacy echoed that of communities across early modern Europe and suggest a broadly shared sexual culture in working communities.[4] In allowing for young people to have a wide spectrum of intimacy that was regarded as acceptable, intimate partners, their families, and communities delineated licit desire as publicly observed, stable relationships between young people of similar rank spread over months and with the knowledge of kin and friends. When young people were monogamous within these parameters, they were permitted to engage in a wide range of intimacy without damaging their honor, reputations, or futures. Even intercourse attracted no negative comment in the context of predicted marriage. When couples' relationships became illicit, defined quite narrowly as failure to marry in the case of pregnancy, young men were expected to remedy the situation by some means. The prospect or experience of detention in prison during the legal investigation was no doubt a spur to some kind of resolution.

This sexual culture was widespread and central in working communities but it was not the only one. Elites had a distinctive sexual culture that was important and remains visible, but still only one of many. Young heterosexual workers in ongoing relationships with peers that were headed toward marriage were the vast majority of residents of any community, but men and women involved in casual sex, prostitution, same sex sex, or subject to coercion and violence by employers or other predators were participants in different, if sometimes overlapping, sexual cultures. For these men and women, access to support systems was probably much more limited than for young women and men when marriage was the relationship goal. Most obviously, young women whose casual relationships left them pregnant were probably less able to mobilize support networks or to file a paternity suit to seek a court-ordered award. They were probably far more likely to have to use the Hôtel-Dieu if they were without male partners to fund paid services, and communities might not have been as supportive when young women's own behavior seemed problematic.

Regulation of reproduction was local and uneven throughout the Old Regime. Local officials, whether in the legal system or part of the social welfare work of the Hôtel-Dieu, joined neighbors in scaffolding intimacy, incentivizing marriage, and mitigating risk when pregnancies proceeded outside of wedlock. Interruptions of reproduction remained mainstays of women's lives. Despite the increases in ambition of seventeenth- and eighteenth-century states to make aspirational moral claims, intimacy and reproduction were areas where states had limited impact. For early modern people, taxes, warfare and civil legal actions were the state issues and processes that most touched their lives. France, like England, had no sex police within the religious or state apparatus. As in England and elsewhere, only the most notorious cases were subject to discipline and then probably only occasionally.[5] Even the Parlement of Paris, France's highest law court, was willing to rein in over-zealous local officials' efforts to intervene in pregnancies, despite the myriad confusions around what royal edicts had required for management of out-of-wedlock pregnancy.

The practitioners of reformed Catholicism did not usually seem intent on disciplining young women specifically or young people generally, as shown by the pastoral care and pragmatic interactions of local clergy with young people about the consequences of intimacy. Moreover, the attitudes of Lyonnais priests and friars in Old Regime Catholic France were largely similar to clergy in Lutheran Sweden or Anglican England, despite occasional elite advocacy of harsher discipline. Even in areas that were actively Calvinist with clergy and consistories who were perhaps more likely to exercise tight control and public shaming, the pattern was not uniform. Ritual stigmatization persisted in Scotland and Geneva through the eighteenth century, but in eighteenth-century Leiden in the Dutch Republic, single mothers were often treated leniently. In Calvinist Nîmes in southern France, the consistory's own commitment to moral discipline in the late sixteenth and early seventeenth century was not aligned with the more pragmatic attitudes of most of the community. Even where the practice of public shaming existed, the religious end goal of the ritual was reconciliation.[6]

The management of reproduction rested on paid work as well as the emotional labor of neighbors, employers, family, and friends. When courts became involved, judges, myriad lesser court officials, midwives, and surgeons were remunerated for the work they did. Notaries were paid for drawing up contracts, the Hôtel-Dieu was paid for receiving childbearing women and foundlings, gravediggers, landladies and wet-nurses were paid. Parents, the young couple, midwives, wet-nurses, landladies, and the Hôtel-Dieu made complaints when promises of payment were not made good. Such payments largely underlay the pragmatic socially and economically acceptable solutions to unplanned pregnancies out-of-wedlock.

As the Old Regime drew to a close, the markers of licit intimacy in young people's relationships were typical of those that had prevailed in working communities for decades. In the late 1780s, for example, Catherine Brillat (who decorated hats for a living) and Francois Sallier started to keep company. She recalled that they were equal in rank and property, he proposed marriage to her and initiated the request for her father's consent. Her father agreed and they began to have sex as the marriage contract was drawn up and the banns were called. Although they did not marry when she became pregnant, he referred to her in a letter as "my dear wife" and "my dear one." The priest who baptized their baby recorded the birth as if it was legitimate and described her as Sallier's wife. Marie Grandelemu recalled in the same year that Antoine Millard persuaded her to marry him by emphasizing "the economies" (that is financial practicalities). She had given him money she earned to rent a room where they could live. She emphasized they were equal in rank and age, and their parents consented. Neighbors emphasized that she was "well behaved and worked assiduously" and had never kept company with other young men, and their observations led them to believe they would be married. For all of these reasons, she believed his promises to marry her were sincere and they started to have sex.[7] Catherine, Marie, and their neighbors continued to emphasize equal rank and long-term keeping company as speaking to intentions of marriage; parental consent, community safeguarding, and an incremental transition into marriage that even priests recognized were all still present.

Into the late 1780s, women continued to bring paternity suits that demonstrated continuity in the type of legal support they could expect as well as in other regards. The court continued to support young women in awarding financial support. Increasingly, young women did register simple "declarations" to the court in which they offered to show the babies when they were born as clear intention that they did not have infanticide in mind. Yet these declarations were as much for the women's use as any regulatory scheme. The court ordered that women be given copies to use as they liked, and since most single pregnant women still did not come to court at all, the women who did so evidently had their own purposes. Sometimes they intended to use their copies as sworn affidavits about their situations for the Hôtel-Dieu. On other occasions, the copy may have been a negotiating device. Jeanne Armand, for instance, registered a complaint at the *greffe* (the records office of the courts) naming Jacques Cochet as the father of her child. Three days later she went forward with a paternity suit because she explained that he was still trying to excuse himself from keeping his promises to marry her.[8] These uses aligned with the way paternity suits had been used for decades.

The incremental changes in practices of youthful intimacy that had began to emerge in the decades since the mid-eighteenth century co-existed with older forms. Marie Terrasse, a dressmaker for women, explained that Pierre Vachon had used "half force and half caresses" to secure her agreement to the last favors, while her neighbors affirmed the couple's long-standing appearance of courtship. Magdelaine Moine explained that she "had delivered herself" to S. Callet due to his promises of marriage during an eighteen-month courtship, and "he is the only one she has given such proof of affection [*amitié*]." Pierrette Chatard, who prepared leather that her shoemaker employer used, said "only the affection" she had developed for S. Lavarre drove her to start a relationship with him and she had "no hope of fortune," that is, no property or financial expectation.[9] The 1790 investigation into the circumstances of the dead baby in the sewer also highlighted some changes, both in the rise of new medical knowledge (in a debate about whether the baby had ever taken a breath) and in the exclusive role of surgeons and doctors as the medico-legal experts who confirmed pregnancies, with midwives absolutely absent.

One striking if thinly documented emerging shift lay in young women's occasional claims from the 1760s that they would raise their babies themselves as Roze Ducarre did.[10] This slow turn away from the long-standing routine assignment of custody to fathers perhaps elliptically hints at shifting emotions about parenting and mother-child relations as well as new pragmatic possibilities. If the maternal-child bond had become magnified in prescriptive discussion about the family, this incremental shift also increasingly allowed men to avoid paternal responsibility for the reproductive consequences of their sexual activity.

These emerging shifts by the late 1780s may have been part of wider cultural, political, and intellectual developments associated with the Enlightenment. The second half of the eighteenth century saw widespread perceptions in France about rising illegitimacy, anxieties about morality, and falling birthrates. Among other trends, couples began to marry at younger ages. Given the increasing clarity about the long practice of under-reporting out-of-wedlock births and the rate of population growth, it may be that these fears of an illegitimacy crisis were more about anxiety than fact. Or perhaps they represented changing community attitudes to accepting out-of-wedlock births as predictable. In Lyon, illegitimacy rates were at about 5%–10%

(and perhaps higher with the under-reporting pattern) throughout the Old Regime and evidence does not indicate a shifting rate.[11] While anxieties about such developments are well known, the social history of the choices couples made about their reproductive lives in the Old Regime is less clear.

Indeed, Rousseau himself famously embodied Enlightenment contradictions between the persistence of Old Regime practices and the emergence of new ideas and a new language of family life. The new prescriptive aspirations about ideal families where marriage was based on choice and compatibility with children at the center of family love that Rousseau articulated became potent ideals that middling and elite couples were particularly inspired to emulate. Other prominent *philosophes* did aim to live the life of the new family as part of their own practice. Rousseau's promotion of maternal breastfeeding to replace the use of wet-nurses was one concrete example of the shift toward child-centered parenting. These ideas could be attractive even in working families for whom these new ideals were in reality out of reach.[12] Nevertheless, Rousseau did not marry his long-time domestic partner and abandoned their five children. Broad claims about the Enlightenment and a possible sexual revolution seem likely to pertain to a small group of elite, white, straight men.[13]

The Revolution did bring changes, sometimes briefly and occasionally more persistently, to expressed attitudes toward young couples' intimacy, definitions of licit intimacy, law, and resources. Issues about gender and family became a potent political language and lived experiences of families helped them make sense of and advance some aspects of the revolutionary goals. The emphasis on choice of partners in the new family aligned closely with the choice of government systems that the actors of the Revolution claimed.[14] Young people were more inclined to challenge the paternal consent requirement in court during the early 1790s. Personal ads seeking spouses became a new way to find a spouse and the language of those advertisements articulated innovative ideas about marriage. For example, a Caribbean deputy to the National Assembly, a man who had certainly profited from the labor of enslaved people, advertised in a personal ad in 1791 for a Parisian wife who did not have strong opinions but was a gentle character and fair of face. A woman who answered in print explicitly tied hierarchy in marriage to hierarchies in slavery and asserted that she would reject anyone who had benefited from slavery. The Revolution promised to destigmatize illegitimacy and make all children equals regardless of the legal status of their parents.[15] In such ways, the politics of the Revolution sought to remake the politics of marriage, and ordinary people sometimes saw in the Revolutionary debates an opportunity to remake their own family situations.

Yet for all the promises of change, the Revolution in many ways did not interrupt patterns of courtship, marriage, broken promises to marry, untimely pregnancy, efforts to interrupt reproduction, or the experience of precarity as a central thread of young working people's lives. Historians of France have shown potent continuities that survived the Revolution across a variety of areas, including family life. The legal structure of coverture, for example, continued unchanged throughout the gender "changes" of the era of Revolutions. The extraordinary persistence of asymmetrical gender relations, or what Judith Bennett calls "the patriarchal equilibrium," was much in evidence. The fertility revolution of the early twentieth century is by many measures a far later and more important major marker of change in women's lives and family experiences.[16] Just as supporters of the Revolution could not agree with each other on what new political form should prevail and some people still supported monarchy, changes in family and youthful relationships appeared slowly and unevenly in ways that were often segmented by rank, place of residence, and gender.

Not all changes necessarily marked forward progress toward equality. For example, even if women began to use a language of consent and began to explain the shift to intercourse based on their feelings of love and the pleasure of caresses, their consent to sex and marriage did not impact men's legal rights within marriage. Coverture, usually regarded as a legal and property category, continued to underwrite men's access to women's bodies, especially bodies of women transitioning to wives. Young workers exploring intimacy used a language of affection with each other decades before elite eighteenth-century writers highlighted love as a key expectation for new models of matrimony, but their choice of vocabulary did not equalize women's and men's experiences of intimate relationships and its consequences.

While community and court support in various forms sought to clarify licit intimacy and mitigate the risks associated with it before and after pregnancy in part by holding men firmly responsible for their sexual activity, intimacy posed greater risks to women. These risks were both physical, related to their health and well-being (via pregnancies, use of abortifacients, and childbirths) and emotional and financial through the uncertainties and stresses men caused if they declined marriage and tarried or refused to provide other support. The use of force as a routine part of courtship and verbal pressure that had ample coercive potential remained the norm even as some women moved away from explaining their shift to first intercourse as the result of violence to emphasizing caresses and even romance.

In many regards, the stigma, shaming, and secrecy associated with unmarried motherhood may have been far starker in the nineteenth and twentieth centuries than it was in the sixteenth to eighteenth centuries. If disciplining was exceptional in the Old Regime, women who became single mothers in subsequent centuries widely experienced a lack of support coupled with hostility and harsh institutional responses. If they were not ruined, they were often regarded as ruined.[17] The harshness with which single mothers and their children were treated through much of the twentieth century has become notorious in many European countries. Meanwhile young men walked away, often while their families and communities blamed the women who were their intimate partners. The finding of dead newborn babies' bodies remained and remains a regular occurrence across Europe and the United States.

The extraordinary stories of the ordinary lives of young working people in the Old Regime illuminate up close in one specific historical context the universal experiences associated with premarital intimacy. Uneven progression toward marriage, out-of-wedlock pregnancy, women's ongoing efforts to manage their reproductive health and control their fertility, and community and institutional investment in managing young couples' intimacy and women's reproductive lives remain ever present themes. The configurations of interest, emotion, legitimacy, scandal, and power have factored differently in other contexts, but the threads are ever present. An eighteenth-century garter, rare now but a common if ephemeral fashion trinket in the Old Regime, provides a touchstone for the layers of intimacy young people's lives involved. Produced for a target market of young workers, purchased by one or other partner, and then sent with their baby to the foundling hospital, it is still pinned today in the middle of one of the many bundles of similar records that were filed together with string every quarter. The garter's survival poignantly demonstrates the Old Regime particularities of intimacy as well as the aching continuities.

Notes

Abbreviations

ADR   Archives Départementales du Rhône
AML   Archives Municipales de Lyon

Introduction

1. AML HCL HD G85, 27 April 1768. Lyon's Hôtel-Dieu had multiple functions. Besides sheltering children whose parents gave them up to its care, it also housed the poor and old or those too sick to work as well as poor mothers who delivered babies there.
2. Parents sometimes left items (known as tokens) with babies who were left with foundling hospitals throughout the early modern period. The best recent work on such tokens is in the eighteenth-century British context. Styles describes ribbons generally as the "the very currency of romance, love and courtship" and Holloway notes the erotic connotations of garters as courtship gifts. See John Styles, *Threads of Feeling*, 43–48 and Sally Holloway, *The Game of Love in Georgian England: Courtships, Emotions and Material Culture* (Oxford: Oxford University Press, 2019) 78–79. Garters were also occasionally left as tokens with other Lyon foundlings. Two other babies were left with garters in the summer months after Jean, for example, both with two garters according to the description of their belongings when they arrived. None of these garters are attached to the records now. AML HD HCL G86, 6 July 1768 and 12 September 1768.
3. AML HCL, Hôtel Dieu G85, 27 April 1768.
4. ADR BP3541, 21 January 1683, Dossier of Vignon and Barbier; ADR BP354113, May1682 Dossier of Mignon and Deroche.
5. For the narrative that follows, see ADR BP3263, 30 July 1759, Catherine Eure.
6. For an important call to historians to focus on the persistence of gendered power asymmetries, see Judith Bennett, *History Matters: Patriarchy and the Challenge of Feminism* (Philadelphia: University of Pennsylvania Press, 2007).
7. Carolyn Steedman, *Master and Servant: Love and Labor in the English Industrial Age* (Cambridge: Cambridge University Press, 2010), 177 and passim. Steedman's trenchant critique acknowledges the frequent silencing of women's experiences with intimacy because of the lack of direct sources. For the gap between the much-studied regulation of sexuality and the little understood practice, see Jeremy Hayhoe in a study of rural Burgundy. Jeremy Hayhoe, "Illegitimacy, Inter-Generational Conflict, and Legal Practice," *Journal of Social History* 38, no. 1 (March 2005): 673–684. For projects

that have used court records to fill this gap, see for example, the exemplary work of Laura Gowing, *Domestic Dangers: Women, Words, and Sex in Early Modern London* (Oxford: Oxford University Press, 1996), and Laura Gowing, *Common Bodies: Women, Touch and Power in Seventeenth-century England* (New Haven, CT: Yale University Press, 2003). For France, see Arlette Farge, *Fragile Lives: Violence, Power and Solidarity in Eighteenth-Century Paris*, translated by Carol Shelton (Cambridge, MA: Harvard University Press, 1993). See also Suzannah Lipscomb, *The Voices of Nîmes: Women, Sex and Marriage in Reformation Languedoc* (Oxford: Oxford University Press, 2019) for an effort to use Protestant consistory court records of the sixteenth and early seventeenth centuries to explore women's views of many matters.

8. The dense research for early modern France includes a wide range of work including, but not limited to, the following. For traditional and revisionist approaches to reproduction, see Jean-Louis Flandrin, *Familles, Parenté, Maison, Sexualité* (Paris: Éditions du Seuil, 1984), and Cathy McClive, *Menstruation and Procreation in Early Modern France* (London: Routledge, 2015). For sexuality as a political and legal issue, see Leslie Tuttle, *Conceiving the Old Regime: Pronatalism and the Politics of Reproduction in Early Modern France* (New York: Oxford University Press, 2010); Sarah Hanley, "Engendering the State: Family Formation and State Building in Early Modern France," *French Historical Studies* 16, no. 1 (Spring 1989): 4–27, and Sarah Hanley, "Family and State in early modern France," in Marilyn J. Boxer and Jean H. Quataert (eds.) *Connecting Spheres: Women in the Western World, 1500–Present* (New York: Oxford University Press, 1987), 53–63; Sarah Maza, *Private Lives and Public Affairs:The Causes Celebres of Pre-Revolutionary France* (Berkeley: University of California Press, 1993); Matthew Gerber, *Bastards: Politics, Family, and Law in Early Modern France* (Oxford: Oxford University Press, 2012); Véronique Demars-Sion, *Femmes séduites et abandonnées au 18e siècle: l'exemple du Cambrésis* (Hellemmes: Ester, 1991); Sylvie Steinberg, *Une tache au front: La bâtardise au XVIe et XVII siècles* (Paris: Albin Michel, 2016). For the intertwining of sexuality and economic issues, see Clare Haru Crowston, *Credit, Fashion, Sex: Economies of Regard in Old Regime France* (Durham, NC: Duke University Press, 2013). For sexuality in French Renaissance culture, see Katherine Crawford, *The Sexual Culture of the French Renaissance* (Cambridge: Cambridge University Press, 2010). For work on prostitution, see Erika Maria Benabou, *La prostitution et la police des moeurs au XVIIIe siècle* (Paris: Librairie académique Perrin, 1987); Nina Kushner, *Erotic Exchanges: The World of Elite Prostitution in Eighteenth-Century Paris* (Ithaca, NY: Cornell University Press, 2013), and Clyde Plumazille, *Prostitution et Révolution: Les femmes publiques dans la cite républicanne (1789–1804)* (Ceyzérieu: Champ Vallon, 2016). For men's same sex desire, see the many essays of Rey and Merrick which include Michel Rey, "Police et sodomie à Paris au XVIIIe siècle: Du péché au désordre," *Revue d'histoire moderne et contemporaine* 29, no. 1 (1982): 113–124 and Jeffrey Merrick, "Patterns and Concepts in the Sodomitical Subculture of Eighteenth-Century Paris," *Journal of Social History* 50, no. 2 (2016): 273–306.

9. Jeremy Hayhoe noted, for instance, the gap between the much-studied regulation of sexuality and the little understood practice in a study of rural Burgundy. Hayhoe, "Illegitimacy, Inter-Generational Conflict, and Legal Practice."
10. Nayan Shah, *Stranger Intimacy: Contesting Race, Sexuality and the Law in the North American West* (Berkeley: University of California Press, 2012), esp. 6–9; Nina Kushner, "Adultery and the Ideal of the Good Woman: Infidelity in Eighteenth-Century France," Annual Meeting of the American Historical Association, Denver 2017. (I thank Nina Kushner for sharing her important unpublished work in progress with me.)
11. Litigation over broken promises to marry was a staple of early modern European lawsuits. Important scholarship that indicates the geographic breadth (and see the footnotes for other work related to this topic) includes Abigail Dyer, "Seduction by Promise of Marriage: Law, Sex and Culture in Seventeenth-Century Spain," *Sixteenth Century Journal* 34, no. 2 (Summer 2003): 439–455; Mari Valimaki, "Responsibility of a Seducer: Men, Women and Breach of Promise in Early Modern Swedish Legislation," in *Gender in Late Medieval and Early Modern Europe*, edited by Marianna Muravyeva and Raisa Tovo (New York: Routledge, 2013), and Jeffrey Watt, *The Making of Modern Marriage: Matrimonial Control and the Rise of Sentiment in Neuchâtel, 1550–1800* (Ithaca, NY: Cornell University Press), 1992.
12. For important interventions about modern "silences," see Steedman, *Master and Servant*, and Deborah Cohen, *Family Secrets: Shame and Privacy in Modern Britain* (New York: Oxford University Press, 2013), that examines practices of silence that developed in modern Britain as well as work like Michel Trouillot, *Silencing the Past: Power and the Production of History* (Boston: Beacon Press, 1995).
13. Françoise Bayard, *Vivre à Lyon sous L'Ancien Régime* (Paris: Perrin, 1997), 26, and Maurice Garden, *Lyon et les Lyonnais au XVIIIe siècle* (Paris: Les Belles Lettres, 1970), 37. The usual rate given for illegitimacy in early modern Europe pre-1750 of 3% or less followed by sharp increases after 1750 probably under-represents the extent of illegitimacy, although certainly there might be regional variations. Priests were often willing to presume legitimacy at baptism, as noted here if the father was present or the parents seemed to be involved in the long process of getting married; this complicity means that parish registers are not fully reliable. For the usual rates, see Michael Flinn, *The European Demographic System, 1500–1820* (Baltimore: Johns Hopkins University Press, 1981).
14. Historians have occasional examples of the discretionary nature of reporting even infanticides. Alfred Soman, for example, analyzed an infanticide in a village outside of Paris that was not reported to the local court for six weeks, a delay he argues was due to the community deciding who was responsible. A young German servant was accused, a classic outsider, and Soman argues that the discovery of the baby's body would never have been reported if the community had determined one of their own daughters or wives had been involved. See Alfred Soman, "Le témoignage maquille: Encore un aspect de l'infrajustice a l'époque moderne," in *Les archives du délit: Empreinte de société*, edited by Yves-Marie Berce and Yves Castan (Toulouse: Éditions universitaires du sud, 1990).

15. For examples of couples whose economic independence was constrained (for example, young couples living with parents after marriage or spouses living apart due to work obligations), see Julie Hardwick, *The Practice of Patriarchy: Gender and Household Relations in Early Modern France* (State College: Pennsylvania State University Press, 1998), 64–65.
16. For explorations of power and intimacy, see Shah, *Stranger Intimacy,* and Daina Ramey Berry and Leslie M. Harris, eds., *Sexuality and Slavery: Reclaiming Intimate Histories in the Americas* (Athens: University of Georgia Press, 2018).
17. The historiography of early modern marriage formation in continental Europe has emphasized issues different from those important in the scholarship on England. Diana O'Hara ably summarized the dense debate about English courtship: historians have acknowledged that young couples selected marriage partners with sentiment as well as practicality in mind, and argued about whether choice of spouses primarily reflected primarily personal preference or was inflected by laws and community conventions. Historians of the continent, on the other hand, have emphasized the emergence of new, early modern imperatives, especially innovative requirements for publicity and parental permission, that increased kin and community control over marriage. These innovations were shaped by religious reformations and state formation in the sixteenth and seventeenth centuries as governments took over the regulation of marriage. They have certainly assumed that, outside of elites, young people were able to choose marriage within the parameters of a parental veto, but the overwhelming scholarly emphasis has been on spouses as pragmatic partners. For the historiography on Britain, see Diana O'Hara, *Courtship and Constraint: Rethinking the Making of Marriage in Tudor England* (Manchester: Manchester University Press, 2000), esp. 3–7 for a review of the British historiography from Stone onward. See also Gowing, *Domestic Dangers*. For work on continental Europe that has emphasized increased regulation of marriage as a fundamental feature of state formation, see work such as Hardwick, *The Practice of Patriarchy*, and Julie Hardwick, *Family Business: Litigation and the Political Economies of Daily Life in Early Modern France* (Oxford: Oxford University Press, 2009); Hanley, "Engendering the State," 4–27; Ulrike Strasser, *State of Virginity: Gender, Religion and Politics in an Early Modern Catholic State* (Ann Arbor: University of Michigan Press, 2004). For the pragmatic to companionate marriage debate, see Dena Goodman, "Marriage Choice and Marital Success: Reasoning about Marriage, Love, and Happiness," in *Family, Gender, and Law in Early Modern France*, edited by Suzanne Desan and Jeffrey Merrick (State College: Pennsylvania State University Press, 2009), 26–61. See also the pioneering studies of marriage in eighteenth-century in rural France: Anne Fillon, *Les Trois Bagues aux Doigts: Amours Villeageoises au XVIII siècle* (Paris: R. Lafront, 1989), Françoise Lebrun, *La vie conjugale sous L'Ancien Regime* (Paris: A. Colin, 1975), and Flandrin, *Familles*. For rethinking early modern marriages in the light of history of emotions approaches, see the pioneering work of Katie Barclay, including *Love, Intimacy and Power: Marriage and Patriarchy in*

Scotland, 1650–1850 (Manchester: Manchester University Press, 2014) and Katie Barclay, "Illicit Intimacies: The Imagined "Homes" of Gilbert Innes of Stow and His Mistresses, (1751–1832)," *Gender and History* 27, no. 3 (2015): 576–590.
18. See the subsequent chapters for full discussions of the relevant historiographies alluded to here and throughout this section.
19. For ordinary as an important category of analysis, see Claire Langhamer, "Everyday Love and Emotions in the 20th Century," https://manyheadedmonster.wordpress.com/2013/08/28/claire-langhamer-everyday-love-and-emotions-in-the-20th-century/, accessed 12 June, 2019, and Bianca Premo, *Enlightenment on Trial: Ordinary Litigants and Colonialism in the Spanish Empire* (New York: Oxford University Press, 2017). See also Guillaume Mazeau and Clyde Plumauzille who argue that instead of attention to "romantic illusions of a proto-feminism defended by a few heroines," historians should "pay attention to those millions of ordinary women, who using their discretion, readjusted gender relations [in everyday life] without having wished for it, or foreseen it. As in most moments of uncertainty and political crisis, the vast majority of women like men preferred silence and waiting to spectacular action." Guillaume Mazeau and Clyde Plumauzille, "Penser avec le genre: Trouble dans la citoyenneté révolutionnaire," *La Révolution française: Cahiers de L'Institute d'histoire de la Révolution française* 9 (2015): 17–18.

Chapter 1

1. For the many complex steps of the silk production process and Lyon women's essential roles in it, see Daryl Hafter, *Women at Work in Preindustrial France* (University Park: Pennsylvania State University Press, 2007), 123–142. For the centrality of women to silk production elsewhere in Europe, see Anna Bellavitis, *Women's Work and Rights in Early Modern Urban Europe* (London: Palgrave Macmillan, 2018), 197–208.
2. ADR BP3541 Dossier of Bert and Aymond, 27 July 1682; ADR BP3558 Dossier of Rubard and Fiancon, 15 April 1762.
3. For the use of verbs as more reliable indicators of women's work than social descriptions of occupation, see Maria Ågren, ed., *Making a Living, Making a Difference: Gender and Work in Early Modern European Society* (New York: Oxford University Press, 2016).
4. The inclusion—or not—of the relationship histories was a variable determined locally by jurisdictions. Cities besides Lyon that required histories included Aix, Carcassone. Grenoble, Paris, and Provins, while cities such as Châteaulaudren, Etampes, Laon, and Melun did not require them. Cissie Fairchilds, "Female Sexual Attitudes and the Rise of Illegitimacy: A Case Study," *Journal of Interdisciplinary History* 8, no. 4 (Spring 1978), 630, and Marie-Claude Phan, *Les Amours Illégitimes: histoires de séduction en Languedoc (1676–1786)* (Paris: Editions du Centre national de la recherche scientifique, 1986), 10.
5. A case study of 1760 confirms how unusual going to court was: only 4 of 262 illegitimate babies at the Hôtel-Dieu that year could be matched with paternity suits

in court. Jean-Marcel Bourgeat, "L'abandon d'enfants à Lyon: Origines sociales et géographiques . . . le cas de 1760," *Société des Etudes Historiques Revolutionnaires et Imperials* (novembre 2011), 27.

6. That is, litigation over paternity had much in common with all other forms of litigation. Julie Hardwick, *Family Business: Litigation and the Political Economies of Daily Life in Early Modern France* (Oxford: Oxford University Press, 2009). In addition, a small sub-group who delivered at the Hôtel-Dieu seemed to have been instructed to go to court to collect some financial compensation from fathers they perceived had the means to pay after the mothers or administrators had failed to agree to payment through private negotiations.

7. See chapter 3 for the why and when aspects of these paternity suits, chapter 4 for the prevalence of extralegal settlements about the management of out-of-wedlock pregnancies and other options including efforts to interrupt reproduction, and chapters 5 and 6 for other types of options.

8. David Sabean and Hans Medick's important work on early modern families argued thirty years ago that pragmatic interest and emotion were never mutually exclusive. Hans Medick and David Sabean, eds., *Interest and Emotion: Essays on the Study of Family and Kinship* (Cambridge: Cambridge University Press, 1988). For emotional practices as a methodological category, see Monique Scheer, "Are Emotions a Kind of Practice (and Is That What Makes Them Have a History)? A Bourdieuian Approach to Understanding Emotion," *History & Theory* 51, no. 2 (May 2012): 193–220. For emotions as a set of agreed community norms about what is socially acceptable defined by the group and not simply about individual feelings, see Barbara Rosenwein, *Emotional Communities in the Early Middle Ages* (Ithaca, NY: Cornell University Press, 2006), esp. pp. 24–25.

9. For "observable actions" as key evidence to explore the historicization of emotions, see Scheer, "Are Emotions a Kind of Practice," 218.

10. Young women who brought paternity suits had not infrequently already had one baby with their intimate partner and sometimes more than one. Presumably they would have continued to cohabit without the benefit of marriage if some problem had not prompted the woman to go to court; others surely did continue to cohabit long term.

11. The court showed no interest in disciplining men's sexual violence through these kinds of suits even though they consistently used them to hold men responsible for untimely extra-marital pregnancies by imposing financial penalties and charging them with custody of the offspring. See for instance two suits brought against Louis Portales in October and November 1743. Both young women argued that they had sex with him only after he was violent toward them, and the second noted their neighborhood was full of gossip about his "disorders." The first young woman said he forced her to have sex initially with the help of a procuress who held her hand over her month, and the second claimed that he used a knife to cut off her corset and threatened to kill her if she told anyone he was the father when she was pregnant. Despite two lawsuits and the seemingly wider knowledge that Portales was a sexual predator, the lawsuits ended when he paid the women off via out-of-court settlements and the judges showed no interest in the young women's allegations of violence. ADR BP3552

6 October 1743 Dossier of Draguet and Portales and 21 November 1743 Dossier of Courtois and Portales.
12. Hardwick, *Family Business*. For women who chose to create households together, see Clare Haru Crowston, *Fabricating Women: The Seamstresses of Old Regime France, 1675–1791* (Durham, NC: Duke University Press, 2001), 356-61, and Olwen Hufton, "Women without Men: Women and Men in Britain and France in the Eighteenth Century," *Journal of Family History* (Winter 1984): 355–376. Crowston notes that the high rate of non-marriage among Parisian seamstresses in the eighteenth century (varying between 37% and 48%, depending on the source) so clearly, at least in particular niches, some women did not find matrimony compelling. Our archival evidence of same sex desire as a motive for household formation remains scarce, but see the pioneering work of Jonas Roelens, "A Woman Like Any Other: Female Sodomy, Hermaphroditism, and Witchcraft in Seventeenth-Century Bruges," *Journal of Women's History* 29, no. 4 (Winter 2017).
13. Damoiselle Madelaine Delacroix, for example, explained to the court that her father's financial difficulties in Paris led them to leave that city, and she came to Lyon while he went to Milan. Her intimate partner had deceived her and her father with his offers of help, and when she became pregnant, he sent her to live with his sister in the country. After the baby was born, she claimed, he took the baby who "disappeared." She said she would have preferred to keep the matter "a secret to avoid scandal and dishonor even though she was the victim," but he had extorted a lot of money from her that left her destitute. ADR BP3552 21 July 1742 Dossier of Delacroix and Gaboulet.
14. Historians have discussed these issues at length with regard to women and other participants in the legal process. For a recent overview, see Tim Stretton, "Women, Legal Records, and the Problems of the Lawyer's Hand," *Journal of British Studies* 58, no. 4 (October 2019), 684–700. For the classic statement of the ways in which historians can locate the voices of the plaintiffs amid the complex production of legal texts, see Natalie Zemon Davis, *Fiction in the Archives: Pardon Tales and Their Tellers in Sixteenth-Century France* (Palo Alto, CA: Stanford University Press, 1987).
15. For Lyon's *sénéchausée* court, I examined all surviving material for 1657–1727 (a total of eight boxes, and I sampled within nine boxes (of twenty-two) selected at random for the 1729–1790 decades. No material survives for 1700–1720. The surviving material clearly does not include all petitions that were filed. (In the box for 1727, for instance, eighteen of the twenty cases were dated January and February.) The 1657–1727 boxes include 293 cases and 3,195 pages of evidence. The first box also includes a ninety-page "*livre de déclarations*" that includes 187 statements for the years 1741-1747. Ten claims were found in records of Lyon's church courts for the 1760s and 1770s. As these records are very fragmentary, more paternity claims were likely filed in those jurisdictions than survive.
16. Phan noted that extant "declarations" rarely date from before the late seventeenth century. It is unclear why this is—perhaps royal courts became more popular for paternity claims after the mid-seventeenth century whereas notaries were more often used earlier and the latter often did not retain their records of these kinds of claims, as we will see in chapter 4. Marie-Claude Phan, "Les déclarations de grossesse en

France (XVIe-XVIIIe siècles): Essai institutionnel," *Revue d'histoire moderne et contemporaine* 22 (1975): 72.

17. Work on "declarations" derived from a variety of persons, institutions, and regions to examine illegitimacy include Jacques Depauw, "Amour Illégitime et société à Nantes au XVIII siècle," *Annales: Economies, Sociétés, Civilisations* (juillet–octobre 1972), 1157, (8,000 declarations made in response to a municipal requirement in Nantes, 1725–1788); A. Lottin, "Naissances illégitimes et filles mères à Lille au XVIIIe siècle," *Revue d'histoire, moderne et contemporaine* (avril–juin 1970), 281–282 (declarations of midwives under the conditions of a municipal regulation made in Lille); Phan, *Les Amours illegitimes* (over three hundred "declarations" given primarily to the *sénéchausse* court in Carcassone in southern France between 1676 and 1776); James R. Farr, *Authority and Sexuality in Early Modern Burgundy (1550–1730)* (New York: Oxford University Press, 1995) (eighty-seven declarations made in Dijon between 1619 and 1730); Fairchilds, "Female Sexual Attitudes," 627–667 (3,001 declarations given at the Hôtel-Dieu in Aix-en-Provence, 1727–1789); Jeremy Hayhoe, "Illegitimacy, Inter-Generational Conflict, and Legal Practice," *Journal of Social History* 38, no. 1 (March 2005): 673–684 (late eighteenth-century declarations given to notaries and seigneurial courts in rural Burgundy); Kathryn Norberg, *Rich and Poor in Grenoble, 1600–1814* (Berkeley: University of California Press, 1985), 52–57, 198–215 (fifty "declarations" for 1669–1689—it is unclear to whom they were given—plus 1,100 for 1720–1789 apparently primarily declarations the Hôtel-Dieu required for women to be admitted and written by a variety of people whether notaries, priests, or the city's municipal court). Arlette Farge—*Lives: Violence, Power and Solidarity in Eighteenth-Century Paris*, translated by Carol Shelton (Cambridge, MA: Harvard University Press, 1993), esp. 26-41— explored illegitimacy by examining about one hundred late-eighteenth-century single pregnant women's complaints to Parisian police commissioners about men who seduced and abandoned them. More recently, Matthew Gerber—*Bastards: Politics, Family and Law in Early Modern France* (Oxford: Oxford University Press, 2012), 138–144—innovatively viewed "pregnancy declarations" in terms of jurisprudence about legal paternity, and Cathy McClive—*Menstruation and Procreation in Early Modern France* (London: Routledge, 2015)—made brilliant use of them to explore women's reproductive bodies.

18. For a summary of this viewpoint, see Farr, *Authority and Sexuality*, 117–118. Although historians of other regions have claimed that the occupation of servant was the dominant work profile of unwed mothers, paternity suits brought in Lyon that were employer-servant were only one narrow sector of a much broader spectrum of out-of-wedlock pregnancy among women who brought paternity suits as well as of the larger cohort that did not appear in court. Servants were perhaps a small proportion of the Lyon plaintiffs because Lyon offered many opportunities for women to work in the textile trades or because women who were identified as "servants" in the legal language of social description in fact usually did other kinds of work too so they are in fact over-represented in the records.

19. For the full text of the 1556 Edict and its subsequent reissues, see a Lyonnais archbishop's manual of instructions for parish priests published in 1787. *Rituel du diocese de Lyon imprimé par l'autorité de Monseigneur Antoine de Malvin de Montazet, archevèque et comte de Lyon, primat de France* (Lyon: Aimé Delaroche, 1787), vol. 2, 12, 351–352. For the 1556 text in the standard source for French laws, see François Isambert et al., *Recueil Général des Anciennes Lois Françaises depuis l'an 420 jusqu'à la Révolution de 1789* (Paris, 1829), vol. 13, 471–473.
20. Hanley in 1989 tied this lack of enforcement to what she called a "counterfeit culture" where women collaborated to resist intensified patriarchal management of female reproduction via the family-state compact. Ruff characterized compliance as "reluctant." Sarah Hanley, "Engendering the State: Family Formation and State Building in Early Modern France," *French Historical Studies* 16, no. 1 (Spring 1989): 11; Julius Ruff, *Crimes, Justice, and Public Order in Old Regime France* (London: Routledge, 1984), 169–170.
21. For declarations as legal instruments with many purposes, see (Claire Dolan cited in) Sylvie Brassard, "Le Notaire, La Justice et Le Justiciable: Les déclarations d'abandon de procès dans les actes notariés à Aix-en-Provence (1550–1600)," MA thesis, Université Laval, 2012, 9.
22. For the use of declarations to allege paternity before 1556, see Susan Broomhill, "Le prix d'amour: négociations après des relations sexuelles et des grossesses illegitimes à Paris au début du XVIe siècle," in *Femme en fleurs, femmes en corps: sang, santé, sexualités du Moyen Age aux Lumières*, edited by Cathy McClive and Nicolle Pellegrin (St. Etienne: Publications de l'Université de Saint-Étienne, 2010), 201. Depauw notes that were several different types of *déclarations de grosseses*, including legal actions that had old roots and continued throughout the old regime. Depauw, "Amour Illégitime," 1157.
23. Louis-Sébastian Mercier, *Tableau de Paris*, edited by Gustav Desnoiresterres (Paris, 1853), 215 and 218.
24. For Brillon and other jurists on these issues, see Annie Lefebvre-Telliard, "Marriage in France from the Sixteenth to the Eighteenth Centuries," in *Marriage in Europe, 1400–1800*, edited by Sylvie Seidel Mnchi (Toronto: University of Toronto Press, 2016); J. Fournel, *La séduction, considérée dans l'ordre judiciare* (Paris, 1781) passim and 86, for this error in understanding the terms of the 1556 Edict. For widespread conceptions about the edict and legal efforts to counter them in both local and broader legal prescription, see Véronique Demars-Sion, *Femmes séduites et abandonnées au 18e siècle: L'exemple du Cambrésis* (Lille: Ester, 1992), 116–120.
25. On the municipal and other local initiatives, see Depauw, "Amour Illégitime," 1157; Lottin, "Naissances illégitimes," 281–282; Armand Corre and Paul Aubry, *Documents de criminologie rétrospective: Bretagne, XVIIe et XVIIIe siècles* (Paris, 1895), 471–472; H. Hervot, *La médecine and les médecins à Saint Malo, 1500–1820* (Rennes: Librairie J. Plihon et L. Hommay, 1905), 74–101; Norberg, *Rich and Poor in Grenoble*, 97–98. Depauw acknowledges the very patchy observation of the Nantes regulations. The key early studies (Depauw or Lottin, for example) on illegitimacy that used "declarations" in fact used statements generated by the Hôtel-Dieu or municipal authority

that had nothing to do with the 1556 Edict. These critical distinctions have usually been conflated in subsequent work.

26. For the regulation's introduction and annulment, see Pierre Le Ridant, *Code matrimonial, ou Recueil complet de toutes les loix canoniques et civiles de France . . . sur les questions de mariage. Tome 2 / . . . Nouvelle édition par M***, avocat au Parlement, 1770* (Paris, 1770), 637. For similar restrictions on local efforts to expand regulation of reproduction in Toulouse, see Sylvie Perrier, "La grossesse entre intimité et publicité dans les archives judiciaries de la France d'Ancien Régime," unpublished paper, Family and Justice in the Archives: Histories of Intimacy in Transnational Perspective, Concordia University, May 2019. I thank Sylvie Perrier for sharing her fascinating work in progress with me.
27. *Rituel du diocese*, 401, for the table of contents.
28. ADR BP3543 22 March 1722 Dossier of Armonie and Dambois; ADR BP3551 29 March 1741 Dossier of Montmain [no other name given].
29. This book is filed in the first surviving box of *sénéchausée* records, which date to the 1660s, that is, decades earlier (ADR BP3540). It seems likely that an archivist popped it in to that box for want of knowing what else to do with it. The judges who signed the statements were Riveraulx De Varax and Louis Cholier, both nobles from elite judicial families. For renewed elite interest in morality at this time, see Jay Smith, *Nobility Reimagined: The Patriotic Nation in Eighteenth-Century France* (Ithaca, NY: Cornell University Press, 2005). The arrival of a new official in Carcassone in southern France in 1773 was followed by the introduction of the phrase *plainte et declaration* in court records of paternity suits. Phan, *Les Amours Illégitimes*, 122–123.
30. The "declarations" that Lottin used in his well-known article about illegitimacy in Lille were made by midwives, not young pregnant women.
31. The impact of archival practices on the histories we write has received much attention recently for a wide range of times, places, and subjects. These works include (among others) Ann Laura Stoler, *Along the Archival Grain: Epistemic Anxieties and Colonial Common Sense* (Princeton, NJ: Princeton University Press, 2010); Marisa Fuentes, *Dispossessed Lives: Slavery, Violence and the Archive* (Philadelphia: University of Pennsylvania Press, 2016), and a special issue of *French Historical Studies* (April 2017). For France, see also Arlette Farge, *Le gôut de l'archive* (Paris: Éditions du Seuil, 1989). For early modern archival practices in particular, the essays in "The Social History of the Archive: Record Keeping in Early Modern Europe," *Past and Present* 230, suppl. #11 (November 2016), and Kate Peters, Alexandra Walsham, and Lisebeth Corens, eds., *Archives and Information in the Early Modern World* (New York: Oxford University Press, 2018).
32. Phan, "Les déclarations de grossesse," 72.
33. ADR BP3541 27 July 1682 Dossier of Bert and Aymond; ADR BP3558 15 April 1762 Dossier of Rubard and Fiancon.
34. In Lyon, the first use of *déclaration en grossesse* as the case descriptor in an extant document was in 1732 (ADR BP 3549 Dossier of Berthier and Chaquet 19 January 1732) but it was used very rarely until the second half of the eighteenth century. In

Carcassone, for example, the term *plainte* was used exclusively until 1773 when the term *plainte et déclaration* appeared. Phan, *Les Amours Illégitimes* 122–123.

35. Cissie Fairchilds wrote in 1978 that declarations were "required by French law of women about to give birth to illegitimate children." By this account, the 1556 Edict's goal was public humiliation. The source of this information is unclear as she cites a 1975 article that notes declarations were not required. Julius Ruff claimed in 1984 that "the edict of Henry II required registration with judicial authorities of all pregnancies." Sarah Hanley claimed in a series of influential articles that the edict required single women to register their pregnancies and that midwives were required to identify and report the name of the fathers: "women were required to declare a pregnancy officially and to birth a child before witnesses." Fairchilds, "Female Sexual Attitudes," 630. (Fairchilds's declarations were all taken at the Aix Hôtel-Dieu in the eighteenth century and seem in fact to be a local institutional project only.) Ruff, *Crimes, Justice, and Public Order*, 169–170. Sarah Hanley, "The Marriage Pact," in *Connecting Spheres*, edited by Marilyn J. Boxer and Jean H. Quaetaert (New York: Oxford University Press, 1987), 56. See also Hanley, "Engendering the State." For the existence of the same error about the edict and required declarations in French scholarship, see, for instance, Olga Cragg and Rosenna Davison, *Sexualité, marriage et famille au XVIIIe siècle*, (Québec City: Les Presses de L'Université Laval, 1998), 244, who cite Yvonne Knibiehler and Catherine Fouquet, *Histoire des Mères du moyen age à nos jours* (1982, repr.; Paris: Montalba, 1977). On that page they refer to a "procedure" which went as follows—during childbirth, "they asked her who the father was while threatening her with death and flames of hell if she lied" (my translation) which they cite from Yvonne Knibiehler, *Les pères aussi ont une histoire* (Paris: Hatchette, 1987).

36. For an able summary of this framework, see Katherine Crawford, *European Sexualities, 1400–1800* (Cambridge: Cambridge University Press, 2007). Historians also linked reformed religion to the state project of disciplining female morality. For two important examples (among many), see Ulrike Strasser, *State of Virginity: Gender, Religion, and Politics in an Early Modern Catholic State* (Ann Arbor: University of Michigan Press, 2004) and Farr, *Authority and Sexuality*.

37. Historians who noted from the 1970s onward that the edict did not require declarations include Phan, "Les déclarations de grossesse," 61–88; Phan, *Les Amours Illégitimes*, 5; Depauw, "Amour Illégitime"; Jean-Louis Flandrin, "A Case of Naivete in the Use of Statistics," *Journal of Interdisciplinary History* 9, no. 2 (Autumn 1978), 310; Demar-Sion, *Femmes séduites et abandonées*, 112–124; and Gerber, *Bastards: Politics, Family, and Law*, 138–139.

38. These confirmation biases were so powerful that, apparently, a generation of historians and peer reviewers neglected the original text of the edict and overlooked the work of historians who pointed out that the edict did not require declarations. Anglophone historians, including myself, who repeated this claim routinely cited secondary scholarship usually identified "declarations" as a key example of the emergence of an early modern disciplinary state in which the regulation of family and female sexuality was a core project. See, among many possible examples, the following iterations of what the 1556 Edict required of pregnant single women: Kirsten

Gager, *Blood Ties and Fictive Ties: Adoption and Family Life in Early Modern France* (Princeton, NJ: Princeton University Press, 1996), 64 ; Leslie Tuttle, *Conceiving the Old Regime: Pronatalism and the Politics of Reproduction in Early Modern France* (New York: Oxford University Press, 2010), 70) McClive, *Menstruation and Procreation*,152–164; Broomhill, "Le Prix d'Amour," 224. I myself took this requirement as fact—see, for example, Julie Hardwick, "Policing Paternity: Historicizing Masculinity and Sexuality in Early-Modern France," *European Review of History*, 22, no. 4 (2015), 645.

39. For discussions of this jurisprudence, see Demars-Sion, *Femmes séduites*, and Gerber, *Bastards*.
40. For the importance of recognizing state claims as ambitious rhetoric that were far from translatable into practice without local support, see Steve Hindle, *The State and Social Change in Early Modern England, c. 1550–1640* (London: Palgrave Macmillan, 2002).For the ways in which courts of first instance tended to confirm neighborhood opinion and regional laws, see Hardwick, *Family Business*. In French historiography, the emphasis on state expansion through collaboration with local elites or elite families is associated with the work of William Beik, *Absolutism and Society in Seventeenth-Century France: State Power and Provincial Aristocracy in Languedoc* (Cambridge: Cambridge University Press, 1985), and Sarah Hanley's many articles. For a striking example of state interest in combining taxation and families, see the 1666 Edict passed under Louis XIV and his chief minister, Colbert, that promised tax exemption to fathers of ten living, legitimate children, discussed in Tuttle, *Conceiving the Old Regime*.
41. Lyon's Old Regime history has been explored in some classic social histories. For the Old Regime overall, see Françoise Bayard, *Vivre à Lyon sous l'ancien régime* (Paris: Perrin, 1997) and Maurice Garden, *Lyon et les Lyonnais au XVIIIe siècle* (Paris: Les Belles Lettres, 1970), 90–92. For important studies of aspects of Lyon's history, see Jean-Pierre Gutton, *La Société et les Pauvres: l'exemple de la généralité de Lyon, 1534–1789* (Paris: Les Belles Lettres, 1971); Anne Montenach, *Espaces et pratiques du commerce alimentaire à Lyon au XVIIe siècle: l'économie du quotidien* (Grenoble: Presses Universitaire de Grenoble, 2009); and the work of Olivier Zeller on a wide range of early modern topics.
42. For the domestic impact of a global economy in areas far from port cities, see Emma Rothschild, "Isolation and Economic Life in Eighteenth-Century France," *American Historical Review* 19, no. 4 (October 2014): 1055–1082, and Julie Hardwick, "Fractured Domesticity in the Old Regime: Families and Colonialism at Home in Eighteenth-Century France," *American Historical Review* 124, no. 4 (October 2019): 1267–1277. For Lyon and the consumer revolution, see Julie Hardwick, "Parasols and Poverty: Production, Reproduction and the Consumer Revolution," in *Market Ethics and Law c.1300–1850*, edited by Simon Middleton and James Shaw (New York: Routledge, 2017).
43. For city size and migration see Garden, *Lyon et Les Lyonnais*, 34 and 25–81; Philip Benedict, "Overview," in Philip Benedict, ed., *Cities and Social Change in Early*

Modern France (New York: Routledge, 1992), 24 (also provides a comparison to the sizes of other cities); Bayard, *Vivre à Lyon*, 105–115.

44. W. Gregory Monahan, *Year of Sorrows: The Great Famine of 1709 in Lyon* (Columbus: Ohio State University Press, 1993); Garden, *Lyon et les Lyonnais*; Bayard, *Vivre à Lyon*.

45. AM Lyon HCL HD G73 19. The archives of the Hôtel-Dieu for the abandoned children section include many examples of spouses who left, as well as one spouse's departure that tipped the other into crisis. While the scale of child surrender in Lyon has been well documented as has the terrifying mortality rates of those children, much work remains to be done on the lived experiences of those involved. For important work on different aspects of the abandonment of children at the Hôtel-Dieu, see Garden, *Lyon et Les Lyonnais* and Gutton, *La Société et les Pauvres*. For challenging lived experiences of Lyon workers in the 1760s, see Hardwick, "Parasols and Poverty," and "Fractured Domesticity."

46. Bellavitis, *Women's Work and Rights*, 197–208; Jan De Vries, *The Industrious Revolution: Consumer Demand and the Household Economy, 1650 to the Present* (Cambridge: Cambridge University Press, 2009).

47. Declarations of female textile workers in Lille (actually made by midwives about their clients) accounted for more than 50% of the total and servants less than 20% according to Lottin, "Naissance Illégitimes," 35. Much research in recent years has explored women's work in textiles and other kinds of non-domestic labor, including Hafter, *Women at Work*; Janine Lanza, *From Wives to Widows in Early Modern Paris: Gender, Economy, and Law* (New York: Routledge, 2007); Crowston, *Fabricating Women*; and Montenach, *Espaces et pratiques du commerce alimentaire*.

Although historians of female servants traditionally regarded their labor as devoted narrowly to domestic work, the great Lyon historian Jean-Paul Gutton observed almost fifty years ago that women described as servants did all kinds of commercial work for their employers. Steedman has recently emphasized the importance of textile work for English rural servants and Kushner has reiterated that the French word "servant" in the eighteenth century encompassed domestic labor and industrial work. Gutton, *La Société et les Pauvres;* Carolyn Steedman, *Master and Servant: Love and Labour in the English Industrial Age* (Cambridge: Cambridge University Press, 2007); Nina Kushner, *Erotic Exchanges: The World of Elite Prostitution in Eighteenth-Century Paris* (Ithaca, NY: Cornell University Press, 2013), 46.

For the classic historiography of servants in eighteenth-century France, see Cissie Fairchilds, *Domestic Enemies: Servants and Their Masters in Old Regime France* (Baltimore: Johns Hopkins University Press, 1984), and Sarah Maza, *Servants and Their Masters in Old Regime France: The Uses of Loyalty* (Princeton, NJ: Princeton University Press, 1983). On servants in England, see for 1560–1640 Eleanor Hubbard, *City Women: Money, Sex and the Social Order in Early Modern London* (Oxford: Clarendon Press, 2014), and for the eighteenth century, Steedman, *Master and Servant*.

More broadly, gender historians in early modern Europe have acknowledged the complexities of women's work hidden by labels like "servants." See Ågren, *Making a Living, Making a Difference*.

48. Hardwick, *Family Business*. See also the discussions of the fluid nature of early modern "household" spaces in Ågren, *Making a Living, Making a Difference* and Amanda Vickery, *Behind Closed Doors: At Home in Georgian England* (New Haven, CT: Yale University Press, 2010).
49. See the editors' introduction and Randolph Trumbach's essay for age as a key organizer of sexuality in Sarah Toulalan and Kate Fishers, eds., *The Routledge History of Sex and the Body, 1500 to the Present* (New York: Routledge, 2013).
50. For European and Lyonnais marriage demographics, see Michael Flinn, *The European Demographic System, 1500–1820* (Baltimore: Johns Hopkins University Press, 1981) and Garden, *Lyon et les Lyonnais*, 90–92.
51. Flinn, *The European Demographic System*; Garden, *Lyon et les Lyonnais*, 90–92. For Lyon illegitimacy rates in the 5%–10% range, see Garden, *Lyon et les Lyonnais*, 37, and Bayard, *Vivre à Lyon*, 186. For the likely under-registration of out-of-wedlock births, see chapter 4.
52. For age of puberty as around sixteen in eighteenth-century France, see Anne Jacobson Schutte, Thomas Kuehn, and Silvana Seidel Menchi, eds., *Time, Space, and Women's Lives in Early Modern Europe* (Kirksville, MO: Truman State University, 2001), 66; for the rarity of "precocious" marriage, that is, for one or both partners to be younger than twenty, except for elite families, see Jean-Pierre Bardet, "Early Marriage in Pre-Modern France," *History of the Family* 6, no. 3 (2001): 345–363.
53. Priests seemed quite willing to record children as legitimate if the father was present at the baptism (as was often the case in these relationships), regardless of the couple's legal marital status, so children born out of wedlock were likely under-recorded by some significant amount in parish registers. See chapter 4.
54. ADR BP3543 17 July 1743 Dossier of Pitra and Matton. For an image of one workspace of a *batteur d'or* that evokes the "co-existence" Pitra described, see the engraving in Diderot's *Encyclopédie*—available at https://fr.wikipedia.org/wiki/Batteur_d%27or#/media/File:Atelier_de_batteur_d%E2%80%99Or_XVIIIe_si%C3%A8cle.jpg, accessed 1 March 2019. For elite concern in Lyon in 1707 about the mobility of *tourneuses* and the essential work they did, see *Statuts et Reglements que le Roy veut & entend être observe en l'Art et Metier de Tireurs, Ecacheurs & Fileurs d'Or & D'Argent en la ville de Lyon* (Lyon nd) 82 and 112.
55. ADR BP5344 23 October 1724 Dossier of Martin and Louis. Martin's trajectory was likely very similar to that of young women in other big cities as well as Lyon. See Kushner, *Erotic Exchanges*, 46.
56. Historians have debated the impact of migration on relationships between men and women at later moments in the life course. Maurice Garden observed very low rates of remarriage by widows in Lyon, and he argued that this was likely due to the constant stream of young women moving to the city and available for matrimony as well as labor. Janine Lanza suggested that the low rate of remarriage for Lyon widows might have been due not only to competition from younger women but because of the unusual amount of paid work available to women, including widows, that meant they

did not feel pressure to remarry. Garden, *Lyon et les Lyonnais*, 92; Lanza, *From Wives to Widows*, 157.
57. Hafter, *Women at Work*, 133.
58. *Statuts et règlemens que le roy veut et entend être observés en l'art et métier de Tireurs, Ecacheurs & Fileurs d'Or & d'Argent de la ville de Lyon* (A Lyon a depense de la commaunte, ND) 82–83 for the 1707 debates, 111–112 for the 1733 debates. These workers produced silk and gold thread to be used in luxury textiles.
59. *Statuts et règlemens*, 32 and passim. On servants doing essential work of commerce by transporting goods between households, see Ågren, *Making a Living, Making A Difference*.
60. Weavers were usually male while draw girls usually pulled the cords of looms, but wives of master weavers were allowed to have looms. Hafter, *Women at Work*, 133.
61. ADR BP3541 22 October 1680.
62. Laura Gowing, "The Haunting of Susan Lay: Servants and Mistresses in Seventeenth-Century England," *Gender and History* 14, no. 2 (August 2002): 183–201. In Lyon, see, for instance, Marie Aymin's account of working as a servant for a tailor, Claude Francois, and his wife; after the wife died, Francois began to proposition Aymin and offered to marry her. ADR BP 3446 20 February 1726 Dossier of Aymin and Francois.
63. This is not to say that young women employed as textile workers never experienced sexual harassment from their employers. See, for instance, Anne Martin's account of what she framed as entirely non-consensual sex with the son of her employer who subsequently threatened to kill her if she blamed him for her pregnancy. ADR BP 5344 23 October 1724 Dossier of Martin and Louis.

Chapter 2

1. ADR BP 3544 1 November 1723 Dossier of Perricaud and Pillot.
2. For politics, economies, and law as intrinsic to street life, see Karin Sennefelt, "The Politics of Hanging Around and Tagging Along: Everyday Practices of Politics in Eighteenth-Century Stockholm," *Past and Present* 203, supplement 4 (January 2009): 172–190; Anne Montenach, "Formal and Informal Economy in an Urban Context: The Case of the Food Trade in Seventeenth-Century Lyon," in *Shadow Economies and Irregular Work in Urban Europe, 16th to 20th Centuries*, edited by Thomas Buchner and Philip Hoffman-Rehnitz (Berlin: LIT Verlag, 2011); Julie Hardwick, *Family Business: Litigation and the Political Economies of Daily Life in Early Modern France* (Oxford: Oxford University Press, 2009), 71–74.
3. This is not to say that a broad range of licit intimacy was restricted to cities but to insist that city life configured it in specific ways. For observations about the wide scope of physical intimacy before marriage among young couples in rural France in the eighteenth century (in the area around Le Mans in the Loire Valley), see Anne Fillon, *Les Trois Bagues aux Doigts: Amours Villeageoises au XVIII siècle* (Paris: R. Laffont, 1989), 217–221.

4. ADR BP3543 3 March 1721 Dossier of Ruedy and Michel; ADR BP3551 16 November 1740 Dossier of Rang and Millot.
5. ADR BP3541 17 December 1680 Dossier of Ferraud and Terme; BP 3442 23 July 1687 Dossier of Chauvet and De Juif; ADR BP3542 5 March 1688 Dossier of Joanon and Marcou.
6. ADR BP3544 8 June 1724 Dossier of Valouey and Richard; ADR BP3551 5 August 1740 Dossier of Clerc and Flacheron.
7. ADR BP3541 17 February 1683.
8. Joan DeJean, *How Paris Became Paris: The Invention of the Modern City* (London: Bloomsbury, 2014), 132–142. Paris was probably not quite as exceptional as DeJean suggests, as many of its new features were shared with other large cities across Europe, including Lyon. It was likely very exceptional in the number of travel guides devoted to it, and these provide the core evidence base for her excellent book.
9. ADR BP3552 4 January 1744 Dossier of Moulin and Fontrobert.
10. For the spread of street lighting in Paris, in Lyon, and elsewhere in Europe, see DeJean, *How Paris Became Paris*, 132–142; Jean Baptiste Monfalcon, *Histoire Monumentale de de Lyon*, vol. 6 (Lyon: Bibliotheque de la ville, 1866), 26; Phillip Benedict, *Cities and Social Change in Early Modern France* (New York: Routledge, 1989), 46–47.
11. For the importance of the streets as social and political sites, see Colin Jones, "Meeting, Greeting and Other 'Little Customs of the Day' on the Streets of Late Eighteenth-Century Paris," *Past and Present* 203, supplement 4 (2009): 144–171, and Sennefelt, "The Politics of Hanging Around and Tagging Along."
12. ADR BP3540 18 December 1663 Dossier of Recorneau and Favery.
13. ADR BP3542 27 October, 1686 Dossier of Caron and Demin; ADR BP3541 13 December 1682 Dossier of Minquet and Dumarets; ADR BP3542 17 October 1686 Dossier of Namy and Bergeron.
14. ADR BP3541 17 February 1683 Dossier of Ollier and Guillemin; ADR BP3541 13 November 1669 Dossier of Cossard and Duplot.
15. ADR BP3541 1 July 1684 Dossier of Florin and Cognard.
16. ADR BP3545 6 March 1725 Dossier of Quentin and Delphin.
17. ADR BP 3545 19 July 1725 Dossier of Marie Maugard and Jean Ravier; ADR BP 3551 19 October 1740 Dossier of Tronchet and Estodat.
18. ADR BP3545 6 March 1725 Dossier of Quentin and Delphin.
19. ADR BP3541 22 October 1680 Dossier of Roussin and Chabanassy; ADR BP5342 28 May 1689 Dossier of Chana and Ramel; ADR BP 3545 19 July 1725 Dossier of Maugard and Ravier.
20. ADR BP3551 2 June 1740 Dossier of Grissonet and Peysonnaux.
21. ADR BP3551 15 April 1741 Dossier of Michaud and Ripert.
22. ADR BP3540 6 February 1668 Dossier of Deluis and Gaultier.
23. ADR BP3549 5 August 1730 Dossier of Gillet and Feraud; ADR BP3549 15 September 1730 Dossier of Durand and Riviere; ADR BP3543 21 March 1721 Dossier of Chabry and Boyer.

24. ADR BP 3551 5 August 1749 Dossier of Clerc and Flacheron; ADR BP 3551 23 June 1749 Dossier of Lalaneure and Rossaly; ADR BO3540 25 April 1669 Dossier of Priere and Rambaud.
25. ADR BP 3549 15 September 1730 Dossier of Thillier and Gaylart.
26. ADR BP3549 26 November 1730 Dossier of Duchene and Poully.
27. ADR BP3549 21 November 1741 Dossier of Planet and Cheville; ADR BP3543 21 March 1721 Dossier of Chabry and Boyer.
28. ADR BP3549 2 March 1732 Dossier of Berger and Chappuis.
29. ADR BP3549 22 July 1730 Dossier of Allegret and Caillat; ADR BP3551 19 October 1740 Dossier of Tronchet and Estodat.
30. ADR BP3541 5 May 1682 Dossier of Pichon and Lucenay; ADR 12G 7 June 1685 procès-verbal Jacques Issac.
31. See the contemporary definition in the *Le Dictionnaire de L'Académie Française* (1694).
32. Few promises to marry are extant in the archives despite many references to them in paternity suits. It is unclear whether women rarely deposited them as evidence or they have not been preserved by court clerks or archivists over time. They were not required as evidence, and their presence or absence does not seem to have made any difference to the outcome of paternity suits.
33. ADR BP3541 14 May 1680 Dossier of Berchet and Flacheron. The paternity case listed her name as Anne Berchet, and it is unclear where the name confusion came from. All subsequent details are also from this dossier.
34. See Julie Hardwick, *The Practice of Patriarchy: Gender and the Politics of Household Authority in Early Modern France* (State College: Pennsylvania State University Press, 1998), and Laurie Nussdorfer, "Writing and the Power of Speech: Notaries and Artisans in Baroque Rome," in *Culture and Identity in Early Modern Europe (1500–1800): Essays in Honor of Natalie Zemon Davis*, edited by Barbara B. Diefendorf and Carla Hesse (Ann Arbor: University of Michigan Press, 1993).
35. ADR BP3558 15 April 1762 Dossier of Rubard and Fiancon.
36. ADR BP3560 17 December 1767 Dossier of Sibert and Chaboud.
37. The rhetoric used in such letters is a striking, rank-specific contrast to the lively elite print culture debate in which seventeenth-century French men and women equated both love and passion with peril and unhappiness. For a summary of this debate, see Stephanie Merrim, *Early Modern Women's Writings and Sor Juana Inés de la Cruz* (Nashville, TN: Vanderbilt University Press, 1999), 95–103.
38. ADR BP3555 28 September 1753 Dossier of Mollard and Dubois; ADR BP3552 26 November 1743 Dossier of Dutremblois and Cadet. A dense epistolary culture between middling and elite intimate partners became common in the eighteenth century. It remains unclear how widespread this culture was among working people because their letters so rarely survive. Although very few elite women pursued paternity suits, Marguerite Chavannes, the daughter of a nobleman, provides a rare window into the expansive culture of letter writing that became integral to intimacy at an elite level as she deposited with the court twenty-seven letters from her partner. ADR BP3541 Dossier of Chavannes and De Cossard. For epistolary culture as an essential

practice of middling and elite intimate relationships in the eighteenth century, see Dena Goodman, "Marriage Choice and Marital Success: Reasoning about Marriage, Love and Happiness ," in *Family and State in Early Modern France*, edited by Suzanne Desan and Jeffrey Merrick (University Park: Pennsylvania State University Press, 2009), 26–61, and Sally Holloway, *The Game of Love in Georgian England: Courtship, Emotions and Material Culture* (Oxford: Oxford University Press, 2019).

39. For gifts and courtship in England, see Diana O'Hara, *Courtship and Constraint: Rethinking the Making of Marriage in Tudor England* (Manchester: Manchester University Press, 2000), 57–87; Laura Gowing, *Domestic Dangers: Women, Words, and Sex in Early Modern London* (Oxford: Oxford University Press, 1996), esp. 159–166; Holloway, *The Game of Love*.

40. As witnesses were not asked specifically about gifts, such tokens were probably more common than suggested by the number of references in these records. ADR BP3540 6 February 1657 Dossier of Cottelier and Bernier; ADR BP3540 1 May 1676 Dossier of Decert and Devaux; ADR BP3542 23 July 1687 Dossier of Chauvet and De Juif; ADR BP3541 22 October 1680 Dossier of Roussin and Chabanassy. The only other types of gifts mentioned in these records were a wooden chest and a silver tobacco box.

41. ADR BP3543 23 July 1720 and 28 July 1720. Jean-Paul Gutton, *La Société et les Pauvres: l'exemple de la généralité de Lyon 1534–1789* (Paris: Les Belles Lettres, 1971), 69–78 for estimates of working men's wages.

42. ADR BP 3540 1 July 1674 Dossier of Lyonnet and Moulet.

43. ADR BP3555 28 September 1753 Dossier of Dubois and Mollard; ADR BP3540 19 June 1658 Dossier of Peyrieu and Peyssillon.

44. For the context-specific meaning of objects, see John Styles, "Objects and Emotions: The London Foundling Hospital Tokens, 1741–1760," https://emotionalobjects.wordpress.com/2013/11/11/181/, accessed 12 March 2019.

45. ADR BP3560 17 December 1767 Dossier of Sibert and Chabord.

46. Historians have debated the extent of early modern popular knowledge about sex and reproduction. For England, Mary Fissell has argued that there was much discussion about sex in cheap print culture, albeit often erroneous in terms of accuracy; Laura Gowing, however, has suggested that knowledge about reproduction was the preserve of married women. For France, Cathy McClive has argued that no stark divide existed in knowledge of reproduction and attitudes toward possession of that knowledge between married and unmarried women. Mary Fissell, *Vernacular Bodies: The Politics of Reproduction in Early Modern England* (New York: Oxford University Press, 2004); Laura Gowing, *Common Bodies: Women, Touch and Power in Seventeenth-Century England* (New Haven, CT: Yale University Press, 2003); Cathy McClive, *Menstruation and Procreation in Early Modern France* (London: Ashgate, 2015).

47. BP3549 28 November 1728 Dossier of Frederville and Briquet.

48. ADR BP3540 21 August 1677 Dossier of Official and Pinardy; ADR BP 3543 30 June 1721 Dossier of Rangeard and Mercier.

49. ADR BP3560 17 December 1767 Dossier of Sibert and Chaboud.

50. See, for instance, ADR 3541 5 July 1683.

51. See Julie Hardwick, "Early Modern Perspectives on the Long History of Domestic Violence: The Case of Seventeenth-Century France," *Journal of Modern History* 78, no. 1 (March 2006): 1–36; and Hardwick, *Family Business*, 183–221, for definitions and negotiations about the legitimate and acceptable use of force as opposed to the use of force categorized as excessive and abusive.

52. As Amy Stanley noted, historians have often skirted the issue of sexual violence due to incomplete evidence (also often the case today) or "suggested women seized on cultural narratives about seduction and coercion to explain themselves." Amy Stanley, "Writing the History of Sexual Assault in the Age of #METOO," *Perspectives on History* (November 2018). Historians have noted the occurrence of such accounts across Europe between 1500 and 1800. For Spain, see Abigail Dyer, "Seduction by Promise of Marriage: Law, Sex and Culture in Seventeenth-Century Spain," *Sixteenth Century Journal* 34, no. 2 (Summer 2003): 439–455, and Renato Barahona, *Sex Crimes: Honor and the Law in Early Modern Spain* (Toronto: University of Toronto Press, 2003), 62–69. Historians who have observed the consistent descriptions of use of force have explained them in various ways. Women's complaints to the Paris police in the late eighteenth century for "seduction and abandonment" (legally defined as a crime where men had seduced women with no intention of marriage and then disappeared before or during a resulting pregnancy) routinely alleged the use of force and Arlette Farge speculated that the women drew on deep memories of Sleeping Beauty to shape their complaints—that is, young women drew on oral popular culture tradition to frame a narrative about their circumstances. Elizabeth Cohen argued in her analysis of the Artemesia Gentileschi rape case in early seventeenth-century Rome that women used a prescribed legal script in rape cases in which violence was a trope because that is what cases required to be successful. Anna Clark and Katie Barclay noted that "forcible seduction" was considered routine in courtships in England and Scotland because men expected to have to use violence to overcome women's modesty and engage their desire. For the argument that "forcible seduction" was routine in England and Scotland, see Julie Gammon, "Researching Sexual Violence, 1660–1800: A Critical Analysis," and Katie Barclay, "From Rape to Marriage: Questions of Consent in Eighteenth-Century Britain," in *Interpreting Sexual Violence, 1660–1800*, edited by Anne Greenfield (London:Pickering and Chatto, 2013),. See also Arlette Farge, *Fragile Lives: Violence, Power and Solidarity in Late Eighteenth-Century Paris*, translated by Carol Shelton (Cambridge, MA: Harvard University Press, 1993), 36–38; Elizabeth Cohen, "The Trials of Artemisia Gentileschi: A Rape as History," *Sixteenth Century Journal* 31, no. 1 (Spring 2000), 47–75.

53. For comparisons of the narratives of intercourse between couples in ongoing consensual relationships made in paternity suits as opposed to legal actions that alleged rape, see Julie Hardwick, "Peril Stories: Sexual Violence and Domesticity in early modern Europe," in *The Routledge History of the Domestic Sphere in Europe: Sixteenth to Nineteenth Century*, edited by Joachim Eibach and Margaret Lanzinger (Abingdon: Routledge, 2020) . See also the arguments of Cohen (who contends that the use of violence was not marked as rape by early moderns in the way modern society does) and Karin Jansson who argues that the shifting definition of acceptable

(licit) or unacceptable (rape) male behavior in terms of sex depended on rank and marital status as well as occupation. Cohen, "Trials of Artemisia Gentileschi"; Karin Jansson, "English Summary of *Conceptualizing Rape: Gendered Notions of Violence in Sweden 1600–1800*" (PhD Thesis, University of Uppsala, 2002).

54. Sharon Block, *Rape and Sexual Power in Early America* (Chapel Hill: University of North Carolina Press, 2006); Garthine Walker, "Everyman or Monster? The Rapist in Early Modern England, 1600–1750," *History Workshop Journal* 76, no. 1 (Autumn 2013): 5–31, and "Rape, Acquittal and Culpability in Popular Crime Reports in England, 1670 –1750," *Past and Present* 220, no.1 (August 2013): 115–142.

55. Alecia Simmons, "Embodying Sexual Violence in the Civil Courts: On Promises, Coverture and Consent," unpublished paper. I thank Alecia Simmons for sharing her work in progress with me. For failures of married men to meet their obligations that could lead courts and communities as well as wives to seek redress, such as excessive domestic violence or financial mismanagement, see Hardwick, *Family Business*.

56. ADR BP 3551 2 June 1740 Dossier of Grissonet and Peyssonaux.

57. ADR BP3551 16 November 1740 Dossier of Vincent and Moulin; ADR BP3549 20 January 1730 Dossier of Trenet and Francois; ADR BP 3551 16 November 1740 Dossier of Rang and Milot.

58. A few surviving copies of the Lyon Affiches from 1761 to 1774 have been digitized. A search for *danse* returns many entries for *maitres de danses* offering lessons and for their opening of *salles de danse*. Paris travelers described lavish, purpose-built dance halls that were quite different in that regard from the Lyon dance halls that were rooms in regular buildings, but the dancing master supervised dances and spectators were likely very similar. Luc-Vincent Thiéry, *Almanach du voyageur à Paris contenant une description sommaire . . . Ouvrage utile aux citoyens, et indispensable pour l'Etranger* (Paris, 1784), 602–603.

59. ADR BP 3551 Dossier of de Moulin and Vincent 29 October 1740; ADR BP 3449 20 January 1730 Dossier of Trenet and Francois; ADR BP 3551 16 November 1740 Dossier of Rang and Milot. Eighteenth-century city dancing masters made very modest livings, comparable to those of shopkeepers or artisans; Garden, *Lyon et le Lyonnais*, 90. For an unusually explicit articulation of earlier types of dancing, see Cottillier and Bernier who went with some friends to a parish feast day celebration where they danced and Bernier said she danced so well he never wanted to dance with anyone else (ADR BP 3540 6 June 1657). For the long-term implications of the rise of commercial leisure (including dance halls) for young people's dating habits, especially the quid pro quo aspect of young men "treating" or paying for their girlfriends, see Kathy Peiss, *Cheap Amusements: Working Women and Leisure in Turn-of-the-Century New York* (Philadelphia: Temple University Press, 1986). For the rise of new forms of paid entertainment in eighteenth-century Paris that included dances, see Robert Isherwood, *Farce and Fantasy: Popular Entertainment in Eighteenth-Century Paris* (New York: Oxford University Press, 1986).

60. ADR BP3549 16 June 1730 Dossier of Bornier and Burel.
61. ADR BP3549 27 June 1731 Dossier of Cagny and Gonnet; ADR BP 3549 16 June 1730 Dossier of Brun and Bodet; ADR BP 3549 15 September 130 Dossier of Thillier and Gaylart.
62. ADR BP 3551 20 September 1740 Dossier of Anger and Blain; ADR BP 3551 4 October 1740 Dossier of Privat and Lefebvre; ADR BP 3551 8 August 1741 Dossier of Blanc and Clement; ADR 10G3811 7 May 1768 Dossier of Favard and Belleville. Privat's reference to a promise of an establishment picked up what became an occasional theme that references to run a small business, with a partner or individually.
63. BP3561 29 April 1768 Dossier of Thervenin and Martin.
64. ADR BP3551 5 August 1740 Dossier of Clerc and Flacheron.

Chapter 3

1. ADR BP3543 16 March 1720 Dossier of Rougemond and Reposte; ADR BP 3544 11 September 1724 Dossier of Transchard and Montainier; ADR BO3543 4 January 1721 Dossier of Silvester and Chosellard.
2. Scholarship on the emerging history of early modern masculinity has framed a many-faceted register in which age, rank, reputation, sexuality, race, ethnicity, and competing priorities complicated male privileges and obligations. Patricia Simons and Katherine Crawford have emphasized the centrality of pleasure, and not just procreation, in normative elite discourses about male sexuality. Historians of many regions have shown that early modern masculinity was not a homogenous category, and access to what is often called patriarchal privilege was by no means uniform among men. For a sampling of this rich scholarship, see Patricia Simons, *The Sex of Men in Premodern Europe: A Cultural History* (Cambridge: Cambridge University Press, 2011); Katherine Crawford, *The Sexual Culture of the French Renaissance* (Cambridge: Cambridge University Press, 2010); Alexandra Shepard, *The Meaning of Manhood in Early Modern England*, Oxford Studies in Social History (New York: Oxford University Press, 2003); Julie Hardwick, *Family Business: Litigation and the Political Economies of Daily Life in Early Modern France* (Oxford: Oxford University Press, 2009), 108–110 and 199–200; Julie Hardwick, "Early Modern Perspectives on the Long History of Domestic Violence: The Case of Seventeenth-Century France," *Journal of Modern History* 78, no. 1 (March 2006): 1–36; Julie Hardwick, "Policing Paternity: historicizing masculinity and sexuality in early modern France," *European Review of History: Revue Européene d'histoire* 22, 4 (2015): 643-57; Alexandra Shepard, "Brokering Fatherhood: Illegitimacy and Paternal Rights and Responsibilities in Early Modern England," in *Remaking English Society: Social Relations and Social Change in Early Modern England*, edited by Steve Hindle, Alexandra Shepard, and John Walter, 41–64 (Woodbridge, UK: Boydell Press, 2013); Bernard Capps, "The Double Standard Revisited: Plebian Women and Male Sexual Reputation in Early Modern England," *Past and Present* 162 (1999): 70–100;

Edward Behrend-Martinez, "Taming Don Juan: Limiting Male Sexuality in Early Modern Spain," *Gender and History* 24, no. 2 (August, 2012): 333–352; Edward Behrend-Martinez, "Spain Violated: Foreign Men in Spain's Heartland," *European Review of History: Revue Européene d'histoire* 22, 4 (2015): 579–594.

3. See Katherine Crawford, *European Sexualities, 1400–1800* (Cambridge: Cambridge University Press, 2007),146 and passim, for an excellent summary of the work on the impact of expanded regulation of sexuality. For important work on this issue for England, see Martin Ingram, *Church Courts, Sex and Marriage in England, 1570–1640* (Cambridge: Cambridge University Press, 1990); Martin Ingram, *Carnal Knowledge: Regulating Sex in England, 1470-1600* (New York: Cambridge University Press, 2017).

4. ADR BP 3541 28 July 1682 Dossier of Mulatier and Priou; ADR BP3542 12 October 1686 Dossier of Demen and Carron; ADR BP 3543 19 February 1721 Dossier of Bonnard and Cartier; ADR BP3543 9 February 1721 Dossier of Girard and Biton.

5. ADR BP3541 22 October 1681 Dossier of Roussin and Chabanassy; ADR BP3544 22 October 1723 Dossier of Martin and Louis. Young women were extremely vulnerable when their intimate partners were their employers, a group highlighted in the historiography of illegitimacy, not least because marriage was often not feasible. Three examples show the particular varieties of challenges they could face. Andree Ganot worked for Sr. Mazard, a shoemaker, in 1685 and his "promises" and "hopes of marriage" led her to have intercourse with him, but when he "abandoned" her, she moved from her mother's to a neighborhood just outside the city because she was "ashamed" of being pregnant in front of her own neighborhood. Pierrette Benoist asked a surgeon to tell her employer she was pregnant after they had had sex several times, a strategy that suggests she was apprehensive. Her anxiety was fulfilled when her employer asked her to name one of his apprentices as the father and promised he would take care of her if she did so. She did not want to make a false claim and even discussed the request with her mother who replied it would "be on her conscience" if she did. When she did not, he refused to do anything for her. Marie Chambre explained that she had been deprived of her wages as well as dishonored when her employer refused to marry her. ADR BP 3541 1 September 1685 Dossier of Ganot and Mazard; ADR BP3551 24 December 1740 Dossier of Benoist and Dessiateur; ADR BP3551 7 September 1741 Dossier of Chambre and Marquin.

6. ADR BP 3551 22 February 1741 Dossier of Groble and Virey.

7. ADR BP 3545 7 March 1725 Dossier of Lauchausee and Perron; ADR BP3543 20 July 1720 Dossier of Burraud and Royer; ADR BP3545 Dossier of Leurat and Champetre 22 January 1725; ADR BP3543 23 October 1723 Dossier of Anne Martin and Antoine Louis.

8. ADR BP3543 12 February 1720 Dossier of Legout and Falconnet.

9. ADR BP3540 15 September 1670 Dossier of Vacheron and Hugouin. Notably, Vacheron did not explain, nor did the court ask her, why she had not filed a paternity suit sooner. Perhaps her patience was simply worn out with Hugouin's promises that he

would eventually marry her and she wanted him to clarify the status of their long relationship, or perhaps some other grievance had motivated her. Historians have found it very difficult to establish the extent of cohabitation without official marriage due to the lack of documentation. For some context in different settings, see Allyson Poska, *Women and Authority in Early Modern Spain: The Peasants of Galicia* (Oxford: Oxford University Press, 2006), and Ginger S. Frost, *Living in Sin, Co-habiting as Husband and Wife in Nineteenth-Century England* (Manchester: Manchester University Press, 2008).
10. ADR BP 3545 9 May 1725 Dossier of Rozet and Bouin.
11. ADR BP 3543 13 January 1720 Dossier of Fournais and Mallet.
12. For an example of how these obligations worked out in a different context, see Katie Barclay, "Illicit Intimacies: The Imagined 'Homes' of Gilbert Innes of Stow and His Mistresses (1751–1832)," *Gender and History* 27, no. 3 (2015): 576–590.
13. Julie Hardwick, *The Practice of Patriarchy: Gender and the Politics of Household Authority in Early Modern France* (University Park: Pennsylvania State University Press, 1998), 18.
14. ADR BP3542 13 July 1697 Dossier of Morel and Poullin. The father successfully objected to the proposed marriage.
15. ADR BP3544 23 March 1724 Dossier of Bruyart and Picart; ADR BP3541 15 June 1685 Dossier of Berthaud and Poulet; ADR BP3543 23 July 1720. Dossier of Rozet and Michaud.
16. ADR BP3560 17 December 1767 Dossier of Pierette and Chaboud; ADRBP 3542 23 July 1687 Dossier of Chauvet and De Juif.
17. ADR BP3540 20 July 1673 Dossier of Colombet and Grandon.
18. ADR BP3551 29 October 1740 Dossier of Moulin and Vincent.
19. ADR BP3551 20 September 1740 Dossier of Anger and Blain.
20. ADR BP3552 12 December 1742 Dossier of Berger and Duplaignant.
21. ADR BP3542 8 July 1697 Dossier of Brouillard and Duvert; ADR BP3552 23 April 1741 Dossier of Maison and Laurent.
22. For general patterns of litigation, see Hardwick, *Family Business*.
23. ADR BP3540 1 May 1676 Dossier of Decert and Duvaux; ADR BP 3543 16 March 1720 Dossier of Rougemond and Reposte; ADR BP3542 24 May 1689 Dossier of Bourjon and Berthet.
24. ADR BP3551 5 April 1741 Dossier of Laurat and Cassart; ADR BP3551 29 March 1741 Dossier of Montmain and (no name given).
25. ADR BP3540 1 May 1677 Dossier of Goujardy and Bonjour; ADR BP3540 17 May 1668 Dossier of Renauol and Lacoste; ADR BP3544 11 January 1723 Dossier of Perricaud and Pillot.
26. ADR BP3551 4 October 1740 Dossier of Privat and Le Febvre.
27. For requirements in other cities that young women who used the Hôtel-Dieu services make a "declaration," see, for example, Kathryn Norberg, *Rich and Poor in Grenoble, 1600–1814* (Berkeley: University of California Press, 1985), 198. These could then be used in paternity suits. I have seen no evidence about such a requirement at the Lyon

Hôtel-Dieu, but it appears that they prompted some young women to file paternity suits if they had not made private arrangements for payment.

28. The boxes for 1725 and 1726, for example, include twenty-seven cases associated with the Hôtel-Dieu out of a total of forty-two cases and they were often clustered, such as four on the same day in August 1726. Women who came to the court for payment to be made to the Hôtel-Dieu were also less likely to be in long-term stable consensual relationships, perhaps because the longer term stable consensual relationships were more likely to have their arrangements decided in extra-judicial ways as we will see in chapter 4. A case study of 1760 that shows only four of 262 illegitimate babies at the Hôtel-Dieu that year could be matched with "declarations" in court. Jean-Marcel Bourgeat, "L'abandon d'enfants à Lyon: Origines sociales et géographiques . . . le cas de 1760," *Société des Etudes Historiques Revolutionnaires et Imperials* (novembre 2011), 27.
29. ADR BP3542 23 September 1687 Dossier of Chauvet and De Juif.
30. These kinds of arrangements are discussed in chapter 4.
31. ADR BP3540 Dossier of Dart and Barrot (no first names as the witness statements are the only surviving evidence) 14 December 1674; ADR BP3551 26 April 1741 Dossier of Dugoin and Ballet.
32. ADR BP3546 20 February 1726 Dossier of Aymin and Francois.
33. Examples include ADR BP3549 5 August 1730 Gillet and Feraud; ADR BP3551 30 November 1741 Dossier of Mann and Hera; ADR BP 3543 16 March 1720 Dossier of Rougemond and Reposte.
34. For legal action as a way to repair honor in a variety of early modern Spanish crimes involving sexuality, see Renato Barahona, *Sex Crimes, Honour, and Law in Early Modern Spain: Vizcaya, 1528–1735* (Toronto: University of Toronto Press, 2003).
35. ADR BP3542 21 November 1721 Dossier of Faury and Matteron.
36. ADR BP3540 15 September 1670 Dossier of Vacheron and Hugonin.
37. Mortality rates of wet-nursed babies were extremely high, and rural parish priests seemingly did not always record in their parish registers the deaths of many Lyon babies who were temporary visitors. See Maurice Garden, *Lyon et les Lyonnais au XVIIIe siècle* (Paris: Les Belles Lettres, 1970), 116–140.
38. ADR BP3540 15 September 1670 Dossier of Vacheron and Hugouin. The size of the financial award was exceptional and it is unclear why the judges awarded it. Although women quite often brought paternity suits after the birth of a baby or even a second baby, perhaps the length of their relationship and the five children seemed to signal a deception that justified a larger compensation.
39. ADR BP3540 14 November 1663 Dossier of Joubert and Bonjour.
40. For the state of prisons, see Nicole Castan, *Justice et repression en Languedoc à L'Epoque Des Lumieres* (Paris: Flammarion, 1980), 222–228. ADR BP3542 20 December 1743 Dossier of Duon and Eyroux.
41. ADR BP3542 15 May 1688 Dossier of Gabet and Benoist; ADR BP3542 26 May 1689 Dossier of Chana and Ramel; ADR BP3540 28 August 1676 Dossier of Julien; ADR BP3540 4 July 1683 Dossier of Carler and de la Frasser.

42. ADR BP 3540 25 May 1659 Dossier of Bourdan and Puzin; ADR BP 3540 June 19 1658 Dossier of Peyssillon and Lucie Peyrieu; ADR BP 3541 July 5 1685 Dossier of Blanchin and Marest; ADR BP3552 23 April 1741 Dossier of Maison and Laurent.
43. ADR BP3540 29 January 1658 Dossier of Beaujollon and Bichon. Joseph-Michel-Antoine Servan, *Discours de Monsieur S***, ancient avocat général au parlement de ****, dans un procès sur une déclaration de grossesse* (Lyon, 17***). The royal prosecutor imposed this highly gendered interpretation on the circumstances even while he acknowledged that in the wake of Beaujallon's complaint to the court, sergeants had caught Bichon trying to flee the city dressed as a woman, a strategy that might seem to imply that Bichon thought he indeed had something to run away from. For the moralizing strain among the elite judiciary in seventeenth- and eighteenth-century France, see James R. Farr, *Authority and Sexuality in Early Modern Burgundy (1550–1730)* (New York: Oxford University Press, 1995), and Jay Smith, *Nobility Reimagined: The Patriotic Nation in Eighteenth-Century France* (Ithaca, NY: Cornell University Press, 2005). Smith notes that Servan was a prominent Enlightenment legal reformer as well as a prosecutor in the parlement of Grenoble, not far from Lyon, who emphasized renewed commitment to morality as the foundation to counter increased corruption. Smith, *Nobility Reimagined*, 170. For Servan's subsequent career as a proponent of criminal justice reform, see also Sarah Maza, *Private Lives and Public Affairs: The Causes Célèbres of Prerevolutionary France*, 237–240 (Berkeley: University of California Press, 1993).
44. ADR BP 3540 15 September 1670 Dossier of Madeline Vacheron and Jean Paul Hugouin. For elite jurisprudence's commitment to compulsory marriage, see Matthew Gerber, *Bastards: Politics, Family, and Law in Early Modern France* (Oxford: Oxford University Press, 2012), 139–142.
45. For examples of the court offering men marriage or payment and custody in the seventeenth century, see ADR BP 3540 16 May 1668 Dossier of Chambery and Vassal, and ADR BP3540 20 December 1668 Dossier of Chau and Razet.
46. ADR 12G 942 17 September, 1751 Dossier of Marie Joseph Butavna and Pierre Odry and Jean Odry.
47. ADR BP3543 18 April 1721 Dossier of Renaud and Joannin; ADR BP3544 8 June 1724. Dossier of Valouey and Richard; ADR BP3545 6 March 1725 Dossier of Quentin and Delphin; ADR BP3544 15 October 1723 Dossier of Riviere and Chazey; ADR BP3544 23 October 1723 Dossier of Martin and Louis.
48. ADR BP3551 16 November 1740 Dossier of Rang and Millot.
49. ADR BP 3540 19 February1658 Dossier of Beaujollon and Bichon. For the legal principle of filation that made men responsible for children born out of wedlock, see Sylvie Steinberg, *Une tache au front: La bâtardise aux XVIe et XVIIe siècles* (Paris: Michel Albin, 2016). For the routine awarding of delivery costs because judges expected that helped protect the child, see Anne Lefebvre-Trillard, *Autour de l'enfant: Du droit canonique et romain médiéval au Code Civil de 1804* (Leiden: Brill, 2008). Children born out-of-wedlock were excluded from other claims such as inheritance on the estate of their father besides basic provision. See Gerber, *Bastards*.

50. For royal efforts to mandate and dictate morality via the *rapt* legislation, see Julius Ruff, *Crime, Justice and Public Disorder in Old Regime France: The Sénéchausées of Liborne and Bazas, 1689–1798* (London: Routledge, 1984). Ruff identified about fifty prosecutions for *rapt* in the local criminal records, most of which were willing elopements or cases where obstacles to marriage existed. That is, consensual relationships in which marriage was possible but where the men refused to marry their partners were not tried as *rapts* in those regions either. Twenty-three cases of *rapt* were prosecuted in Lyon in the Old Regime, with only two involving violence and the rest being between young men and younger women of higher social class. For an example of the eighteenth-century discussion about the forms of *rapts*, see Pierre Francois Muyart de Vouglans, *Les lois criminelles de France: Dans leur ordre naturel* (Paris, 1780), 228–236. For *rapt* prosecutions in Lyon, see Françoise Bayard, *Vivre à Lyon sous l'ancien régime* (Paris: Perrin, 1997), 120.
51. ADR BP 3541 6 March 1679 Dossier of Fournel and Rouillat; ADR BP 3540 16 January 1673 Dossier of Bremont and Scarron; ADR BP3542 13 May 1688 Dossier of Gabet and Benoist.
52. ADR BP3541 18 October 1680 Dossier of Chermin and Laisne; ADR BP3542 16 May 1687 Dossier of Aurilloz and Berty; ADR BP3542 26 July 1686 Dossier of Ferlat and Prevallier; ADR BP3542 23 July 1687 Dossier of Chauvet and De Juif.
53. ADR BP3549 23 June 1731 Dossier of Didier and Conte; ADR BP3551 21 March 1741 Dossier of Reveilly and Barthellier.
54. ADR BP3542 28 May 1689 Dossier of Chana and Ramel; ADR BP3544 23 October 1723 Dossier of Martin and Louis. Note that although female employees (perhaps assisted by their lawyers) routinely presented such interactions as abuse embedded in unequal power relations, and female servants were extremely vulnerable to abuse, at least some interactions at some points may have been more complex. A couple of witnesses noted that Chana reveled "in the privileges of a mistress" Ramel gave her. Although Ramel's wife was alive so Chana could not have anticipated foreseeable marriage, the women noted that masters who abused their authority also offered promises of marriage. In these regards, see the cautionary note of Laura Gowing about the complexity and competition involved in power relations in these kinds of households as well as the possibility that at least sometimes female employees played the hand they had for their own hope of gain. See Laura Gowing, "The Haunting of Susan Lay: Servants and Mistresses in Seventeenth-Century England," *Past and Present* 14, no. 2 (August 2002): 183–201.
55. ADR BP3540 2 December 1660 Dossier of Simonet and Viegeard; ADR BP 3542 13 May 1688 Dossier of Gabet and Benoist; ADR BP3540 9 November 1697 Dossier of Baurand and Berger. The single exception to the routine release with guarantor was in a case when both parties were from a rural area about forty miles north of Lyon and it involved a weaver and a woman who worked for him. The court declined to release him under caution because *rapt* was involved. It was very unusual for rural cases to be referred to the Lyon court and it is unclear why this one was. ADR BP3541 27 June 1685 Dossier of Blanchin and Marest.

56. ADR BP3541 6 February 1683 Dossier of Olier and Guillemin; ADR BP3542 10 September 1689 Dossier of Orset and Reydellet.
57. ADR BP3551 23 June 1740 Dossier of Lalaneure and Rossaly.
58. For similar uses of prison in other cities, including Loudon, Carcassone, and Grenoble, see Edwin Bezzina, "The Protestants of Loudon: The Fragile Existence of a Religious Minority in 17th-Century France," *Social History* 46, no. 90 (May 2013): 35 (a 1665 marriage contract made in prison where future groom was held at the request of the future bride following court action); Marie-Claude Phan, *Les Amours Illégitimes: Histoires de séduction en Languedoc (1676–1786)* (Paris: Editions du Cantre national de la recherche scientifique, 1986); Norberg, *Rich and Poor in Grenoble*, 56. Women were also able to get Spanish courts to imprison their intimate partners to compel them to marry them. See Abigail Dyer, "Seduction by Promise of Marriage: Law, Sex and Culture in Seventeenth-Century Spain," *Sixteenth Century Journal* 34, no. 2 (2003): 439–455. This routine charging of the illegitimate newborn to the father's care was in contrast to the varied arrangements Alexandra Shepard has shown in England at the same time. Shepard, "Brokering Fatherhood."
59. See Hardwick, *Family Business*, for the many other ways in which local courts endorsed community viewpoints rather than introducing regulations associated with state mandates.
60. For courts' refusals in other areas of France to punish women for pregnancy, see Veronique Demar-Sion, *Femmes séduites et abondonnées au 18e siècle: L'exemple du Cambrésis* (Lille: Ester, 1992) and Norberg, *Rich and Poor in Grenoble*, 56–57.
61. Hardwick, "Early Modern Perspectives on the Long History of Domestic Violence"; Ulrike Strasser, *State of Virginity: Gender, Religion, and Politics in an Early Modern Catholic State* (Ann Arbor: University of Michigan Press, 2004); Gerber, *Bastards*.

Chapter 4

1. For the details about the Benoist-Gabet relationship and a copy of the priest's parish register entry, see ADR BP3542 13 May 1688 Dossier of Gabet and Benoist.
2. ADR BP3555 13 June 1753 Dossier of Julliard and Page.
3. For a brief summary of the argument that reproduction is a female realm, see Sarah Toulalan and Kate Fishers, eds., *The Routledge History of Sex and the Body, 1500 to the Present* (London: Routledge, 2013), 8. See also Kim M. Phillips and Barry Reay, *Sex before Sexuality: A Premodern History* (Cambridge: Polity Press, 2011); Laura Gowing, "Secret Births and Infanticide in Seventeenth-Century England," *Past and Present* 156 (August 1997): 87–115. For the classic formulation of oral female-controlled secret networks of contraceptive knowledge as a particular sector of reproductive knowledge, see John M. Riddle, *Eve's Herbs: A History of Abortion and Contraception in the West* (Cambridge, MA: Harvard University Press, 1999). For caveats that do note in passing the involvement of men, albeit in cases that ended in criminal court, see P. Renne Baernstien and John Christopoulos, "Interpreting the Body in Early Modern Italy: Pregnancy, Abortion, and Adulthood," *Past and Present* 223, no. 1

(May 2014): 41–75; Joanne Ferraro, *Nefarious Crimes, Contested Justice: Illicit Sex and Infanticide in the Republic of Venice, 1557–1789* (Baltimore: Johns Hopkins University Press, 2008), 162; Guido Ruggiero, *Binding Passions: Tales of Magic, Marriage, and Power at the End of the Renaissance* (New York: Oxford University Press, 1993), 61–62; Ulinka Rublack, "The Public Body: Policing Abortion in Early Modern Germany," in *Gender Relations in German History: Power, Agency and Experience from the Sixteenth Century to the Twentieth Century*, edited by Lynn Abrams and Elizabeth Harvey (Durham, NC: Duke University Press, 2006). See also John Christopoulos, *Abortion in Early Modern Italy* (Cambridge, MA: Harvard University Press, 2020).

4. For classic arguments about the intensification of the disciplining of extra-marital (above all female) sexuality through legal and religious channels in early modern France, see James Farr, *Authority and Sexuality in Early Modern Burgundy (1550–1730)* (New York: Oxford University Press, 1995), Sarah Hanley, "Engendering the State: Family Formation and State Building in Early Modern France," *French Historical Studies* 16, no. 1 (Spring 1989): 4–27, and Sarah Hanley, "Family and State In Early Modern France: The Marriage Pact," in *Connecting Spheres: Women in the Western World, 1500–Present*, edited by Marilyn J. Boxer and Jean H. Quataert (New York: Oxford University Press, 1987). More recently, see also Matthew Gerber, *Bastards: Politics, Family and Law in Early Modern France* (New York: Oxford University Press, 2012), for the intensification of the stigma of illegitimacy among elites. Similar arguments have been made for other regions of early modern Europe: see, for example, Ulrika Strasser, *State of Virginity: Gender, Religion, and Politics in an Early Modern Catholic State* (Ann Arbor: University of Michigan Press, 2004). For a reading of the Catholic Reformation in Lyon as an important example of the disciplinary paradigm, see Philip Hoffman, *Church and Community in the Diocese of Lyon, 1500–1789* (New Haven, CT: Yale University Press, 1984).

5. ADR BP 3543 25 November 1722 Dossier of Bergeron and Soutel. Bergeron told this narrative to the court in her initial complaint and repeated it in nearly identical terms in her interrogatory.

6. ADR BP3541 15 June 1685 Dossier of Berthaud and Poulet.

7. See Merry Wiesner-Hanks, *Women and Gender in Early Modern Europe* (Cambridge: Cambridge University Press, 2000), 61–62, 78, for the definition of abortion.

8. For the complexities, ambiguities, and uncertainties around menstruation and reproduction, see Cathy McClive, *Menstruation and Procreation in Early Modern France* (London: Routledge, 2015).

9. ADR BP3555 13 June 1753 Dossier of Julliard and Page; ADR 3541 15 June 1685 Dossier of Berthaud and Poulet.

10. ADR 3541 15 June 1685 Dossier of Berthaud and Poulet.

11. ADR BP3541 13 February 1685 Dossier of Faure and Foretz; ADR BP3552 2 October 1743 Dossier of Blanchet and Behal; ADR BP3542 23 July 1687 Dossier of Chauvet and De Juif; ADR BP3555 13 June 1753 Dossier of Julliard and Page; ADR 3541 15 June 1685 Dossier of Berthaud and Poulet.

12. ADR 3541 15 June 1685 Dossier of Berthaud and Poulet; ADR BP3555 13 June 1753 Dossier of Julliard and Page. Evidence is scant for elites, although one barrister in

Grenoble procured six different remedies for his mistress. Kathryn Norberg, *Rich and Poor in Grenoble, 1600–1814* (Berkeley: University of California Press, 1985), 212.

13. ADR 354115 June 1685 Dossier of Berthaud and Poulet; ADR BP3542 16 February 1689 Dossier of Marquet and Bernard; ADR BP3555 13 June 1753 Dossier of Julliard and Page.
14. For a compelling account of a scandal surrounding an elite woman's death from an apparent abortion in Paris in 1660, see Leslie Tuttle, *Conceiving the Old Regime: Pronatalism and the Politics of Reproduction in Early Modern France* (New York: Oxford University Press, 2010), 17–18.
15. ADR BP3541 13 February 1685 Dossier of Faure and Foretz. For evidence of the pattern of men procuring remedies elsewhere, see the brief references to similar dynamics in Grenoble, not far from Lyon, in Norberg, *Rich and Poor in Grenoble*, 99. It is unclear whether some surgeons specialized in facilitating solutions to out-of-wedlock pregnancies, although some notaries and landladies did, as we will see. See McClive, *Menstruation and Procreation*, 126–128, for discussion of several related topics: the 1700 Paris Parlement ruling that ordered surgeons not to bleed any single woman without proof that she was not pregnant; for the well understood associations among surgeons and young women between bleeding and "miscarriages" as well as bleeding to treat a range of medical problems; and concerns about women's ability to use bleedings for miscarriages. Nevertheless, professional censure seems to have been very rare, and surgeons continued to do such bleedings in the eighteenth century as paternity suits reveal.
16. ADR BP3555 13 June 1753 Dossier of Julliard and Page.
17. ADR BP3552 2 October 1753 Dossier of Blanchet and Behal.
18. Court officials in criminal cases for infanticide did inquire about the use of "remedies." See the discussion of possible infanticides in chapter 6.
19. Jean-François Fournel, *Traité de la séduction: Considerée dans l'ordre judiciare* (Paris, 1781)—section on abortion 390–396 and quote on 391. For the Dijon mayor, see James R. Farr, *Authority and Sexuality in Early Modern Burgundy (1550–7130)* (New York: Oxford University Press, 1995), 129–130.
20. I thank Cathy McClive for the numbers of abortion cases in the Lyon criminal court records based on her work in progress. The low rate of prosecution mirrored that of other cities, like Dijon. Farr, *Authority and Sexuality*, 129–130.
21. If women did petition the court for relief, they hired *procureur*s to represent their claims immediately, and men did too if they did not move quickly to out-of-court settlements.
22. ADR BP3543 15 November 1721 Dossier of Arthuad and Croste. She filed her complaint with the court the same day.
23. ADR BP 3547 22 May 1727 Dossier of Chevallier and Sivol; ADR BP3541 16 January 1673 Dossier of Bremont and Scarron; ADR 12G 418 5 January 1774 Dossier of Beaujollit and Cottet.
24. ADR BP3558 1 April 1762 Dossier of Buy and Duvernay.
25. See Julie Hardwick, *The Practice of Patriarchy: Gender and Household Authority in Early Modern France* (State College: Pennsylvania State University Press, 1998), esp. 17–49. For the breadth of occasions when individuals paid notaries to draw up records

they might want to use for many purposes, see Hardwick, *Practice of Patriarchy*, 46–48, and Laurie Nussdorfer, "Writing and the Power of Speech: Notaries and Artisans in Baroque Rome," in *Culture and Identity in Early Modern France, 1500–1800: Essays in Honor of Natalie Davis*, edited by Carla Hesse and Barbara Diefendorf (Ann Arbor: University of Michigan Press, 1993).

26. Dolan, quoted in Sylvie Brassard, "Le Notaire, La Justice et Le Justiciable: Les déclarations d'abandon de procès dans les actes notariés à Aix-en-Provence (1550–1600)," MA thesis, Université Laval, 2012, 9.
27. ADR BP3541 17 April 1673 Dossier of Bezan and Croizet.
28. ADR BP3542 16 February 1689 Dossier of Riboullet and Quint. Riboullet's tactic did not work, as a couple of weeks later she was left "without resources" to deliver the baby at the Hôtel-Dieu whose officials recommended to her that she go to court to get him to keep his promises; she deposited a copy of the notarized declaration record with the court the same day she started her lawsuit.
29. ADR BP3541 16 February 1685 Dossier of Phillipon and Savoyard. For another example, see ADR BP3540 13 December 1663 Dossier of Boucher and Lalive. Very few examples survive in the notarial records. This one is a copy of the original submitted with the court complaint.
30. ADR BP3541 16 February 1685 Dossier of Phillipon and Savoyard.
31. *Supplement au nouveau et parfait Notaire de Jean Cassan contenant des nouveuax modeles de contracts et acts dresses sue le stile des plus habiles notaires & dans les terms les plus usitez*. Recueil par F. B. Dev... ancien maître clerc de notaires à Paris (Paris: Chez Theodore Legras,1728), 177 and 287. The agreement for galanterie first appeared in the *La science parfaite des notaires ou le Moyen de faire un parfait notaire: Nouvelle Edition* (Paris: Chez Legras, 1752), Tome II, 452. I consulted the 1764 version. The introduction of the term *galanterie* links to the emergence of *galanterie* as a cultural code as well as literary genre from the mid-seventeenth century although the word had a loaded range of meanings and implications. Did the handbook updater see the term as one of veiled disdain for love as a frivolous game, or had the term had become part of a popular vocabulary for dalliances where marriage was not the intent? This remains unclear. For the rise of the concept, see Alain Viala, *La Galanterie: Une mythologie française* (Paris: Seuil, 2019) as well as Viala's earlier work on the subject.
32. *Supplement au nouveau et parfait Notaire de Jean Cassan*, 177.
33. ADR BP3542 2 March 1688 Dossier of Faure and Saunier.
34. As in all litigation, the majority of single women's paternity claims did not go as far as sentencing: some women may have dropped their claim completely for whatever reason, but many more either married or made a settlement. For the general pattern of a low proportion of court actions proceeding to sentencing, see Julie Hardwick, *Family Business: Litigation and the Political Economies of Daily Life in Early Modern France* (Oxford: Oxford University Press, 2009), 76. For that pattern in these legal actions, see chapter 3.
35. ADR BP3544 18 May 1723 Dossier of Ballard and Berger.
36. ADR BP 3543 21 March 1721 Dossier of Ruedy and Michel; ADR BP 23 October 1723 Dossier of Martin and Louis. Other surviving examples of men who agreed

to sign out-of-court settlements while in prison during the course of a lawsuit for paternity include ADR BP3544 6 June 1724 Dosser of Cretin and Dupasquier and 8 June 1724 Dossier of Valouey and Richard. Probably much more often, court documents did not record such settlements. No copy of the Martin-Louis agreement survives so the terms are not clear, but since witnesses had affirmed their steady relationship despite his denials, likely they reached a private settlement that included some compensation.

37. ADR BP3541 15 June 1683 Dossier of Blanquemet and DeLeon.
38. ADR BP3542 23 May 1687 Dossier of Fontanel and Rey. See chapter 6 for the acceptance that it was not criminal to abandon a baby in a safe place, and the father's boutique certainly constituted a safe place.
39. ADR 10G3811 29 August 1765 Dosser of Tripier and Bourgeois.
40. ADR BP3540 15 September 1673 Dossier of Sallomon and Ragon.
41. ADR BP3455 13 June 1753 Dossier of Julliard and Page. The role of the notary was recorded subsequently when Julliard filed a paternity suit, asking that Page keep his promises to marry her or provide compensation.
42. ADR BP3555 28 September 1753 Dossier of Dubois and Mollard.
43. ADR BP3541 18 October 1684 Dossier of Lacroisette and Massias.
44. Historians have done little work on *désistements* despite the massive use of court records of the last five decades or more and the historiographical interest in out-of-court settlements broadly categorized as *"infrajustice"* or informal dispute resolution. (I have omitted the accent when referring to eighteenth-century documents that did not use it.)This neglect is partly because the notarial archives contain few *désistements* (or declarations that pertained to pregnancy), despite the high number of all legal actions that were resolved out of court and even fewer *désistements* to do with personal matters. For historians' interest in informal dispute resolution as a parallel to or integral part of the judicial system, known in French historiography as "infrajustice," and the practical intertwining in people's legal choices between formal and informal dispute resolution, see Hardwick, *Family Business*, 57–87. Brassard's excellent master's thesis on *désistements* in Aix focuses on the procedure and users, but her sample includes very few dealing with issues about court claims to do with sexuality. She points out that the absence of attention is in part due to archivists' practices because such acts were termed "unclassifiable," due to the variety of their contents, and thus have been ignored. See Brassard, "Le Notaire, La Justice et Le Justiciable," 8. Nicole Castan suggested in a study of southern France that looked at *accomodements* between 1779–90 that agreements between unwed couples must have been common even if they were not usually registered. Nicole Castan, *Justice et Répression en Languedoc à l'époque des lumières* (Paris: Flammarion, 1980), 20–22.
45. For the Grenoble apothecary, see Norberg, *Rich and Poor in Grenoble*, 200. For the Loire notary and the very low rate of survival of such acts in extant notarial records, because notaries did not register them, see Anne Fillon, "Fréquentation, Amour, Mariage au XVIIIe siècle dans les villages du Sud du Maine (1ère partie)," *Annales de Bretagne et des pays de l'Ouest* 93, no. 1 (1986): 47. For the terms of the 1693 *Contrôle des Acte*s, and the many efforts after 1693 to ensure that notaries registered

all acts within two weeks, see Jean Nicolas Guyot, *Repertoire universal et raisonne de jurisprudence civil*, vol. 42 (Paris 1781), 277. This legislation built on the sixteenth-century Edict of Villars-Cotteret.
46. Stuart Carroll argues for a reassertion of the clerical role of mediation as part of reformed Catholicism, albeit his focus is mostly on elites. Stuart Carroll, *Blood and Violence in Early Modern France* (London: Oxford University Press, 2006), 225.
47. ADR BP3555 28 September 1753 Dubois and Mollard. For the argument that priests sometimes chose "presumed legitimacy," see Gerber, *Bastards*, 12. It is impossible to assess how often priests' decisions glossed over out-of-wedlock births rather than flagging them as illegitimate.
48. AML HCL HD G92 1 March 1771; ADR BP3575 5 April 1787 Brillat and Sallier.
49. For the internal missions of monastic orders and friars' roles in cities as well as rural areas, see Mita Choudhury, *The Wanton Jesuit and the Wayward Saint: A Tale of Sex, Religion, and Politics in Eighteenth-Century France* (University Park: Pennsylvania State University Press, 2015), esp. 26–41; Dominique Delandres, *Croire et Faire Croire: Les missions francaises au XVIIe siècle (1600–1650)* (Paris: Fayard, 2003); Barbara Diefendorf, *Planting the Cross: Catholic Reform and Renewal in Seventeenth-Century France* (New York: Oxford University Press, 2019), esp. 63–129. For the internal missions in and around Lyon, see Bernard Dompnier, *Enquête au pays de frères des anges: Les Capucins de la province de Lyon and XVIIe et XVIIIe siècles* (Saint Etienne: Publications de l'Univerісté de Saint-Etienne, 1993); and Françoise Bayard, *Vivre à Lyon sous l'ancien régime* (Paris: Perrin, 1997), 133–137. For the seventeenth-century French Catholic church overall, see Joseph Bergin, *Church, Society and Religious Change in France, 1580–1730* (New Haven, CT: Yale University Press, 2009).
50. Dompnier, *Enquête au pays de frères des anges*. Dompnier did not identify the number of Capuchins who lived in the city of Lyons. Choudhury notes that Toulon (a city of about 20,000) had about forty secular clergy (parish priests) and over 230 friars during the first half of the eighteenth century. Choudhury, *Wanton Jesuit and Wayward Saint*, 28.
51. For a full list of Eudes's publications, see http://www.idref.fr/026936798, accessed 20 May 2019.
52. Jean Eudes, *Le Bon Confesseur ou Avertissements aux Confesseurs . . . Specialement les Missionaires* (Rouen: Chez Benoist Vignieu, 1635), 213–220. Eudes also encouraged confessors to ask married women if they were afraid of having more children or if they used remedies to prevent having them.
53. ADR BP3542 6 January 1689 Dossier of Bariou-Dumas.
54. ADR BP3541 21 July 1685 Dossier of Solore and Du Colombe; ADR BP3541 16 February 1685 Dossier of Faure and Foretz; ADR BP3542 28 May 1689 Dossier of Chana and Ramel.
55. ADR BP3547 22 May 1744 Dossier of Chevallier and Sivol.
56. ADR BP 3551 21 March 1741 Dossier of Revilly and Berthellier; ADR BP3552 17 July 1742 Dossier of Patra and La Fay. Priests, of course, could vary in their responses.

A witness for Anne Roussin said she had told another person that she had gone to a nearby town, Romans, to confess, but the priest there denied her absolution. ADR BP3551 22 October 1680 Dossier of Roussin and Chabanassy.
57. ADR BP3541 4 July 1683 Dossier of Carlet (Loubat's father) and Frasser; ADR BP3542 7 July 1697 Dossier of Brouillard and Duvert.
58. ADR BP3541 27 July 1684 Dossier of Grateloupe (mother of Ruffard) and Gay; ADR BP3543 30 August 1721 Dossier of Murat and Prost. For friars' involvement with care workers, see chapter 5.
59. ADR BP3542 3 February 1689 Dossier of Faure and Saunier (Faure did not mention the men's first names in either her initial complaint or her interrogatory and no other information survives); ADR BP3541 27 July 1682 Dossier of Bert and Aymond; for guarantors, see ADR BP 35414 July 1683 Dossier of Carler and Frasser (kin); ADR BP3542 30 September 1687 Dossier of Cornet and Farget; ADR BP3522 10 February 1743 Dossier of Blanchet and Behal; ADR BP 3542 28 February1687 Dossier of Gras and Bouvier February.
60. Mulatier did start work for the new employer, but within days he and his wife had became exasperated by her pregnancy and said they did not want to be involved. ADR BP3541 28 July 1682 Dossier of Mulatier and Priou.
61. ADR BP3541 28 July 1682 Dossier of Mulatier and Priou
62. For a compelling argument about the pragmatic attitudes of legal and religious authorities in early modern Italy based on a micro-history of an elite family, see Baerstien and Christopoulos, "Interpreting the Body in Early Modern Italy."
63. For a brief summary of the historiography of the varied means of informal dispute resolution outside of the court system (termed "infrajustice" by French historians), see Hardwick, *Family Business*, 59. The roles of notaries and clergy as mediators is noted in Benoit Garnot, "Justice, Infrajustice, Parajustice et Extrajustice dans la France d'Ancien Régime," *Crime, Histoire & Sociétés* 4, no. 1 (2000). Little work exists on such mediation practices. For the role of clergy as mediators in elite families, see Carroll, *Blood and Violence*, and for the role of priests as mediators between unmarried women and the Hôtel-Dieu in Grenoble, see Norberg, *Rich and Poor in Grenoble*, 193–194.

Chapter 5

1. ADR BP3542 6 January 1689 Dossier of Bariou-Dumas.
2. Bruyere disagreed with Bariou and Dumas about what she was owed, so she asked Bariou's father, Antoine, to pay her for the work she had done for his daughter and granddaughter. Antoine immediately started a court action to get Dumas to pay.
3. For out-of-wedlock childbirth as a site of tension, see Laura Gowing, "Secret Births and Infanticide in Seventeenth-Century England," *Past and Present* 156, no. 1 (August 1997): 87–115. For such births as matters of state in which women were either allies

of the state or collaborators with single mothers, see Sarah Hanley, "Family and State in Early Modern France: The Marriage Pact," in *Connecting Spheres: Women in the Western World, 1500–Present*, edited by Marilyn J. Boxer and Jean H. Quataert, 53–63 (New York: Oxford University Press, 1987), 65, and Sarah Hanley, "Engendering the State: Family Formation and State Building in Early Modern France," *French Historical Studies* 16, no. 1 (Spring 1989): 15–27. For out-of-wedlock births as matters of shame and stigma in urban working parishes that were bastions of clandestine "maternity wards" where desperate and terror-stricken women hid their shame from elites and families, see James R. Farr, *Authority and Sexuality in Early Modern Burgundy (1550–1730)* (New York: Oxford University Press, 1995), 111–112. For the claim, based on the famous 1780s Parisian rapporteur, Louis-Sébastian Mercier, that Parisian midwives sheltered unmarried girls in their apartments in total secrecy, see Nina Rattner Gelbert, *The King's Midwife: A History and Mystery of Madame Coudray* (Berkeley: University of California Press, 1999), 27–29. It is unclear whether a pattern might have emerged in late eighteenth-century Paris that was different from that of other cities then or earlier, or whether Mercier was an unreliable narrator of lived experience. For the growing stigmatization of illegitimacy among elites, see Matthew Gerber, *Bastards: Politics, Family and Law in Early Modern France* (Oxford: Oxford University Press, 2012). For important interventions in rethinking gender and many forms of work, see Maria Ågren et al., *Making a Living, Making a Difference: Making a Living in Early Modern European Society* (New York: Oxford University Press, 2016); ; Anne Montenach, "Legal Trades and Black Markets: Food Trades in Lyon in the late Seventeenth and Early Eighteenth Centuries," in *Female Agency in the Urban Economy: Gender in European Towns, 1640–1830*, edited by Anne Montenach and Deborah Simonton (New York: Routledge, 2013); Daryl M. Hafter, "Women in the Underground Business of Eighteenth-Century Lyon," *Enterprise and Society* 2, no. 1 (March 2001): 11–40; Sharon Strocchia, "Introduction: Women and Healthcare in Early Modern Europe" and the other articles in the same special issue of *Renaissance Studies* 28, no. 4 (September 2014). For the importance of locating women who made a living from various aspects of sexuality as part of the job market and as part of a larger frame of how the sexual economy runs through social relations and the gendered division of labor, see Clyde Plumauzille, *Prostitution et Révolution: Les Femmes Publiques dans la Cité Républicaine* (Paris: Champ Vallon, 2016), 46–47.
4. ADR BP3540 19 December 1663 Dossier of Recorneau and Favary; ADR BP3542 24 July 1687 Dossier of Chauvet and De Juif.
5. ADR BP3540 19 December1663 Dossier of Recorneau and Favary; ADR BP3542 26 May 1683 Dossier of Charmeton and Janot.
6. ADR BP3542 2 March 1689 Dossier of Faure and Saunier.
7. ADR BP3542 2 May 1687 Dossier of Perne and Guerin; and 13 May 1682 Dossier of Mignot and Deroche.
8. ADR BP3542 13 May 1687 Dossier of Blanc and Frillat. The couple and Blanc's employer and neighbor were all silk workers. Blanc's mother made the paternity complaint to the court on 2 May 1687 about a week after the couple left.

9. ADR BP3542 24 July 1687 Dossier of Chauvet and De Juif; ADR BP 3543 18 April 1721 Dossier of Garnier (Joannin's widowed mother) and Renaud.
10. ADR BP3541 1 September 1685 Dossier of Ganot and Mazard; ADR BP3541 21 July 1685 Dossier of Solore and Du Colombe; ADR BP3542 29 January 1689 Dossier of Crespu and Bourdillion.
11. ADR BP 3542 11 September 1689 Dossier of Orset and Reydellet.
12. ADR BP3542 29 July 1688 Dossier of Marguerite Granger and Francois Berne; ADR BP 3542 13 May 1688 Dossier of Henriette Gabet and Francois Benoist.
13. ADR BP 3542 24 July 1686 Dossier of Chenu [mother of Allary) and Laval. Not all couples relied on rented rooms, although other solutions, as with the mother's family, are very difficult to trace.
14. Louise Bourgeois, *Midwife to the Queen of France: Diverse Observations*, translated by Stephanie O'Hara and edited by Alison Klairmont Lingo (Toronto: University of Toronto Press, 2017), 270.
15. For a brief overview of the debates about and regulation of midwives as medical practitioners, see Susan Broomhill, *Women's Medical Work in Early Modern France* (Manchester: Manchester University Press, 2004), 16–43. For an argument that male critiques were misplaced, see Liane McTavish, *Childbirth and the Display of Authority in Early Modern France* (Aldershot: Ashgate, 2005), 8. Jacques Gélis, *Fertility, Pregnancy and Birth in Early Modern Europe*, translated by Rosemary Morris (Cambridge: Polity Press, 1991), 96–138, provides an overview of early modern midwifery. For a very interesting analysis based on archival records as well as prescriptive accounts of midwifery in a major early modern city, see Doreen Evenden, *The Midwives of Seventeenth-Century London* (Cambridge: Cambridge University Press, 2000).
16. ADR BP5342 13 May 1688 Dossier of Gabet and Benoist. For the licensing of midwives elsewhere with its examinations of competency in Saint Malo and Paris, see Blanchard Hervot, *La médecine and les médecins à Saint Malo: 1520–1800* (Rennes: Librairie J. Plihon et L. Hommay, 1905), 74–80, and Gelbert, *The King's Midwife*, 25.
17. ADR BP3542 5 March 1688 Dossier of Brosset and Robert; ADR BP3542 6 January1689 Dossier of Bariou and Dumas.
18. ADR BP5342 13 May 1688 Dossier of Gabet and Benoist; ADR BP3542 23 May 1687 Dossier of Fontanel and Rey. For the Grenoble Hôtel-Dieu procuring this ruling from the local *parlement*, see Kathryn Norberg, *Rich and Poor in Grenoble, 1600–1814* (Berkeley: University of California Press, 1985), 97–98.
19. For an overview of wet-nursing in eighteenth- and nineteenth-century France, see George D. Sussman, *Selling Mothers' Milk: The Wet-Nursing Business in France, 1715–1914* (Champaign: University of Illinois Press, 1982). This focuses primarily on regulation and mortality statistics and includes very little about wet-nurses or their charges. For the pervasive use of wet-nurses in Lyon, see Maurice Garden, *Lyon et les Lyonnais au XVIIIe siècle* (Paris: Les Belles Lettres, 1970), 107–140. For a summary of the work of wet-nurses in England, see Linda Campbell, "Wet-Nurses in Early Modern England: Some Evidence from the Townshend Archive," *Medical History*

33 (1989): 360–370. For impressive work that focuses on the rural wet-nurses taking care of London nurslings, see Valerie Fildes, "The English Wet-Nurse and Her Role in Infant Care 1538–1800," *Medical History* 32 (1988): 142–173. For Spain, based on prescriptive literature, see Emilie L. Bergman, "Milking the Poor: Wet-Nursing and the Sexual Economy of Early Modern Spain," in *Marriage and Sexuality in Medieval and Early Modern Iberia*, edited by Eukene Lacarra Lanz (New York: Routledge, 2014).

20. ADR 8B1080-1; AML HCL 28 October, 1767 Charité G294.
21. ADR BP3542 28 February 1687; AML HCL HD G86 8 December 1768.
22. See, for instance, the correspondence in ADR 8B 1260-1 and 2 and ADR 8B876-15.
23. See Julie Hardwick, "Parasols and Poverty: Production, Reproduction and the Consumer Revolution," in *Market Ethics and Practices c.1300–1850*, edited by Simon Middleton and James Shaw, 129–149 (New York: Routledge, 2017).
24. ADR BP3542 6 January 1689 Dossier of Bariou-Dumas; ADR BP3543 18 April 1721 Dossier of Joannin and Renaud.
25. ADR BP3542 29 January 1689 Dossier of Crespu and Bourdillion; Valérie Pourret, "Fille-mères et amours illégitimes en Lyonnais de 1672 à 1790," *Mémoire de maîtrise, Université Lumière Lyon II* (1996), 33–34. Pourret notes that Charron was rare in admitting why she had come from Lyon to deliver, but she was not the only one who did so. The absence of a partner willing and able to pay for in-town arrangements may have been one key variable in where deliveries took place.
26. ADR BP3542 22 July 1686 Dossier of Jeanne Vollet and Pierre Douin; ADR BP 3542 12 May 1683 Dossier of Catherine Bouvier and Guichard Gras.
27. For midwives promising to safeguard family secrets as part of their oaths, see Marie-Claude Phan, "Les déclarations de grossesse en France (XVIe–XVIIIe siècles): Essai institutionnel." *Revue d'histoire modern et contemporaine* 22, no. 1 (January–March 1975): 86.
28. ADR BP3542 6 January 1689 Dossier of Bariou and Dumas.
29. Louis-Sebastian Mercier, *Tableau de Paris*, edited by Gustav Desnoiresterres (Paris, 1853), 215 and 218. For the argument that the edict required midwives to report out-of-wedlock births, see Hanley, "Family and State," 65 and "Engendering the State," 15–27.
30. The Brest order was issued as a printed regulation now in the municipal archives according to Armand Corre and Paul Aubry, *Documents de criminologie rétrospective: Bretagne, XVIIe et XVIIIe siècles* (Paris, 1895): 471–472. The order continued that such witnesses were charged with responsibility for any "inconveniences which could arise" and with the feeding of the babies. For St. Malo, see Hervot, *La médecine and les médecins à Saint Malo*, 74–101. For the Lyon regulation's introduction and annulment, see Pierre Le Ridant, *Code matrimonial, ou Recueil complet de toutes les loix canoniques et civiles de France . . . sur les questions de mariage*. Vol. 2 . . . *Nouvelle édition par M***, avocat au Parlement, 1770* (Paris, 1770), 637.
31. By the 1720s, St. Malo officials seemed to enforce at least some parts of those obligations on occasion. In 1727, St. Malo officials brought a court case against a midwife who had not declared an illegitimate birth and imposed a substantial fine of 100 *livres*. By 1737, at least the occasional midwife complied, and officials recorded their

visit with such a midwife to quiz the mother of the baby about the details of the situation. See Hervot, *La médecine and les médecins à Saint Malo*, 74–101.
32. AML HH 71—correspondence 1750–1773.
33. ADR 12 G 418 3 October 1653 and 9 July 1664. It is hard to know whether these fragments, in a small folder of church court documents, were part of a larger pattern of visits. Very few Catholic church court records survive for Lyon or for any region of France.
34. For midwives as legal medical experts in court cases, see Cathy McClive, "Blood and Expertise: The Trials of the Female Medical Expert in the Ancien Regime Courtroom," *Bulletin of the History of Medicine* 82, no. 1 (2008): 86–108, and "Masculinity on Trial: Penises, Hermaphrodites and the Uncertain Male Body in Early Modern France," *History Workshop Journal* 68, no. 1 (2009): 45–68.
35. ADBP3542 2 June 1688 and 30 September 1689.
36. ADR BP3542 12 September 1687 Dossier of Roland and Aurillon; ADR BP 3542 2 June 1688 Rapport of Parisot and Zacharie for Elizabeth Charavry. The Lyonnais medico-legal experts, whether male or female, did not seem to articulate in these short reports whether they gave priority to "quickening" as the preferred sign of pregnancy; Cathy McClive found this to be so with medico-legal experts elsewhere. The perceived advantage of quickening as a marker was that it could be verified by a third party, it indicated that the pregnancy was firm and the baby was animated, and there was no longer any possibility for abortion. Perhaps local practices developed their own formats for the reports or perhaps the brevity of others did not lend themselves to clarifications such as these. Cathy McClive, *Menstruation and Procreation in Early Modern France* (London: Routledge, 2015), 190–191.
37. For the lack of certainty among medical practitioners as well as pregnant women as well as for the diagnoses of molar pregnancies, see Cathy McClive, "The Hidden Truths of the Belly: The Uncertainties of Pregnancy in Early Modern Europe," *Social History of Medicine* 15, no. 2 (2002): 209–227 (based primarily on French texts and legal briefs) and McClive, *Menstruation and Procreation*, passim. ADR BP3552 17 July 1743 Dossier of Pitra and Matton. Pitra had provided a long list of other indicators of pregnancy including loss of appetite, nausea, headaches, and stomachaches.
38. For the regularization of medico-legal reports, if not the standardization of practice, see McClive, "Blood and Expertise," 89.
39. ADR BP3544 22 February 1724 Dossier of Phillipe and Pretement. I thank Cathy McClive for sharing her expertise about the 1723 reporting requirements (private correspondence, April 2016).
40. In an interesting example of the incomplete records, Motton's report is the only surviving piece of one paternity suit. ADR BP3557 16 February 1727.
41. ADR BP3542 12 September 1687; ADR BP3542 12 September 1687 Dossier of Roland and Aurillon; ADR BP3542 12 October 1686 Dossier of Denem and Caron; ADR BP3542 12 March 1688 Dossier of Faure and Saunier.
42. I thank Cathy McClive for this information about the fee.
43. The reports for paternity suits files in 1788 and 1789 (ADR BP5375) were done exclusively by male medical professionals.

44. ADLA BP3542 23 July 1686 Dossier of Chenu (for Allary) and Laval; ADR BP3542 13 May 1688 Dossier of Gabet and Benoist.
45. For the complex braiding of affection and financial provision, see Katie Barclay," Illicit Intimacies: The Imagined 'Homes' of Gilbert Innes of Stow and His Mistresses (1751–1832)," *Gender and History* 27, no. 3 (2015): 576–590.
46. A year later, when Dubois became pregnant a second time, her relationship with Mollard became contentious and her father grew frustrated with Mollard's failure to marry her as well as his daughter's refusal to cut off ties with him. The father filed a legal complaint that revealed the circumstances of the initial pregnancy and birth. ADR BP 3555 28 September 1753 Dossier of Dubois and Mollard.
47. Pourret, "Fille-mères," 124–126.
48. Garden, *Lyon et les Lyonnais*, 116–140, used the phrase "devoured" to capture how city babies disappeared in rural parishes where priests failed to register the deaths at wet-nurses.
49. For the importance of a reconsideration of the definitions of work to include care work and other forms of "domestic" labor, see Jane Whittle, "A Critique of Approaches to 'Domestic Work': Women, Work and the Preindustrial Economy," *Past and Present* 243, no. 1 (May, 2019): 35–70.
50. Farr, *Authority and Sexuality*, passim, and Gerber *Bastards*, passim.

Chapter 6

1. ADR BP3552 26 November 1743 Dossier of Dutremblois and Noel.
2. ADR BP3544 19 January 1723 Dossier of Berthier and Estephe.
3. For the designation of parts of churchyards for such cadavers, see reports about the findings of dead babies' bodies filed in ADR10G3811, including 11 January1764, 23 January 1766, and 4 July 1781; for the remains of baby bodies in a Rennes drain, see Olwen Hufton, *The Poor of Eighteenth-Century France, 1750–1789* (Oxford: Clarendon Press, 1974), 349; for the baby remains in a barn wall, see Maria Ågren, ed., *Making a Living, Making a Difference: Gender and Work in Early Modern European Society* (New York: Oxford University Press, 2016), 1.
4. John Boswell, *The Kindness of Strangers: The Abandonment of Children in Western Europe from Late Antiquity to the Renaissance* (Chicago: University of Chicago Press, 1998), 428–434; Matthew Gerber, *Bastards: Politics, Family and the Law in Early Modern France* (Oxford: Oxford University Press, 2012); John Styles, "Objects and Emotions: The London Foundling Hospital Tokens, 1741-1760," keynote paper presented at conference, Emotional Objects: Touching in Emotions in History, http://emotionalobjects.wordpress.com/2013/11/11/181/. See also Jean Pierre Bardet, "Enfants abandonnés et enfants assistés à Rouen dans la seconde moitié du XVIII siècle," *Annales du Démographie Historique* (1973): 19–47.
5. For the rise of institutions as means of discipline or what historians referred to as "the great enclosure" of the seventeenth century, see the classic and magisterial study of the poor in Lyon by Jean-Pierre Gutton, *La société et les pauvres: L'exemple*

de la généralité de Lyon, 1534-1789 (Paris: Les Belles Lettres, 1971), esp. 295-360. Revisionist efforts press to re-frame the institutions as early providers of institutionalized welfare services rather than sites of discipline; see, for example, James B. Collins, *The State in Early Modern France* (Cambridge: Cambridge University Press, 1995), 190-191. For analytical emphasis on users of such institutions, see Julia Gossard, "Breaking a Child's Will: Eighteenth-Century Parisian Juvenile Detention Centers," *French Historical Studies* 42, no. 2 (2019): 239-259; Jean-Pierre Gutton, "L'insertion sociales des enfants recueillis par la Charité de Lyon au XVIIIe siècle," in *Lorsque l'enfant grandit: Entre dependence et autonomie*, edited by Jean-Pierre Bardet (Paris: Presses de l'Université de Paris-Sorbonne, 2003). For the choices of poor and unmarried pregnant women in Paris in using such institutions for a much later period, primarily from the mid-nineteenth century, see Rachel Fuchs, *Poor and Pregnant in Paris: Strategies for Survival in the Nineteenth Century* (New Brunswick, NJ: Rutgers University Press, 1992).
6. For very thoughtful and sympathetic work on infanticide through criminal codes that highlight single women as infanticidal mothers because they were outsiders with few other choices, see in particular Laura Gowing, "Secret Births and Infanticide in Seventeenth-Century England," *Past and Present* 156, no. 1 (August 1997): 87-115, and Ulinka Rublack, *The Crimes of Women in Early Modern Germany* (New York: Oxford University Press, 2001), 163-196. Case studies in France similarly conclude that prosecuted women were on the margins of subsistence and extremely vulnerable. Farr, *Authority and Sexuality*, 124-156; Alfred Soman, "Anatomy of an Infanticide Trial: The Case of Marie-Jeanne Bartonnet (1724)," in *Changing Identities in Early Modern France*, edited by Michael Wolfe, 248-272 (Durham, NC; Duke University Press, 1997); Robert Muchembled, "Fils de Caïn, enfants de Médée. Homicide et infanticide devant le parlement de Paris (1575-1604)," *Annales Histoire, Sciences Sociales* 62, no. 5 (September–October 2007): 1063-1094; Stéphane Minveille, "Marie Bonfils, une veuve accusée d'infanticide dans le Bordelais de la fin du xviie siècle," *Dix-septième siècle* 4, no. 249 (2010): 623-643. For an overall summary of the established trajectory, see Margaret Brannan Lewis, *Abortion and Infanticide in Early Modern Germany* (London: Routledge, 2016).
7. Soman, "Anatomy of an Infanticide Trial," 248.
8. For examples of long gaps between the abortion or infanticide and prosecution, see Alfred Soman, "Le témoginage maquille: Encore un aspect de l'infrajustice à l'époque moderne," in *Les archives du délit: Empreinte de société*, edited by Yves-Marie Berce and Yves Castan (Toulouse: Éditions universitaires du sud, 1990); Cornelia Hughes Dayton, "Taking the Trade: Abortion and Gender Relations in an Eighteenth-Century New England Village," *William and Mary Quarterly* 48, no. 1 (January 1991): 19-41; Joanne Ferraro, *Nefarious Crimes, Contested Justice: Illicit Sex and Infanticide in the Republic of Venice, 1557-1789* (Baltimore: Johns Hopkins University Press, 2008), 116-157.
9. Paternity suits are especially valuable because, while the surviving records for the Lyon Hôtel-Dieu records include a large number of dossiers for admitted abandoned babies, the sick and the elderly, no dossiers survive for pregnant mothers who delivered there before the Revolution. It is unclear whether this lacuna is due to the

loss of this particular series of records or whether—like the informal settlements notaries made record of but did not register—they were deliberately set aside. Eighteenth-century rules for the Hôtel-Dieu refer to the registers for women who delivered there as "secret." See Ennemond Fayard, *Histoire administrative de l'oeuvre des enfants trouvés, abandonnés et orphelins de Lyon, suivie des noms des recteurs et administrateurs des hospices et hôpitaux, depuis la fondation de l'hospice de la Charité jusqu'en 1859* (Paris: Guillaume & Cie, 1859), 58–130, for the history of the Hôtel-Dieu's handling of abandoned children to 1783.

10. For the brief phase of regulation in Lyon and its annulment, see Lefebvre-Trillard, "Marriage in France." ADR BP3544 19 January 1723 Dossier of Berthier and Estephe; ADR BP3551 29 October 1740 Dossier of Demoulin and Vincent.

11. ADR BP3542 12 May 1689 Dossier of Devilliard and Perret.

12. AML HD G075 *Registre de remise des enfants exposés et abandones à la Charité 1660–1671* (Note the catalog description is wrong. The document includes babies from 1652 and the description on it is "*Acte et l'estat. Des enfants de l'hostel dieu remises a rvrd Dame de la Charite Le Dimanche XIe jour d'apuril 1660 34e Carrés transferés à la Charité.*") It described the mothers of fifteen of the 187 illegitimate babies at the Hotel-Dieu between 1652 and 1670 as "*filles debauchées.*" The mid eighteenth-century edition of the rules did use that term. *Statuts et Reglements Generaux de Hotel-Dieu de la ville de Lyon*, Aime Delaroche, 1756), 149–152. For the 1760 register categories (with no use of debauched girl or apparent euphemism), see Jean-Marcel Bourgeat, "L'abandon d'enfants à Lyon: Origins sociales et géographiques, differences de statuts et avenir des enfants abandonnés—le cas de 1760," *Société des Etudes Historiques Révolutionnaires et Impériales* (novembre 2011).

13. ADR BP5344 1724 12 July 1724 Dossier of Thirugien and Deporte; ADR 10G3811 7 May 1764 Dossier of Favard and Belleviel.

14. ADR BP3542 12 May 1689 Dossier of Devilliard and Perret; ADR BP3541 27 July 1684 Dossier of Ruffard and Gay; BP3542 2 March 1689 Dossier of Faure and Saulnier.

15. ADR BP 3541 21 January 1683 Dossier of Vignon and Barbier. Elite anxiety about working class girls and their offspring produced some other small initiatives. For example, the Hôpital de la Providence was established in 1707 by pious elite women to shelter poor children whose family environment was judged to be harmful and educate them until they were twenty-one. The only surviving records show five admissions of young children whose parents were debauched and one for an adult daughter whose parents said her "libertinage" required her to be detained. ADR 44 H 122 (Communautes de filles repenties—Providence).

16. ADR BP3542 16 February 1689 Dossier of Marquet and Bernard.

17. ADR BP3541 5 May 1689 Dossier of the rectors of the Hôtel-Dieu (for Pernon) and Tardieu.

18. ADR BP3542 16 February 1689 Dossier of Riboullet and Quinet.

19. ADR 11G309 1 July 1712.

20. *Reglements pour les domestiques du Grand Hotel-Dieu de Lyon* (Aime Delaroche: Lyon, 1754), 89–97; *Statuts et reglements generaux de l'hôpital général de Notre-Dame de*

Pitié du Pont du Rhône et Grand Hotel-Dieu de la ville de Lyon (Aime Delaroche: Lyon, 1756), 149–152 and 170–183.
21. ADR 29 August 1765 Dossier of Tripier and David. The rector addressed the negotiating party simply as "dear sir" so it is not clear whom he was dealing with, although it does not appear to have been the father; it may have been the notary or perhaps a third party.
22. ADR BP5344 12 July 1724 Dossier of Thirugien and Deporte; ADR BP5343 19 February 1721 Dossier of Bonnard and Cartier.
23. See, for example, the ticket included with ADR BP BP3552 2 October 1743, the testimony that the alleged father had paid the Hotel-Dieu to take the first baby the couple had together in ADR BP3555 28 September 1753, and a letter to a Hotel-Dieu rector about admission that acknowledged receipt of a billet included with ADR10G3811 29 August 1765.
24. ADR BP3544 18 May 1723 Dossier of Ballard and Tavernier; ADR BP3544 6 June 1724 Dossier of Cretin and Dupasquier; ADR BP 3551 2 June 1741 Dossier of Clerc and Marchand.
25. ADR BP3551 Dossier of Privat and Lefebvre 4 October 1740. Subsequently Privat told her mother who did not like the way the agreement had been made, perhaps in part due to the exclusion of the parents. The mother "took advice" (perhaps legal) and they decided Privat would file a paternity suit despite the agreement, apparently thinking they might get more financial compensation by that path. Privat asked for 250 *livres* but the court awarded the customary rate of 120. Lefebvre objected to having to pay an extra 120 *livres* when he had paid out of court earlier. The surviving record does not clarify how that dispute was resolved.
26. The Hôtel-Dieu in Grenoble, seventy miles west of Lyon, had an even more supportive stance. The rectors there procured a ruling from the Grenoble Parlement in 1705 that allowed new mothers to get legal permission to leave their unsupported babies on the doorsteps of their fathers. Norberg, *Poor of Grenoble*, 97–98.
27. ADR 10G3811 "Proces-verbal de levee de cadavre d'un enfant nouveau ne," 7 April 1781.
28. For elite anxiety in the form of legislation and prosecution in early modern France, see Soman, "The Anatomy of an Infanticide Trial."
29. Bourgeat, "L'Abandon d'Enfants"; ADR BP3263 30 July 1759 Catherine Eure.
30. ADR BP3263 30 July 1759 Catherine Eure; ADR BP3542 12 May 1689 Dossier of Ducoin and Jouainin; ADR BP3542 6 January 1689 Dossier of Bariou and Dumas.
31. Kristen Elizabeth Gager, *Blood Ties and Fictive Kin: Adoption and Family Life in Early Modern France* (Princeton, NJ: Princeton University Press, 1996), 137, suggests that the customary punishment for abandonment was whipping, but no evidence of such punishment survives for Lyon, and Gerber finds little effort at prosecution in Paris. Gerber, *Bastards*, 134–147.
32. For examples of routinized responses, see the many dossiers of babies that survive in the Hôtel-Dieu archives in AML, and the handful of surviving reports in the church court archives, in particular ADR10G3811.

33. ADR10G3811 3 January 1768.
34. AML HD G075 *Registre de remise des enfants exposés et abandonés à la Charité 1660–1671* (covers the years 1652–1670). The register shows that 238 children were recorded, of whom 51 were deemed legitimate and 187 illegitimate. Only 51 of the illegitimate babies (just over two a year and a little over a quarter of the total) were abandoned in the first two weeks of their lives. This register includes only children who survived to return from their wet-nurses to the care of the Hôtel-Dieu as six-year-olds.
35. Fayard, *Histoire Administrative*, 449. This rapid increase in the number of children charged to public care parallels that in Paris. See Bourgeat, "L'abandon d'enfants à Lyon," 10–17, for shifting proportions of legitimate and illegitimate children over the course of the eighteenth century.
36. McClive, personal communication—for numbers of infanticides prosecuted in Lyon between 1720 and 1790 (the records are missing for 1700–1720); Gerber, *Bastards*; Soman, "Anatomy of an Infanticide Trial."
37. ADR BP 3291 27 January 1763 Dossier of Pierrette Nicoud; ADR BP3009 18 July 1724.
38. ADR BP 3041 21 June 1728 Dossier of Marguerite Rebourdin.
39. They no doubt prompted her to make a legal claim against the father for unkept promises when the baby was a week old. She framed their relationship as a stable one in which she had had sex in the expectation of marriage, and he had made no effort to keep his promises. ADR BP5344 3 March 1724 Dossier of Sage and Berlier.
40. ADR BP2974 2 July 1715.
41. ADR BP3542 28 February 1687 Dossier of Bouvier and Gras. Gras claimed the wet-nurse had left the baby at the Hôtel-Dieu when he did not pay her and he had subsequently made arrangement with the Hôtel-Dieu to pay for his daughter's expenses there. ADR BP3543 18 April 1721 Dossier of Garnier and Renaud. Renaud claimed and witnesses affirmed that he had gone to the wet-nurse and required her to go with him to take the baby to the Hôtel-Dieu and to "keep it a secret."
42. ADR BP3540 19 December1663 Dossier of Recorneau and Favary; ADR BP3542 9 February 1723 Dossier of Ducat and Rigieur; ADR BP3543 21 November 1721 Dossier of Faury and Materon; ADR BP 3142 7 December 1742 Dossier of Antoine Riche; ADR BP3263 30 July 1759 Catherine Eure. See also chapter 4 for the use of this language of keeping safe or losing the baby.
43. ADR BP 3142 7 December 1742 Antoine Riche.
44. ADR 11G311 5 January 1631; ADR 10G3811 11 January 1764; ADR 11G314 21 September 1784.
45. The reports are filed opaquely in local church court records in the modern cataloging system and typically titled "procès-verbaux" in the original notation. Archivists sorted them together with a variety of other deaths like drownings, killed by carriages, and the occasional suicide. Only a very small number of church court records survive for the entire city for the seventeenth and eighteenth centuries, so many more must have been made originally. Seventeen of the reports date from 1676 to 1788. The gaps are extensive—no reports at all survive, for example, between 1683 and 1739.

46. James R. Farr, *Authority and Sexuality in Early Modern Burgundy (1550-1730)* (New York: Oxford University Press, 1995), 126-133, notes that infanticide and abortion were very difficult to prove, so the number of cases tried represents only an unknown fraction of incidence.
47. Archives Départmentales de Loire-Atlantique B6667 7 and 15 May 1653.
48. For an argument that these factors allowed married couples to engage in infanticide without prosecution, see Gregory Hanlon and Simone Caffari, "Infanticidio dei coppie sposati nella Toscana moderna nella prima età moderna," *Quaderni Storici* 38, n.113 (August 2003): 453-498.
49. ADR 10G3811 21 May 1771.
50. ADR 10G3811 1 November 1764.
51. Intentional killing of newborns could take many of these silent death forms. See, for instance, eighteenth-century English cases where the mother confessed to putting her finger down a newborn's throat to stop it crying, or the baby's body was found with a cloth stuffed in its mouth. Sarah Fox, "'The Woman Was a Stranger': Childbirth and Community in Eighteenth-Century England," *Women's History Review* 28, no. 3 (2019): 421-436, https://doi.org/10.1080/09612025.2018.1473067.
52. ADR 11G313 2 September 1743.
53. Garthine Walker suggestively sought to explore the mindset of mothers in these kinds of situations through their actions. She describes two single women in England who tried themselves to dig their dead babies' graves in churchyards, and another who hid the dead baby under an egg basket in the residence where she lived. See Garthine Walker, "Just Stories: Telling Tales of Infant Death in Early Modern England," in *Culture and Change: Attending to Early Modern Women*, edited by Margaret Mikesell and Adele Seeff (Newark: University of Delaware Press, 2003), and Garthine Walker, "Child-Killing and Emotion in Early Modern England and Wales," in *Death, Emotion and Childhood in Premodern Europe*, edited by Katie Barclay, Kimberley Reynolds, and Ciara Rawnsley (London: Palgrave Macmillan, 2016).
54. ADR 11G313 24 April 1744 and 17 September 1743.
55. ADR BP 3555 13 June 1753 Dossier of Julliard and Page.
56. For the early modern emergence of the gap between bed and wall (the *ruelle* in French) as a particular site of intimacy and privacy, see Orest Ranum, "The Refuges of Intimacy," in *Passions of the Renaissance*, vol. 3, *A History of Private Life*, edited by Roger Chartier (Cambridge, MA: Belknap Press, 1989), 218-225.
57. The events involving Gimet are recorded in ADR BP 3009 18 July 1724 Louise Gimet and ADR BP3544 11 January 1725 Louise Gimet. The 1725 record was in fact the sentence from a criminal investigation that archivists at some sorting stage included in the *déclarations de grossesse* classification. It shows that she was tried, found guilty, and sentenced to be branded on her right shoulder with a fleur de lis, whipped "at the usual places around the city" while carrying a card" girl who concealed her pregnancy and then banished from the jursidiction and fined 10 *livres*. Two married women who were tried with her (presumably the neighbors) were discharged. She was then sent to Paris with the material from her case and it is unclear what, if anything, subsequently

happened. This appears to be the only instance of its kind in Lyon in the eighteenth century.
58. As always, official investigations began only after someone had notified a legal official.
59. For the Marseilles reports (in the form of *procès-verbaux* in a folder dated 1750–1789), see Agnès Barroul, "Du geste à la parole: Infanticide et abandon d'enfants à Marseilles à la fin due XVIIIè siècle," in *Marseillaises: Les femmes et la ville, des origins à nos jours*, edited by Yvonne Knibiehler et al. (Paris: Côtés-Femmes, 1993), 148–160 and 380–381.
60. Fox, "The Woman Was a Stranger," argues that proximity and the history (or lack thereof) of personal interactions shaped community responses to a variety of childbirth events in eighteenth-century England.
61. ADR BP 3555 13 June 1753 Dossier of Julliard and Page.
62. Maurice Garden, *Lyon et les Lyonnais au XVIIIe siècle* (Paris: Les Belles Lettres, 1970), 116–140.
63. The well-known Marseilles example of a rigorous approach to women who were judged promiscuous still affected only a small group of women whose actions were in striking contrast to the conventions of licit intimacy for single women; the initiative there was driven by a specific local circumstance, that is, the character of Marseilles as a city with a high number of transient men. In Marseilles, as in Lyon, policing of women's sexuality was a matter of local regulation, was sporadic, and was mostly tied to a small number of women whose intimate relationships were defined as casual. Marseilles established a "Refuge" for debauched women whose neighbors and family had denounced them. Georg'Ann Cattelona has argued that female denouncers there regulated female sexuality in ways that in part served the purposes of the patriarchal state and in part protected ordinary women from accusations of misconduct. The *sénéchausée* in Marseilles began to register pregnancy declarations regularly from 1735. The Parlement of Provence in 1745 ordered judges to "sequester" with midwives or surgeons women who reported their pregnancies, or they were to be admitted to the Refuge. The requirement was hardly enforced, and less than 20% of the women detained claimed promise of marriage. Rather, they were accused of engaging in behavior defined as illicit and characterized by poverty, instability, and isolation that contrasted with expectations of licit intimacy in relationships leading to marriage. See Georg'Ann Cattelona,"Control and Collaboration: The Role of Women in Regulating Female Sexual Behavior in Early Modern Marseilles," *French Historical Studies* 18, no. 1 (Spring 1993): 13–33; Yvonne Knibiehler, "L'accueil des mères pauvres XVIIIe–XXe siècles," in *Marseillaises: Les femmes et la ville, des origins à nos jours*, edited by Yvonne Knibiehler et al. (Paris: Côtés-Femmes, 1993), 236–239.
64. Historians have found evidence of delays in alerting authorities in a wide range of regions. See, for example, Alfred Soman, "Le témoignage maquille: Encore un aspect de l'infrajustice à l'époque modern," in *Les archives du délit: Empreinte de société*, edited by Yves-Marie Bercé and Yves Castan, 99–109 (Toulouse: Éditions universitaires du sud, 1990), and Dayton, "Taking the Trade."

65. The mortality rate for children who became wards of foundling hospitals was horrifying even by pre-modern standards. Olivier Zeller describes the chances of survival for babies placed at wet-nurses by the Hôtel-Dieu in the eighteenth century as "minimal." Maurice Garden estimated that from half to three-quarters of foundling babies placed with wet-nurses by the Hôtel-Dieu died before the age of six and the mortality rates increased in the eighteenth century as the number of abandoned children the Hôtel-Dieu had to place with wet-nurses grew. Over 90% of children abandoned as infants in Rouen died before their first birthday compared to about 38% of children who were placed at wet-nurses by their parents. Sussman estimates that for France as a whole in the eighteenth century, the mortality rate in the first year of life for abandoned newborns was 65% to 90%, more than twice that for babies sent to wet-nurses by their parents (25% to 40%) and three times that of babies nursed by their mothers (about 20%). Oliver Zeller, "La Place des Miseraux et des Malades à Lyon, de l'Ancien Régime à nos jours," in *Villes et Hospitalité*, edited by Anne Gotman (Paris: Edition de la Maison de sciences de l'homme, 2004), 79; Garden, *Lyon et les Lyonnais*, 125–133; Bardet, "Enfants abandonnés et enfants assistés," 27–34; George Sussman, *Selling Mother's Milk: The Wet-Nursing Business in France, 1715–1914* (Champaign: University of Illinois Press, 1982).

Conclusion

1. ADR BP3538 2 March 1790 Dossier of Jeanne Baptiste Guilin.
2. For the essential role of neighbors and other co-residents in observing, supporting, and regulating many aspects of lives in working communities, see Arlette Farge, "Familles: L'honneur et le secret," in *L'Histoire de la vie privée*, vol. 3: *De la Renaissance aux Lumières*, edited by Roger Chartier (Paris: Seuil, 1986), 296, and Nicole Castan, "Le public et le particulier," in *L'Histoire de la vie privée*, vol. 3: *De la Renaissance aux Lumières*, edited by Roger Chartier (Paris: Seuil, 1986), 590; David Garrioch, *Neighborhood and Community in Paris, 1740–1790* (Cambridge: Cambridge University Press, 1986), 16–55. For women's networks as sources of discipline and support for other women, see Georg'Ann Cattelona, "Control and Collaboration: The Role of Women in Regulating Female Sexual Behavior in Early Modern Marseilles," *French Historical Studies* 18, no. 1 (Spring 1993): 13–33, and, for the early years of the Revolution, Roderick Phillips, "Women, Neighborhood and Family in the Late Eighteenth Century," *French Historical Studies* 18, no. 1 (Spring 1993): 1–12.
3. In contrast, historians such as James Farr and Tracey Rizzo have emphasized shaming that changed only when lawyers began to emphasize the victimhood and plight of the betrayed, seduced women, drawing on cultural stereotypes and the sexual double standard to elicit sympathy from judges. The archive of reproduction suggests such situations were outliers in practice. James R. Farr, *Authority and Sexuality in Early Modern Burgundy (1550–1730)* (New York: Oxford University Press, 1995); Tracey Rizzo, *A Certain Emancipation of Women: Gender, Citizenship, and the Causes Celebres of Eighteenth-Century France* (Selingsgrove: Susquehanna University Press, 2004).

4. See Elisabeth S. Cohen, "Straying and Led Astray: Roman Maids Become Young Women circa 1600," and Eleanor Hubbard, "A Room of Their Own: Young Women, Courtship and the Night in Early Modern England," both in *The Youth of Early Modern Women*, edited by Elisabeth S. Cohen and Margaret Reeves (Amsterdam: Amsterdam University Press, 2018).
5. Martin Ingram observed the lack of sex police in early modern England in a comment that has wide applicability to pre-modern European societies. See Ingram, *Church Courts, Sex and Marriage in England, 1570-1640* (Cambridge: Cambridge University Press, 1990), 279–280.
6. Maria Korpiola, "Marriage in Sweden, 1400–1700: Formalism, Collectivism and Control," in *Marriage in Europe, 1400–1800*, edited by Silvana Seidel Menchi (Toronto: University of Toronto Press, 2016), esp. 250; Loraine Chapuis, "Enquêter, Baptiser, réprimer: Le côntrole de la bâtardise à Genève au XVIII siècle (1750–1770)," *Crime, Histoire et Sociétés* 18, no. 1 (2014): 57–79; Griet Vermeesch, "The Legal Agency of Single Mothers: Lawsuits over Illegitimate Children and the Uses of Legal Aid to the Poor in the Dutch Town of Leiden (1750–1810)," *Journal of Social History* 50, no. 3 (2016) 51–73; Suzannah Lipscomb, *The Voices of Nîmes: Women, Sex and Marriage in Reformation Languedoc* (Oxford: Oxford University Press, 2019), 181–273. For the importance of shaming as a religious ritual aimed at eventual reconciliation, see Katie Barclay, "Marriage, Sex and the Church of Scotland: Exploring Non-Conformity among the Lower Orders," *Journal of Religious History*, 43, no. 2 (June 2019), 163–179. It is possible that other aspects might have shaped women's experience of out-of-wedlock birth. Different religious confessions might have produced different philosophies in care institutions or to the baptism of children whose parents were not married. Different legal and cultural practices might have been different too, for women in other regions did raise their babies as single mothers whereas Lyonnais women who gave birth out of wedlock usually did not raise their children until at least the late eighteenth century. Nevertheless, at least for the pre-modern period, Vermeesch notes the shift in historiography of many regions to "stress the agency of single mothers, their local belonging and the leniency of local governments towards them" rather than keeping them as victims of strict church and state discipline. See also Jeanette Kamp and Ariadne Schmidt, "Getting Justice: A Comparative Perspective on Illegitimacy and the Use of Justice in Holland and Germany, 1600–1800," *Journal of Social History* 51, no. 4 (Summer 2018): 672–692.
7. ADR BP3575 5 April 1787 Dossier of Brillart and Sallier; ADR BP3575 11 May 1787 Dossier of Grandelemu and Millard.
8. ADR BP 3575 20 March 1787 Dossier of Ducarre and Ferriol; ADR BP3575 8 May 1787 Dossier of Armand and Cochot.
9. ADR BP3575 13 April 1787 Dossier of Terrase and Vachon; ADR BP 3575 23 April 1787 Dossier of Moine and Callet; ADR BP 3585 12 May 1787 Dossier of Chatard and Lavarre.
10. ADR BP3575 20 March 1787 Dossier of Ducarre and Ferriol.
11. For illegitimacy rates of 5% to 10% in Lyon in the Old Regime, see Maurice Garden, *Lyon et les Lyonnais au XVIIIe siècle* (Paris: Les Belles Lettres, 1970), 37, and Françoise

Bayard, *Vivre à Lyon sous l'ancien régime* (Paris: Perrin, 1997), 96. Neither makes any case about increases in illegitimacy across the Old Regime, perhaps because the rates they present are well above the usual estimates. For the case that illegitimacy rates did increase in the eighteenth century, see Yves Blayo, "Illegitimate Birth in France from 1740 to 1829 and in the 1960s," in *Bastardy and Its Comparative History*, edited by Peter Laslett et al. (Cambridge, MA: Harvard University Press, 1980), 278; and Jean Meyer, "Illegitimates and Foundlings in Pre-Industrial France," in *Bastardy and Its Comparative History*, edited by Peter Laslett et al. (Cambridge, MA: Harvard University Press, 1980), 249–257.

12. For the attractions of Rousseau even in Lyon's working communities for whom his ideals were absolutely unattainable, see Julie Hardwick, "Fractured Domesticity in the Old Regime: Families and Colonialism at Home in Eighteenth-Century France," *American Historical Review* 124, no.4 (October, 2019): 1267-1277. For Rousseau's purchase as an inspiration for lived experience in middling and elite families, see Robert Darnton, "Readers Respond to Rousseau: The Fabrication of Romantic Sensitivity," in Robert Darnton, *The Great Cat Massacre and Other Episodes in French Cultural History* (New York: Basic Books,1984); Dena Goodman, "Marriage Choice and Marriage Structure: Reasoning about Marital Happiness in Eighteenth-Century France," in *Family, Gender, and Law in Early Modern France*, edited by Suzanne Desan and Jeffrey Merrick, 26–61 (University Park: Pennsylvania State University Press, 2009.. For the exemplary performance of new family life by other *philosophes*, see Meghan Roberts, *Sentimental Savants: Philosophical Families in Enlightenment France* (Chicago: University of Chicago Press, 2016).

13. Historians of England in particular have argued for a sexual revolution in the eighteenth century tied to new ideas of the Enlightenment, secularization, new forms of print culture, and a new emphasis on pleasure and penetrative sex. See various iterations in, for example, Tim Hitchcock, *English Sexualities, 1700–1800* (London: Palgrave Macmillan, 1997); Dror Wharman, *The Making of the Modern Self: Identity and Culture in Eighteenth-Century England* (New Haven, CT: Yale University Press, 2006); and Faramerz Dabhoiwala, *The Origins of Sex: A History of the First Sexual Revolution* (New York: Oxford University Press, 2012). For an important revisionist correction, see William Gibson and Joanne Begiato, *Sex and the Church in the Long Eighteenth Century: Religion, Enlightenment and the Sexual Revolution* (London: I. B Taurus, 2017). Historians of France have argued that a new elite interest in pleasure as well as sex is evident in the sixteenth century. See Katherine Crawford, *The Sexual Culture of the Renaissance* (Cambridge: Cambridge University Press, 2010).

14. For insightful reflections on what is now a vast field, see Suzanne Desan, "Recent Historiography on the French Revolution and Gender," *Journal of Social History* 52, no. 3 (2019): 566–574, and Guillaume Mazeau and Clyde Plumazille, "Penser avec le genre: Trouble dans la citoyenneté," *La Révolution française: Cahiers de l'Institut d'histoire de la Révolution françaises* 9 (2015): 17–18.

15. For young people's litigation to challenge parental consent in the early 1790s and many other examples of the symbiotic relationships between political discourse and

lived experience, see Suzanne Desan, *The Family on Trial in Revolutionary France* (Berkeley: University of California Press, 2004). For the two personal ads, see Desan, *Family On Trial*, 47. For an early nineteenth-century innovation in personal ads that involved highly and commercially curated formulations of the attractions of new kinds of courtships, see Andrea Mansker, "'Marriages by the *Petites Affiches*': Advertising Love, Marital Choice and Commercial Matchmaking in Napoléon's Paris," *French Historical Studies* 41, no. 1 (2018): 1–31.

16. For the persistence of coverture as critical, see Goodman, "Marriage Choice and Marriage Structure." For emphasis on continuities, see Judith Bennett, *History Matters: Patriarchy and the Challenge of Feminism* (Philadelphia: University of Pennsylvania Press, 2006); Sarah Knott, *Mother Is a Verb: An Unconventional History* (New York: Farrar, Straus and Giroux, 2019).

17. Rachel Fuchs analyzes the "grief ridden lives" of single mothers in nineteenth-century Paris with few options and little support, and Deborah Cohen describes unwed motherhood in early twentieth-century Britain as a "life-wrecking disaster" that was a source of tremendous stigma. Rachel Fuchs, *Poor and Pregnant in Paris: Strategies for Survival in the Nineteenth Century* (New Brunswick, NJ: Rutgers University Press, 1992); Deborah Cohen, *Family Secrets: Shame and Privacy in Modern Britain* (New York: Oxford University Press, 2013), 124–155.

Bibliography

Archival sources

This book is based primarily on research in Lyon at the Archives Départementales du Rhône (ADR) and the Archives Municipales de Lyon (AML). To complement the specific information in the notes, I highlight for the use of future researchers the most useful series for this project.

At the ADR, a variety of legal records are especially rich. In particular, the series G records (the few surviving church court records for Lyon parishes that include reports about finding dead babies' bodies as well as a variety of other public disorder matters), and the series B documents that include the criminal records of the *sénéchausée* and the material catalogued as *Déclarations de Grossesse* are important resources.

At the AML, the extensive records of the Hôtel-Dieu held in the ACL HD and ACL Charité series are particularly valuable and hold a wide range of interesting material.

Published Primary Sources

De Ferriere, Claude. *La science parfaite des notaires ou le Moyen de faire un parfait notaire . . . tant en matière Civile que Bénéficiale Nouvelle Editi*on. Paris: Chez Legrad, 1752.

Eudes, Jean. *Le Bon Confesseur ou Avertissements aux Confesseurs . . . pour exercer saintement leur Office*. Lyon: Chez Benoist Vignieu, 1635.

Fournel, Jean François. *Traité de la séduction: Considérée dans l'ordre judiciaire*. Paris, 1781.

Guyot, Jean Nicolas. *Répertoire universel et raisonne de jurisprudence civile, criminelle, canonique et bénéficiale; ouvrage de plusieurs jurisconsultes*,vol. 42. Paris 1785.

Isambert, François et al. *Recueil Général des Anciennes Lois Françaises depuis l'an 420 jusqu'àla Révolution de 1789*, vol. 13. Paris, 1829.

Le Dictionnaire de L'Académie Françoise, dedié au Roy, vol. 1. Paris: 1694.

Le Ridant, Pierre. *Code matrimonial, ou Recueil complet de toutes les loix canoniques et civiles de France, . . . sur les questions de mariage. Nouvelle édition par M***, avocat au Parlement, 1770*, vol. 2. Paris, 1770.

Mercier, Sebastian. *Tableau de Paris*. Edited by Gustav Desnoiresterres. Paris, 1853.

Muyart de Vouglans, Pierre François. *Les lois criminelles de France: Dans leur ordre naturel*. Paris, 1780.

Reglements pour les domestiques du Grand Hotel-Dieu de Lyon. Aime Delaroche: Lyon, 1754.

Rituel du diocèse de Lyon imprimé par l'autorité de Monseigneur Antoine de Malvin de Montazet, archevêque et comte de Lyon, primat de France, vol. 2. Lyon, 1787.

Servan, Joseph-Michel-Antoine. *Discours de Mr. S***, ancien avocat general au parlement de ***; dans un procès sur une déclaration de grossesse*. Lyon: Chez Joseph-Sulpice Grabit, 17***.

Statuts et reglemens généraux de l'Hôpital général de Notre-Dame de Pitié du Pont du Rhône et Grand Hôtel-Dieu de la ville de Lyon. Lyon : Aime Delaroche, 1756.

Statuts et reglemens que le Roy veut et entend être observés en l'Art et Métier de Tireurs, Ecacheurs et Fileurs d'Or et d'Argent de la Ville de Lyon. Lyon: 1709.

Supplement au nouveau et parfait Notaire de Jean Cassan contenant des nouveuax modeles de contracts et acts dresses sue le stile des plus habiles notaires & dans les termes les plus usitez. Recueil par F. B. Dev . . . ancien maître clerc de notaires à Paris. Paris: Chez Theodore Legras,1728.

Thiéry, Luc Vincent. *Almanach du voyageur à Paris, contenant une description sommaire... Ouvrage utile aux citoyens, et indispensable pour l'Etranger*. Paris, 1787.

Secondary Works

Ågren, Maria, ed. *Making a Living, Making a Difference: Gender and Work in Early Modern European Society*. New York: Oxford University Press, 2016.

Baernstien, P. Renée and John Christopoulos. "Interpreting the Body in Early Modern Italy: Pregnancy, Abortion, and Adulthood." *Past and Present* 223, no. 1 (May 2014): 41–75.

Barahona, Renato. *Sex Crimes, Honour, and the Law in Early Modern Spain: Vizcaya, 1528–1735*. Toronto: University of Toronto Press, 2003.

Barclay, Katie. "Illicit Intimacies: The Imagined 'Homes' of Gilbert Innes of Stow and His Mistresses (1751–1832)." *Gender and History* 27, no. 3 (2015): 576–590.

Barclay, Katie. *Love, Intimacy and Power: Marriage and Patriarchy in Scotland, 1650–1850*. Manchester: Manchester University Press, 2014.

Barclay, Katie. "Marriage, Sex and the Church of Scotland: Exploring Non-Conformity among the Lower Orders." *Journal of Religious History* 43, no. 2 (June 2019): 163–179.

Barclay, Katie. "From Rape to Marriage: Questions of Consent in Eighteenth-Century Britain." In *Interpreting Sexual Violence, 1660–1800*, edited by Anne Greenfield, 35–44. London: Routledge, 2013.

Barclay, Katie, Kimberley Reynolds, and Ciara Rawnsley, eds. *Death, Emotion and Childhood in Premodern Europe*. London: Palgrave Macmillan, 2016.

Bardet, Jean-Pierre. "Early Marriage in Pre-Modern France." *History of the Family* 6, no. 3 (2001): 345–363.

Bardet, Jean-Pierre. "Enfants abandonnés et enfants assistés à Rouen dans la seconde moitié du XVIII siècle." *Annales du Démographique Historique* (1973): 19–47.

Barroul, Agnès. "Du geste à la parole: Infanticide et abandon d'enfants à Marseilles à la fin due XVIIIè siècle." In *Marseillaises: Les femmes et la ville, des origines à nos jours*, edited by Yvonne Knibiehler et al., 148–160. Paris: Côtés-Femmes, 1993.

Bayard, Françoise. *Vivre à Lyon sous l'ancien régime*. Paris: Perrin, 1997.

Behrend-Martinez, Edward. "Taming Don Juan: Limiting Male Sexuality in Early Modern Spain." *Gender and History* 24, no. 2 (August 2012): 333–352.

Behrend-Martinez, Edward. "Spain Violated: Foreign Men in Spain's Heartland." *European Review of History: Revue Européene d'Histoire* 22, 4 (2015): 579-594.

Beik, William. *Absolutism and Society in Seventeenth-Century France: State Power and Provincial Aristocracy in Languedoc*. Cambridge: Cambridge University Press, 1985.

Bellavitis, Anna. *Women's Work and Rights in Early Modern Urban Europe*. London: Palgrave Macmillan, 2018.

Benabou, Erica-Marie. *La prostitution et la police des mœurs au XVIIIe siècle*. Paris: Librairie académique Perrin, 1987.

Benedict, Philip, ed. *Cities and Social Change in Early Modern France*. New York: Routledge, 1989.

Bennett, Judith. *History Matters: Patriarchy and the Challenge of Feminism*. Philadelphia: University of Pennsylvania Press, 2006.

Bergin, Joseph. *Church, Society and Religious Change in France, 1580-1730*. New Haven, CT: Yale University Press, 2009.

Bergman, Emilie L. "Milking the Poor: Wet-Nursing and the Sexual Economy of Early Modern Spain." In *Marriage and Sexuality in Medieval and Early Modern Iberia*, edited by Eukene Lacarra Lanz, 90-116. New York: Routledge, 2014.

Berry, Daina Ramey and Leslie M. Harris, eds. *Sexuality and Slavery: Reclaiming Intimate Histories in the Americas*. Athens: University of Georgia Press, 2018.

Bezzina, Edwin. "The Protestants of Loudon: The Fragile Existence of a Religious Minority in Seventeenth-Century France." *Histoire sociale/Social History* 46, no. 91(May 2013): 1-41.

Blayo, Yves. "Illegitimate Birth in France from 1740 to 1829 and in the 1960s." In *Bastardy and Its Comparative History*, edited by Peter Laslett et al. Cambridge, MA: Harvard University Press, 1980.

Block, Sharon. *Rape and Sexual Power in Early America*. Chapel Hill: University of North Carolina Press, 2006.

Brassard, Sylvie. "Le Notaire, La Justice et Le Justiciable: Les déclarations d'abandon de procès dans les actes notariés à Aix-en-Provence (1550-1600)." MA thesis, Université Laval, 2012.

Broomhill, Susan. "Le prix d'amour: Négotiations après des relations sexuelles et des grossesses illegitimes à Paris au début du XVIe siècle." In *Femmes en fleurs, femmes en corps: Sang, santé, sexualités du Moyen Age aux Lumières*, edited by Cathy McClive and Nicolle Pellegrin. St. Etienne: Publications de l'Université de Saint-Étienne, 2010.

Broomhill, Susan. *Women's Medical Work in Early Modern France*. Manchester: Manchester University Press, 2004.

Boswell, John. *The Kindness of Strangers: The Abandonment of Children in Western Europe from Late Antiquity to the Renaissance*. Chicago: University of Chicago Press, 1988.

Bourgeat, Jean-Marcel. "L'abandon d'enfants à Lyon: Origines sociales et géographiques, differences de statuts et avenir des enfants abandonnés—le cas de 1760." *Société des Études Historiques Révolutionnaires et Imperials*, Novembre 2011.

Bourgeois, Louise. *Midwife to the Queen of France: Diverse Observations*. Translated by Stephanie O'Hara and edited by Alison Klairmont Lingo. Toronto: University of Toronto Press, 2017.

Campbell, Linda. "Wet-Nurses in Early Modern England: Some Evidence from the Townshend Archive." *Medical History* 33 (1989): 360-370.

Capps, Bernard. "The Double Standard Revisited: Plebian Women and Male Sexual Reputation in Early Modern England." *Past and Present* 162 (February 1999): 70-100.

Carroll, Stuart. *Blood and Violence in Early Modern France*. Oxford: Oxford University Press, 2006.
Castan, Nicole. *Justice et répression en Languedoc à l'Époque Des Lumières*. Paris: Flammarion, 1980.
Castan, Nicole. "Le public et le particulier." In *L'Histoire de la vie privée*, vol. 3: *De la Renaissance aux Lumières*, edited by Roger Chartier. Paris: Seuil, 1986.
Cattelona, Georg'Ann. "Control and Collaboration: The Role of Women in Regulating Female Sexual Behavior in Early Modern Marseilles." *French Historical Studies* 18, no. 1 (Spring 1993): 13-33.
Chapuis, Loraine. "Enquêter, Baptiser, réprimer: Le côntrole de la bâtardise à Geneve au XVIII siècle (1750-1770)." *Crime, Histoire et Sociétés* 18, no. 1 (2014): 57-79.
Choudhury, Mita. *The Wanton Jesuit and the Wayward Saint: A Tale of Sex, Religion, and Politics in Eighteenth-Century France*. University Park: Pennsylvania State University Press, 2015.
Christopoulos, John. *Abortion in Early Modern Italy*. Cambridge, MA: Harvard University Press, 2020.
Cohen, Deborah. *Family Secrets: Shame and Privacy in Modern Britain*. New York: Oxford University Press, 2013.
Cohen, Elisabeth S. "Straying and Led Astray: Roman Maids Become Young Women circa 1600." In *The Youth of Early Modern Women*, edited by Elisabeth S. Cohen and Margaret Reeves. Amsterdam: Amsterdam University Press, 2018.
Cohen, Elizabeth S. "The Trials of Artemisia Gentileschi: A Rape as History." *Sixteenth Century Journal* 31, no. 1 (Spring 2000): 47-75.
Cohen, Elizabeth S. and Margaret Reeves, eds. *The Youth of Early Modern Women*. Amsterdam: Amsterdam University Press, 2018.
Collins, James B. *The State in Early Modern France*. Cambridge: Cambridge University Press, 1995.
Corre, Armand and Paul Aubry. *Documents de criminologie rétrospective: Bretagne, XVIIe et XVIIIe siècles*. Paris, 1895.
Cragg, Olga and Rosena Davison. *Sexualité, mariage et famille au XVIIIe siècle*. Québec City: Les Presses de L'Université Laval, 1998.
Crawford, Katherine. *European Sexualities, 1400-1800*. Cambridge: Cambridge University Press, 2007.
Crawford, Katherine. *The Sexual Culture of the French Renaissance*. Cambridge: Cambridge University Press, 2010.
Crowston, Clare Haru. *Credit, Fashion, Sex: Economies of Regard in Old Regime France*. Durham, NC: Duke University Press, 2013.
Crowston, Clare Haru. *Fabricating Women: The Seamstresses of Old Regime France, 1675-1791*. Durham, NC: Duke University Press, 2001.
Curtis, Sarah A. and Stephen L. Harp, eds. "Archives in French History." Special issue, *French Historical Studies* 40, no. 2 (April 2017).
Dabhoiwala, Faramerz. *The Origins of Sex: A History of the First Sexual Revolution*. New York: Oxford University Press, 2012.
Darnton, Robert. "Readers Respond to Rousseau: The Fabrication of Romantic Sensitivity." In Robert Darnton, *The Great Cat Massacre and Other Episodes in French Cultural History*. New York: Basic Books,1984).
Davis, Natalie Zemon. *Fiction in the Archives: Pardon Tales and Their Tellers in Sixteenth-Century France*. Palo Alto, CA: Stanford University Press, 1987.

Dayton, Cornelia Hughes. "Taking the Trade: Abortion and Gender Relations in an Eighteenth-Century New England Village." *William and Mary Quarterly* 48, no. 1 (January 1991): 19–49.

DeJean, Joan. *How Paris Became Paris: The Invention of the Modern City*. London: Bloomsbury, 2014.

Deslandres, Dominique. *Croire et faire croire: Les missions françaises au XVIIe siècle, 1600–1650*. Paris: Fayard, 2003.

Demar-Sion, Veronique. *Femmes séduites et abandonnées au 18e siècle: L'exemple du Cambrésis*. Lille: Ester, 1992.

Depauw, Jacques. "Amour Illégitime et société à Nantes au XVIII siècle." *Annales: Économies, Sociétés, Civilisations* (July–October, 1972): 1155–1182.

Desan, Suzanne. *The Family on Trial in Revolutionary France*. Berkeley: University of California Press, 2004.

Desan, Suzanne. "Recent Historiography on the French Revolution and Gender." *Journal of Social History* 52, no. 3 (2019): 566–574.

Desan, Suzanne and Jeffrey Merrick, eds. *Family, Gender, and Law in Early Modern France*. University Park: Pennsylvania State University Press, 2009.

De Vries, Jan. *The Industrious Revolution: Consumer Behavior and the Household Economy, 1650 to the Present*. Cambridge: Cambridge University Press, 2008.

Diefendorf, Barbara. *Planting the Cross: Catholic Reform and Renewal in Seventeenth-Century France*. New York: Oxford University Press, 2019.

Diefendorf, Barbara B. and Carla Hesse, eds. *Culture and Identity in Early Modern Europe (1500–1800): Essays in Honor of Natalie Zemon Davis*. Ann Arbor: University of Michigan Press, 1993.

Dompnier, Bernard. *Enquête au pays des frères des anges: Les Capucins de la province de Lyon and XVIIe et XVIIIe siècles*. Saint Etienne: Publications de l'Univeristé de Saint-Etienne, 1993.

Dyer, Abigail. "Seduction by Promise of Marriage: Law, Sex and Culture in Seventeenth-Century Spain." *Sixteenth Century Journal* 34, no. 2 (Summer 2003): 439–455.

Evenden, Doreen. *The Midwives of Seventeenth-Century London*. Cambridge: Cambridge University Press, 2000.

Fairchilds, Cissie. *Domestic Enemies: Servants and Their Masters in Old Regime France*. Baltimore: Johns Hopkins University Press, 1984.

Fairchilds, Cissie. "Female Sexual Attitudes and the Rise of Illegitimacy: A Case Study." *Journal of Interdisciplinary History* 8, no. 4 (Spring 1978): 627–667.

Farge, Arlette. "Familles: L'honneur et le secret." In *L'Histoire de la vie privée*, vol. 3: *De la Renaissance aux Lumières*, edited by Roger Chartier. Paris: Seuil, 1986.

Farge, Arlette. *Fragile Lives: Violence, Power and Solidarity in Eighteenth-Century Paris*. Translated by Carol Shelton. Cambridge, MA: Harvard University Press, 1993.

Farge, Arlette. *Le goût de l'archive*. Paris: Éditions du Seuil, 1989.

Farr, James R. *Authority and Sexuality in Early Modern Burgundy (1550–1730)*. New York: Oxford University Press, 1995.

Fayard, Ennemon, *Histoire administrative de l'œuvre des enfants trouvés, abandonnés et orphelins de Lyon, suivie des noms des recteurs et administrateurs des hospices et hôpitaux, depuis la fondation de l'hospice de la Charité jusqu'en 1859*. Paris: Guillaume et Cie, 1859.

Ferraro, Joanne M. *Nefarious Crimes, Contested Justice: Illicit Sex and Infanticide in the Republic of Venice, 1557–1789*. Baltimore: Johns Hopkins University Press, 2008.

Fildes, Valerie. "The English Wet-Nurse and Her Role in Infant Care 1538–1800." *Medical History*, 32 (1988): 142–173.
Fillon, Anne. "Fréquentation, Amour, Mariage au XVIIIe siècle dans les villages du Sud du Maine (1ère partie)." *Annales de Bretagne et des pays de l'Ouest* 93, no. 1 (1986): 45–76.
Fillon, Anne. *Les Trois Bagues aux Doigts: Amours Villageoises au XVIII siècle*. Paris: R. Laffont, 1989.
Fissell, Mary E. *Vernacular Bodies: The Politics of Reproduction in Early Modern England*. Oxford: Oxford University Press, 2004.
Flandrin, Jean-Louis. *Familles: Parenté, maison, sexualité dans l'ancienne société*. Paris: Hachette, 1976.
Flandrin, Jean-Louis. "A Case of Naivete in the Use of Statistics." *Journal of Interdisciplinary History* 9, no. 2 (Autumn 1978): 309–315.
Flinn, Michael W. *The European Demographic System, 1500–1820*. Baltimore: Johns Hopkins University Press, 1981.
Fox, Sarah. "'The Woman Was a Stranger': Childbirth and Community in Eighteenth-Century England." *Women's History Review* 28, no. 3 (2019): 421–436.
Frost, Ginger S. *Living in Sin, Co-Habiting as Husband and Wife in Nineteenth-Century England*. Manchester: Manchester University Press, 2008.
Fuchs, Rachel G. *Poor and Pregnant in Paris: Strategies for Survival in the Nineteenth Century*. New Brunswick, NJ: Rutgers University Press, 1992.
Fuentes, Marisa J. *Dispossessed Lives: Enslaved Women, Violence, and the Archive*. Philadelphia: University of Pennsylvania Press, 2016.
Gager, Kirstin Elizabeth. *Blood Ties and Fictive Ties: Adoption and Family Life in Early Modern France*. Princeton, NJ: Princeton University Press, 1996.
Gammon, Julie. "Researching Sexual Violence, 1660–1800: A Critical Analysis." In *Interpreting Sexual Violence, 1660–1800*, edited by Anne Greenfield, 13–22. London: Routledge, 2013.
Garden, Maurice. *Lyon et les Lyonnais au XVIIIe siècle*. Paris: Les Belles Lettres, 1970.
Garnot, Benoît. "Justice, Infrajustice, Parajustice et Extrajustice dans la France D'Ancien Régime." *Crime, Histoire et Sociétés* 4, no. 1 (2000).
Garrioch, David. *Neighborhood and Community in Paris, 1740–1790*. Cambridge: Cambridge University Press, 1986.
Gelbart, Nina Rattner. *The King's Midwife: A History and Mystery of Madame du Coudray*. Berkeley: University of California Press, 1999.
Gélis, Jacques. *History of Childhood: Fertility, Pregnancy and Birth in Early Modern Europe*. Translated by Rosemary Morris. Cambridge: Polity Press, 1991.
Gerber, Matthew. *Bastards: Politics, Family, and Law in Early Modern France*. Oxford: Oxford University Press, 2012.
Gibson, William and Joanne Begiato. *Sex and the Church in the Long Eighteenth Century: Religion, Enlightenment and the Sexual Revolution*. London: I. B. Taurus, 2017.
Goodman, Dena. "Marriage Choice and Marital Success: Reasoning about Marriage, Love, and Happiness." In *Family, Gender, and Law in Early Modern France*, edited by Suzanne Desan and Jeffrey Merrick, 26–61. University Park: Pennsylvania State University Press, 2009.
Gossard, Julia M. "Breaking a Child's Will: Eighteenth-Century Parisian Juvenile Detention Centers." *French Historical Studies* 42, no. 2 (April 2019): 239–259.
Gowing, Laura. *Common Bodies: Women, Touch and Power in Seventeenth-Century England*. New Haven, CT: Yale University Press, 2003.

Gowing, Laura. *Domestic Dangers: Women, Words, and Sex in Early Modern London*. Oxford: Oxford University Press, 1996.
Gowing, Laura. "The Haunting of Susan Lay: Servants and Mistresses in Seventeenth-Century England." *Gender and History* 14, no. 2 (August 2002): 183–201.
Gowing, Laura. "Secret Births and Infanticide in Seventeenth-Century England." *Past and Present* 156, no. 1 (August 1997): 87–115.
Greenfield, Anne, ed. *Interpreting Sexual Violence, 1660–1800*. London: Routledge, 2013.
Gutton, Jean-Pierre. *La société et les pauvres : l'exemple de la généralité de Lyon, 1534-1789*. Paris: Les Belles Lettres, 1971.
Gutton, Jean-Pierre. "L'insertion sociales des enfants recueillis par la Charité de Lyon au XVIIIe siècle." In *Lorsque l'enfant grandit: entre dépendance et autonomie*, edited by Jean-Pierre Bardet. Paris: Presses de l'Université de Paris-Sorbonne, 2003.
Hafter, Daryl M. and Nina Kushner, eds. *Women and Work in Eighteenth-Century France*. Baton Rouge: Louisiana State University Press, 2015.
Hafter, Daryl. *Women at Work in Preindustrial France*. University Park: Pennsylvania State University Press, 2007.
Hafter, Daryl. "Women in the Underground Business of Eighteenth-Century Lyon." *Enterprise and Society* 2, no. 1 (March 2001): 11–40.
Hanley, Sarah. "Engendering the State: Family Formation and State Building in Early Modern France." *French Historical Studies* 16, no. 1 (Spring 1989): 4–27.
Hanley, Sarah. "Family and State in Early Modern France: The Marriage Pact." In *Connecting Spheres: Women in the Western World, 1500–Present*, edited by Marilyn J. Boxer and Jean H. Quataert, 53–63. New York: Oxford University Press, 1987.
Hanley, Sarah. "The Family, the State, and the Law in Seventeenth- and Eighteenth-Century France: The Political Ideology of Male Rights versus an Early Theory of Natural Rights." *Journal of Modern History* 78, no. 2 (June 2006): 289–332.
Hanlon, Gregory and Simone Caffari. "L'Infanticidio di coppie sposate in Toscana nella prima età moderna." *Quaderni Storici* 38, no. 113 (August 2003): 453–498.
Hardwick, Julie. "Early Modern Perspectives on the Long History of Domestic Violence: The Case of Seventeenth-Century France." *Journal of Modern History* 78, no. 1 (March 2006): 1–36.
Hardwick, Julie. *Family Business: Litigation and the Political Economies of Daily Life in Early Modern France*. Oxford: Oxford University Press, 2009.
Hardwick, Julie. "Fractured Domesticity in the Old Regime: Families and Colonialism at Home in Eighteenth-Century France." *American Historical Review* 124, no.4 (October 2019): 1267–1277.
Hardwick, Julie. "Parasols and Poverty: Conjugal Marriage, Global Economy, and Rethinking the Consumer Revolution." In *Market Ethics and Practices c.1300–1850*, edited by Simon Middleton and James Shaw, 129–149. New York: Routledge, 2017.
Hardwick, Julie. "Policing Paternity: Historicising Masculinity and Sexuality in Early-Modern France." *European Review of History/Revue européenne d'histoire* 22, no. 4 (2015): 643–657.
Hardwick, Julie. *The Practice of Patriarchy: Gender and the Politics of Household Authority in Early Modern France*. University Park: Pennsylvania State University Press, 1998.
Hardwick, Julie. "Sexual Violence and Domesticity in Early Modern Europe." In *The Routledge History of the The Domestic Sphere in Europe: Sixteenth to Nineteenth century*, edited by Joachim Eibach and Margaret Lanzinger. New York: Routledge, 2020.
Haumont, Bernard and Alain Morel, eds. *La société des voisins: partager un habitat collectif*. Paris: Éditions de la Maison des sciences de l'homme, 2005.

Hayhoe, Jeremy. "Illegitimacy, Inter-Generational Conflict, and Legal Practice in Eighteenth Century Northern Burgundy." *Journal of Social History* 38, no. 1 (Spring 2005): 673–684.

Hervot, Blanchard. *La médecine and les médecins à Saint Malo, 1500–1820*. Rennes: Librairie J. Plihon et L. Hommay, 1905.

Hindle, Steve, Alexandra Shepard, and John Walter, eds. *Remaking English Society: Social Relations and Social Change in Early Modern England*. Woodbridge, UK: Boydell Press, 2013.

Hindle, Steve. *The State and Social Change in Early Modern England, 1550–1640*. Early Modern History: Society and Culture. London: Palgrave Macmillan, 2002.

Hitchcock, Tim. *English Sexualities, 1700–1800*. London: Palgrave Macmillan, 1997.

Hoffman, Philip T. *Church and Community in the Diocese of Lyon, 1500–1789*. New Haven, CT: Yale University Press, 1984.

Holloway, Sally. *The Game of Love in Georgian England: Courtship, Emotions and Material Culture*. Oxford: Oxford University Press, 2019.

Hubbard, Eleanor. *City Women: Money, Sex and the Social Order in Early Modern London*. Oxford: Oxford University Press, 2014.

Hubbard, Eleanor. "A Room of Their Own: Young Women, Courtship and the Night in Early Modern England." In *The Youth of Early Modern Women*, edited by Elisabeth S. Cohen and Margaret Reeves. Amsterdam: Amsterdam University Press, 2018.

Hufton, Olwen. *The Poor of Eighteenth-Century France, 1750–1789*. Oxford: Clarendon Press, 1974.

Hufton, Olwen. "Women without Men: Widows and Spinsters in Britain and France in the Eighteenth Century." *Journal of Family History* (Winter 1984): 355–376.

Ingram, Martin. *Church Courts, Sex and Marriage in England, 1570–1640*. Cambridge: Cambridge University Press, 1990.

Isherwood, Robert. *Farce and Fantasy: Popular Entertainment in Eighteenth-Century Paris*. New York: Oxford University Press, 1986.

Jansson, Karin. "Conceptualizing Rape: Gendered Notions of Violence in Sweden 1600–1800." PhD diss., University of Uppsala, 2002.

Jones, Colin. "Meeting, Greeting and Other 'Little Customs of the Day' on the Streets of Late Eighteenth-Century Paris." Supplement 4, *Past and Present* 203 (2009): 144–171.

Kamp, Jeanette and Ariadne Schmidt. "Getting Justice: A Comparative Perspective on Illegitimacy and the Use of Justice in Holland and Germany, 1600–1800." *Journal of Social History* 51, no. 4 (Summer 2018): 672–692.

Kaplan, Steven Laurence. *The Bakers of Paris and the Bread Question, 1700–1775*. Durham, NC: Duke University Press, 1996.

Knibiehler, Yvonne. *Les pères aussi ont une histoire*. Paris: Hachette, 1987.

Knibiehler, Yvonne. "L'accueil des mères pauvres XVIIIe–XXe siècles." In *Marseillaises: Les femmes et la ville, des origines à nos jours*, edited by Yvonne Knibiehler et al., 236–245. Paris: Côtés-Femmes, 1993.

Knibiehler, Yvonne and Catherine Fouquet. *Histoire des mères du Moyen-Âge à nos jours*. 1982, repr.; Paris: Montalba, 1977.

Knibiehler, Yvonne et al., eds. *Marseillaises: Les femmes et la ville, des origines à nos jours*. Paris: Côtés-Femmes, 1993.

Knott, Sarah. *Mother Is a Verb: An Unconventional History*. New York: Farrar, Straus and Giroux, 2019.

Korpiola, Maria. "Marriage in Sweden, 1400–1700: Formalism, Collectivism and Control." In *Marriage in Europe, 1400–1800*, edited by Silvana Seidel Menchi. Toronto: University of Toronto Press, 2016.

Kushner, Nina. "Adultery and the Ideal of the Good Woman: Infidelity in Eighteenth-Century France." Unpublished Paper. Presented at the Annual Meeting of the American Historical Association, Denver 2017.

Kushner, Nina. *Erotic Exchanges: The World of Elite Prostitution in Eighteenth-Century Paris*. Ithaca, NY: Cornell University Press, 2013.

Langhamer, Claire. "Everyday Love and Emotions in the 20th Century." *The Many Headed Monster* (Blog). August 28, 2013. https://manyheadedmonster.wordpress.com/2013/08/28/claire-langhamer-everyday-love-and-emotions-in-the-20th-century/.

Lanza, Janine M. *From Wives to Widows in Early Modern Paris: Gender, Economy, and Law*. New York: Routledge, 2007.

Lebrun, Françoise. *La vie conjugale sous L'Ancien Régime*. Paris: A. Colin, 1975.

Lefebvre-Trillard, Anne. *Autour de l'enfant: Du droit canonique et romain médiéval au Code Civil de 1804*. Leiden: Brill, 2008.

Lefebvre-Trillard, Anne. "Marriage in France from the Sixteenth Century to the Eighteenth Century: Political and Juridical Aspects." In *Marriage in Europe, 1400–1800*, edited by Sylvie Seidel Menchi, 261–293. Toronto: University of Toronto Press, 2016.

Lewis, Margaret Brannan. *Infanticide and Abortion in Early Modern Germany*. London: Routledge, 2016.

Lipscomb, Suzannah. *The Voices of Nîmes: Women, Sex and Marriage in Reformation Languedoc*. Oxford: Oxford University Press, 2019.

Lottin, Alain. "Naissances illégitimes et filles-mères à Lille au XVIIIe siècle." *Revue d'histoire, moderne et contemporaine* 17, no. 2 (April–June 1970): 278–322.

Mansker, Andrea. "'Marriages by the *Petites Affiches*': Advertising Love, Marital Choice and Commercial Matchmaking in Napoléon's Paris." *French Historical Studies* 41, no. 1 (2018): 1–31.

Maza, Sarah. *Private Lives and Public Affairs: The Causes Célèbres of Pre-Revolutionary France*. Berkeley: University of California Press, 1993.

Maza, Sarah. *Servants and Masters in 18th-Century France: The Uses of Loyalty*. Princeton, NJ: Princeton University Press, 1983.

Mazeau, Guillaume and Clyde Plumauzille. "Penser avec le genre: Trouble dans la citoyenneté révolutionnaire." *La Révolution française: Cahiers de L'Institute d'histoire de la Révolution française* 9 (2015): 1–28.

McTavish, Lianne. *Childbirth and the Display of Authority in Early Modern France*. Alershot: Ashgate, 2005.

Medick, Hans and David Warren Sabean, eds. *Interest and Emotion: Essays on the Study of Family and Kinship*. Cambridge: Cambridge University Press, 1988.

Merrick, Jeffrey. "Patterns and Concepts in the Sodomitical Subculture of Eighteenth-Century Paris." *Journal of Social History* 50, no. 2 (2016): 273–306.

Merrim, Stephanie. *Early Modern Women's Writing and Sor Juana Inés de la Cruz*. Nashville, TN: Vanderbilt University Press, 1999.

McClive, Cathy. "Blood and Expertise: The Trials of the Female Medical Expert in the Ancien Régime Courtroom." *Bulletin of the History of Medicine* 82, no. 1 (2008): 86–108.

McClive, Cathy. "The Hidden Truths of the Belly: The Uncertainties of Pregnancy in Early Modern Europe." *Social History of Medicine* 15, no. 2 (2002): 209–227.

McClive, Cathy. "Masculinity on Trial: Penises, Hermaphrodites and the Uncertain Male Body in Early Modern France." *History Workshop Journal* 68, no. 1 (2009): 45–68.

McClive, Cathy. *Menstruation and Procreation in Early Modern France*. London: Ashgate, 2015.

McClive, Cathy and Nicolle Pellegrin, eds. *Femme en fleurs, femmes en corps: sang, santé, sexualités du Moyen Age aux Lumières*. St. Etienne: Publications de l'Université de Saint-Étienne, 2010.

Monahan, W. Gregory. *Year of Sorrows: The Great Famine of 1709 in Lyon*. Columbus: Ohio State University Press, 1993.

Monfalcon, Jean Baptiste. *Histoire Monumentale de Lyon*, vol. 6. Lyon: Bibliothèque de la ville, 1866.

Montenach, Anne. *Espaces et pratiques du commerce alimentaire à Lyon au XVIIe siècle: l'économie du quotidien*. Grenoble: Presses Universitaire de Grenoble, 2009.

Montenach, Anne. "Formal and Informal Economy in an Urban Context: The Case of Food Trade in Seventeenth-Century Lyon." In *Shadow Economies and Irregular Work in Urban Europe, 15th to Early 20th centuries*, edited by Thomas Buchner and Philip Hoffman-Rehnitz, 91–106. Berlin: LIT Verlag, 2011.

Montenach, Anne. "Legal Trades and Black Markets." In *Female Agency in the Urban Economy: Gender in European Towns, 1640–1830*, edited by Deborah Simonton and Anne Montenach, 17–34. New York: Routledge, 2013.

Muchembled, Robert. "Fils de Caïn, enfants de Médée: Homicide et infanticide devant le parlement de Paris (1575–1604)." *Annales, Histoire, Sciences Sociales* 62, no. 5 (September–October 2007): 1063–1094.

Norberg, Kathryn. *Rich and Poor in Grenoble, 1600–1814*. Berkeley: University of California Press, 1985.

Nussdorfer, Laurie. "Writing and the Power of Speech: Notaries and Artisans in Baroque Rome." In *Culture and Identity in Early Modern France: Essays in Honor of Natalie Zemon Davis*, edited by Barbara Diefendorf and Carla Hesse, 103–118. Ann Arbor: University of Michigan Press, 1993.

O'Hara, Diana. *Courtship and Constraint: Rethinking the Making of Marriage in Tudor England*. Manchester: Manchester University Press, 2000.

Peiss, Kathy. *Cheap Amusements: Working Women and Leisure in Turn-of-the-Century New York*. Philadelphia: Temple University Press, 1986.

Perrier, Sylvie. "La grossesse entre intimité et publicité dans les archives judiciaries de la France d'Ancien Régime." Unpublished paper. Presented at the panel "Family and Justice in the Archives: Histories of Intimacy in Transnational Perspective," Concordia University, May 2019.

Peters, Kate, Alexandra Walsham, and Lisebeth Corens, eds. *Archives and Information in the Early Modern World*. New York: Oxford University Press, 2018.

Phan, Marie-Claude. *Les Amours Illégitimes: histoires de séduction en Languedoc (1676–1786)*. Paris: Editions du Centre national de la recherche scientifique, 1986.

Phan, Marie-Claude. "Les déclarations de grossesse en France (XVIe–XVIIIe siècles): essai institutionnel." *Revue d'histoire moderne et contemporaine* 22, no. 1 (January–March 1975): 61–88.

Phillips, Kim M. and Barry Reay. *Sex before Sexuality: A Premodern History*. Cambridge: Polity Press, 2011.

Phillips, Roderick. "Women. Neighborhood and Family in the Late Eighteenth Century." *French Historical Studies* 18, no. 1 (Spring 1993): 1–12.

Plumauzille, Clyde. *Prostitution et Révolution: Les femmes publiques dans la cite républicaine (1789-1804)*. Ceyzérieu: Champ Vallon, 2016.

Poska, Allyson M. *Women and Authority in Early Modern Spain: The Peasants of Galicia*. Oxford: Oxford University Press, 2005.

Pourret, Valérie. "Fille-mères et amours illégitimes en Lyonnais de 1672 à 1790." *Mémoire d'maîtrise*, Université Lumière Lyon II, 1996.

Premo, Bianca. *Enlightenment on Trial: Ordinary Litigants and Colonialism in the Spanish Empire*. New York: Oxford University Press, 2017.

Ranum, Orest. "The Refuges of Intimacy." In *Passions of the Renaissance: A History of Private Life*, vol. 3, edited by Roger Chartier, 207–264. Cambridge, MA: Belknap Press, 1989.

Rey, Michel. "Police et sodomie à Paris au XVIIIe siècle: Du péché au désordre." *Revue d'histoire moderne et contemporaine* 29, no. 1 (1982): 113–124.

Riddle, John M. *Eve's Herbs: A History of Abortion and Contraception in the West*. Cambridge, MA: Harvard University Press, 1999.

Rizzo, Tracey. *A Certain Emancipation of Women: Gender, Citizenship, and the Causes Celebres of Eighteenth-Century France*. Selingsgrove: Susquehanna University Press, 2004.

Roberts, Meghan. *Sentimental Savants: Philosophical Families in Enlightenment France*. Chicago: University of Chicago Press, 2016.

Roelens, Jonas. "A Woman Like Any Other: Female Sodomy, Hermaphroditism, and Witchcraft in Seventeenth-Century Bruges." *Journal of Women's History* 29, no. 4 (Winter 2017): 11–34.

Roper, Lyndal. *The Holy Household: Women and Morals in Reformation Augsburg*. New York: Oxford University Press, 1989.

Rosenwein, Barbara. *Emotional Communities in the Early Middle Ages*. Ithaca, NY: Cornell University Press, 2006.

Rothschild, Emma. "Isolation and Economic Life in Eighteenth-Century France." *American Historical Review* 119, no. 4 (October 2014): 1055–1082.

Rublack, Ulinka. *The Crimes of Women in Early Modern Germany*. New York: Oxford University Press, 2001.

Rublack, Ulinka. "The Public Body: Policing Abortion in Early Modern Germany." In *Gender Relations in German History: Power, Agency and Experience from the Sixteenth Century to the Twentieth Century*, edited by Lynn Abrams and Elizabeth Harvey, 57–80. Durham, NC: Duke University Press, 1996.

Ruff, Julius R. *Crime, Justice, and Public Order in Old Regime France: The Sénéchausées of Libourne and Bazas, 1696–1789*. London: Routledge, 1984.

Ruggiero, Guido. *Binding Passions: Tales of Magic, Marriage, and Power at the End of the Renaissance*. New York: Oxford University Press, 1993.

Scheer, Monique. "Are Emotions a Kind of Practice (And Is That What Makes Them Have a History)? A Bourdieuian Approach to Understanding Emotion." *History and Theory* 51 (May 2012): 193–220.

Schutte, Anne Jacobson, Thomas Kuehn, and Silvana Seidel Menchi, eds. *Time, Space, and Women's Lives in Early Modern Europe*. Sixteenth Century Essays and Studies. Kirksville, MO: Truman State University, 2001.

Sennefelt, Karin. "The Politics of Hanging Around and Tagging Along: Everyday Practices of Politics in Eighteenth-Century Stockholm." *Past and Present* 203, Supplement 4 (2009): 172–190.

Simons, Patricia. *The Sex of Men in Premodern Europe: A Cultural History*. Cambridge: Cambridge University Press, 2011.
Shah, Nyan. *Stranger Intimacy: Contesting Race, Sexuality, and the Law in the North American West*. Berkeley: University of California Press, 2011.
Shepard, Alexandra. "Brokering Fatherhood: Illegitimacy and Paternal Rights and Responsibilities in Early Modern England." In *Remaking English Society: Social Relations and Social Change in Early Modern England*, edited by Steve Hindle, Alexandra Shepard, and John Walter, 41–64. Woodbridge, UK: Boydell Press, 2013.
Shepard, Alexandra. *The Meaning of Manhood in Early Modern England*. Oxford Studies in Social History. New York: Oxford University Press, 2003.
Simmons, Alecia. "Embodying Sexual Violence in the Civil Courts: On Promises, Coverture and Consent." Unpublished paper.
Simons, Patricia. *The Sex of Men in Premodern Europe: A Cultural History*. Cambridge Social and Cultural Histories. Cambridge: Cambridge University Press, 2011.
Smith, Jay. *Nobility Reimagined: The Patriotic Nation in Eighteenth-Century France*. Ithaca, NY: Cornell University Press, 2005.
Soman, Alfred. "Anatomy of an Infanticide Trial: The Case of Marie-Jeanne Bartonnet (1742)." In *Changing Identities in Early Modern France*, edited by Michael Wolfe, 248–272. Durham, NC: Duke University Press, 1997.
Soman, Alfred. "Le témoignage maquille: Encore un aspect de l'infrajustice à l'époque moderne." In *Les archives du délit: Empreinte de société*, edited by Yves-Marie Bercé and Yves Castan, 99–109. Toulouse: Éditions universitaires du sud, 1990.
Stanley, Amy. "Writing the History of Sexual Assault in the Age of #METOO." *Perspectives on History*. September 24, 2018. https://www.historians.org/publications-and-directories/perspectives-on-history/november-2018/writing-the-history-of-sexual-assault-in-the-age-of-metoo.
Steedman, Carolyn. *Master and Servant: Love and Labour in the English Industrial Age*. Cambridge: Cambridge University Press, 2007.
Steinberg, Sylvie. *Une tache au front: La bâtardise au XVIe et XVIIe siècles*. Paris: Albin Michel, 2016.
Stéphane, Minvielle. "Marie Bonfils, une veuve accusée d'infanticide dans le Bordelais de la fin du xviie siècle." *Dix-septième siècle* 4, no. 249 (2010): 623–643.
Stoler, Ann Laura. *Along the Archival Grain: Epistemic Anxieties and Colonial Common Sense*. Princeton, NJ: Princeton University Press, 2009.
Strasser, Ulrike. *State of Virginity: Gender, Religion, and Politics in an Early Modern Catholic State*. Ann Arbor: University of Michigan Press, 2004.
Stretton, Tim. "Women, Legal Records, and the Problems of the Lawyer's Hand." *Journal of British Studies* 58, no.4 (October, 2019): 684–700.
Strocchia, Sharon T., ed. "Women and Healthcare in Early Modern Europe." Special issue, *Renaissance Studies* 28, no. 4 (September 2014).
Styles, John. "Objects and Emotions: The London Foundling Hospital Tokens, 1741–1760." Keynote paper presented at Emotional Objects: Touching in Emotions in History Conference. Available online. November 11, 2013. https://emotionalobjects.wordpress.com/2013/11/11/181/.
Styles, John. *Threads of Feeling: The London Foundling Hospital's Textile Tokens 1740–1770*. London: Foundling Museum, 2010.
Sussman, George D. *Selling Mother's Milk: The Wet-Nursing Business in France, 1715–1914*. Champaign: University of Illinois Press, 1982.

Trouillot, Michel-Rolph. *Silencing the Past: Power and the Production of History.* Boston: Beacon Press, 1995.
Toulalan, Sarah and Kate Fishers, eds. *The Routledge History of Sex and the Body, 1500 to the Present.* New York: Routledge, 2013.
Tuttle, Leslie. *Conceiving the Old Regime: Pronatalism and the Politics of Reproduction in Early Modern France.* New York: Oxford University Press, 2010.
Välimäki, Mari. "Responsibility of a Seducer? Men, Women and Breach of Promise in Early Modern Swedish Legislation." In *Gender in Late Medieval and Early Modern Europe*, edited by Marianna Muravyeva and Raisa Maria Tovo, 191–204. New York: Routledge, 2013.
Viala, Alain. *La Galanterie: Une mythologie française.* Paris: Seuil, 2019.
Vickery, Amanda. *Behind Closed Doors: At Home in Georgian England.* New Haven, CT: Yale University Press, 2010.
Walker, Garthine. "Child-Killing and Emotion in Early Modern England and Wales." In *Death, Emotion and Childhood in Premodern Europe*, edited by Katie Barclay, Kimberly Reynolds, and Ciara Rawnsley, 151–171. London: Palgrave Macmillan, 2016.
Walker, Garthine. "Everyman or Monster? The Rapist in Early Modern England, c. 1600–1750." *History Workshop Journal* 76, no. 1 (Autumn 2013): 5–31.
Walker, Garthine. "Just Stories: Telling Tales of Infant Death in Early Modern England." In *Culture and Change: Attending to Early Modern Women*, edited by Margaret Mikesell and Adele Seeff, 98–115. Newark: University of Delaware Press, 2003.
Walker, Garthine. "Rape, Acquittal and Culpability in Popular Crime Reports in England, c. 1670–1750." *Past and Present* 220, no. 1 (August 2013): 115–142.
Walsham, Alexandra. "The Social History of the Archive: Record-Keeping in Early Modern Europe." *Past and Present* 230, no. 11 Supplement (November 2016): 9–48.
Watt, Jeffrey. *The Making of Modern Marriage: Matrimonial Control and the Rise of Sentiment in Neuchâtel, 1550–1800.* Ithaca, NY: Cornell University Press, 1992.
Wharman, Dror. *The Making of the Modern Self: Identity and Culture in Eighteenth-Century England.* New Haven, CT: Yale University Press, 2006.
Whittle, Jane. "A Critique of Approaches to 'Domestic Work': Women, Work and the Pre-industrial Economy." *Past and Present* 243, no. 1 (May 2019): 35–70.
Wiesner-Hanks, Merry. *Women and Gender in Early Modern Europe.* Cambridge: Cambridge University Press, 2000.
Zeller, Oliver. "La Place des Miseraux et des Malades à Lyon, de l'Ancien Régime à nos jours." In *Villes et Hospitalité*, edited by Anne Gotman, 79–102. Paris: Edition de la Maison de sciences de l'homme, 2004.

Index

For the benefit of digital users, indexed terms that span two pages (e.g., 52–53) may, on occasion, appear on only one of those pages.

abandoned children, costs of caring for, 29
abandonment of infants, 13–14, 150–51, 155–56, 157–58, 171–72, 173
    assistance with, 157–58, 183–84
    of dead babies, 188–89, 192
    to fathers, 127
    frequency of, 184
    gossip about, 5–6
    Hôtel-Dieu and, 5–6, 13, 140–41, 155–56, 176, 183–84, 187–88, 190–91, 198, 223n45, 255n65
    institutions and, 171–72, 173
    mortality rates and, 255n65
    punishment for, 127, 251n31
    safeguards against, 97, 176
    safe places for, 183–84, 241n38
abandonment of women, 61, 69, 78–79, 82–83, 92–93, 96, 109, 135, 146, 163–65, 229n52
    See also seduction
abortifacients, 112, 113, 119–20, 138
abortion, 137–38, 191–92, 193–95, 196–97, 247n36
    dangers of, 110–11, 118
    definitions of, 13, 110–11, 116, 247n36
    prosecutions of, 120–21, 184–85
    See also menstruation, restoration of
    See also remedies
abuse. *See* violence
affection. see *amitié*
affection, language of, 43–44, 74–75, 209
age of legal majority, 85
age, as organizer of sexuality, 36–37, 105, 207–8
Allary, Anne, 148–49, 163–64
amitié, 58–59, 75–76, 114, 207
Anger, Suzanne, 75–76, 88–89

apothecaries, 118
archive of reproduction, 7–9, 14, 16, 19–42, 202, 203–4, 227n32
    See also paternity suits
archives, organization of, 24, 26, 29–31, 86–87, 241n44, 252n45
Armonie, Nicole, 28
autopsies, of infants, 182–83, 190–92, 196–97
Aymond, Pierre, 18, 30

Ballard, Jacqueline, 126, 180–81
banns, 67, 70, 83, 85–86, 93, 131, 206
baptism
    Edict of 1556 and, 25–27, 91
    fathers and, 164–65
    legitimacy and, 110, 118–19, 122, 130–31, 165, 202, 206, 213n13, 224n53
    local knowledge and, 141, 153–54, 155–56, 165
    records of, 1–2, 7–8, 20–21, 102,
Bariou, Antoine, 140, 141–42, 152, 162, 243n2
Bariou, Catherine, 133, 243n2
Bariou, Claire, 140–42, 150, 152–54, 155f, 155–56, 157, 162, 167
Beaujollon, Francoise, 101–2, 235n43
de Beaulieu, Elizabeth, 133, 140–41, 142, 153–54
Behal, Gilbert, 117, 119–20
Bennett, Judith, 209
Benoist, Andre, 163, 164
Benoist, Francois, 100–1, 107, 110, 121, 148, 150–51
Berger, Fleurie, 89–90
Bergeron, Leonarde, 113–14

Bert, Francoise, 18, 30, 136
Berthaud, Antoinette, 85–86, 114, 116–18
Berthier, Helaine, 169–71, 183–84
Bichon, Louis, 101–2, 235n43
Blain, Benoit, 75–76, 88–89,
Block, Sharon, 69
bloodletting, 110–11, 115–16, 118–19, 239n15
Bonnard, Francoise, 81, 180
Bouin, Jean, 84
Bourgeois, Louise, 149
Bouvier, Catherine, 136, 152, 155, 187
Brest, 27, 157–58
Brillat, Catherine, 131, 206
Brillon, Pierre, 26–27
Brothers, 55, 136–37
Brouillard, Florie, 91, 135
Bruyere, Catherine, 140–41, 142, 150, 152–54, 167, 243n2
Burial grounds, for infants, 171, 182–83, 184, 188–89, 191–92, 195–96
Burials
   clandestine, 13–14, 193–95
   cost of, 105–6
   infant deaths and concern for, 182–83, 189–90, 193–95, 199
Buy, Antoinette, 122–23

cadavers, infant
   discovery of, 171, 182–83, 189–90, 192–93, 201
   disposal of, 169, 192–95
   as evidence, 188–89, 190–91, 192
Calvinism, 205
Caneu, Anne, 150–51
Capuchins, 132, 135
casual sex, 66–67, 96, 204
   See also promiscuity
Catholicism, reformed, 30–31, 32–33, 111–12, 130–32, 138
Chabanassy, Jean, 53–54, 62–63
Chaboud, A., 61–62, 64, 86
Chabry, Antoinette, 54–56
Chana, Marie, 53–54, 100–1, 106–7, 134, 236n54
Charier, Gaspard, 133, 140–41, 153–54
Chauvet, Louise, 47, 62–63, 86, 94, 117, 144, 147

childbirth
   alone, 91, 186, 194–95
   assistance with, 14, 27–28, 88–89, 111–12, 141, 142–43, 162, 167
   dangers of, 78–79, 117–18, 143, 163–64, 168
   at Hotel-dieu, 94, 154, 173–82
   prevalence of out-of-wedlock, 11–12, 27, 107, 168, 202, 207–8, 242n47
   reporting of, 27, 110, 130, 169–70, 174, 206, 207–8
   reputation and, 14–15, 142, 154
childcare, 82, 91, 92, 142, 151, 152, 177
children, financial responsibility for, 29, 79, 82, 104, 130, 152
Clerc, Francoise, 47–48, 76–77
clergy, 111–12, 121, 130–36, 138, 205
coercion, 22–23, 68–70, 73, 76, 176–77, 209–10
cohabitation, 22, 37–38, 83–84, 95–96, 98–99, 124, 155, 169, 216n10, 232–33n9
Communal complicity, 10–11, 14–15, 16–17, 112–13, 156–57, 168
   abandonment and, 182–84
   infanticide and, 172–73, 184–85, 187, 188, 189–90, 192, 194–96, 200, 203–4
   See also communities
   See also secrecy
communities
   judgment about immorality by, 163–64, 175–76
   knowledge networks in, 11–12, 23, 55, 87–88, 111–13, 119, 136–39, 154, 156–57, 194–95, 203,
   management of intimacy by, 16–17, 20–21, 37–38, 41–42, 44–45, 56–57, 76–77, 90, 166, 168, 181–82, 200, 203–4
   silence about infant deaths in, 189–90, 192, 197
   urban spaces and, 154, 155f
community safeguarding, 10–11, 12, 16–17, 201–2, 203
   care workers and, 141, 144, 150–51, 162, 165–66
   friends and, 54–55

INDEX   275

infanticide and, 171, 189, 191, 194–96, 197
legal system and, 90, 98, 107, 108
male responsibility and, 109, 136–39, 166
marriage and, 79, 80–81, 87–90
public spaces and, 49–52, 73,
risk mitigation and, 52–58
workplaces and, 40–41, 55, 56–57, 89–90
compatibility, 58, 61–62, 86, 208
concealment,
  of pregnancies, 25–26, 30–31, 123–24, 147–48, 191
  of infant bodies, 13–14, 192–93, 194–97
  confessions, 32–33, 132–35, 138, 140–41, 153–54
consent, 49–50, 73, 75–76, 78–79
  language of, 75, 209
  parental, 80–81, 84–87, 93, 206, 208–9
contraception, 65, 115, 138
Contrôle des Actes (1693), 129–30
convents, 140–41, 153–54
corpses. *See* cadavers
courtship
  stages of intimacy in, 41–42, 44, 85, 128, 140
  narratives of, 22, 24, 70–71, 74–75, 91, 114
  oversight of, 11–12, 44–45, 82–83, 88–89, 91, 156–57, 165
coverture, 69–70, 209
co-workers, 3–4, 38, 39, 40–41, 43, 47, 53–54, 55–56, 88–90
Crespu, Marie, 147–48, 154
custody, 137, 141–42, 143, 169–70, 177, 207
  agreements for, 91, 95, 99, 163–65
  paternal, 20, 79–80, 96, 97–98, 102, 103, 104, 106, 108–9, 124–25, 151

dancing, 73–74, 132–33, 230n58, 230n59
De Jean, Joan, 48
De Juif, Jean, 62–63, 86, 94, 117, 144, 147
de Moulin, Barbe, 73–74, 174
De Varax, Riveraulx, 220n29
debauchery, 103, 173–75, 176–77, 178, 199
Decert, Isabeau, 62–63, 92–93

déclarations de grossesse, see pregnancy declarations
deference, 84–86
Delacroix, Damoiselle Madelaine, 217n13
delivery, costs of, 5–6, 20, 82, 91, 92, 94, 96–97, 105–6, 137, 198
Delphin, Vital, 51, 52–53, 103
Demen, Elizabeth, 49–50, 81
demographics of marriage and sexuality, 33, 36–37
Deroche, Louis, 4–5, 145–46.
désistements, 89–90, 124–25, 126, 127, 128–29, 134–35, 241n44
Devaux, Daniel, 62–63, 92–93
Devilliard, Nicole, 174, 175
Dijon, 120
discipline
  female sexuality and, 12, 24–42, 101–2, 108, 109, 111–12, 173–74, 210
  institutions and, 111–12, 130–31, 135–36, 138, 158–59, 167, 172, 173–74, 199, 204–5
  male sexuality and, 36, 79–80, 108, 162, 173–74
  as state formation project, 7, 30–31
discretion, 100–1, 138–39, 145–46, 147, 149, 155–57, 213n14
disorder, 41, 52, 176–77, 203–4, 216–17n11
doctors, 149, 162
domestic servants, 18–19, 34–35, 40, 78–79, 174, 218n18, 223n47
domestic spaces, 18–19, 34–35, 45–46, 50, 68, 70–72, 73
Dominicans, 132
double standard, 14–15, 80, 98–99, 255n3
dowries, 16, 86–87
Du Colombe, Richard, 134, 147–48
Dubois, Benigne, 62, 63–64, 128–29, 131, 165, 248n47
Dumaretz, Estienne, 47, 49–50
Dumas, Jean, 140–42, 150, 152–54, 155f, 155–56, 162, 167, 183–84, 243n2
Duplaignant, Joseph, 89–90
Dutremblois, Marie, 62, 169, 170–71, 194–95
Duvert, Claude, 91, 135

economy of reproduction, 13, 76, 167, 168
Edict on Clandestine Pregnancy (1556), 25–32, 91, 123, 157–58, 167, 174, 219n19, 219–20n25, 221n35, 221–22n38
emotional labor, 152, 163–68, 205
emotions, 16, 19, 21–22, 44, 60, 76, 80–81, 82, 84–85, 87, 128, 141–42, 163, 168, 202
  infant deaths and, 194, 196–97
  language of, 58–59, 73
  material culture and, 58, 61–64
  observations of, 163–64
employer-employee intimate relationships, 41, 106–7, 134, 147–48, 173–74, 176–77, 180, 218n18, 232n5, 236n54
employers, 79, 82, 86, 87–88, 89–90, 232n5
  intervention in intimacy by, 56–57, 89–90
Enlightenment, 96, 201–2, 207–8, 257n13
Estephe, Nicolas, 169–71
Eudes, Jean, 132–33
Eure, Catherine, 5–6, 183–84, 187–88
extra-judicial settlements. *See* infrajustice

false accusations, 28–29, 82–83, 101–2, 103, 126, 127–28, 129, 150–51, 180, 232n5
false conception, 159–60
families
  ideals of, 201–2, 207–9
  regulation of, 31–32
  supervision by, 23, 80–81, 84–87, 94, 119, 136–39
family tensions, settlements and, 128–29
Faure, Catherine, 118–19, 134
Faure, Jacqueline, 125–26, 145, 175
Faury, Francoise, 96–97, 187–88
Favard, Michelle, 75–76, 175
Favary, Jean Baptiste, 49, 144, 187–88
fertility
  intercourse and, 72–73, 77, 78–79, 80–81, 83, 108
  management of, 36, 65, 110–12, 113–21. *See also* remedies

Fiancon, Jean Claude, 18, 30, 60, 61
fille de joie, 63–64
filles debauchées, 174–75, 250n12
financial responsibility, 91, 96–97, 103, 105, 106, 164
Flacheron, Antoine, 55, 59–60, 59*f*
Flacheron, Phillipe, 47–48, 55, 76–77
Fontanel, Magdelaine, 127, 150–51, 241n38
force, licit intimacy and, 44, 45–46, 67–73, 75–76, 209–10, 229n52
Foucault, Michel, 31
foundling hospitals, 171–72, 183, 211n2, 255n65
  See also Hôtel-Dieu
Fournel, Jean-François, 26–27, 120
Franque, Andree, 187–88
French Revolution, 208–9
Friars, 32–33, 130–32, 133, 135–36
friends, intervention in relationships by, 38, 49–50, 54–55, 79, 136, 194–96

Gabet, Henriette, 100–1, 110, 121, 148, 150, 163, 164
galanterie, 240n31
Ganot, Andree, 147–48, 232n5
Gaylart, Pierre, 55, 75
gender
  labor and, 34–35
  political language of, 208–9
  power and, 14–16, 65, 66, 78–79, 108
  pregnancy and, 112–13, 117–18, 168
  sexuality and, 37, 41–42, 57, 65, 80, 108
generational tensions, 85–86, 87, 114, 129
Gerber, Matthew, 171–72
gifts, 1, 18, 58, 62–64, 228n40
Gillet, Fleurie, 54–55, 96
Gimet, Louise, 194–97, 254n57
godparents, 110, 136–37, 145, 178–79
gossip, 5–6, 10, 13–14, 50–51, 57, 89–90, 122–23, 158–59, 188, 216–17n11
Gowing, Laura, 41
Gras, Guichard, 136, 152, 155, 187, 252n41
Grenoble Parlement, 150–51, 251n26

INDEX   277

Grenoble, 103
Grissonet, Claudine, 54, 57, 73
guarantors, 100, 107, 136, 236n55
Guillemin, Jean, 48, 50

heteronormativity, 16–17, 22–23
heterosociabilty, 3–4, 36, 38–42, 48, 73, 133
honor, 24, 26, 48, 82–83, 91–98, 100–1, 105–6, 129–30, 181, 196–97
Hopital de la Providence, 250n15
Hôtel-Dieu (Grenoble), 27, 251n26
Hôtel-Dieu (Lyon), 7, 173–82, 211n1, 216n6, 234n28, 240n28, 251n23
  abandonment and, 155–56, 169–71, 172, 187–88
  administrators of, 94, 180–81
  admission by force to, 174–75
  babies charged to, 177–78
  as community resource, 199
  costs claimed by, 123, 126, 152,
  maternity care and, 160–61, 178, 198
  men's negotiations with, 152–53, 179–80
  as negotiating tactic, 180–81
  poverty and, 142–43, 178–79
  rectors of, 177–78, 181, 195–96, 199
  uses of, 197–98
  voluntary admissions to, 179
household spaces, 71
households, 5, 34–35, 40, 63, 70
Hugonin, Jean Paul, 83–84, 98–99, 232–33n9

illegitimacy
  destigmatizing of, 208–9
  incentive for priests to minimize, 131
  rates of, 36, 79, 207–8, 213n13, 252n34
  stigmatization of, 142, 167
illicit intimacy, 50–53, 55–58, 99, 108, 138, 173–78, 204
imprisonment
  of male intimate partners, 20, 79, 91, 95–96, 98–101, 106, 107, 108–9, 126
  female intimate partners, 126
infant mortality, 171–72, 185, 191
  emotions and, 166

  foundling hospitals and, 255n65
  of wet-nursed babies, 97, 151, 197–98, 234n37
infanticide, 171–73, 186, 187–88, 206–7
  concealment and, 13–14, 30–31,
  Edict of 1556 and, 25–27, 29, 91
  elite anxiety about, 183
  intentional, 198, 253n50
  investigations of, 7, 192
  prevention of, 97, 158–59, 181–82, 183
  proof of, 185–86
  prosecution of, 172–73, 184–88, 203–4
  situational, 170–71, 173, 189, 190–91, 196–97, 198
informal settlements. See infrajustice
informants, 175–76
infrajustice, 8, 9, 20–21, 28–29, 41, 79, 83–84, 104, 121–22, 144, 166, 241n44, 243n63
intention to marry, intimacy and, 54, 55–57
intercourse
  commitment to marry and, 36, 37, 45–46, 54, 57–58, 63, 66, 67–68, 75
  use of force in, 44, 45–46, 67–73, 75–76, 209–10, 229n52
  interior spaces, 45–46, 68, 70–71, 74

Joannin, Aymee, 103, 147
Julliard, Anne, 110–11, 116, 117–18, 119, 128, 194–95, 197–98

knowledge, about sex and reproduction, 65, 138, 228n46
Kushner, Nina, 9

landladies, 57, 111–12, 142, 143–49, 158–59
latrines, infanticide and, 185–87, 188, 201
Laval, Janot, 148–49, 163–64
Lefebvre, Jean, 75–76, 181, 251n25
legal claims. See paternity suits
leisure, 48, 230n59
literacy, 60, 127–28
local knowledge networks, 12–13, 89–90, 122–23, 141–42, 154, 173, 194–96

local policies, 102, 109, 158, 174
locked doors, 45–46, 70–72, 73
Loire Valley, 129–30
Louis, Antoine, 82–83, 103, 106–7, 126

Maison, Phillberte, 91
male responsibility, 12, 79, 99, 118, 130, 137–38, 146
    community enforcement of, 88–90, 108, 150–51, 177
    court enforcement of, 98, 108
    Hôtel-Dieu enforcement of, 173, 199
Marquet, Izabeau, 117–18, 176
marriage contracts, 83, 85, 86–87
Marseilles, 197, 254n63
Martin, Anne, 38–39, 82–83, 103, 106–7, 126
Martin, Ysabeau, 59–60
masculinity, 46, 68–70, 108–9, 231–32n2
material culture of intimacy, 19, 58–64
maternity care
    costs of, 177, 181
    Hôtel-Dieu and, 178, 181–82, 198
Matteron, Barthelemy, 96–97, 187–88
menstruation
    missed as proof of pregnancy, 159–60, 185–86
    restoration of, 13, 65, 110–12, 115–17, 118–19, 120
Mercier, Louis-Sébastian, 26–27, 64, 157
Metereau, Marie, 189–91
Michaud, Charles, 63, 85–86
midwives, 149–53
    bureaucratic roles of, 157–62
    Edict of 1556 and, 25–27, 28, 157
    regulation of, 27, 29, 149, 150, 156–57, 162
    requirement to report births, 28, 29
migrants, 18–19, 23, 33, 34–35, 38–39, 88–89, 198, 224–25n56
Minquet, Marguerite, 47, 49–50
miscarriage, 115, 169, 188, 194–95
miscarriage, induced, 110–11, 119, 169
mole, see false conception
Mollard, Louis, 62, 63–64, 128–29, 131, 165, 248n47
money, gifts of, 63–64
monogamy, 22, 23, 37–38, 45, 46–47, 83–84, 108, 204

Montmain, Estimette, 28, 93
morality, elite concern about, 28–29, 101–2, 203–4
Motton, Justine, 160–61
Moulin, Barbe, 73–74, 88, 174,
Mulatier, Jeanne, 81, 136–37

Nantes, 27, 189–90
National Assembly, 208–9
neglect, 169, 185, 186, 189, 190–91, 192
neighborhoods
    confessors as part of, 133
    geography of networks in, 153–54
neighbors, 43, 46, 47, 55–56, 57, 79, 83–84, 87–88, 91, 119, 128–29, 165, 206
networks, 12, 23, 55, 111–13, 121, 136, 149, 169, 199
newspapers, 74, 152
Noel, Francois, 169, 170–71, 194–95
notaries, 59–60, 85, 93, 112, 121, 123, 124–25, 127–28, 129–30
nuns, 178

Olier, Janne, 48, 50, 107
Orset, Aymee, 107, 147–48
outdoor spaces, 48, 50
out-of-court settlements, 95, 121–30, 240–41n36
    legal officials and, 121–30
    templates for, 124–25
    See also désistements
    See also infrajustice

Page, Francois, 110–11, 117, 119, 128, 194–95, 197–98
Parish priests, 134–35
Parlement of Paris, 27–28, 157–58, 172–73, 174, 204–5
Parlement of Provence, 254n63
paternity suits
    costs of, 121
    court awards for, 90, 91, 96–97
    courts' goals in, 107
    goals of, 94–98
    motives for, 92, 177, 216n10,
    narratives of intimacy in, 9, 20–21, 24, 114–15,
    as negotiating tactic, 95–96
    rarity of, 24, 215–16n5

restoring reputations through, 66–67, 96
support for women in, 99, 102, 103–4
Perricaud, Margeurite, 43, 70–71, 93
Perrouset, Barthelemy, 88, 174
Peyrieu, Lucie, 63–64, 101
Peyssillon, Pierre, 63–64, 101
Peyssonaux, Benoit, 54, 57, 73
Phan, Marie-Claude, 29–30
philosophes, 208
Pillot, Jean, 43, 93
Pitra, Marie, 38–39, 159–60, 247n37
pleasure, 55, 67, 74–75, 202, 209
population growth, 33
Poulet, Louis, 85–86, 114, 116
poverty, 33–34, 142–43, 178–80, 198
pregnancy declarations, 25–30, 78–79, 93, 123–24, 179–80, 206–7, 217–18n16, 218n17, 221n35,
premature birth, 13–14, 169, 185–86, 188–89, 192
Priou, Andre, 81, 136–37
prison, 107, 108, 126, 240–41n36
privacy
  intimacy and, 50–51, 55–56, 67–68, 70–71
  locked doors and, 71
Privat, Claudine, 75–76, 94, 181, 251n25
private spaces, 43, 50–51, 70–71, 73
promiscuity, 114–15, 120, 173–74, 203–4, 254n63
prostitution, 24, 62, 63, 64, 149, 173–74
Protestant reformations, 30–31
public charge, illegitimate children as, 94
public intimacy, 36, 40–41, 45–46
public knowledge, 100–1, 147, 154, 156–57, 201
public shaming, 100, 205
public spaces, 45, 46–47, 73, 176
  regulation of intimacy in, 49, 51–52
  licit intimacy and, 46–47, 48, 49–50, 57
purgatives, 116, 118, 119

Quentin, Jeanne, 51, 52–53, 103
quickening, 13, 110–11, 116, 247n36

Ramel, Joseph, 53–54, 100–1, 106–7, 134, 236n54
Rang, Claudine, 47, 73–74, 103–4
rape, 37, 61, 69–71, 229n52

rapt, 104–6, 236n50, 236n55
Ravier, Jean, 51, 53–54
Recorneau, Anne, 49, 144, 145, 187–88
regulation of intimacy, community members and, 31–32, 52, 54, 55–57
remedies, 65, 110–12, 116, 132–33, 137–38, 143, 169, 171, 187–88, 194–95, 197–98, 239n18
  abortions and, 192
  circulation of, 119
  community ambivalence about, 119
  court questioning about, 114–15
  dangers of, 117–18
  legal views on, 119–21
  male roles in procuring, 113–15, 117, 118
  providers of, 118
  See also abortion
Renaud, Jean, 103, 147, 187, 252n41
rented rooms, 13, 140–42, 143–49, 169–70, 171, 178–79
  claims to anonymity and, 155–56
Reposte, Elie, 78, 92–93
reputation, 13–14, 15, 16, 23, 40–41, 48, 55–56, 77, 78–79, 83, 96, 100–1, 114–15, 142–43, 146, 147, 149, 150–51, 164, 165–66, 174, 196–97
Revilly, Jeanne, 106, 134–35
Rey, Charles, 127, 150–51, 241n38
Reydellet, Antoine, 107, 147–48
Riboullet, Marguerite, 123–24, 177, 240n28
Richard, Jacques, 47–48, 103
Riche, Antoine, 187–88
Rouen, 255n65
Rougemond, Jeanne, 78, 92–93
Rousseau, 208, 257n12
Roussin, Anne, 53–54, 62–63, 82, 242–43n56
Rozet, Antoinette, 63, 85–86
Rubard, Anne, 18, 30, 60, 61
Ruedy, Marie, 47, 126
Ruffard, Marguerite, 135, 175

Sage, Hugette, 186
Sallier, Francois, 131, 206
Saunier, M., 136, 145
scandal, 23, 47–48, 102
secrecy, 10, 55, 71, 91, 129–30, 133, 138–39, 149, 153, 154, 155–57, 166, 173, 194–95, 197–98, 217n13, 252n41

seduction, 22–23, 26–27, 69, 104–5
Servan, Joseph Michel Antoine, 101–2, 103, 235n43
sexual harassment, 225n63
sexual violence, 70–73, 216–17n11, 229n52
Shah, Nayan, 9
shame, 142–43, 147–48, 174–75, 203–4, 243–44n3
shaming, public, 90, 91, 100, 205
Sibert, Pierrette, 61–62, 64, 86
silk industry, 1, 18, 33, 34–35, 36, 39
single motherhood, 82, 96, 143
social rank, 41, 51, 94, 140, 236n50
Solore, Florie, 134, 147–48
St. Malo, 27, 157–58, 246–47n31
Status. *See* social rank
Steedman, Carolyn, 8–9
stigma, 142, 167, 174–75, 205, 208–9, 243n2
stillbirth, 25–26, 169, 196–97
street lighting, 49
suppression d'enfant (disappearance of a baby), 5–6
surgeons, 118–19, 158–60, 161, 162, 191–92, 207, 239n15
St. Morice, 122–23

termination. *See* abortion
Thirugien, Pierette, 175, 180
tokens. *See* gifts
Tripier, Pierrette, 127, 179–80

urban spaces, 3–4, 32–34, 49, 154, 156–57

Vacheron, Madelaine, 83–84, 97, 98–99, 232–33n9
Valouey, Claire, 47–48, 103
Vincent, Pierre, 73–74, 88, 174
violence, 60, 67–69, 70, 75–76, 82–83, 104–5, 136, 175–76, 185, 216–17n11, 236n50

walking out, 3–4, 45, 46–49, 54–55, 66, 68, 73–74,
wet-nurses, 13, 82, 97, 102, 104, 110, 111–12, 140–41, 142, 145, 148, 151–53, 165, 168, 169–70, 181–82, 187, 197–98, 208
women's bodies
discipline of, 70, 83, 209
examination of, 159–60, 161, 168, 201
workplaces, intimacy and, 38, 39, 40–42, 47, 55–56
written promises, 58, 59–60, 59f, 61, 66, 74–75, 148

www.ingramcontent.com/pod-product-compliance
Ingram Content Group UK Ltd.
Pitfield, Milton Keynes, MK11 3LW, UK
UKHW022153230426
12049UKWH00003BA/66